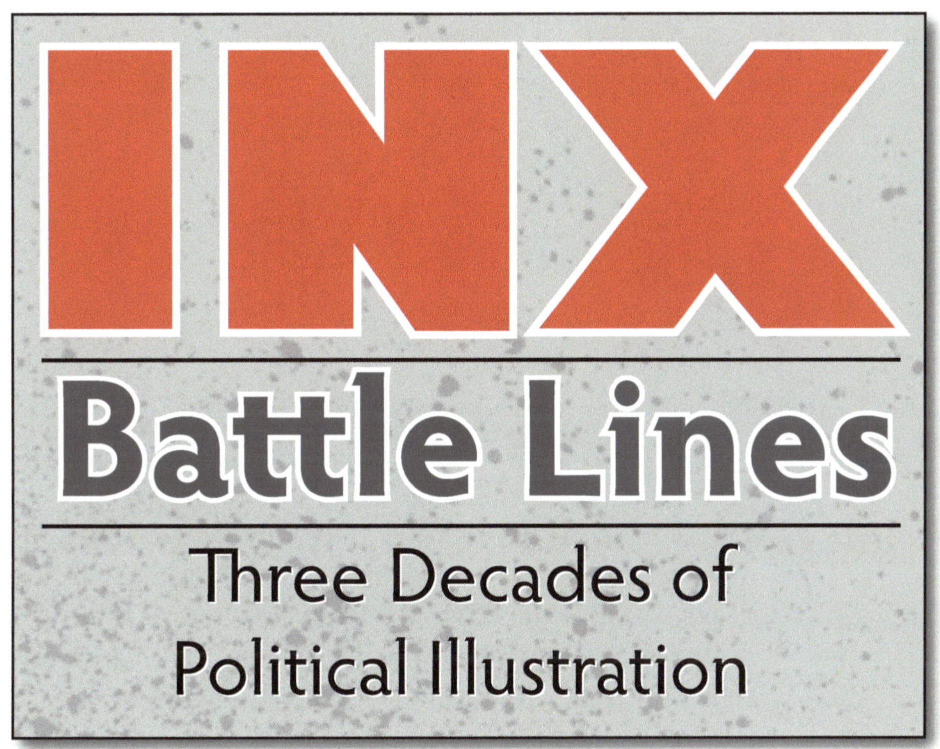

Edited by Martin Kozlowski

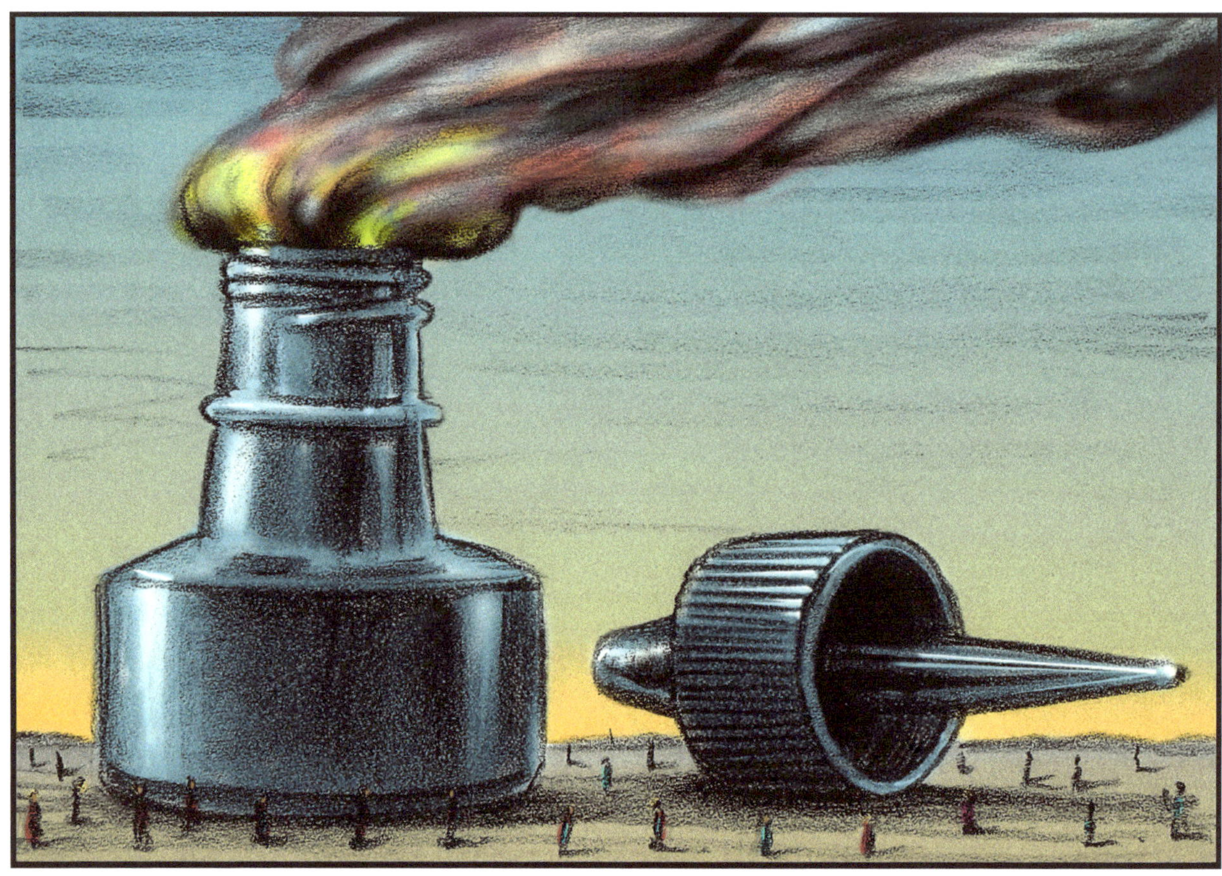

Thomas Kerr • Muslim Cartoon Protests • Coquille Board, Digital Color • 2006

Front cover: Randy Jones (Reagan), Yvonne Buchanan (Clinton),
James Williamson (Bush), and David Chelsea (Obama)
Back cover: Peter Kuper • Terrorism False Alarms • 2003

Special thanks to Felipe Galindo, Randy Jones,
Janusz Kapusta, Thomas Kerr, and Peter Kuper
for helping in the selection of the art for this volume.
Thanks to Barbara Winard for her editorial assistance.

Thanks to all the artists for their wonderful work and camaraderie.

For more on the art and artists in this book, please visit inxart.com.
For more on Now What Media, please visit nowwhatmedia.com.

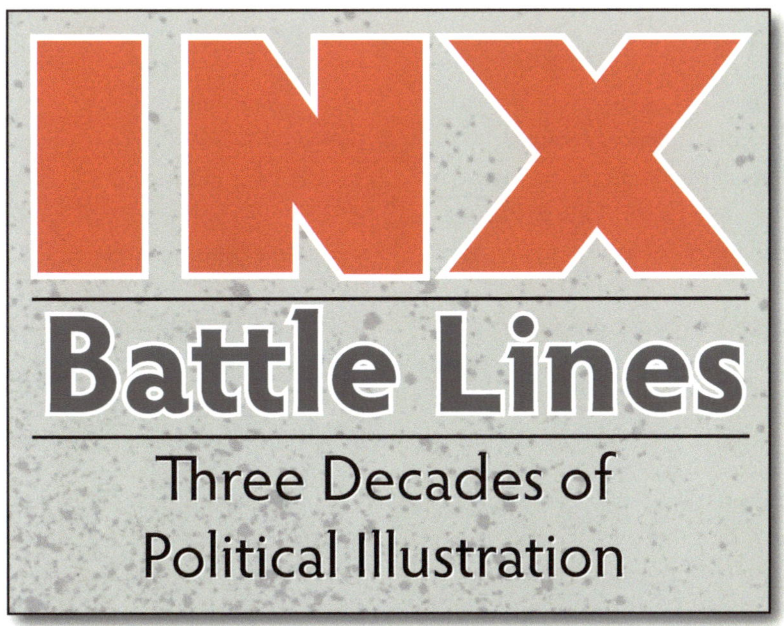

INX
Battle Lines
Three Decades of Political Illustration

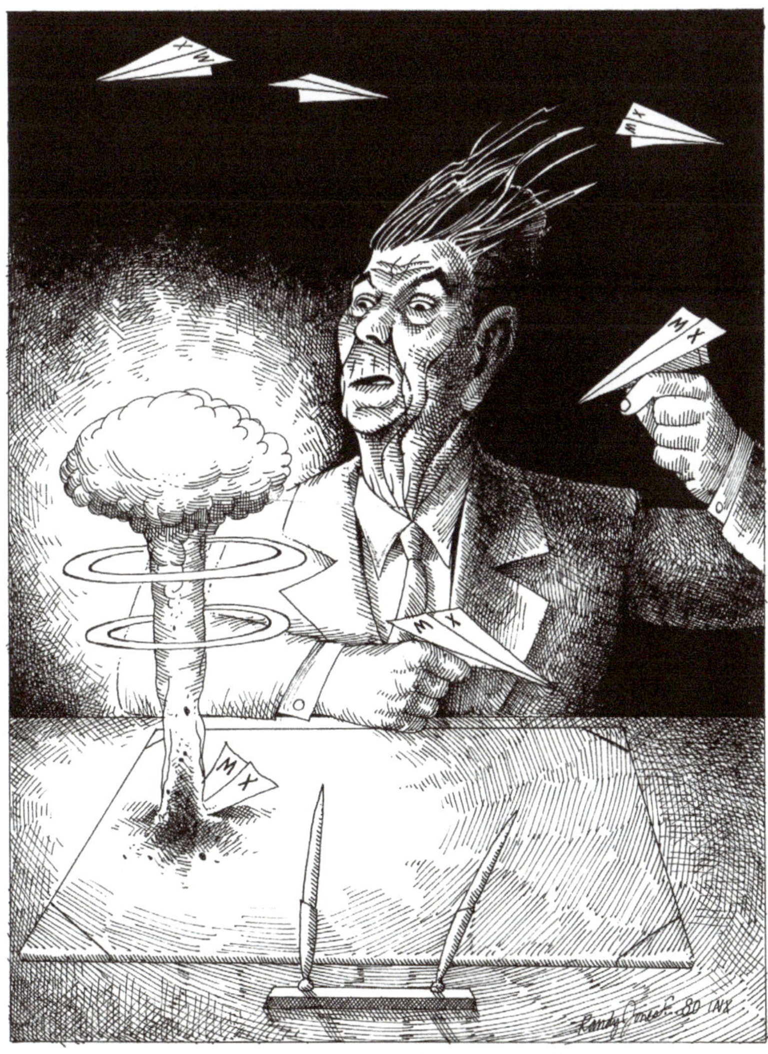

Randy Jones • Reagan & the MX Missile • Pen & Ink • 1980

INX Battle Lines

The history of satirical art is nasty, brutish and long. An acid-tinged line can be traced from Francisco de Goya's etchings exposing Napoleon's nightmarish Spanish campaign to Honoré Daumier's lithographs lampooning the French class system. It links Thomas Nast's bravura engravings in *Harper's Weekly* that cut to Tammany Hall's venal heart with George Grosz's graphic excoriations of decadent post-Weimar Germany.

The line exploded onto thousands of newspaper pages in the 20th Century, needling, jabbing and skewering the powerful and corrupt. In the U.S. it struck like lightning from the pens of Herblock, Mauldin, Conrad, Oliphant, and an army of compatriots. By the 1960s, a Europe rocked by revolutions both political and social gave rise to an increasingly experimental political cartoon that absorbed modernist trends like collage, expressionism, and surrealism.

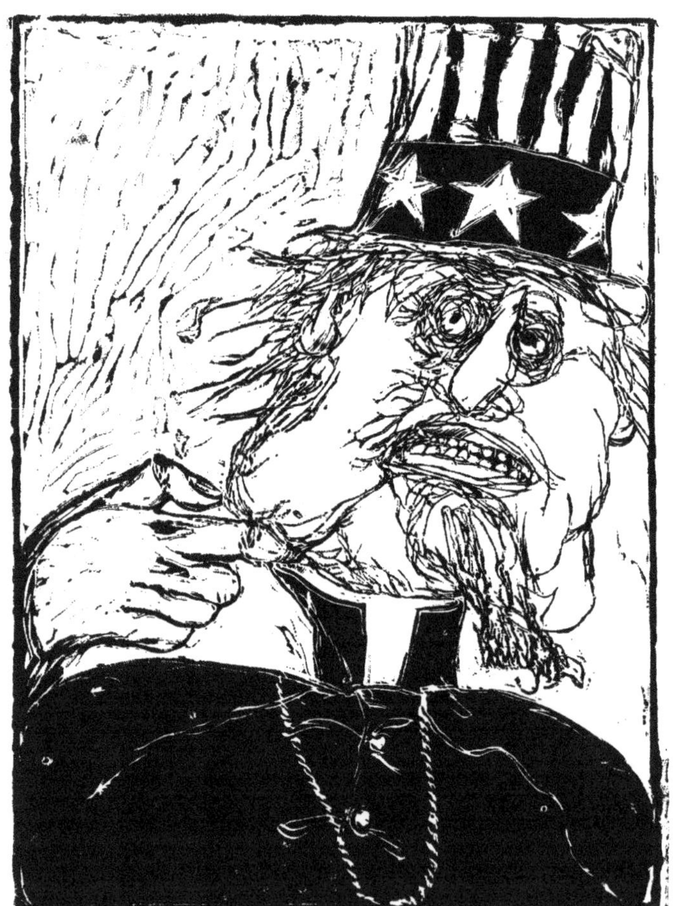

Frances Jetter • Church & State • Print • 1980

Just as the New Wave in European cinema began influencing mainstream Hollywood films, so too did this new graphic sensibility flow westward, specifically onto *The New York Times* Op-ed page. Under the art directorship of first, Jean-Claude Suarés, and then, Steven Heller and Jerelle Kraus, an arguably more sophisticated form of political illustration that eschewed word balloons and captions and emphasized stylistic risk-taking took root and then spread to journals across the country.

This Silver Age gave rise to a younger generation of artists, a new line of innovators eager to expand on the possibilities of the editorial page. However, editors were often wary of this nonverbal form of commentary and less than eager to give the young turks full sway. These restrictions inspired a core of *New York Times* editorial illustrators to form the group INX in 1980, at the dawn of the Age of Reagan.

The founding members were Jean-François Allaux, Bob Gale, Vivienne Flesher, Steven Guarnaccia, Walter Gurbo, Frances Jetter, Randy Jones, Carlos Llerena Aguirre, John MacLeod, Robert Neubecker, Charles Waller, and Oliver Williams. The name INX was a play on "inks," the essential medium employed by these pen and brush artists.

They shared a desire to produce and distribute uncensored political images to the news marketplace, keeping editorial control in the hands of the creators. Free-lancers granted such freedom were galvanized, producing art that was both personal and powerful, even when the remuneration was meager or non-existent.

Camaraderie and passion for the work sustained the group for over three years until the complexities of managing a small business communally caused a rift and drove many members away. Those who remained stabilized INX by negotiating a long-term contract with United Feature Syndicate. Under this new arrangement, the contributors were encouraged to concentrate on their art instead of its promotion and distribution.

At the beginning of each week, four or more artists were commissioned by one of the member art directors Randy Jones, John MacLeod, or Robert Neubecker to contribute illustrations on the topics of the day. For several years

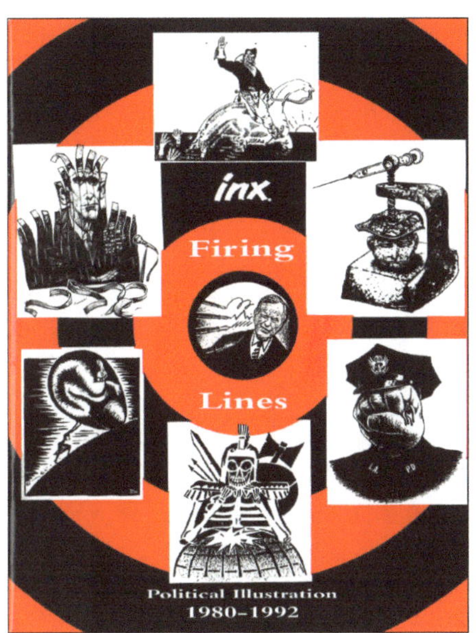

Cover of the catalogue for the Parsons exhibition *INX: Firing Lines* • 1992

that entailed a meeting on Monday at the midtown offices of United Feature, where the artists met and bounced ideas and sketches off one another. Later, the initial communications were made by phone and fax as Peter Kuper and I assumed the roles of co-art directors.

By midweek the finished artwork was dropped off. It was then photostatted, printed onto glossy paper, stapled into 8.5"x11" packages, and syndicated to newspapers in the U.S. and abroad, which over time totaled more than 50 subscribers.

On a good day, the group continued on to a brunch of brainstorming and gossip, a welcome diversion for toilers in an essentially solitary profession. In this loose-limbed fashion, INX generated a body of work composed of over 4,400 images spanning four presidencies, twenty-one years, and the millennial divide.

In early 2002, consolidation of the syndication market had begun and the INX group was unable to negotiate a new contract with United Feature. Facing possible extinction, several of the members banded together to establish a website, inxart.com, and self-syndicate their work in a digital variation on the group's original model. Reflecting advancements in the print technology for newspapers and the explosion of news websites, the online version of INX began featuring full-color art.

In 1992 the first exhibition of INX work, entitled *Firing Lines*, was organized with Parsons School of Design in New York City and opened a few days before the presidential election that saw George Bush the Senior stumble at the finish line. A portion of that show was seen at Parsons in Paris one year later.

In 2001 an extensive retrospective was mounted at St. John's University in Queens, New York, curated by Professor Thomas Kerr, a long-time member artist and inxart.com's web master. *INX: Fever Lines* became the basis of a series of exhibitions that culminated in a show at the Muzeum Karykatury in Warsaw, Poland in 2006, co-organized by INX contributor Janusz Kapusta.

In between, *Fever Lines* had traveled to Syracuse University right after 9/11, the Alberta College of Art and Design in Calgary, Canada, Gallery 9 at *The New York Times*, and several other venues. In 2007, a portion of the exhibition appeared in Oaxaca, Mexico.

For 2012 the exhibition has been broadened to include more recent drawings, and the metaphoric lineage has been extended to *INX Battle Lines*. The work in this book is culled from that selection of the best of more than 6,000 images produced in the last thirty-one years. However, we do regret not having access to more of the early originals.

The fifty-five contributors to this volume represent a wide range of national origins, artistic styles, and, most importantly, opinions. Through INX they've turned a collective eye on an imperfect world and with innumerable lines, scratches, blobs, and blotches left

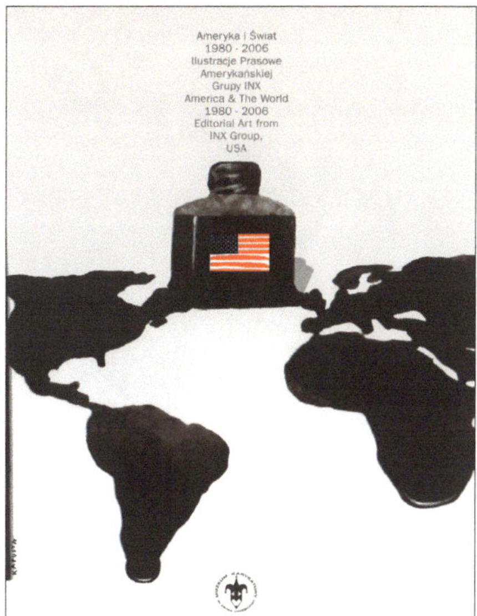

Janusz Kapusta • Catalogue for the INX show in Poland • Watercolor • 2006

an indelible record – a picture history – of the last three decades.

For much more on the artists and their work, and to enjoy fresh lines of attack, please visit inxart.com.

Martin Kozlowski
January, 2012

The 1% Solution

Political cartooning offers its audience a perspective that is at once humorous, provocative, and insightful, very often at the expense of those who inhabit the social strata we've come to know as the 1%. And the celebrities, religious figures, captains of industry and, of course, politicians who serve to warm that upper crust are also prime targets of the satirical artist. Preconceptions, unwitting prejudices and stereotypes can themselves be fodder, punctured by the sharpened nib of the cartoonist's pen. The piebald collective of artists known as INX possesses some of the sharpest pens and most incisive visual wits to be found in any practitioners of the craft in the last three decades.

The INX group has international roots, with members hailing from Argentina, Australia, Canada, Israel, Morocco, Mexico, Poland and Ukraine, but there are some common threads that connect their bodies of work. One clear trend is that they rarely depend on the hackneyed convention of labels to explain the meaning of their images. It is fair to assume that a newspaper reader in any corner of the globe could get the gist of an INX image. And these artists are all students of and adherents to the classical conventions of visual satire. The use of caricature, metaphor, and allegory are to be found in one degree or another in any given INX image.

The word *caricature* draws on the Italian roots *carico* (to load) and *caricare* (to exaggerate). It is one of the more popular types of drawing to be found in the INX canon. The history of caricature is rich, with scholars identifying examples on the walls of the tomb of Egypt's female Pharaoh Hatshepsut, circa 1458 B.C. It's an art that can still amuse both master and slave (read "job creator" and "employee").

INX co-founder Randy Jones continues to produce some of the most scathing broadsides in this mold. His earliest offerings hammered away at the newly-elected president, Ronald Reagan[1], and he's nailed every major U.S. political figure since then, right up to the Republican field of contenders vying for their party's nomination in the 2012 election cycle. Another notable contributor is Martin Kozlowski, the editor of this volume, whose biting line draws inspiration from the work of George Grosz. He graphically gores a range of personages, from maniacal dictators[2] to domestic demagogues[3].

Betsy Scheld, a fondly-remembered contributor who tragically passed away in 1996 at the age of 32, is represented here with the potent *Iron Lady*[4], which depicts Margaret Thatcher wrought from the element of that British Prime Minister's nickname. Cartoonist Tom Hachtman, creator of the underground comic strip classic, *Gertrude's Follies*, gives us *Et Tu, Newt?*[5] which exposes the then Speaker of the House to his own Ides of March.

In language, metaphor is a figure of speech in which a word or phrase is applied to a thing representative or symbolic of something else. To a political cartoonist, the manipulation of visual metaphor is an important tool in transforming sometimes complex situations into essential images. Many INX artists play off of stock icons — Uncle

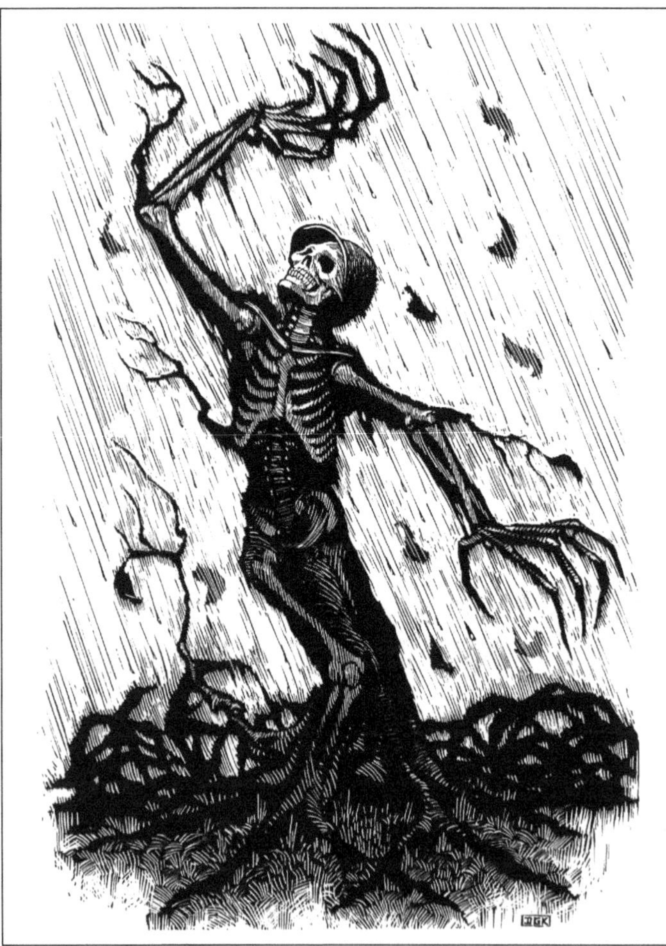

David Klein • Agent Orange • Scratchboard • 1985

Sam, the Republican elephant, the Democratic donkey — and strive to revitalize them in novel ways, while others look to fashion more personal symbols that will still communicate with the viewer. In either case, the aim is to expose the absurdity of human folly.

Janusz Kapusta is well-versed in massaging metaphors. Employing a surrealist sensibility in *Sex & Religion*[6], he encapsulates in one shot the calumny of the abuse cases occurring within the Catholic Church. Giora Carmi takes the very symbol of Switzerland and reimagines it as a muzzle over the mouth of a banker protecting ill-gotten treasure in his piece entitled *Nazi Gold*[7].

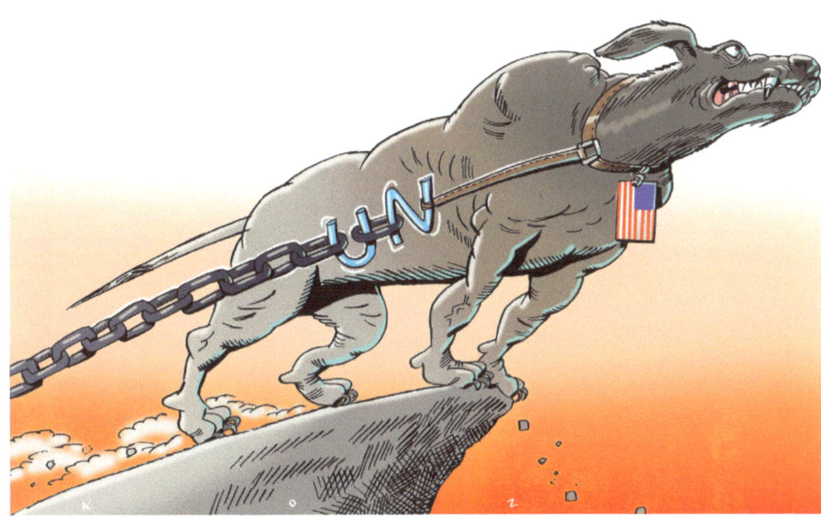

Martin Kozlowski • Dog of War • Pen, Ink & Digital Color • 2003

Allegory can also be found coursing throughout the body of INX work. Horacio Cardo produces an excellent example with his portrait of the hapless *Woody and Mia*[8], showing them at odds in a custody case before no less a historic figure than King Solomon. As with the tale of old, they argue the ownership of their children before the Hebrew king, but in this instance they both refuse to relinquish parentage of the child, resulting in the doll-like tot being torn asunder.

Igor Kopelnitsky spins a stunning allegory with his *Moscow's Act of Terror*[9], wittily playing off Shakespeare's *Hamlet* to deliver a powerful twist. Holding the skull in the manner of the Danish prince, we see a Russian solider contemplating the deaths that had occurred in the storming of the Dubrovka theater.

Whether from Shakespeare or the Bible, the satirist scavenges for source material the reader will recognize. Rob Shepperson's *Iraq's Tower of Babel*[10] is a fine example of the reconstruction of a well-known Old Testament symbol. Allegory springs from parody in versatile Tom Hachtman's *Iraq: Guernica 2003*[11], wherein he updates Picasso's masterpiece to depict the horrors of a modern war.

Editorial cartooning today finds itself in a less than comfortable position. Between incidents like the *Jyllands-Posten* Muhammad cartoon controversy (depicted in Felipe Galindo's *Islamic Cartoon Uproar*[12]), major drops in newspaper circulation, and electronic delivery of content, contemporary editorial artists appear to have the odds stacked against them.

Yet knowing the challenges that existed for earlier cartoonists, it is clear that they did not create in some editorial Eden — the marketplace has always been competitive and, at times, Darwinian. The trials they met often provided fuel for their best work.

Multitudes of corrupt political figures, vain celebrities, and hypocritical religious swindlers will continue to tempt the INX group. No doubt these artists will muster their battle lines, whether at the drawing board or the computer, take careful aim, and fire the satirical salvos that will inform, amuse and delight future readers.

Professor Thomas Kerr
St. John's University
Queens, New York
January 2012

1 – page 11; 2 – page 82; 3 – page 86; 4 – page 25; 5 – page 44; 6 – page 40; 7 – page 54; 8 – page 56; 9 – page 70; 10 – page 76; 11 – page 74; 12 – page 85

1980

Ronald Reagan elected 40th President. Civil war in El Salvador. Mount St. Helens erupts in Washington State. Solidarity Union founded in Poland. INX founded in New York City.

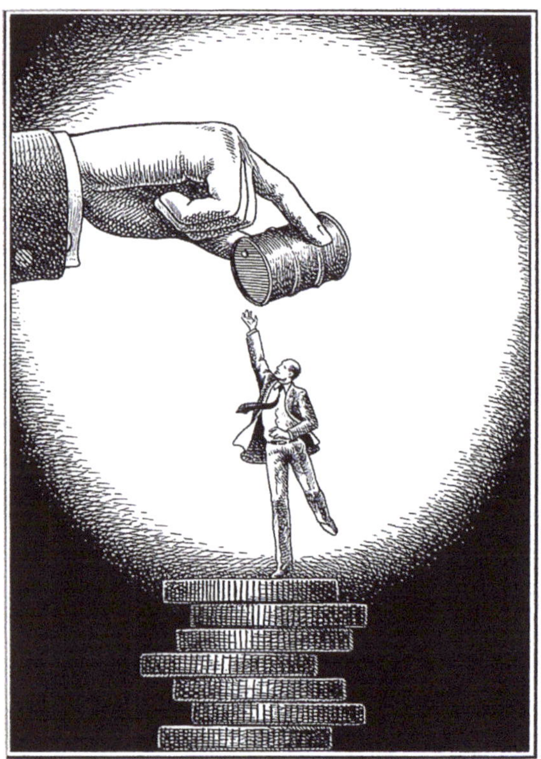

Jean-François Allaux • Oil Leverage • Pen & Ink

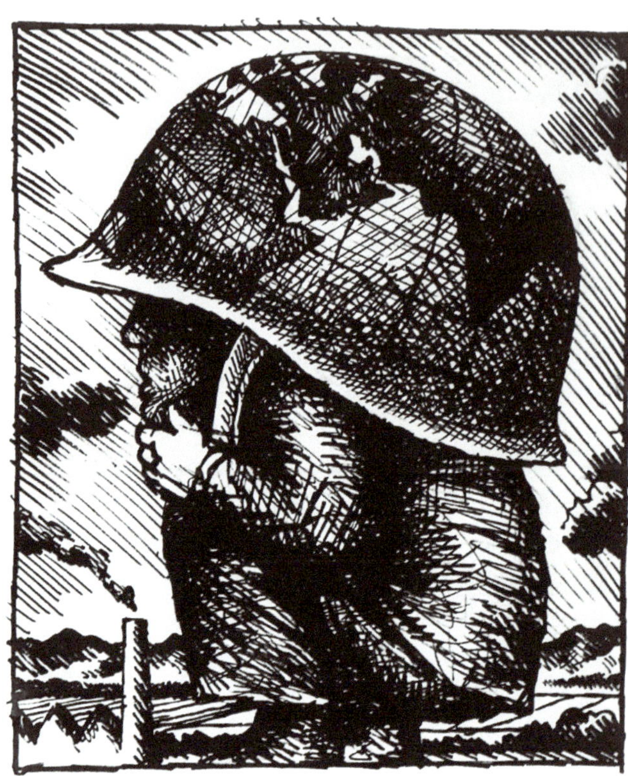

Bob Gale • World at War • Pen & Ink

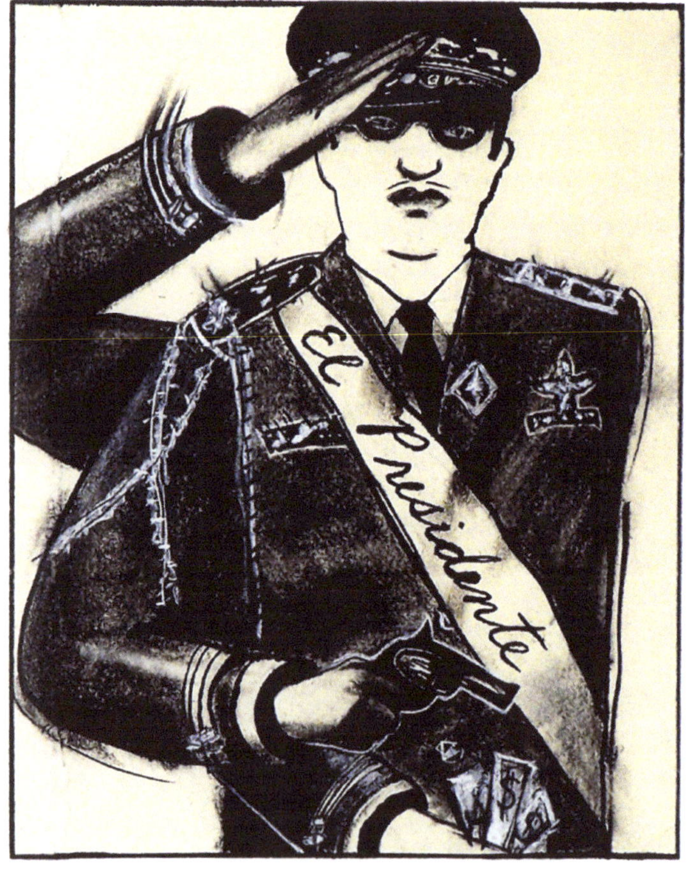

Vivienne Flesher • Latin American Militias • Charcoal

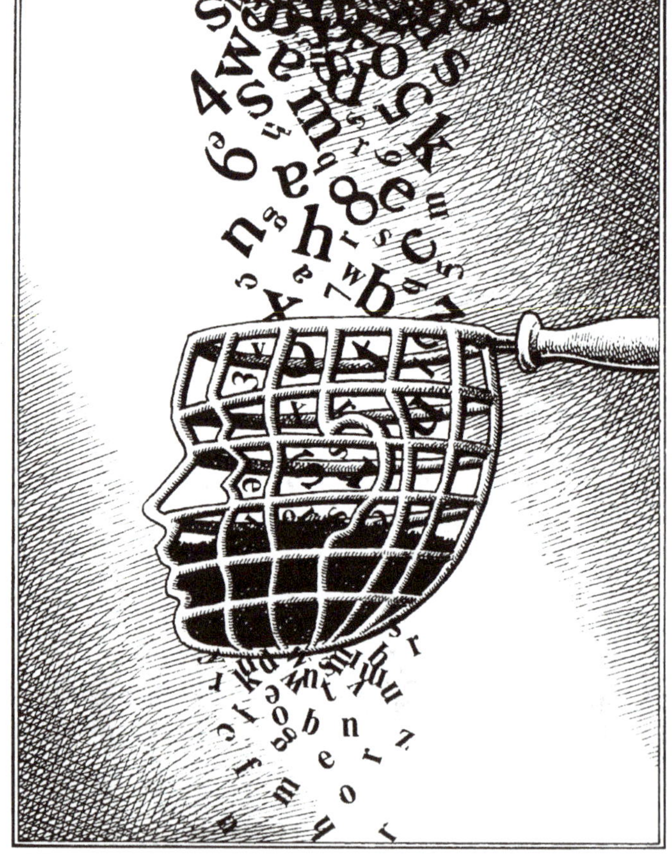

Jean-François Allaux • State of Education • Pen & Ink

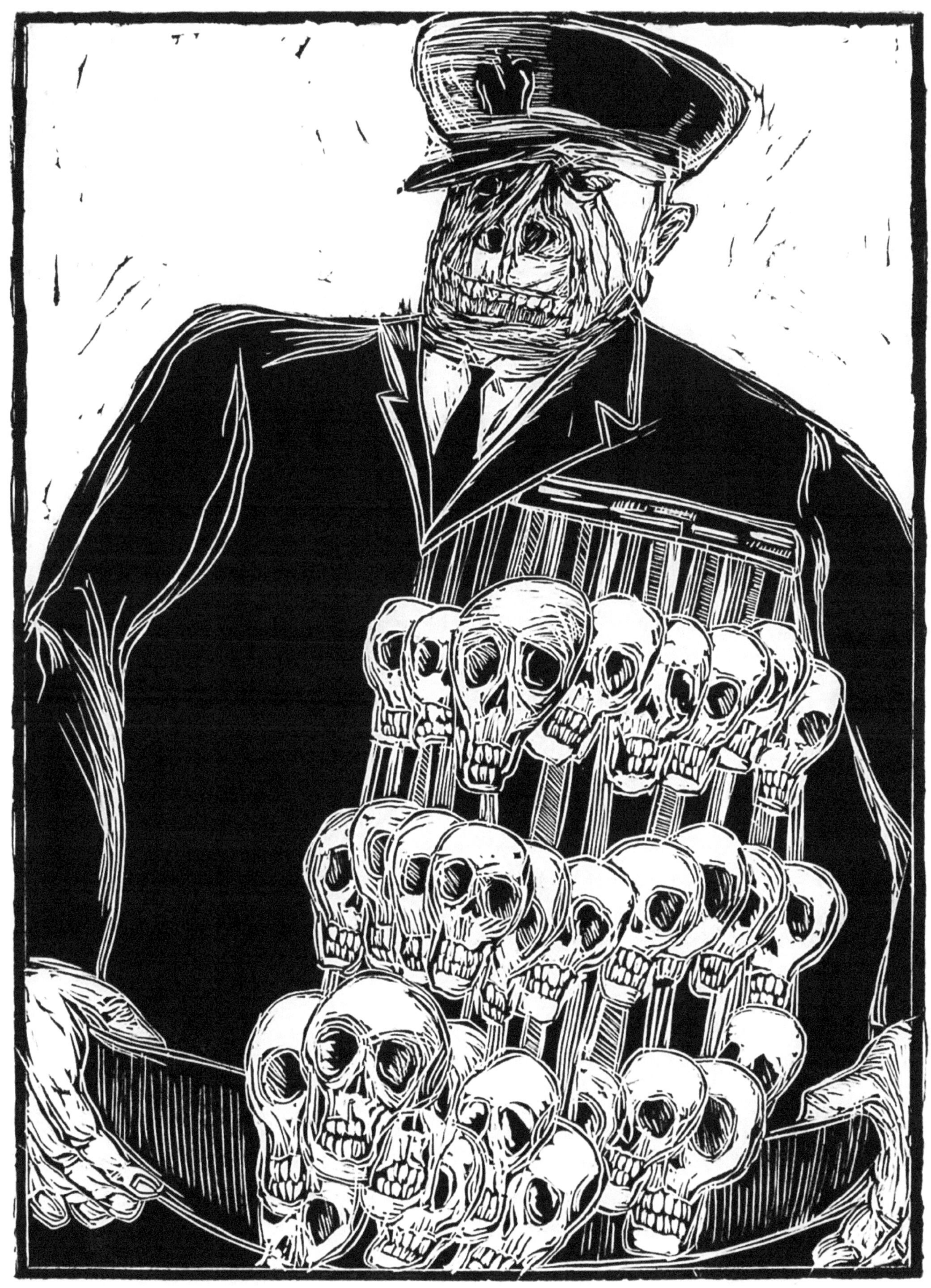

Frances Jetter • El Salvador • Print

U.S. hostages released in Tehran. Assassination attempt on Ronald Reagan by John Hinckley. AIDS virus first identified. Sandra Day O'Connor becomes first woman on Supreme Court.

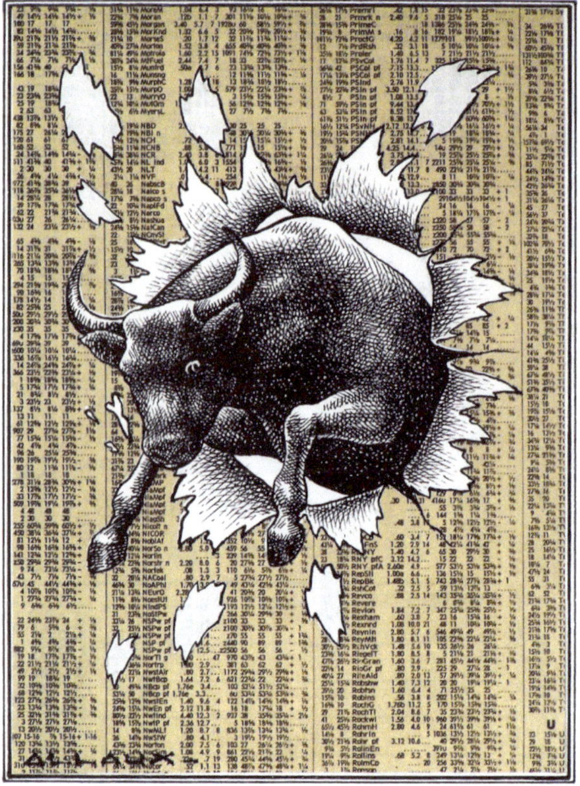

Jean-François Allaux • Bull Market • Pen, Ink, Collage

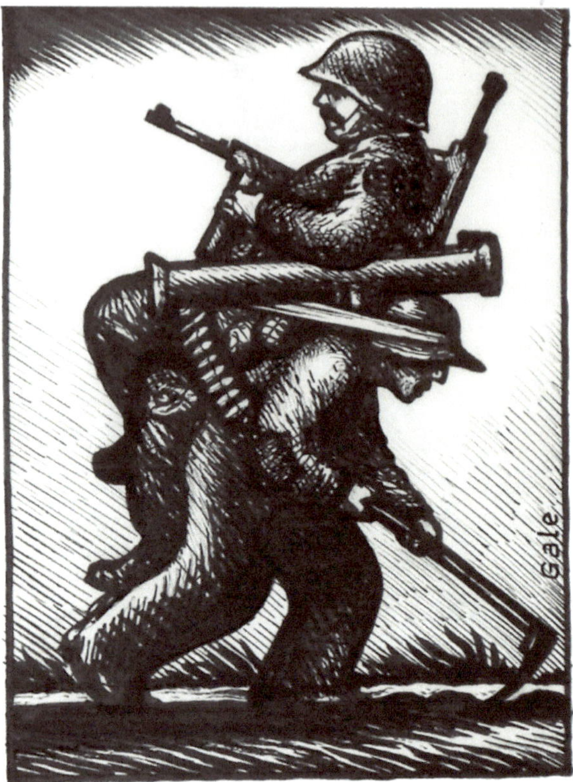

Bob Gale • El Salvador: Refugee's Burden • Pen & Ink

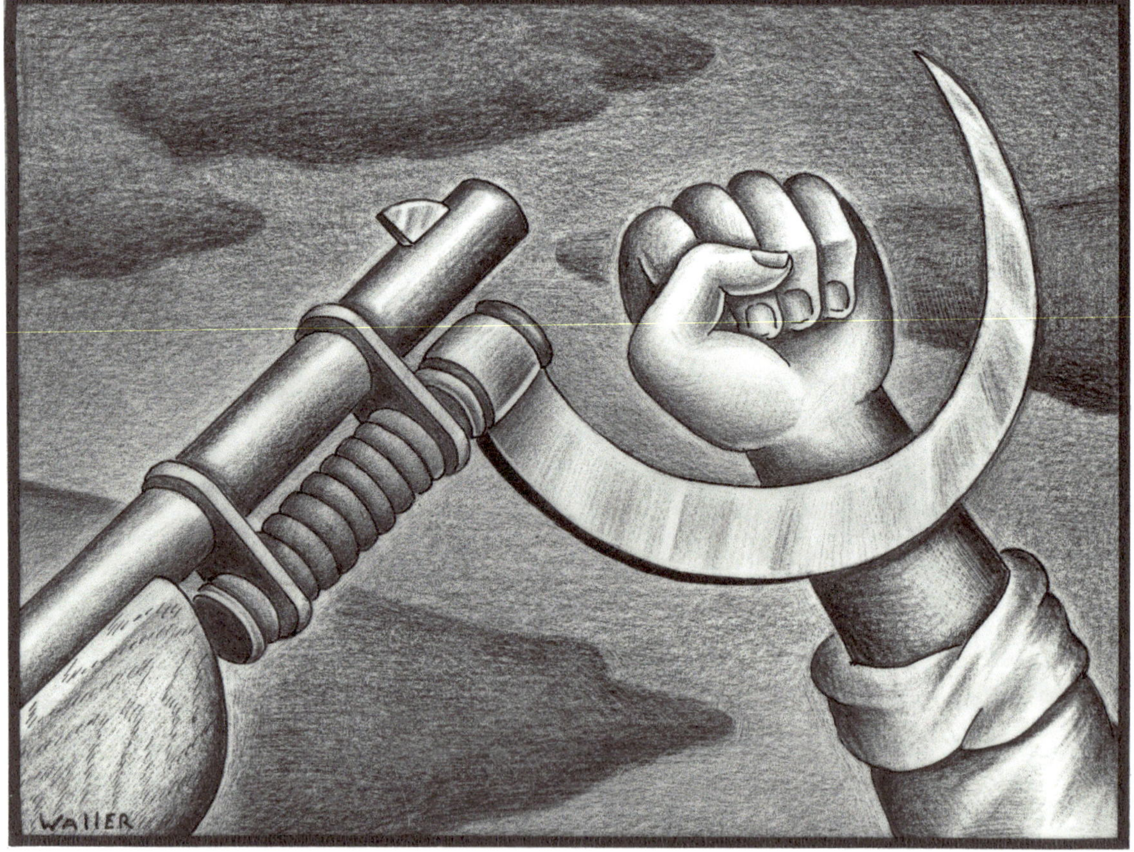

Charles Waller • Confrontation in Poland • Pencil

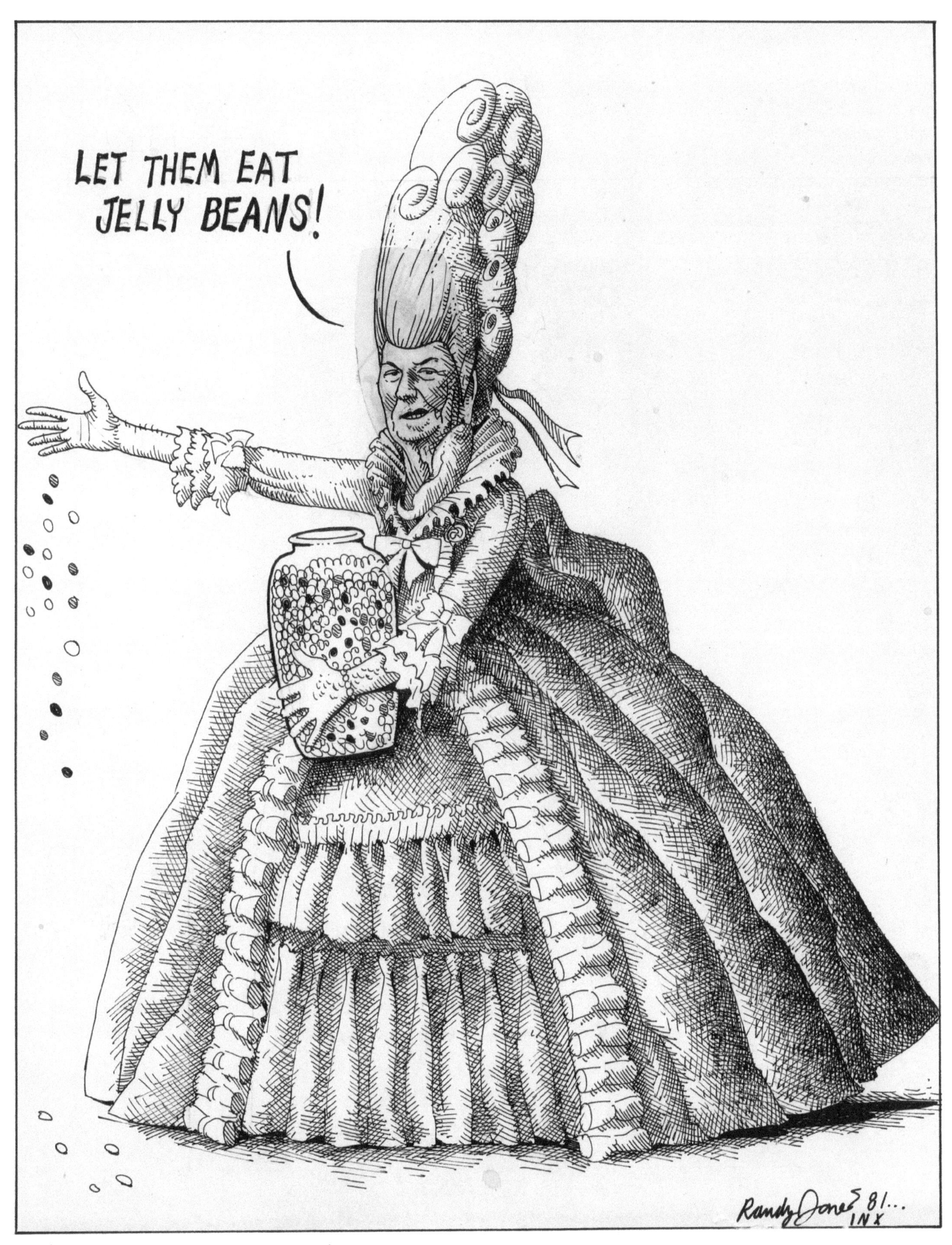

Randy Jones • Ronnie Antoinette • Pen & Ink

Leonid Brezhnev dies in U.S.S.R. United Kingdom goes to war with Argentina over the Falkland Islands. Severe U.S. recession nominally ends in November. Deadline for Equal Rights Amendment passes without sufficient Congressional votes.

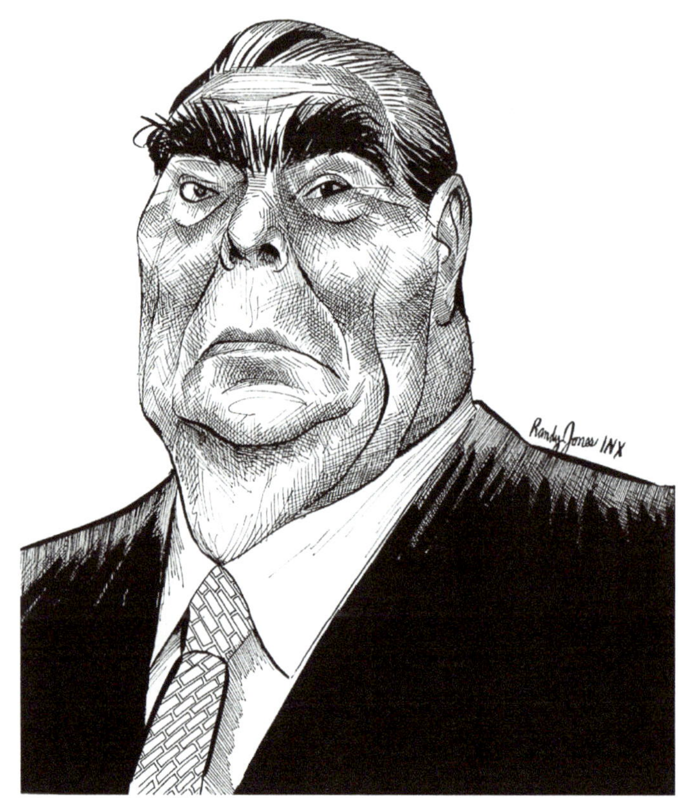

Randy Jones • Brezhnev in Memoriam • Pen & Ink

The earliest INX meetings were convened in a downtown loft in New York City. The group confabbed, sketched, penciled, inked, printed, stuffed, and stamped a weekly package for distribution to a list of subscribers drummed up by a salesman they had hired. It was the first artist owned and operated syndication service in the U.S. This was its original hand-drawn logo:

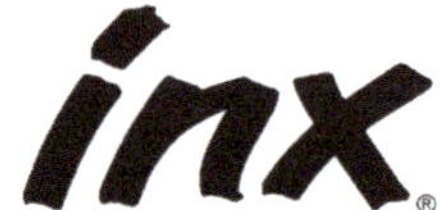

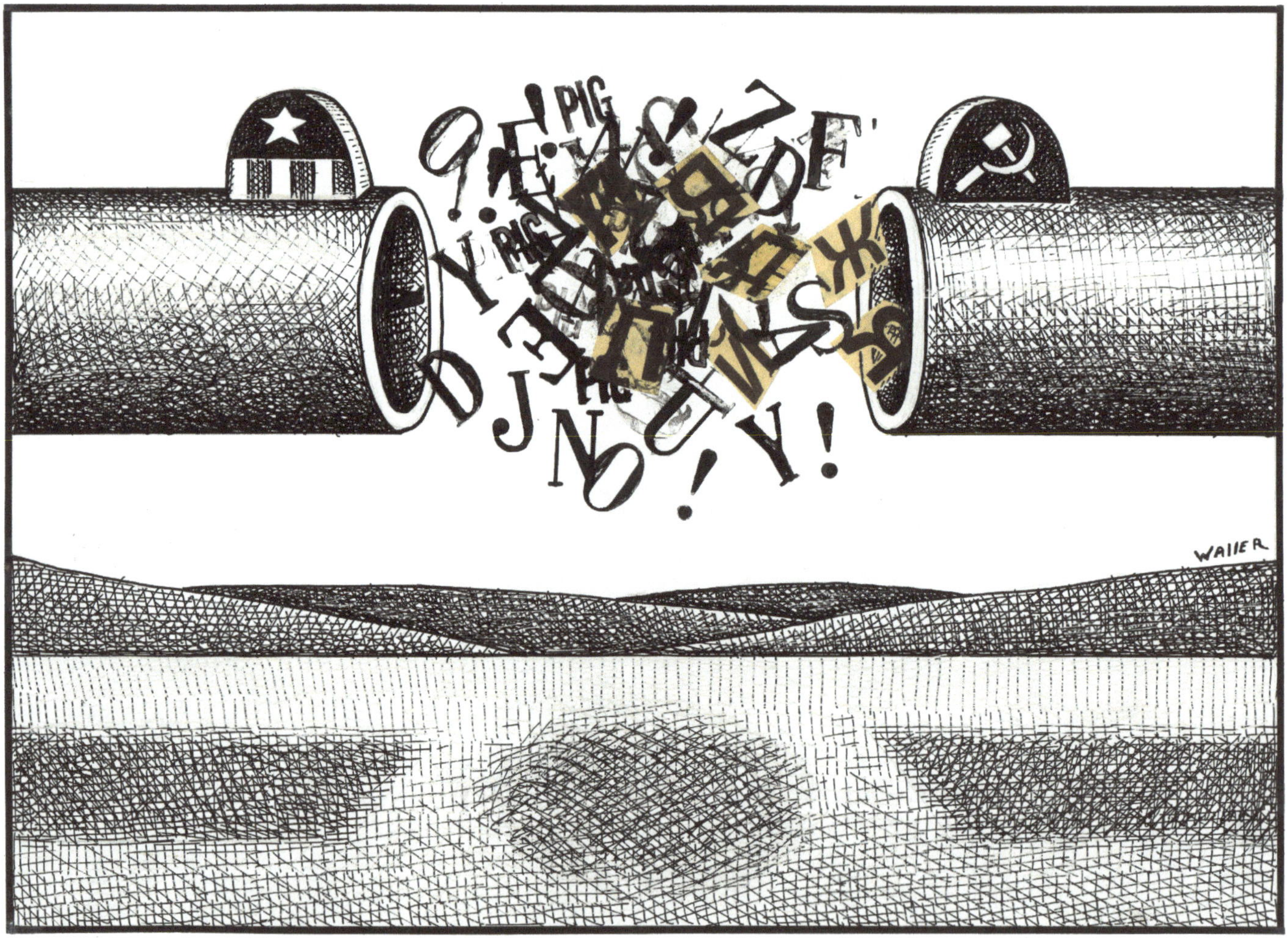

Charles Waller • Propaganda War • Pen, Ink & Collage

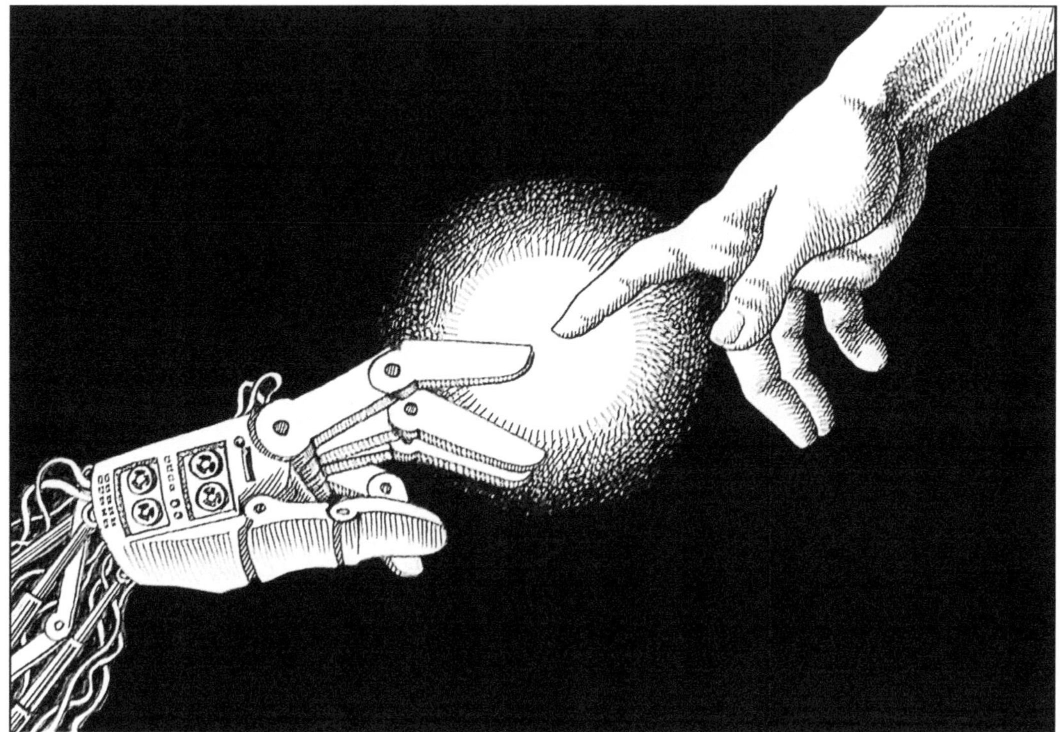

Jean-François Allaux • Automation Creation • Pen & Ink

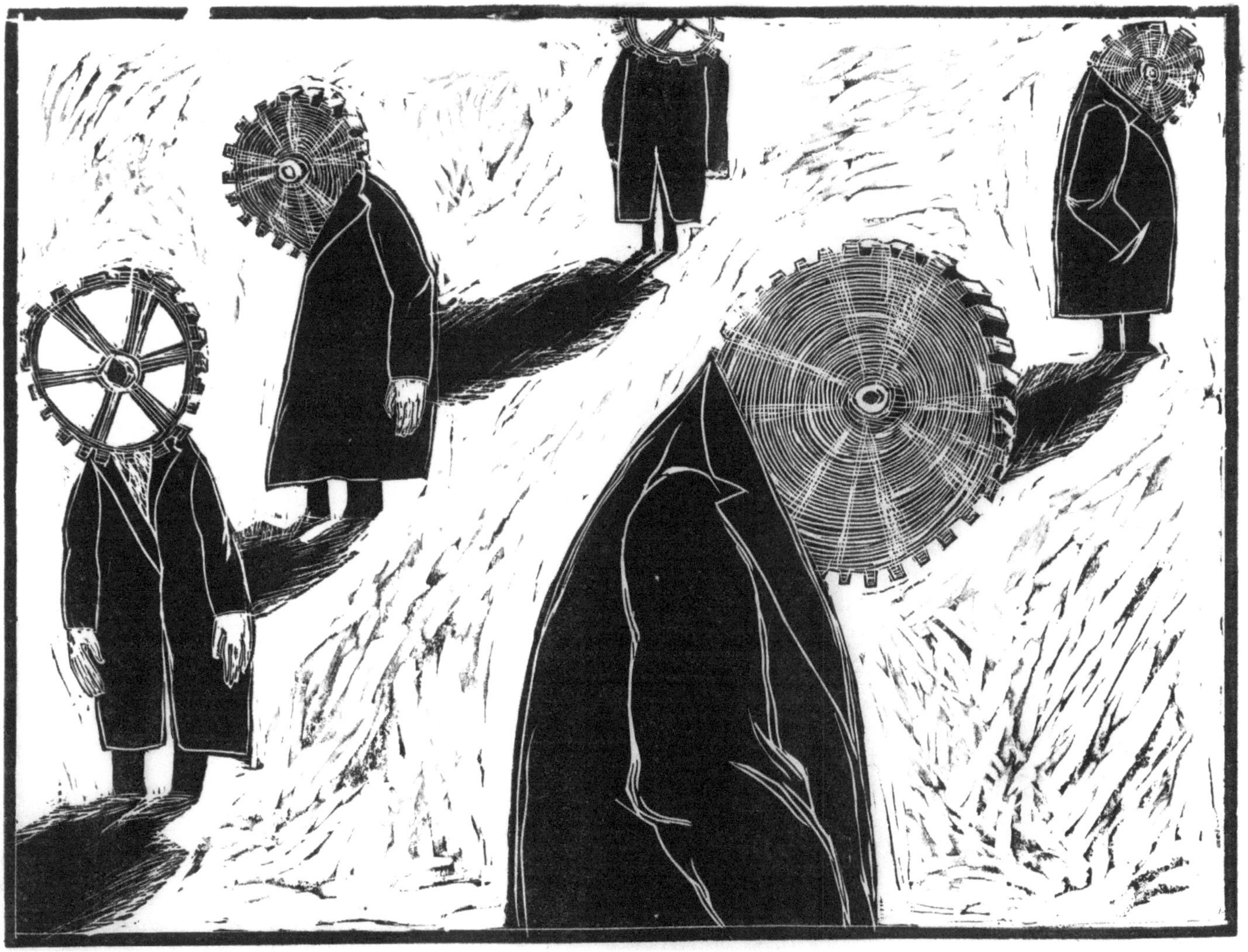

Frances Jetter • Unemployment • Print

1983

241 U.S. Marines killed by suicide bomb in Lebanon. United States invades Grenada. U.S. aids contras against Sandinista government in Nicaragua. End of 1982 war in Lebanon.

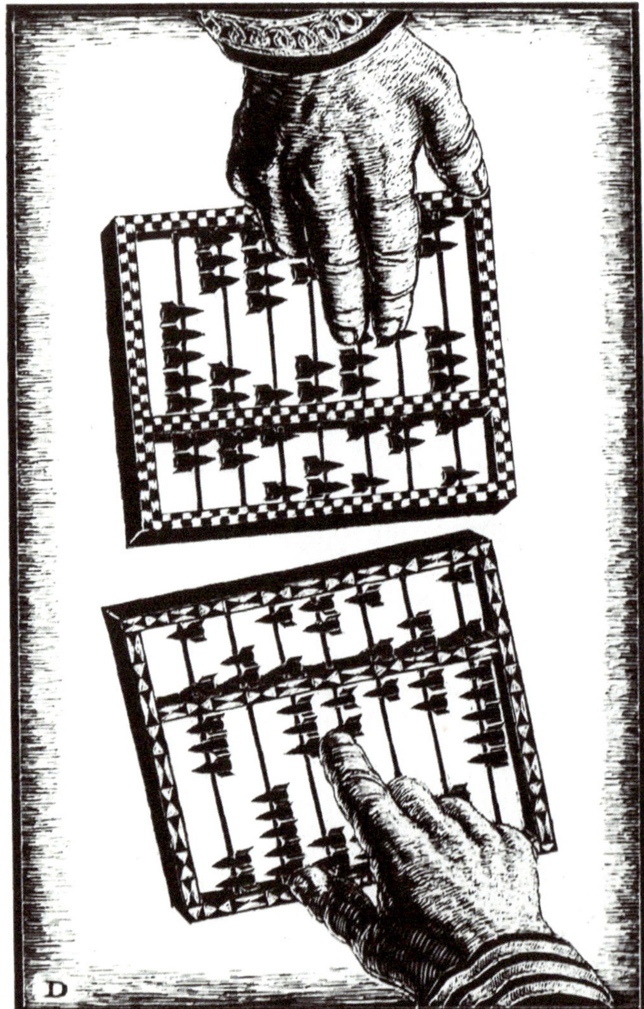

Bob Dahm • Arms Control Calculus • Scratchboard

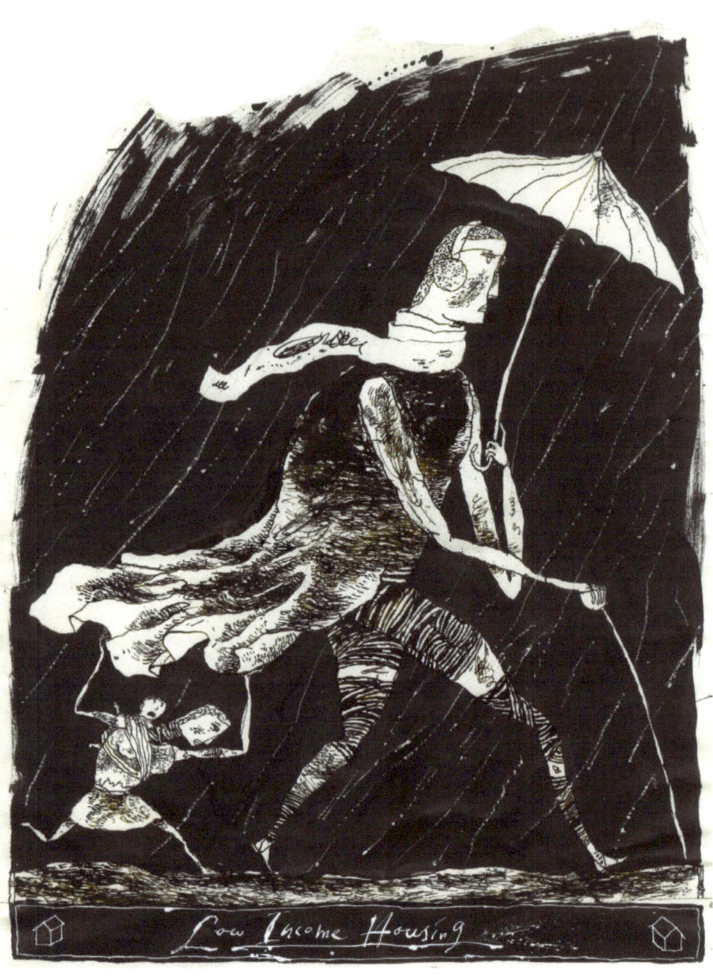

Henrik Drescher • Low Income Housing • Pen & Ink

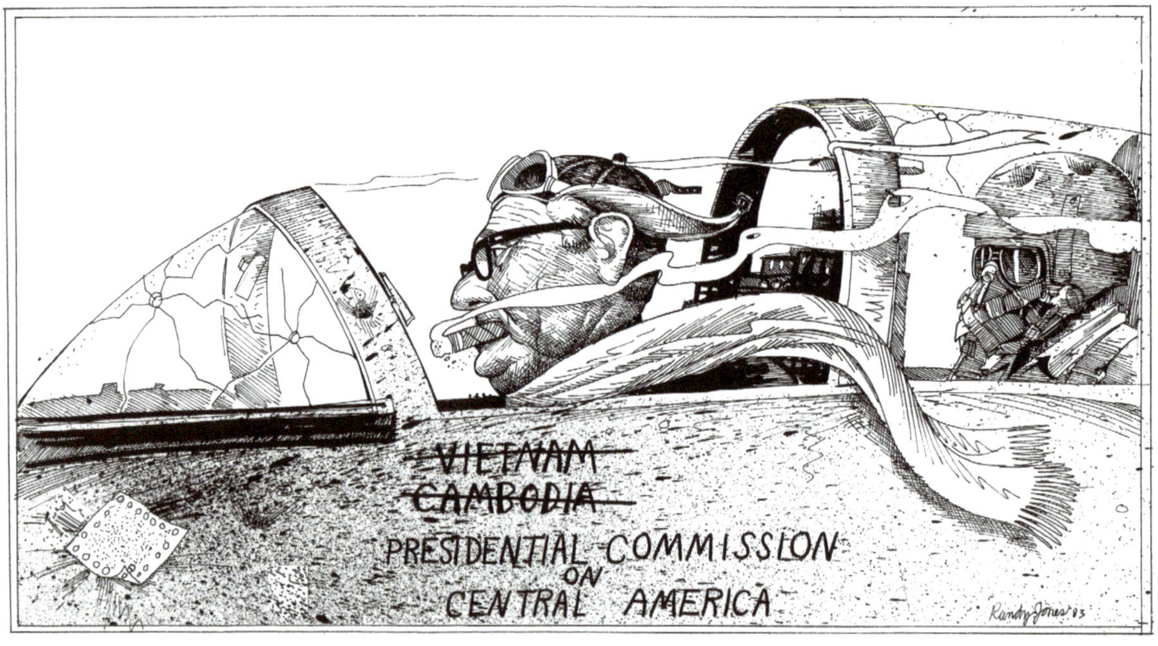

Randy Jones • Kissinger Flying High • Pen & Ink

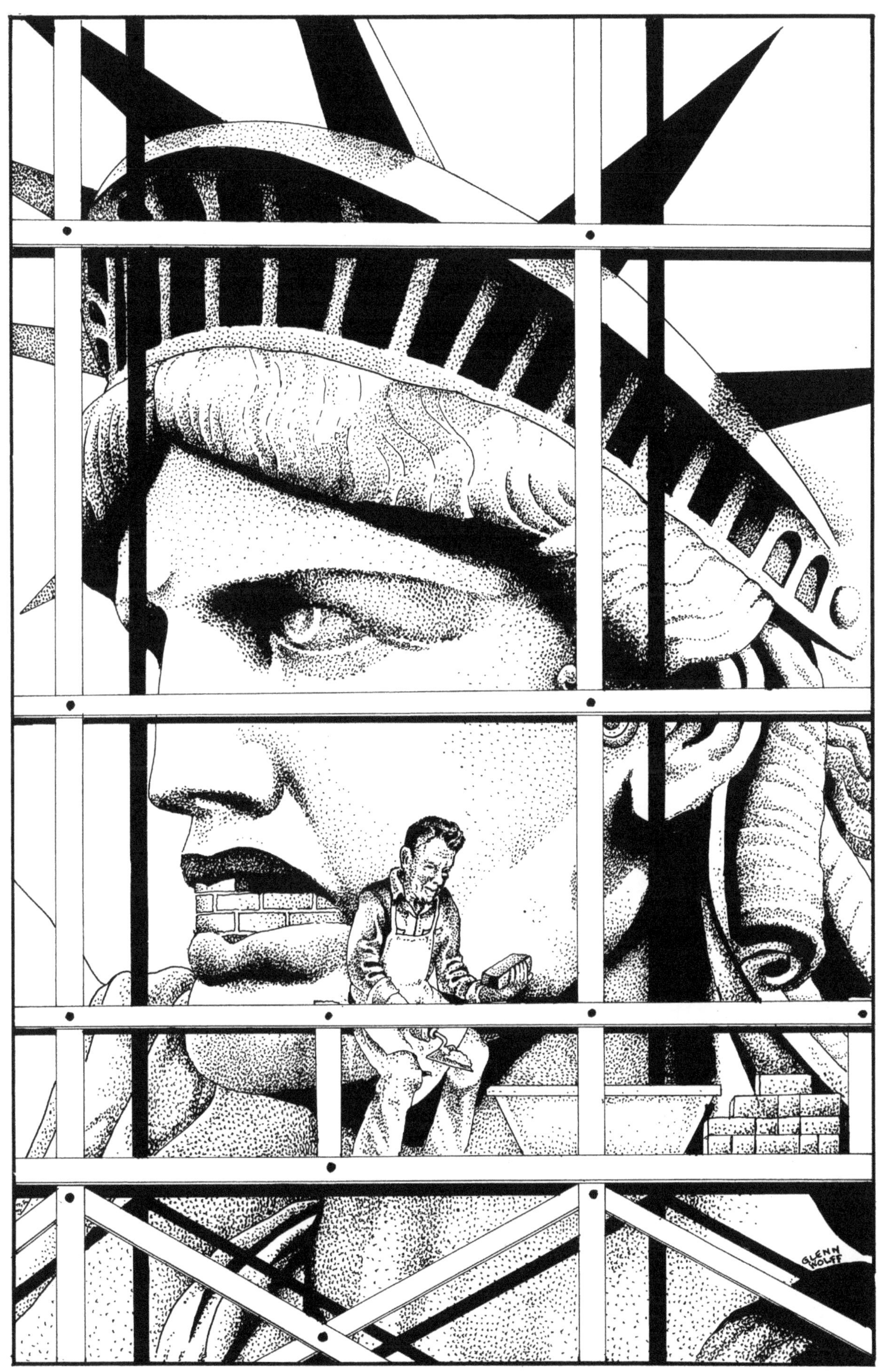

Glenn Wolff • Reagan's Gag Rule • Pen & Ink

1984

Eastern Bloc boycotts LA Summer Olympics. Ronald Reagan defeats Walter Mondale. Drug problem intensifies as crack is introduced. Indira Gandhi assassinated in India.

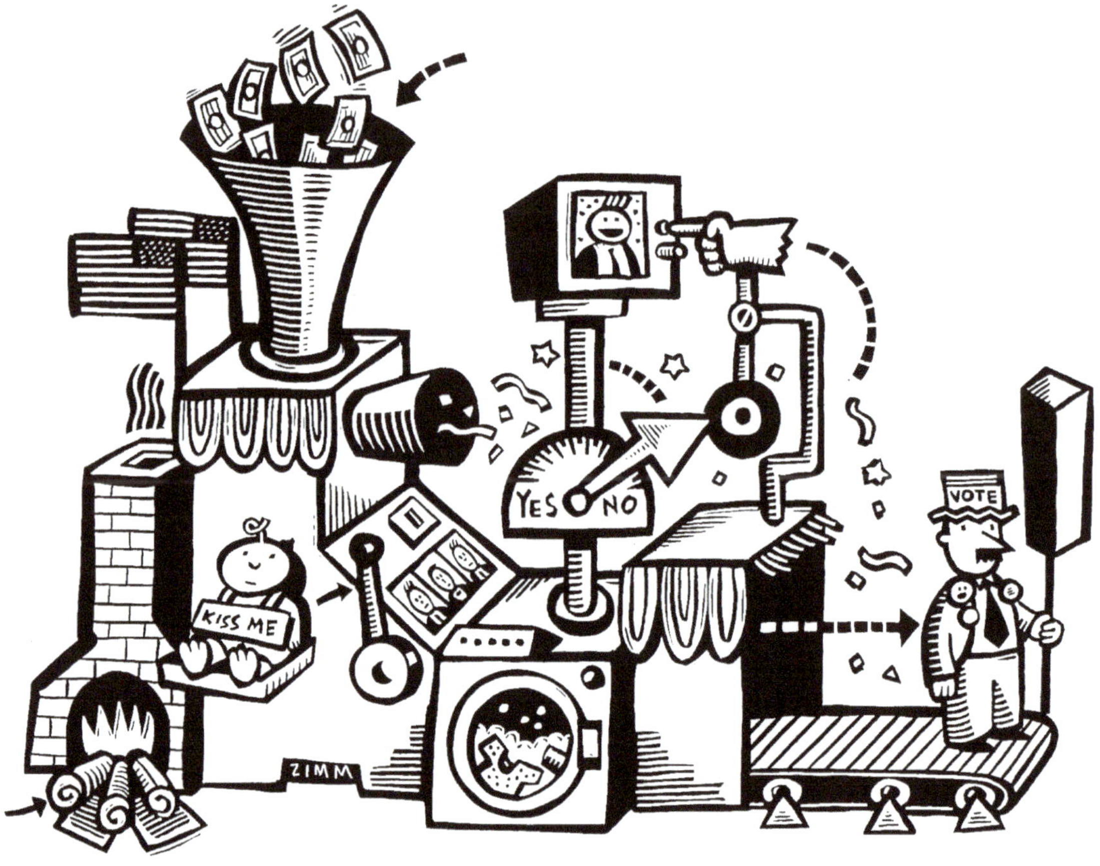

Robert Zimmerman • Campaign Machine • Scratchboard

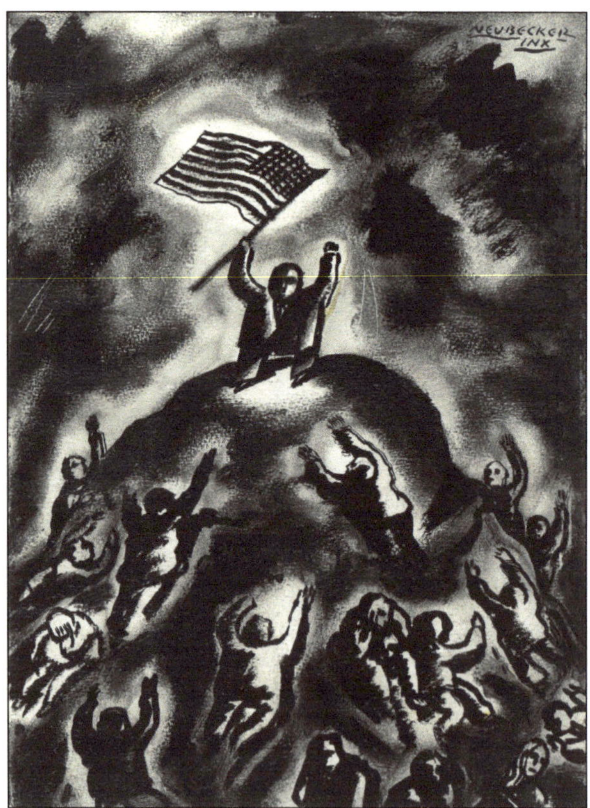

Robert Neubecker • Rally 'Round the Flag • Acrylics

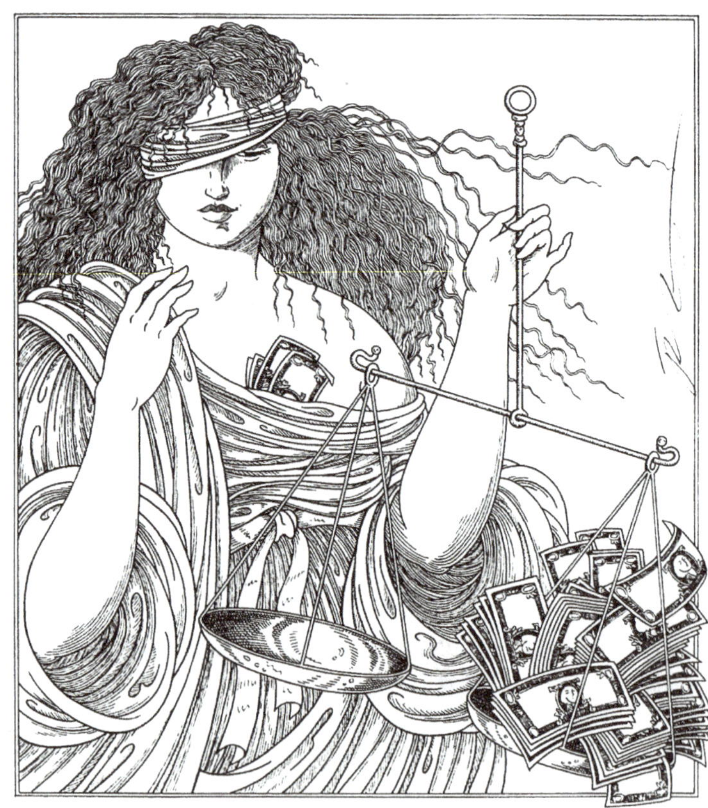

Jill Karla Schwarz • Money & Justice • Pen & Ink

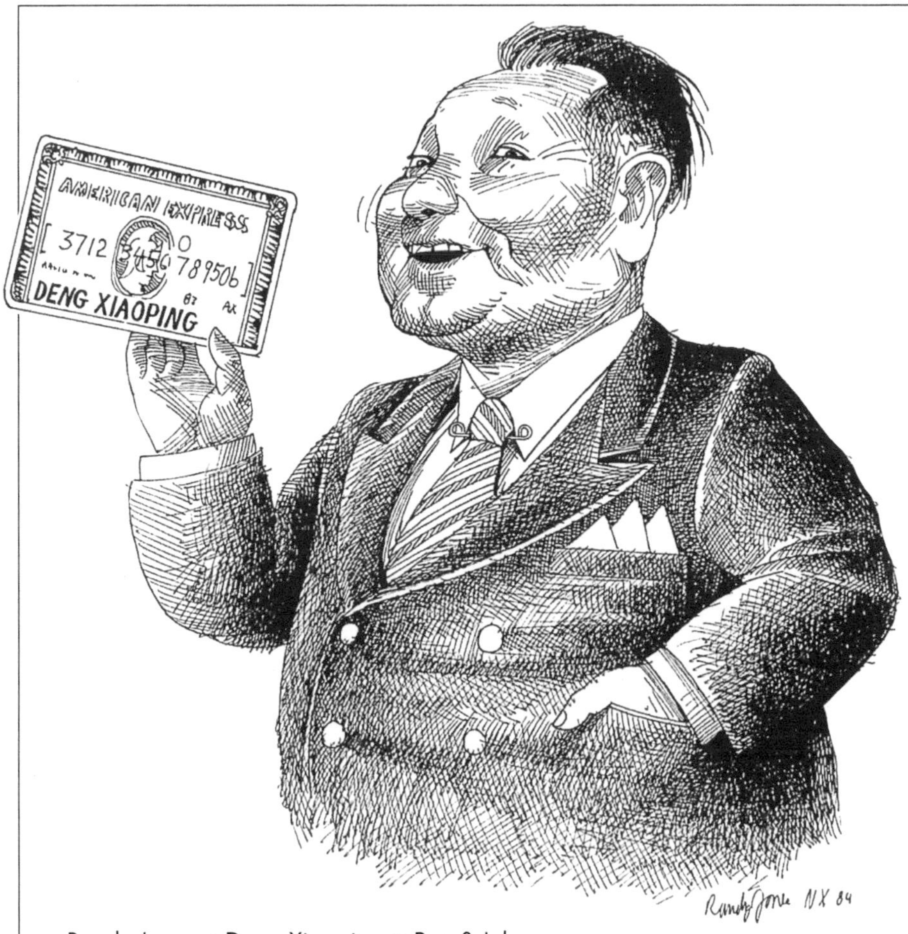

Randy Jones • Deng Xiaoping • Pen & Ink

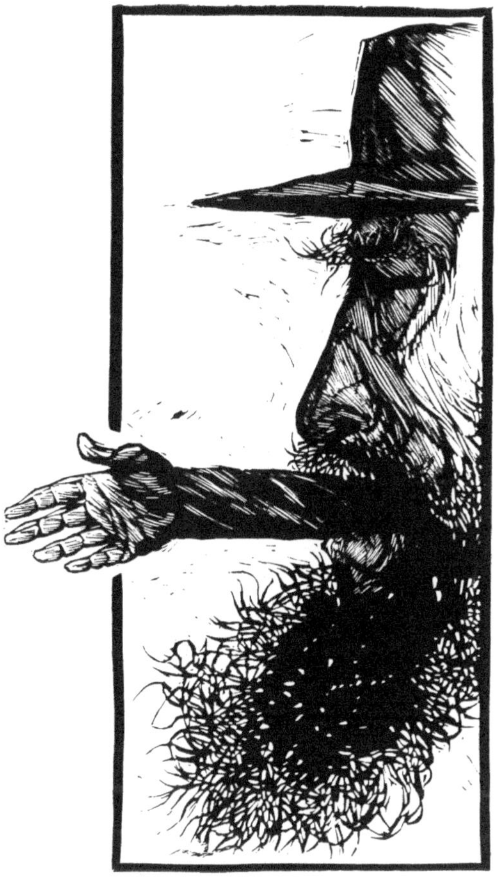

David Klein • Castro Reaches Out • Linocut

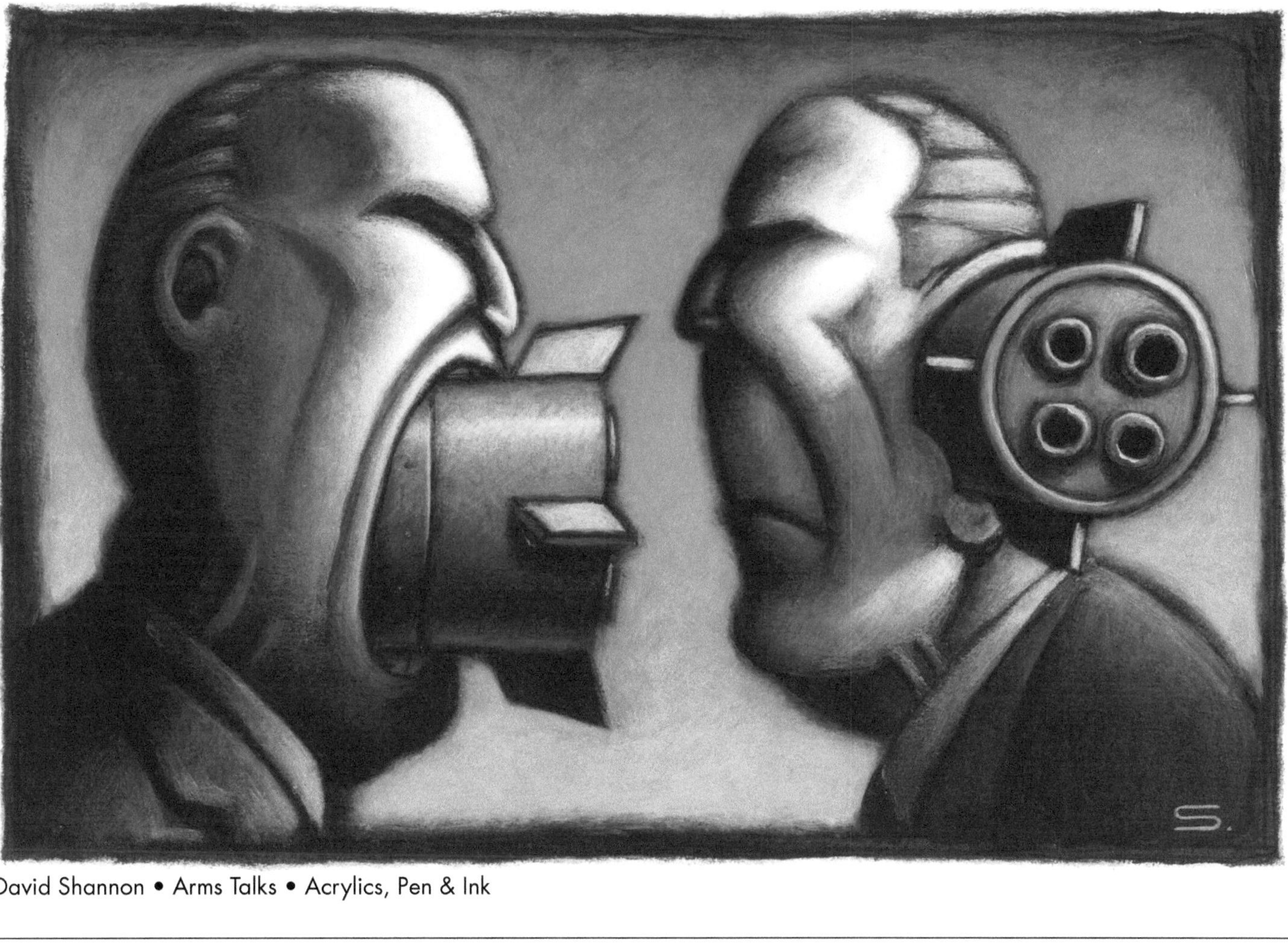

David Shannon • Arms Talks • Acrylics, Pen & Ink

Bernhard Goetz indicted in New York vigilante shooting. *We Are the World* and *Live Aid* organized for famine relief in the Third World. Mikhail Gorbachev becomes Soviet Premier.

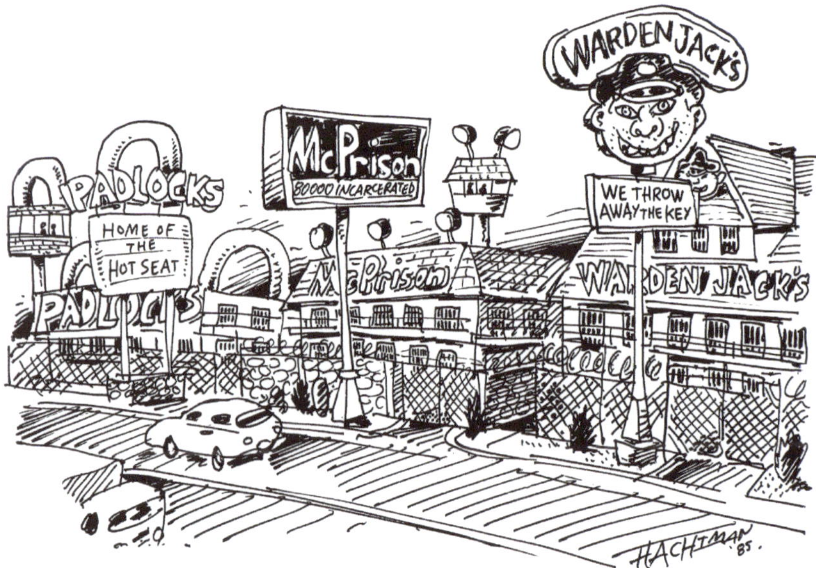

Tom Hachtman • Privatized Prisons • Pen & Ink

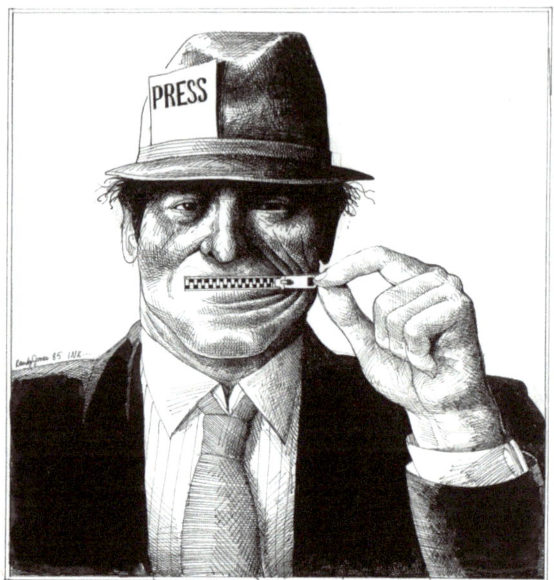

Randy Jones • Muzzled Media • Pen & Ink

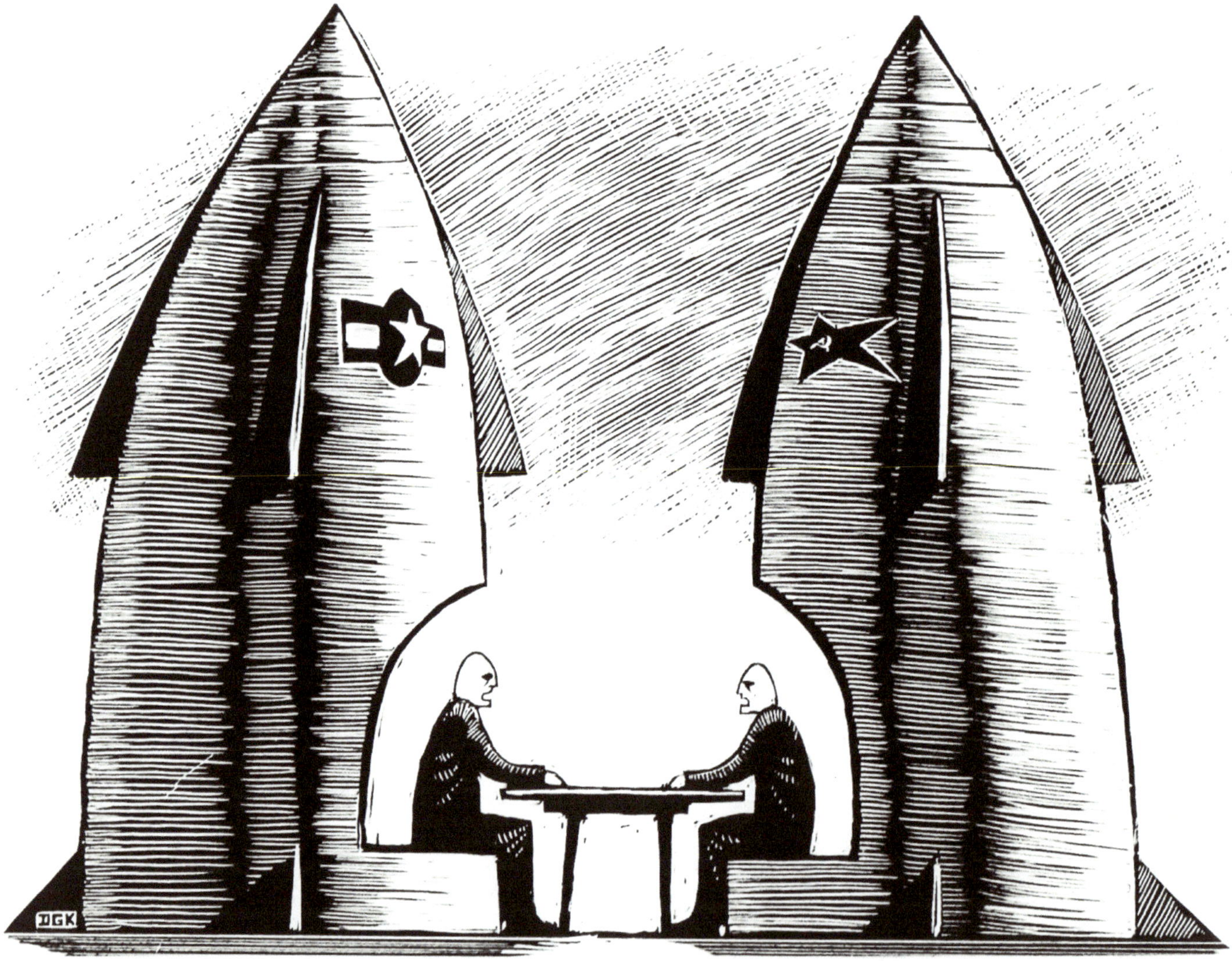

David Klein • Arms Negotiations • Scratchboard

During the years with United Feature Syndicate, home, at the time of *Peanuts* and *Dilbert,* INX was seen on the editorial pages of most of big-market U.S. newspapers including *The Boston Globe, The Chicago Tribune, The Los Angeles Times* and *The Washington Post.* Because most of the artists were New York-based, it wasn't promoted there — they didn't want to compete with cheaper syndicated versions of themselves. United Feature also helped spread the service to journals in Europe and South America where the captionless cartoons needed no translation.

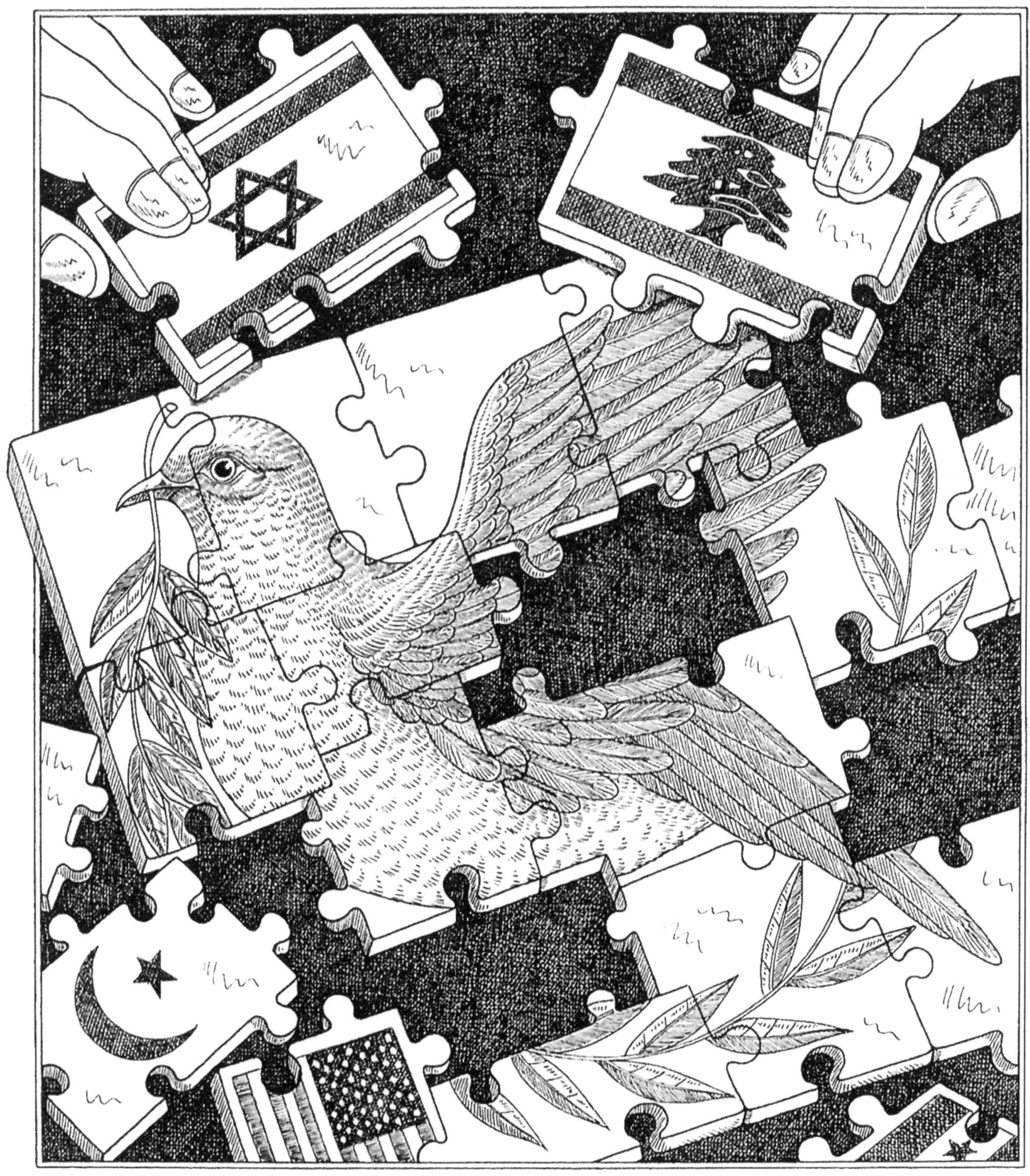

Jill Karla Schwarz • Middle East Peace • Pen & Ink

1986

Iran-Contra scandal erupts. Space shuttle *Challenger* explodes on takeoff killing all seven aboard. Chernobyl nuclear disaster in Ukraine. Fedinand Marcos deposed in Philippines, Corazon Aquino assumes presidency. U.S.S.R. launches Mir space station.

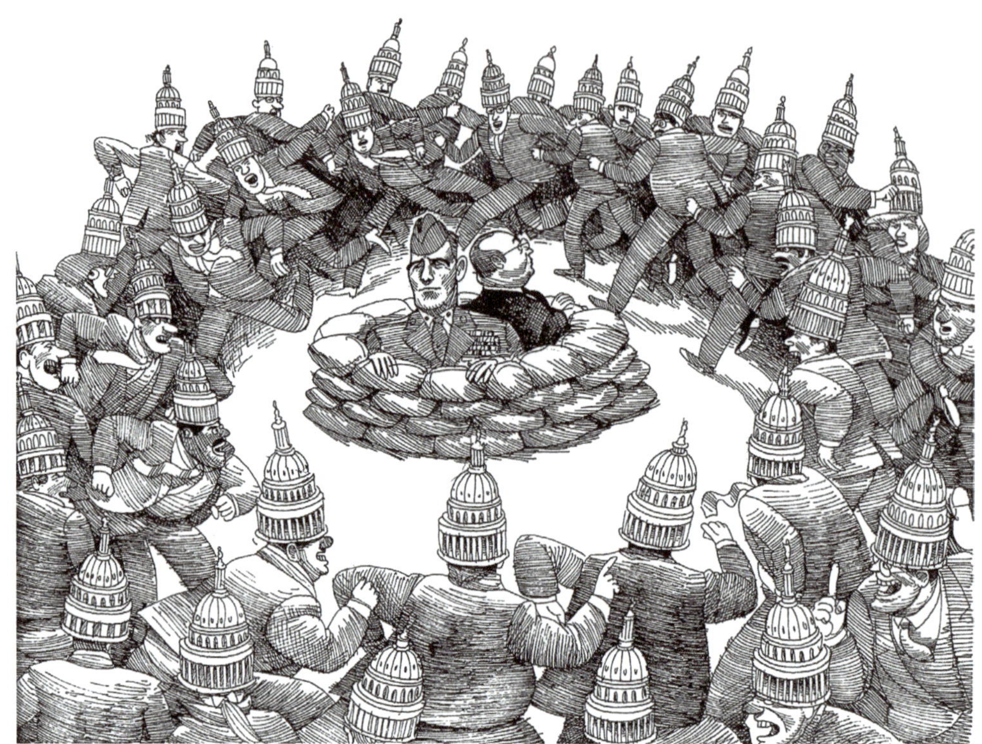

Randy Jones • North's Last Stand • Pen & Ink

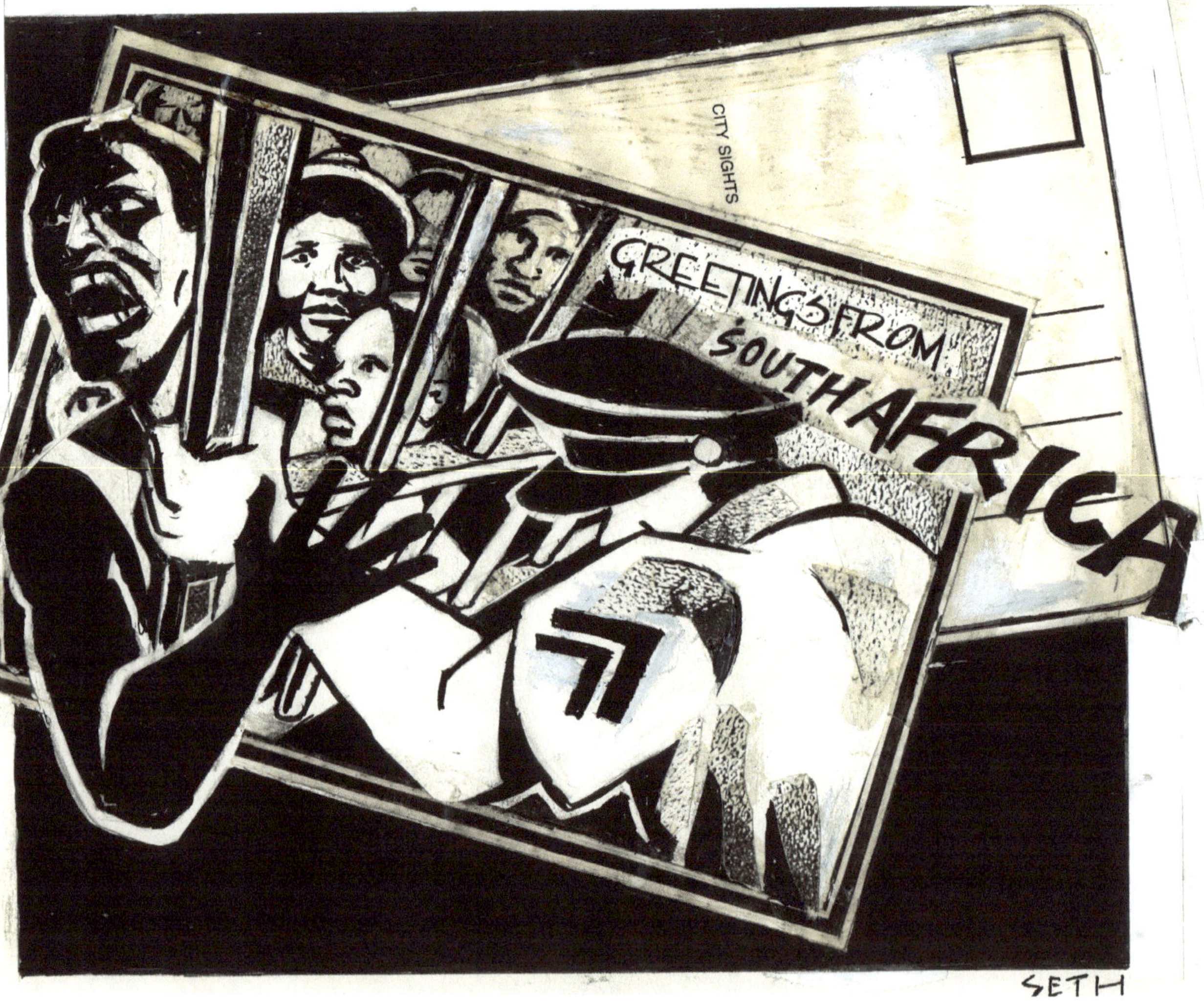

Seth Tobocman • South Africa • Pen, Brush & Ink

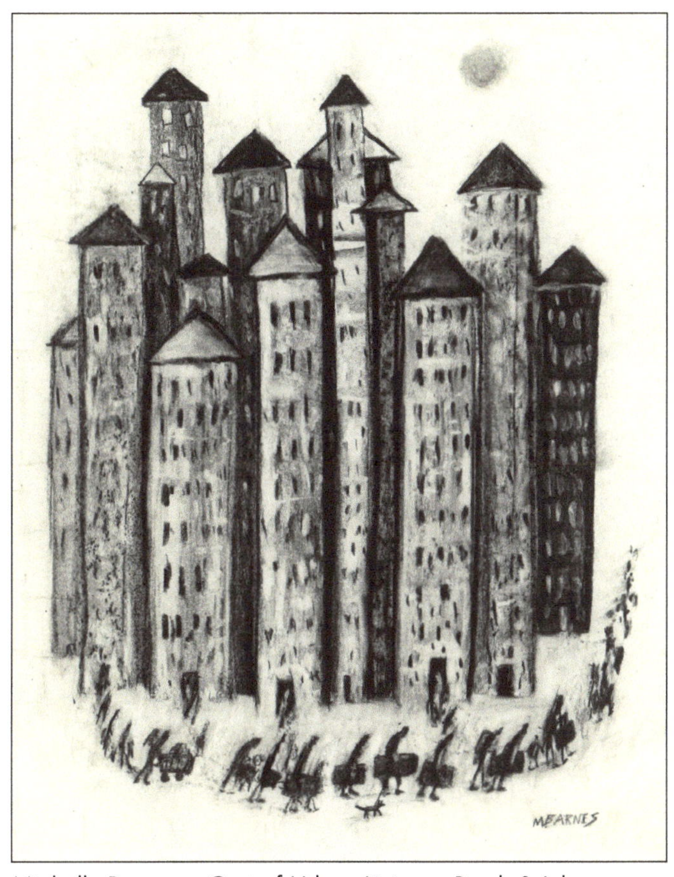

Michelle Barnes • Cost of Urban Living • Brush & Ink

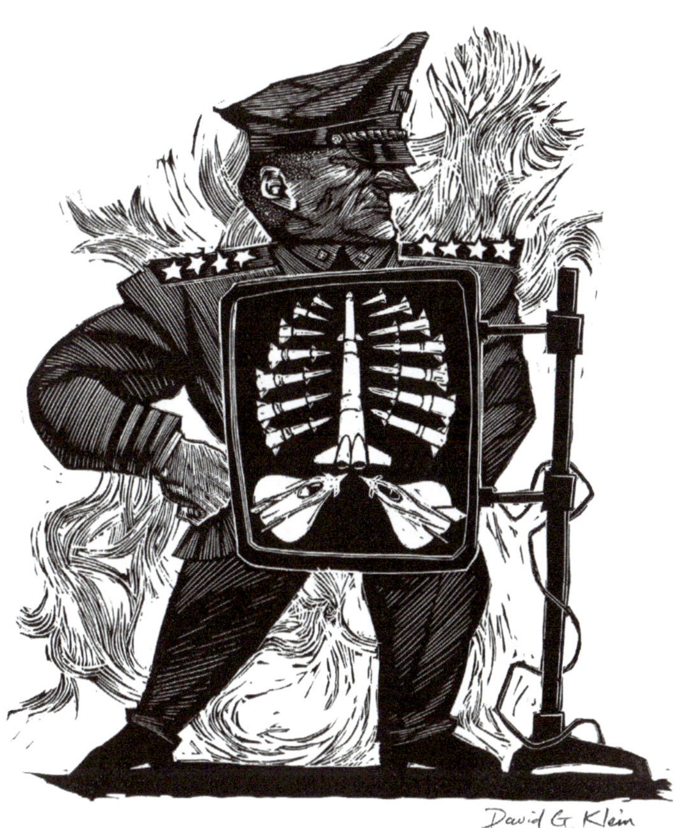

David Klein • Inside the Military • Engraving

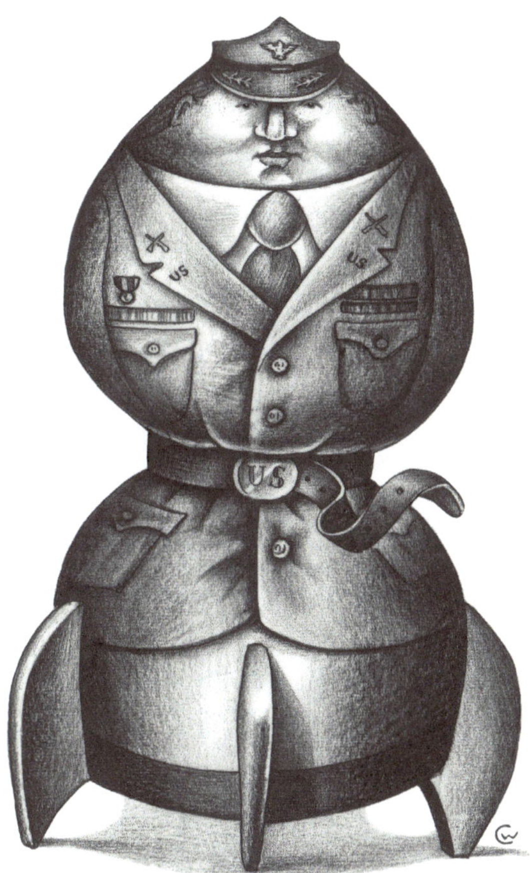

Charles Waller • Defense Spending • Pencil

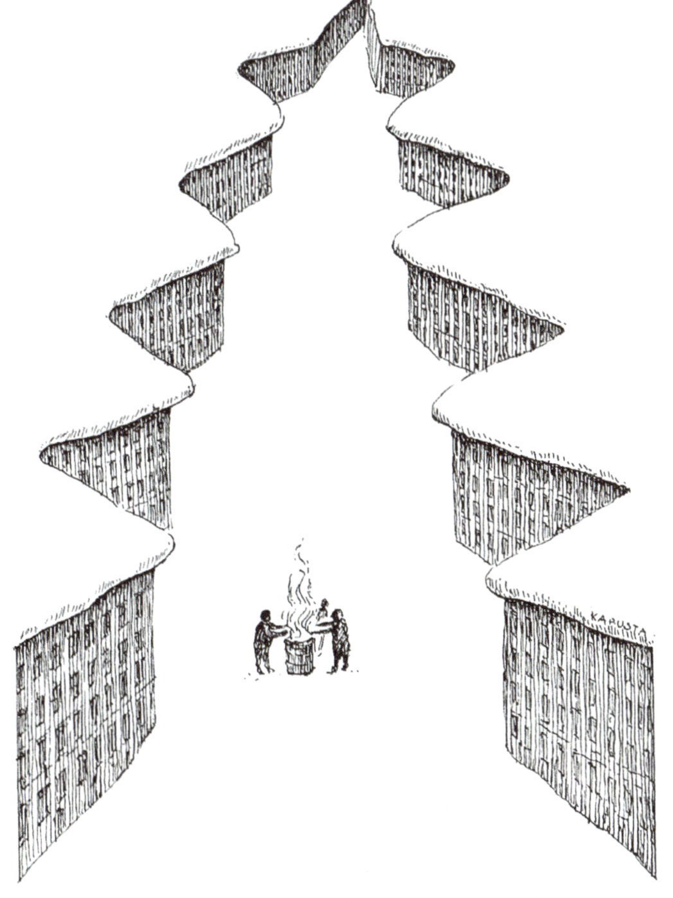

Janusz Kapusta • Christmas in the City • Pen & Ink

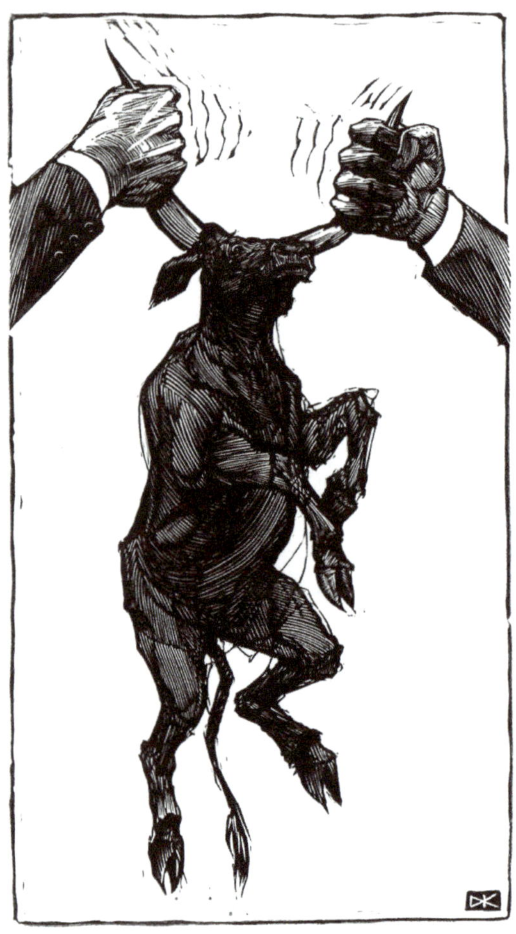

David Klein • Bull By The Horns • Engraving

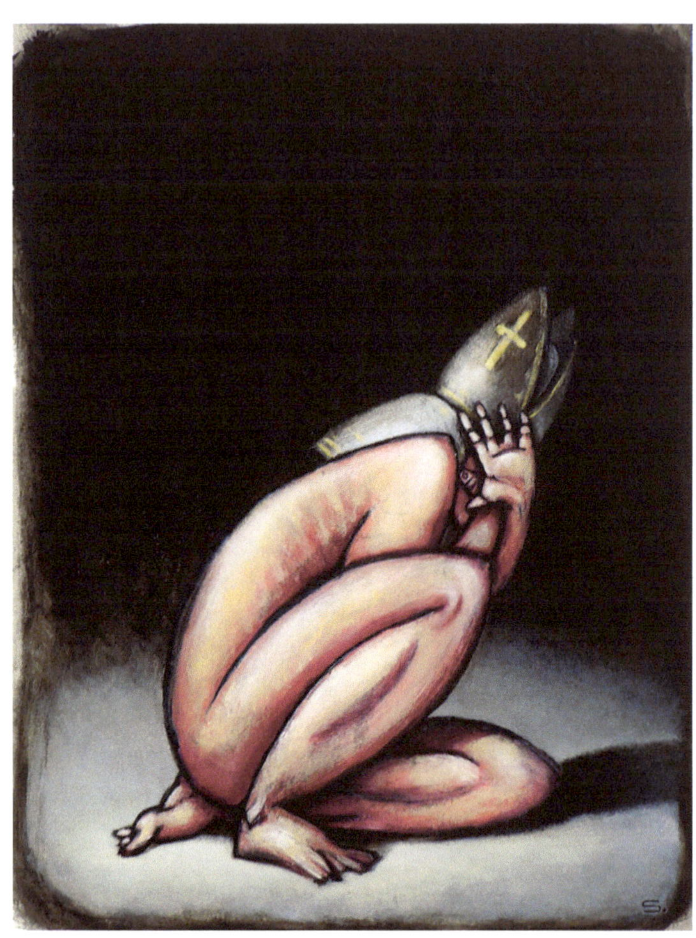

David Shannon • Church Scandals • Acrylics

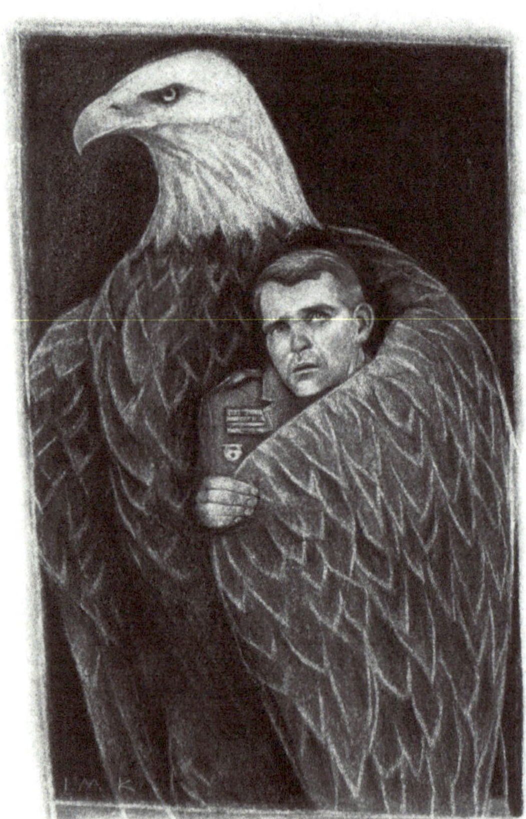

Ira Korman • Ollie North • Charcoal

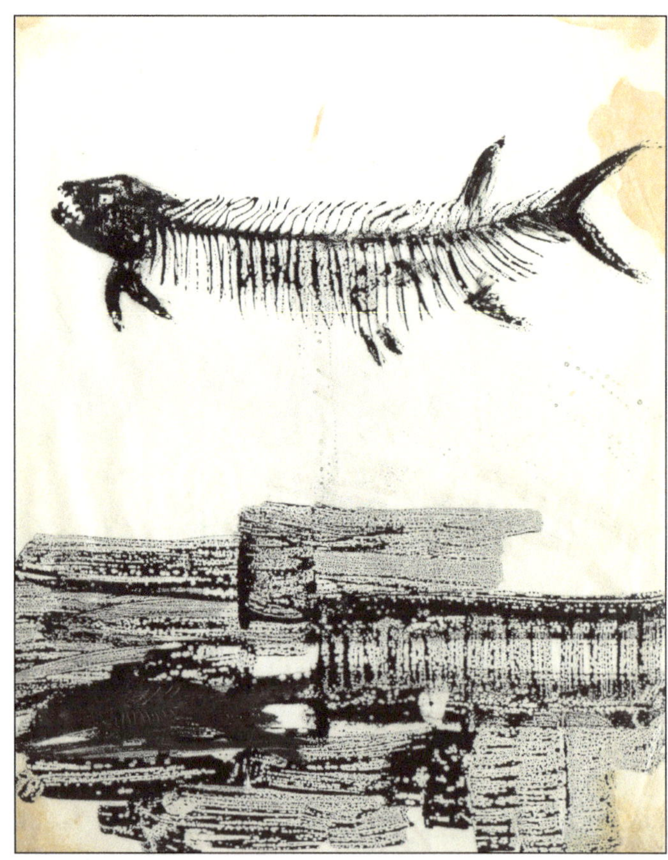

Michelle Barnes • Toxic Spills • Brush & Ink

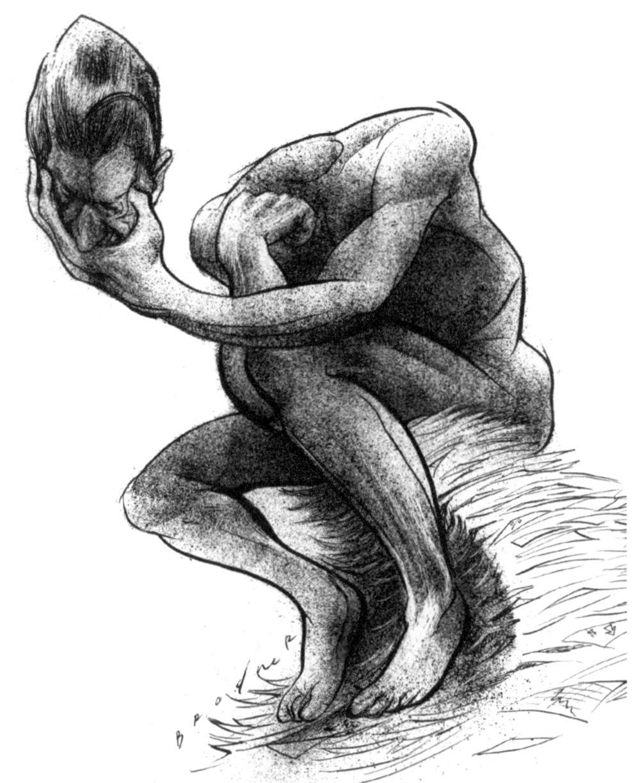

Steve Brodner • Reagan as Thinker • Pen & Ink

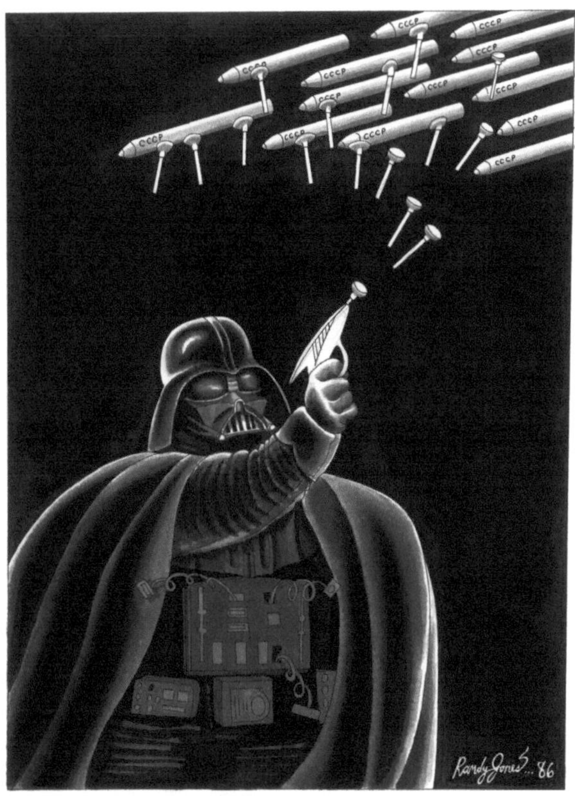

Randy Jones • Star Wars Defense • Pen, Brush & Ink

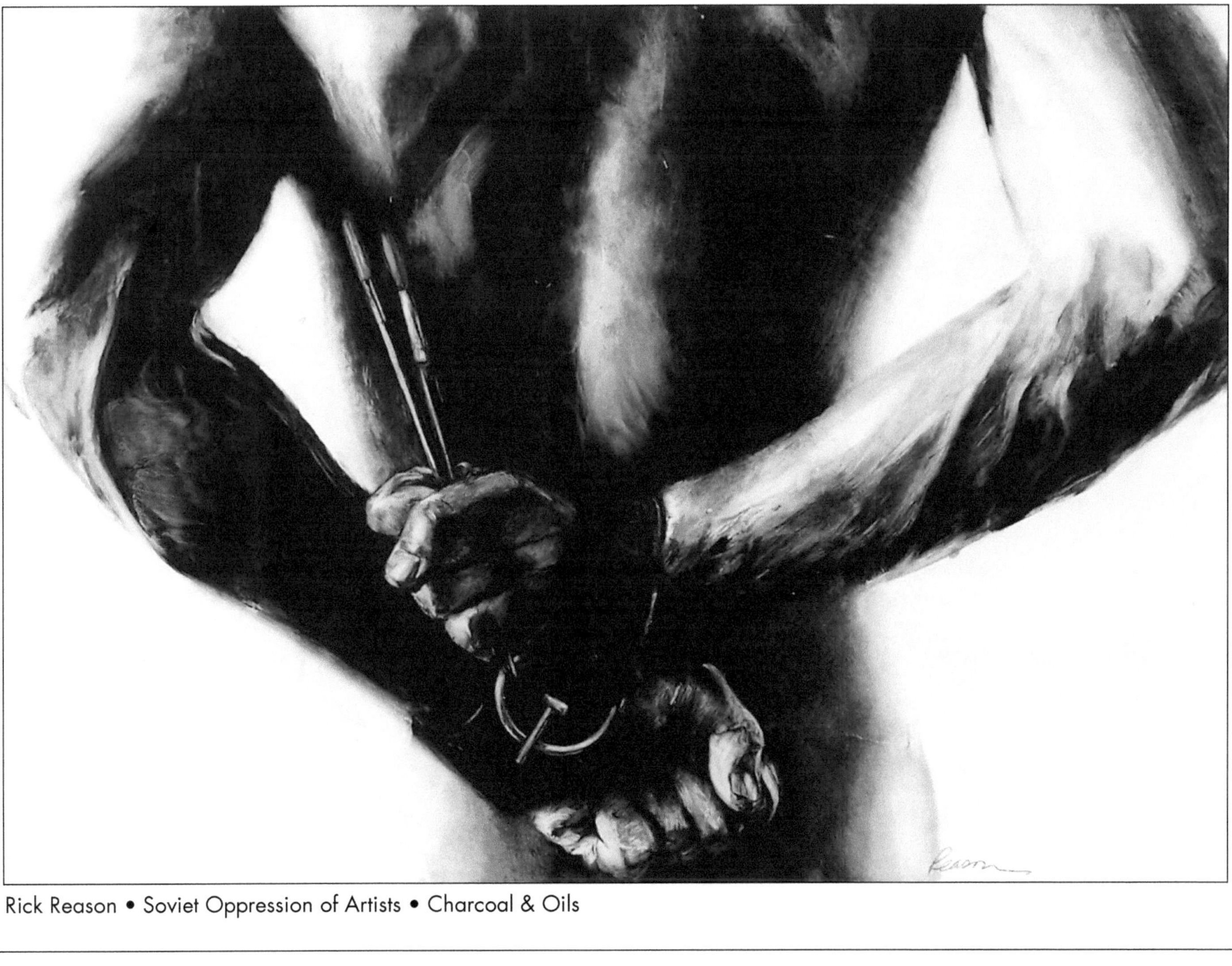

Rick Reason • Soviet Oppression of Artists • Charcoal & Oils

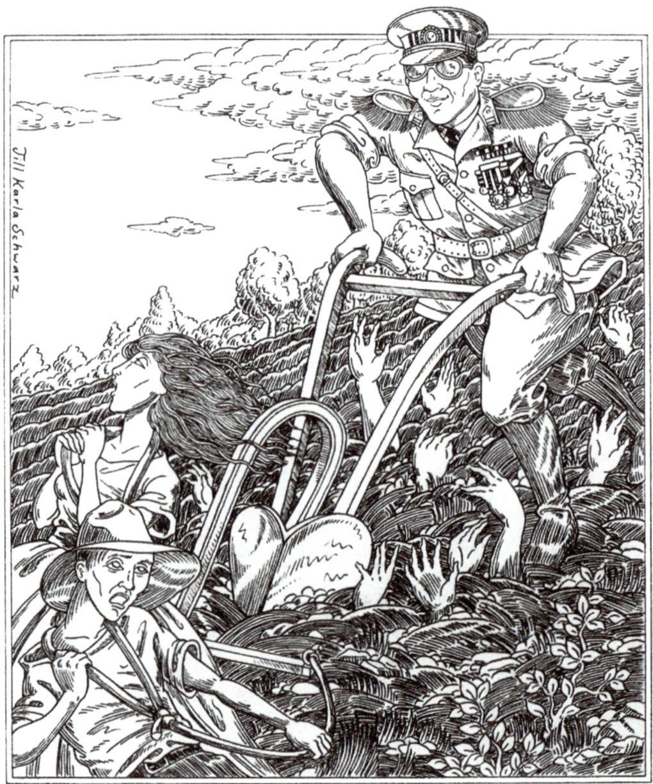

Jill Karla Schwarz • Central America's Grim Harvest • Pen & Ink

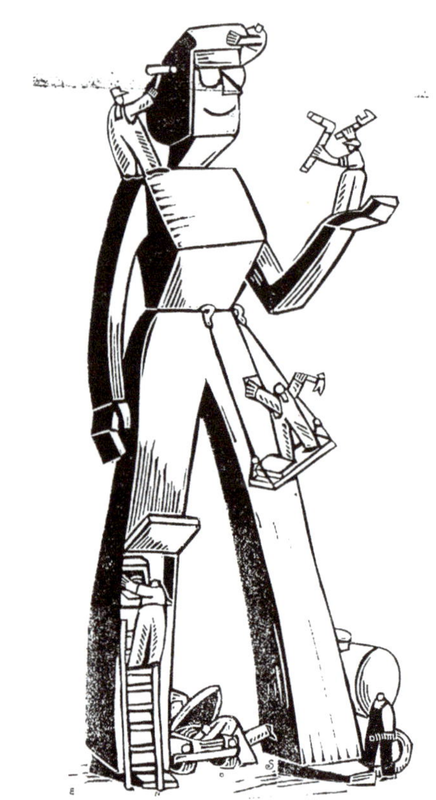

Randall Enos • Women in the Workplace • Linocut

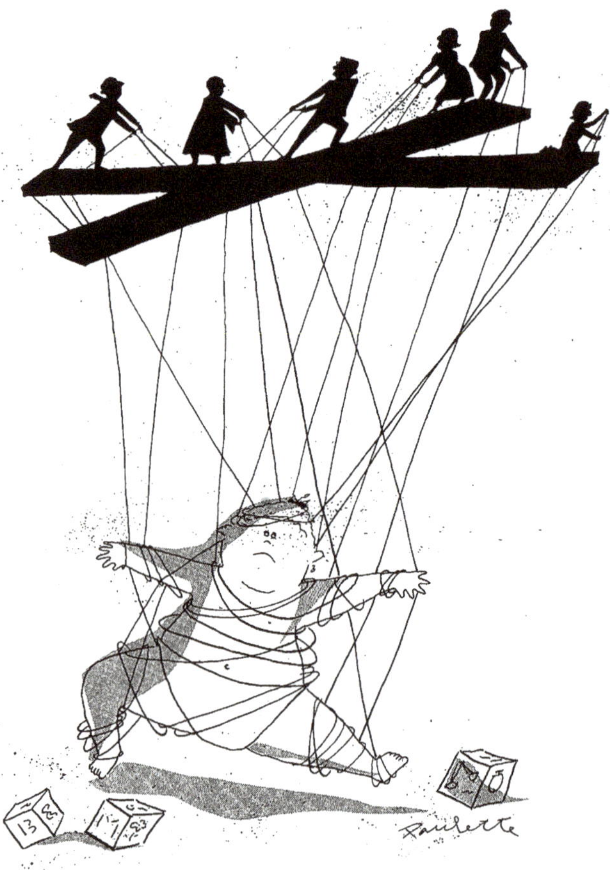

Paulette Bogan • The Custody Battle • Pen & Ink

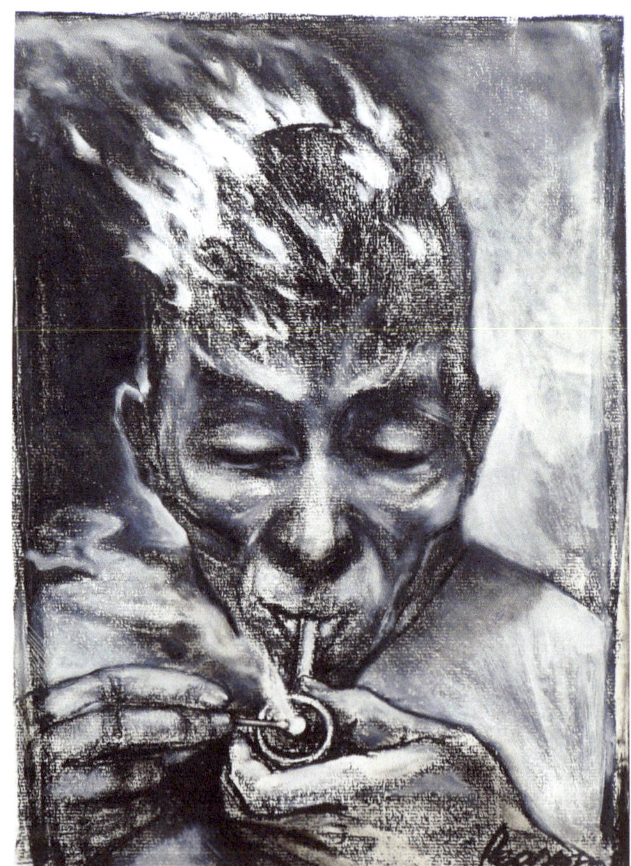

Rick Reason • Crack & Burn • Charcoal & Oils

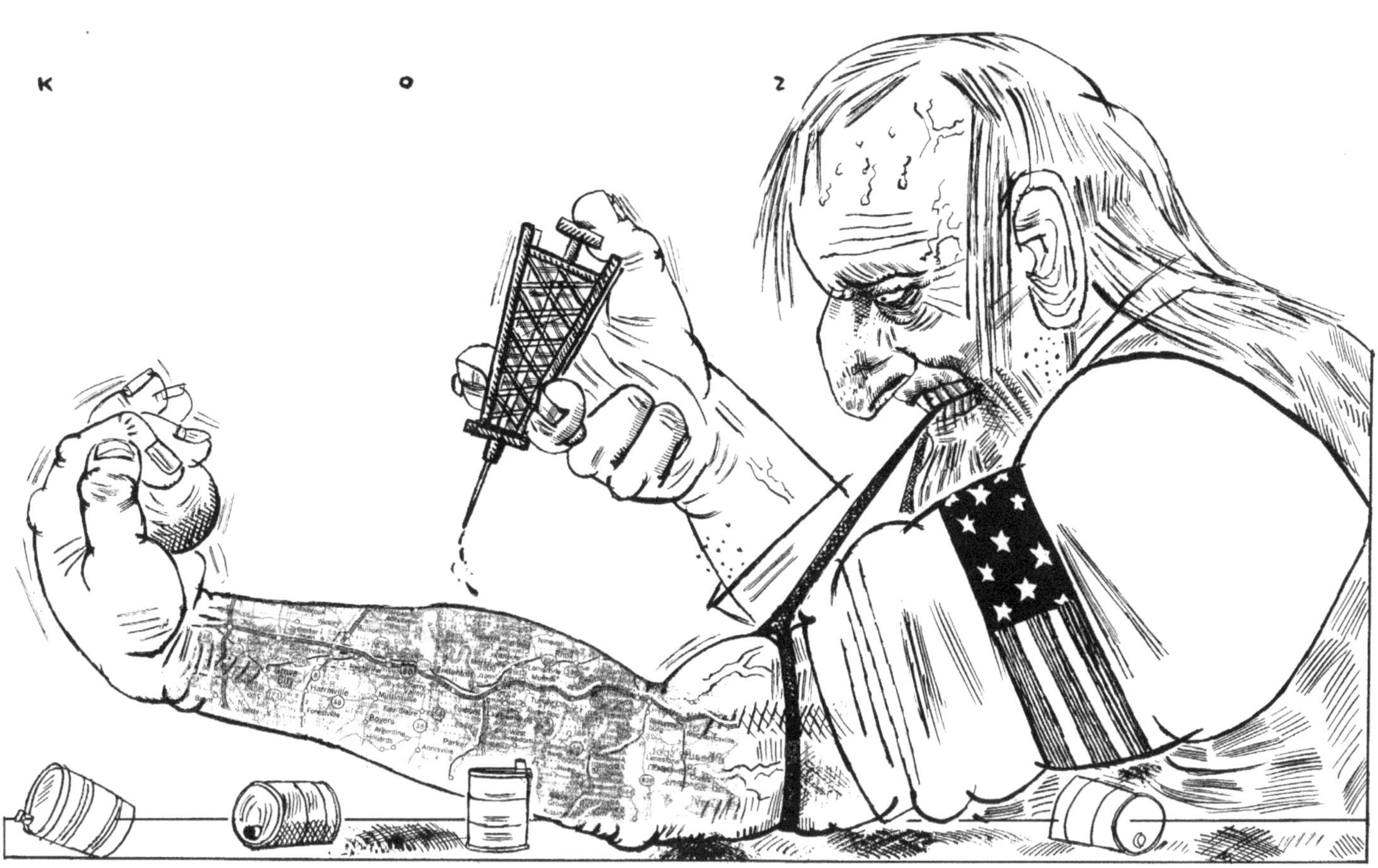

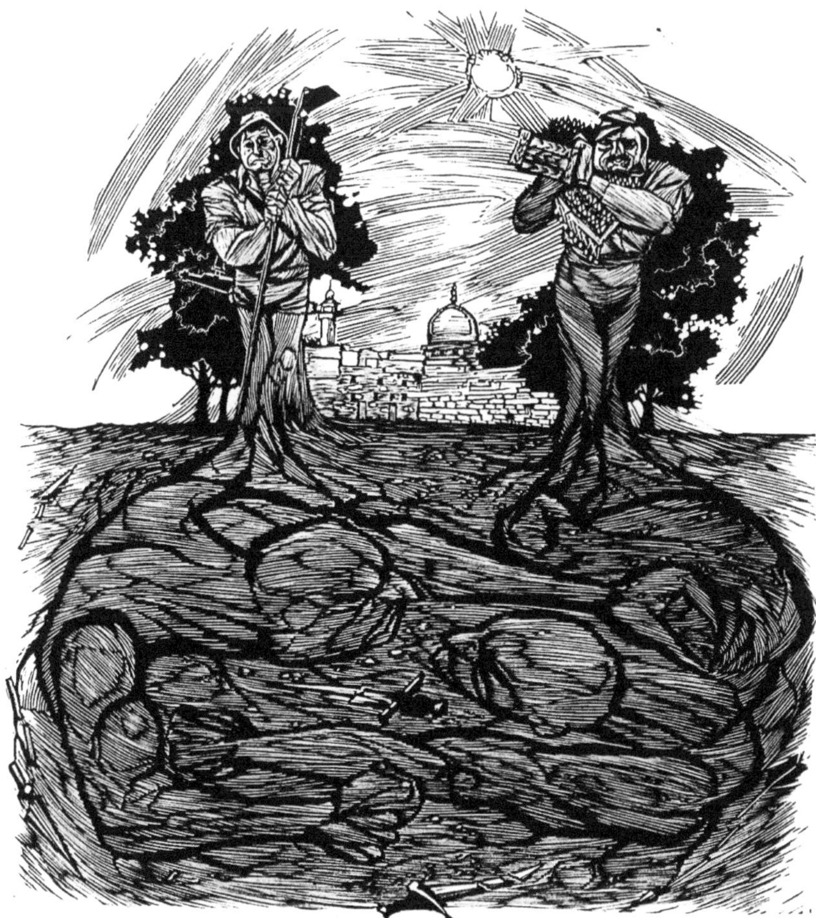

Martin Kozlowski • Uncle Sam's Oil Fix • Pen, Ink & Collage

David Klein • Roots of Middle East Violence • Print

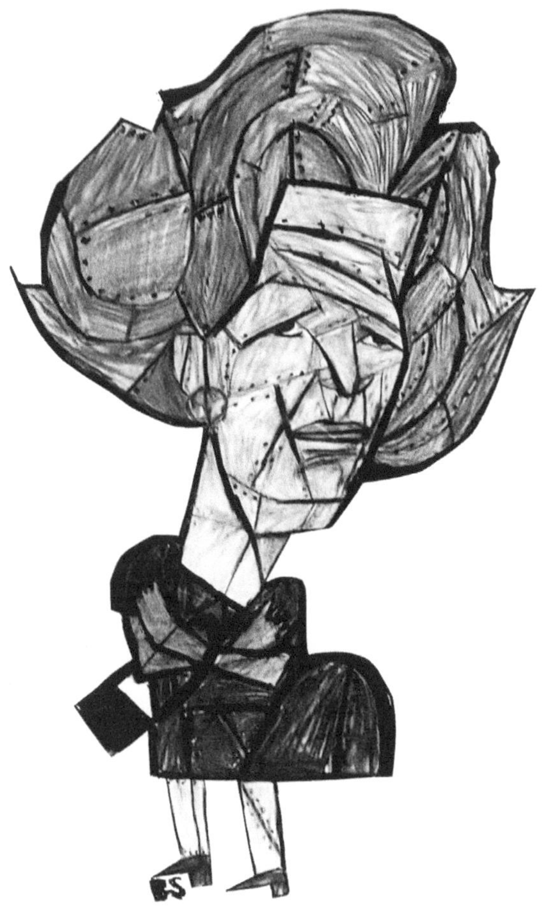

Betsy Scheld • Iron Lady • Mixed Media

1988

George H.W. Bush defeats Michael Dukakis for U.S. presidency. Perestroika begins in U.S.S.R. Iran-Iraq War ends. Pan Am Flight 103 taken down over Lockerbie, Scotland.

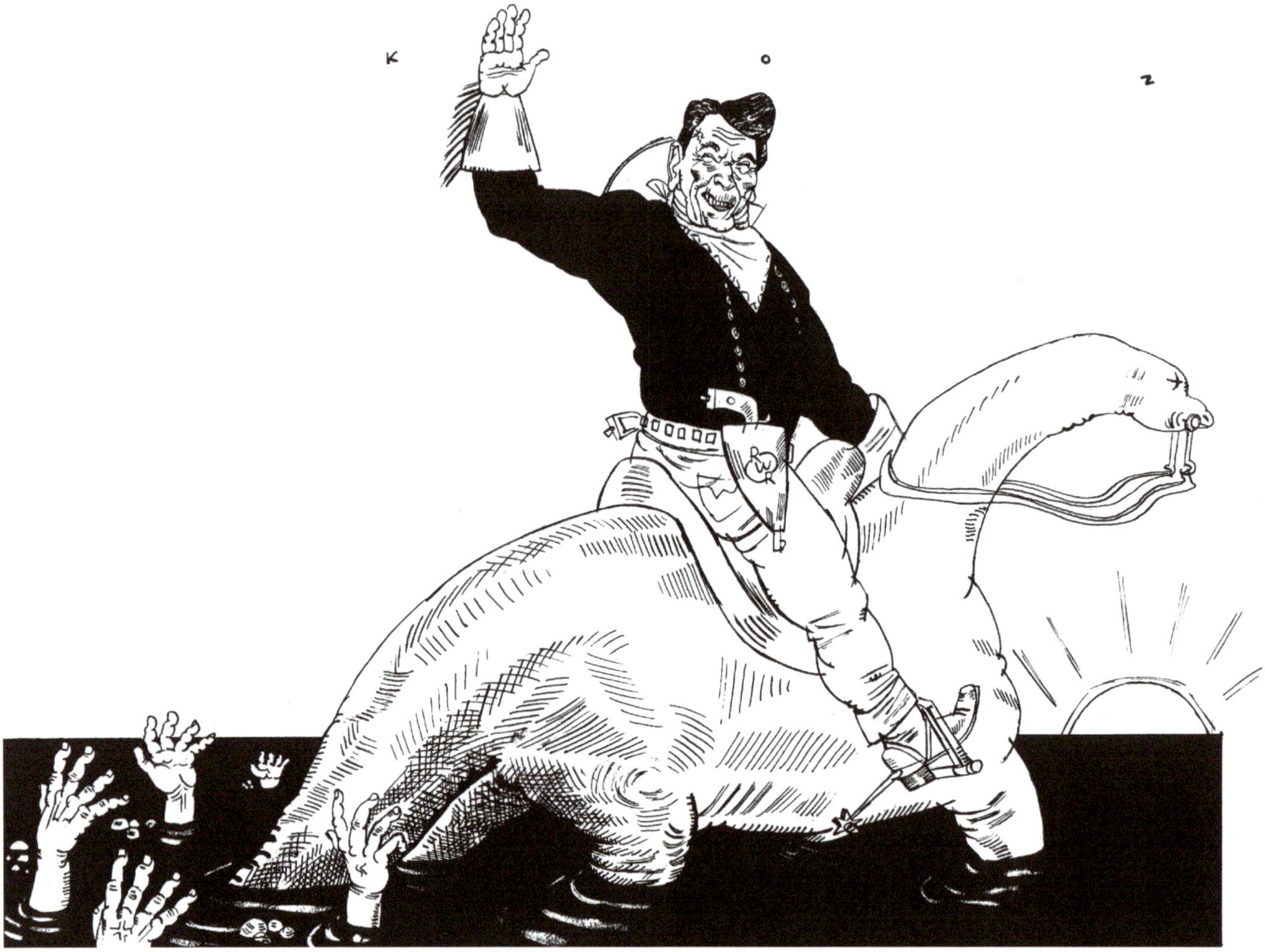

Martin Kozlowski • Reagan Rides Into the Sunset • Pen & Ink

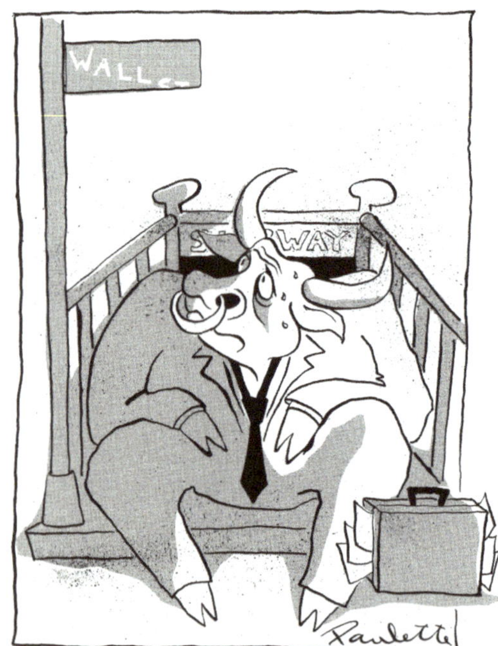

Paulette Bogan • Wall Street Jitters • Pen & Ink

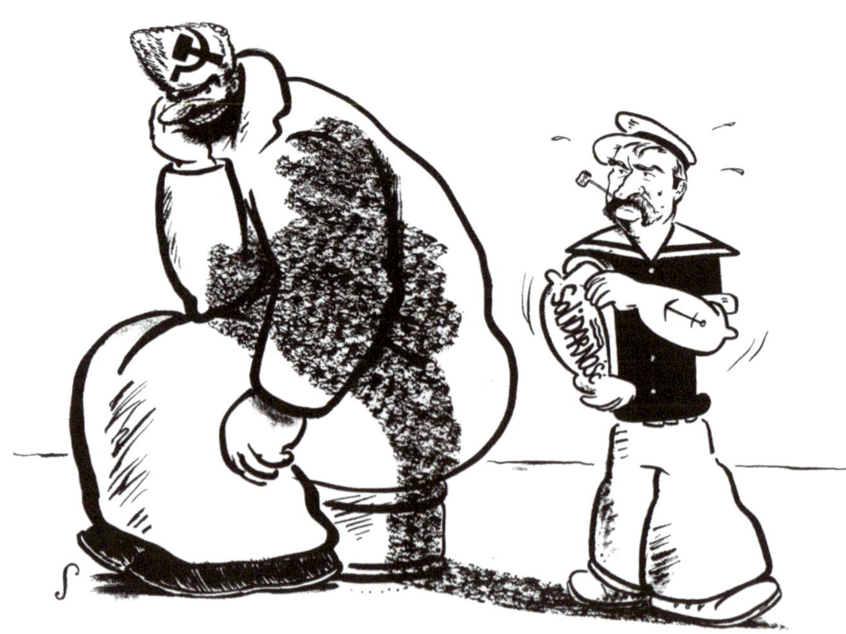

Steven Salerno • Popeye Walesa • Pen & Ink

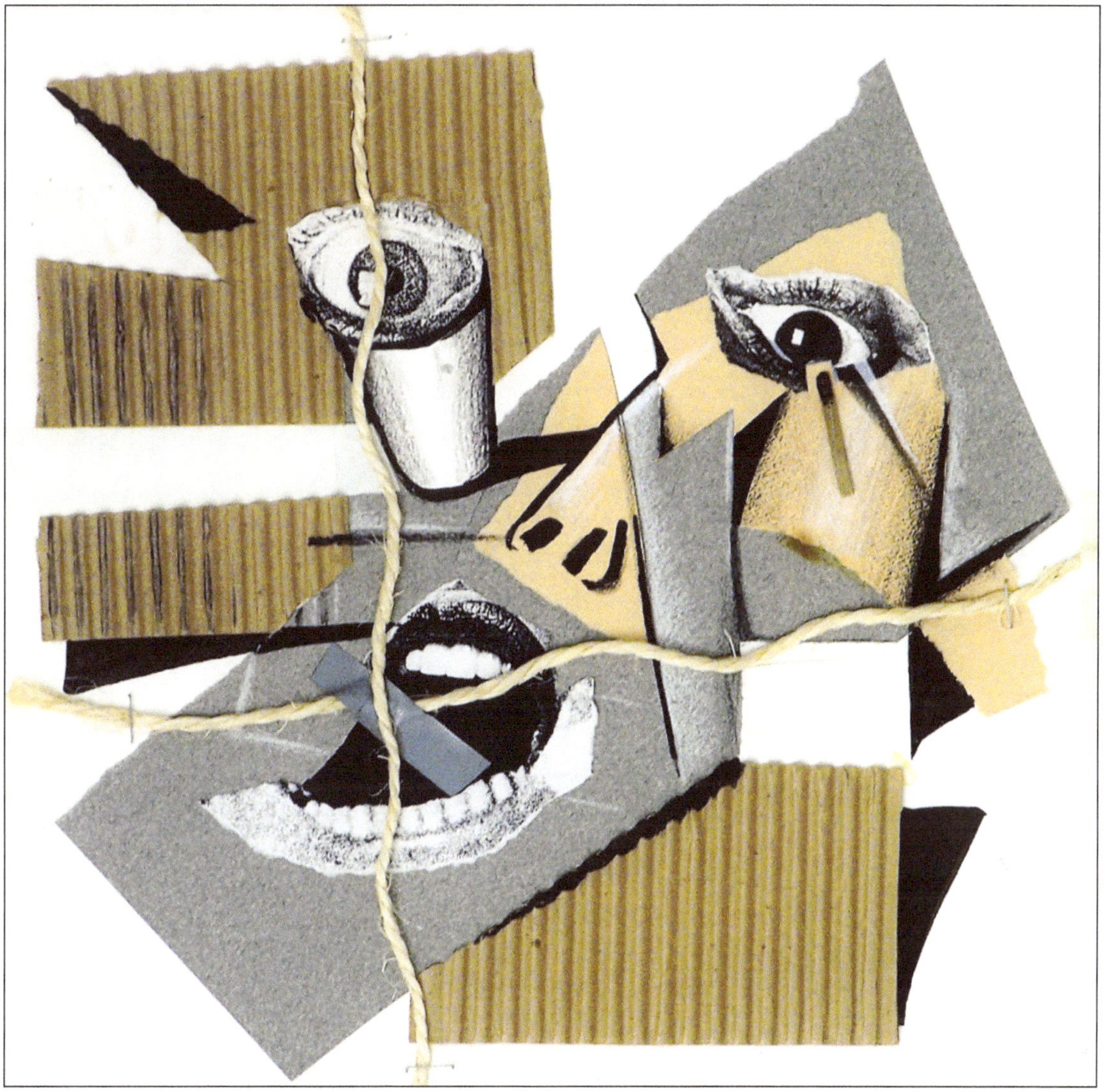

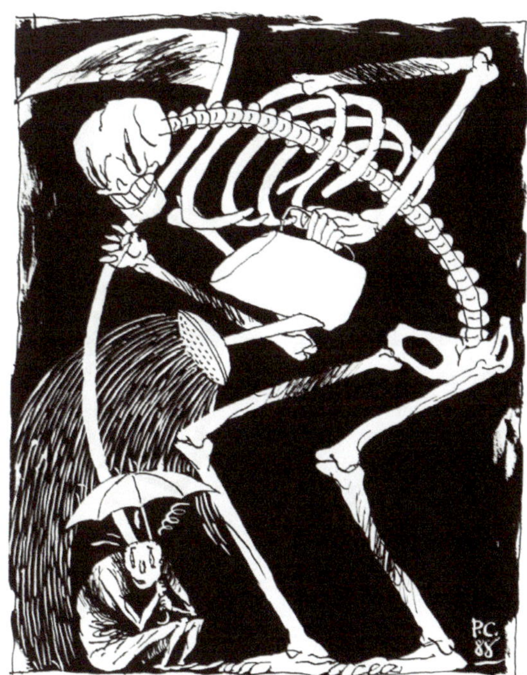

Peter Kuper • Torture • Brush, Ink & Collage

Paul Corio • Acid Rain • Pen & Ink

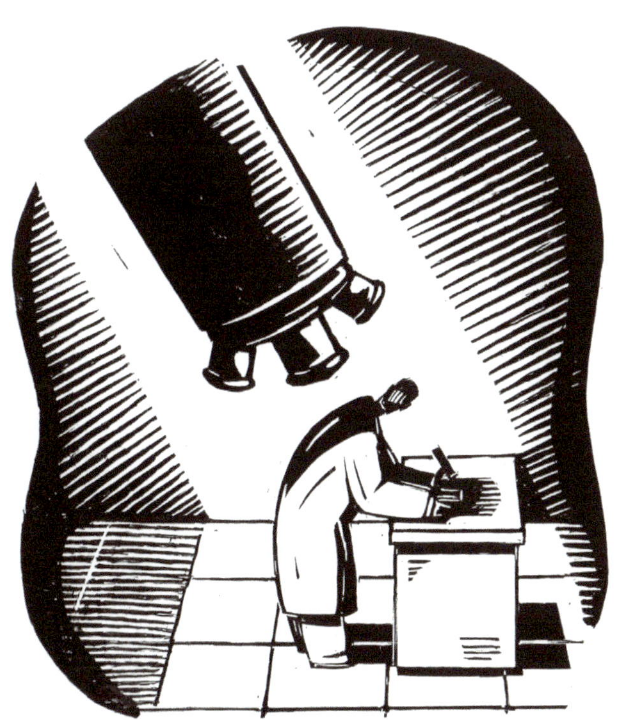

Mark Matcho • Monitoring Scientists • Scratchboard

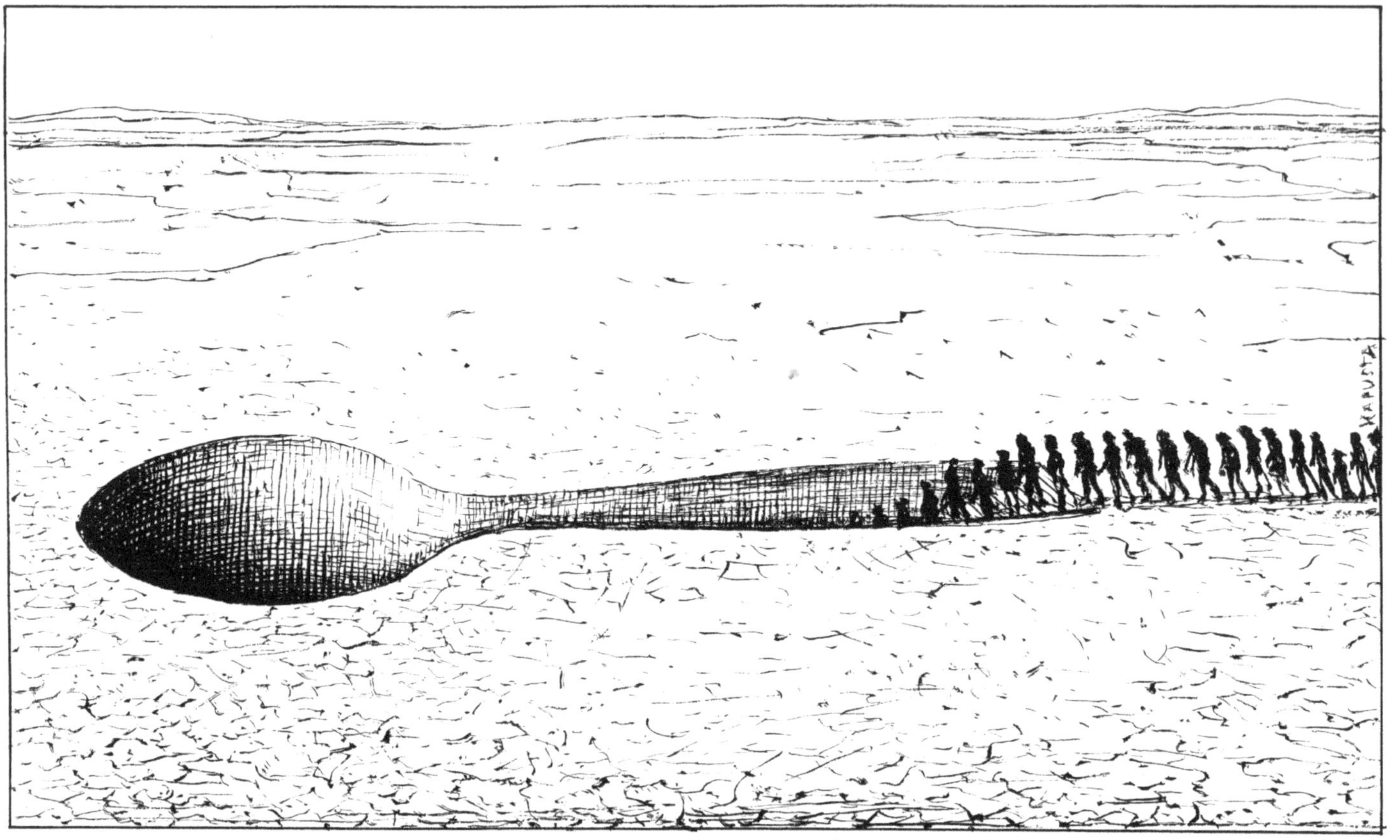

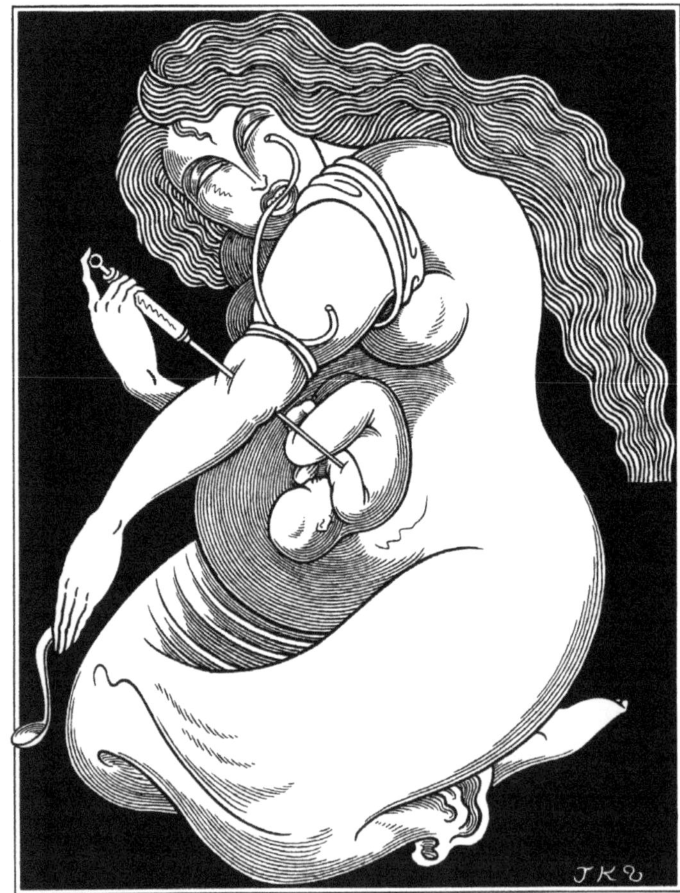

Janusz Kapusta • Drought • Pen & Ink

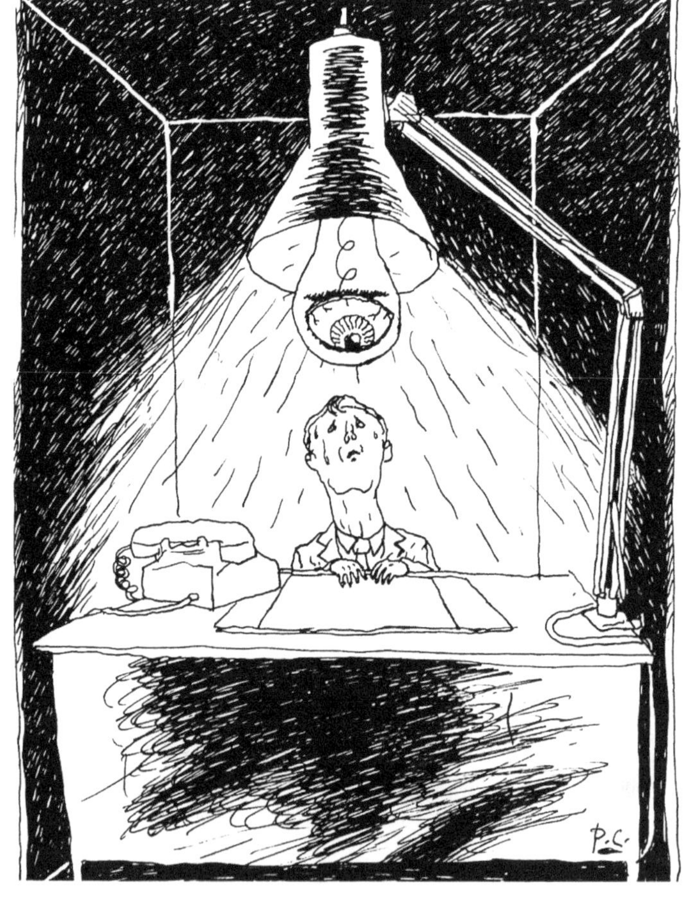

Jill Karla Schwarz • Drugs & Pregnancy • Pen & Ink

Paul Corio • Privacy in the Workplace • Pen & Ink

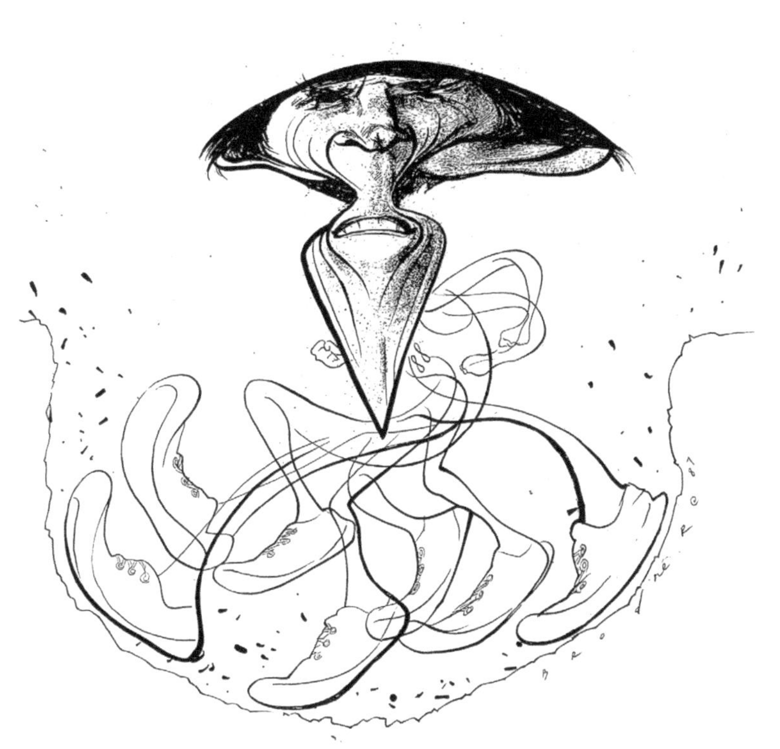

Steve Brodner • Gary Hart • Pen & Ink

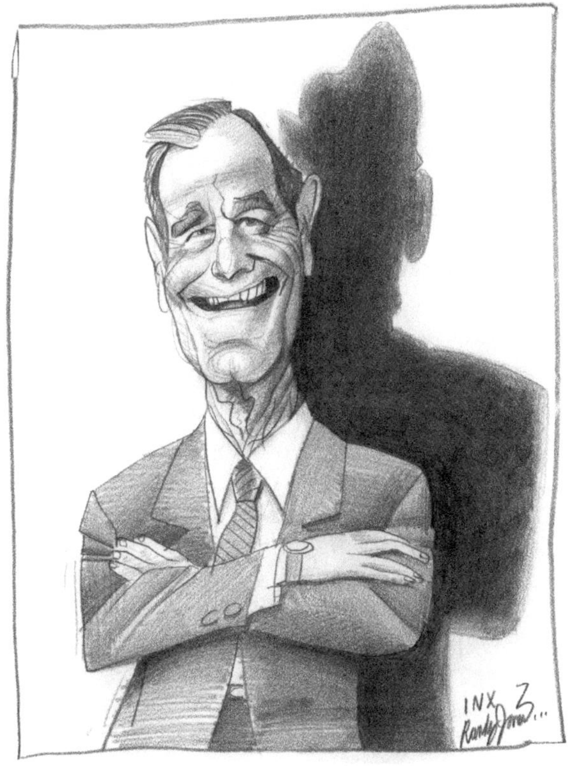

Randy Jones • Bush in Reagan's Shadow • Pencil

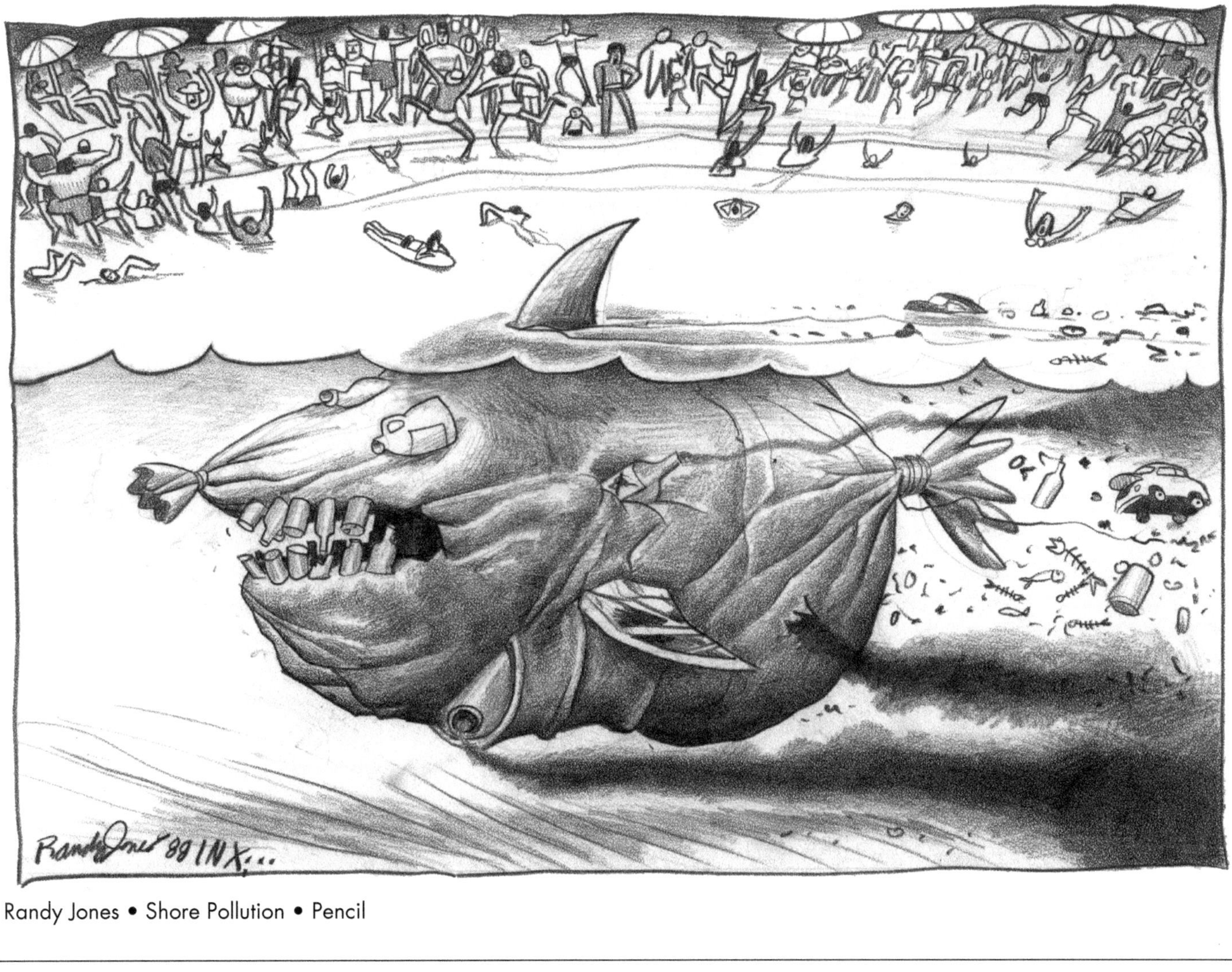

Randy Jones • Shore Pollution • Pencil

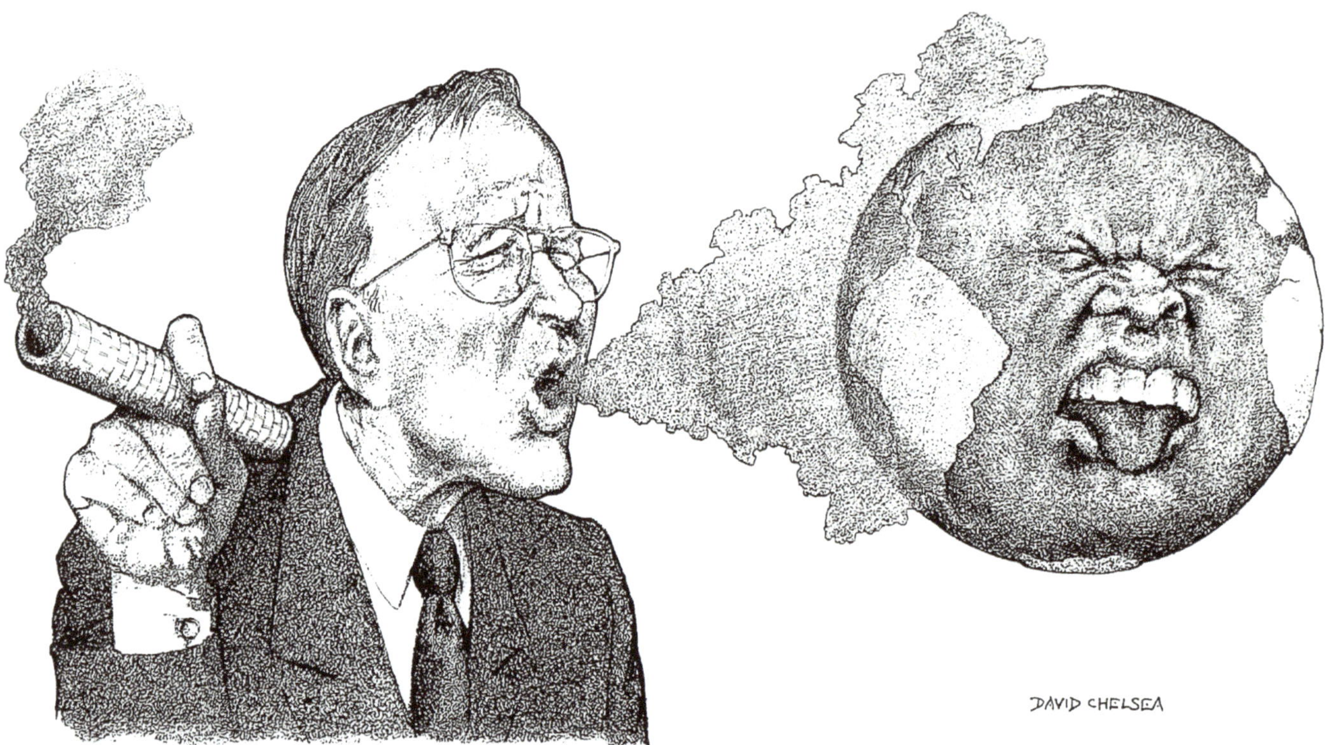

David Chelsea • Bush & the Environment • Pen & Ink

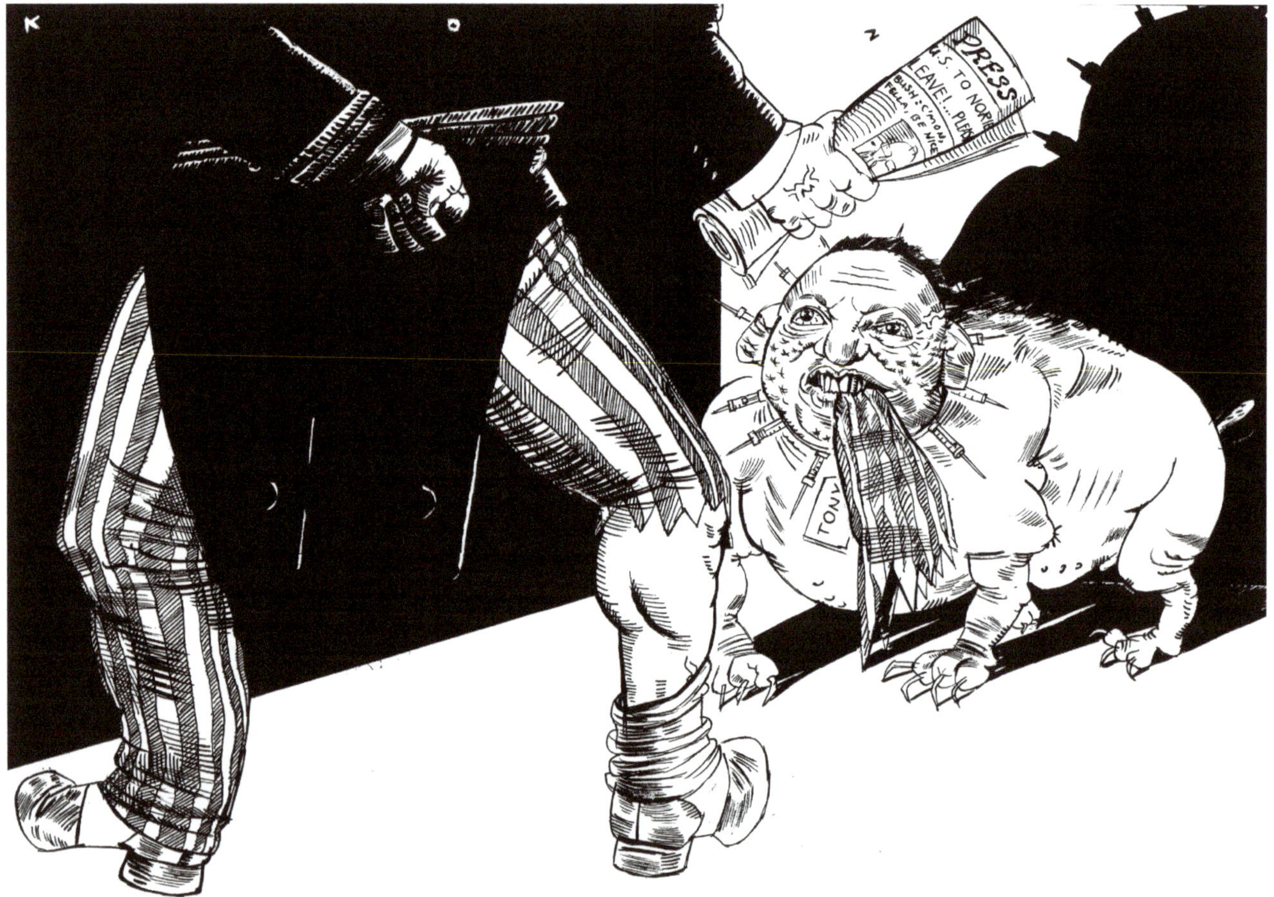

Martin Kozlowski • Panama's Noriega • Pen & Ink

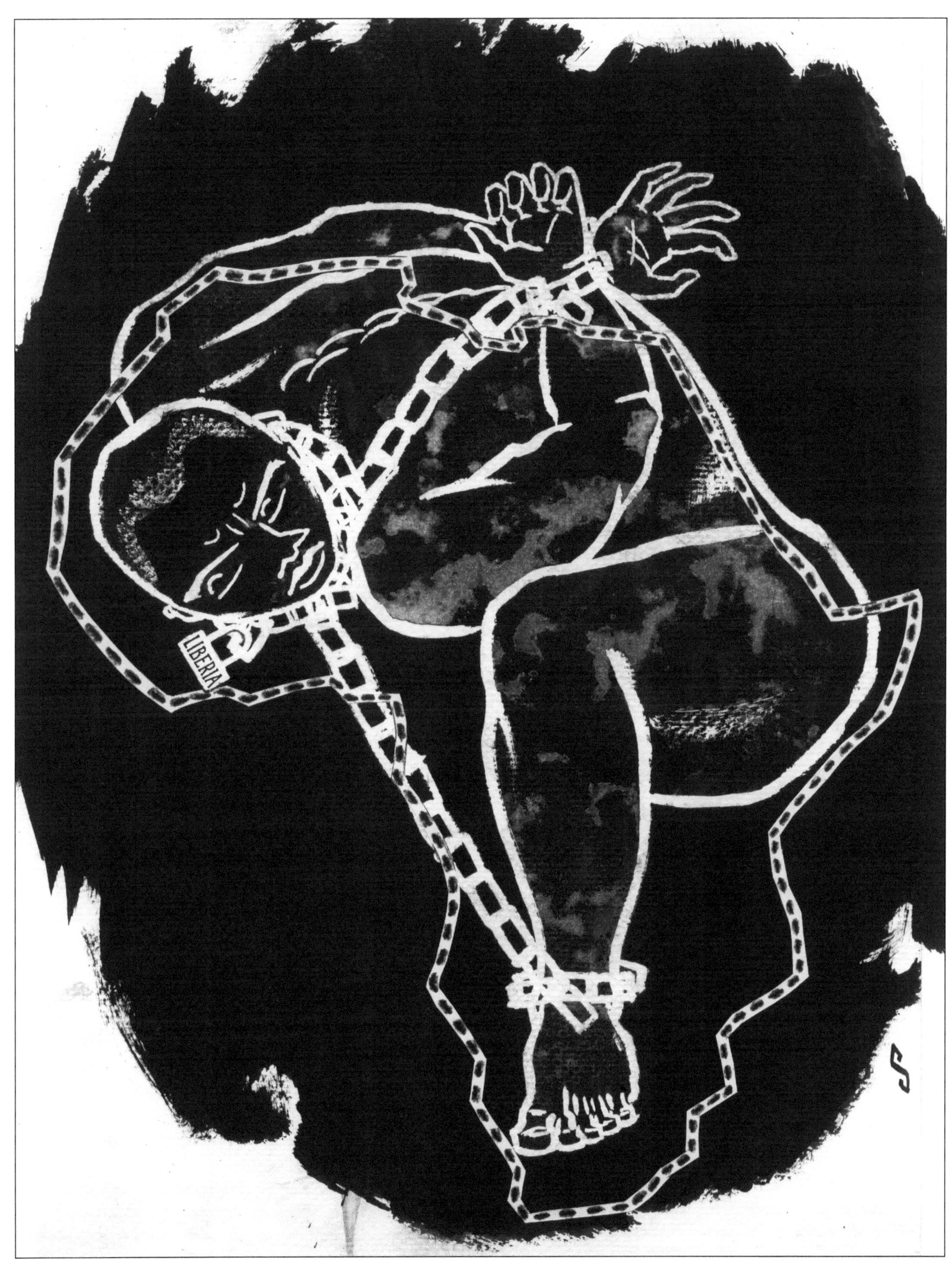

Steven Salerno • Liberia in Chains • Brush & Ink

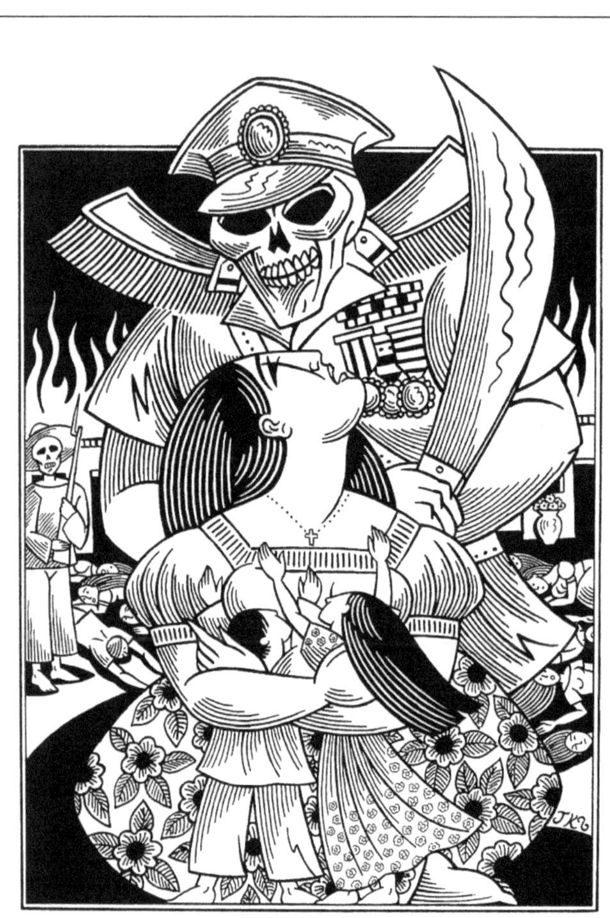

Jill Karla Schwarz • El General • Pen & Ink

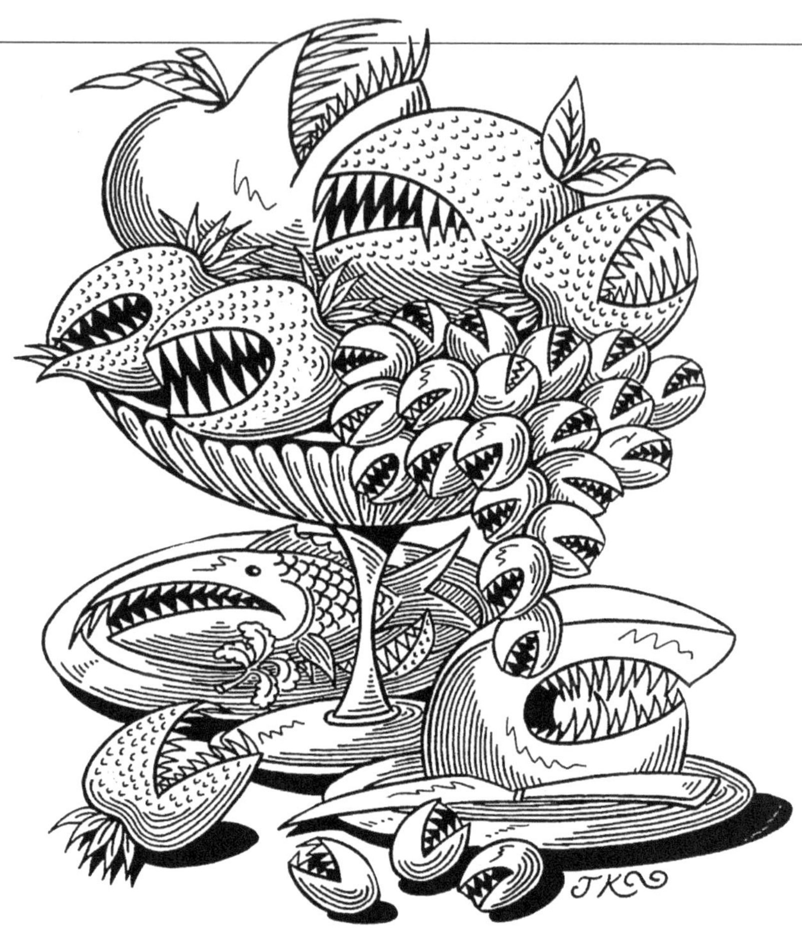

Jill Karla Schwarz • Toxic Food • Pen & Ink

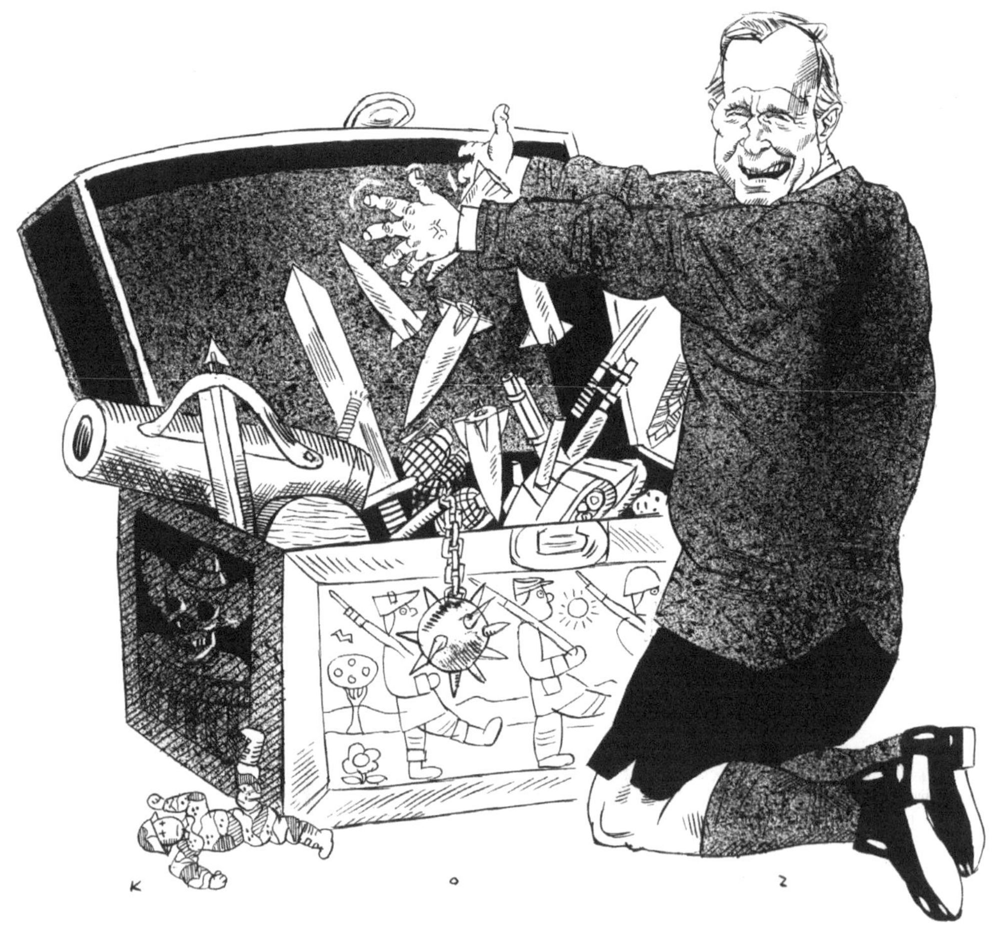

Martin Kozlowski • Bush's War Chest • Pen & Ink

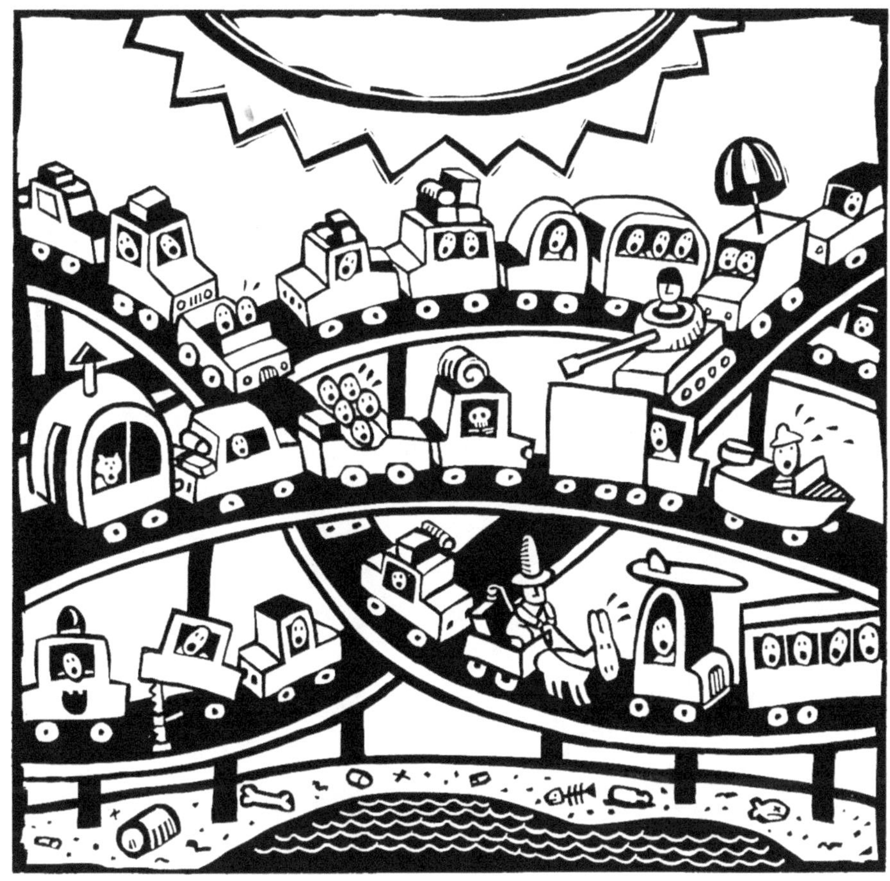

Robert Zimmerman • Summer Getaway • Scratchboard

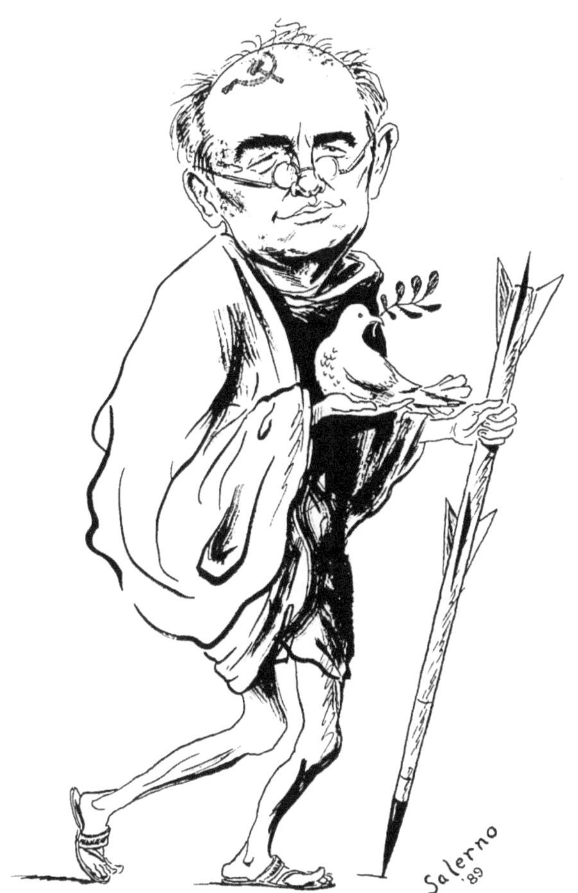

Steven Salerno • Gorby as Gandhi • Pen & Ink

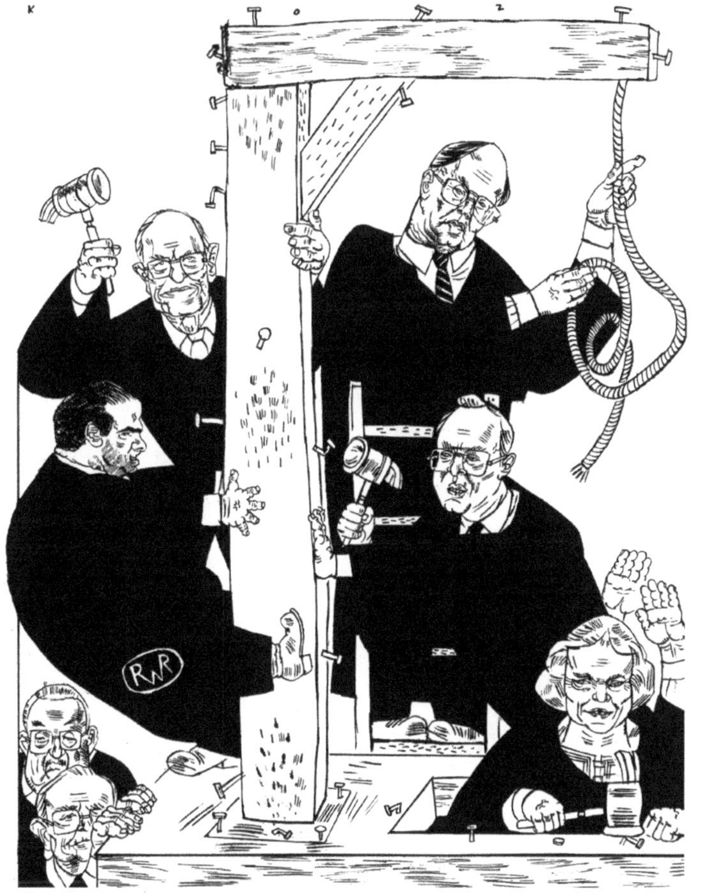

Martin Kozlowski • Supreme Court Death Penalty • Pen & Ink

1990

Iraq invades Kuwait, Gulf War begins. Reunification of Germany. Contra War ends in Nicaragua. Aung San Suu Kyi under house arrest in Myanmar. World Wide Web invented.

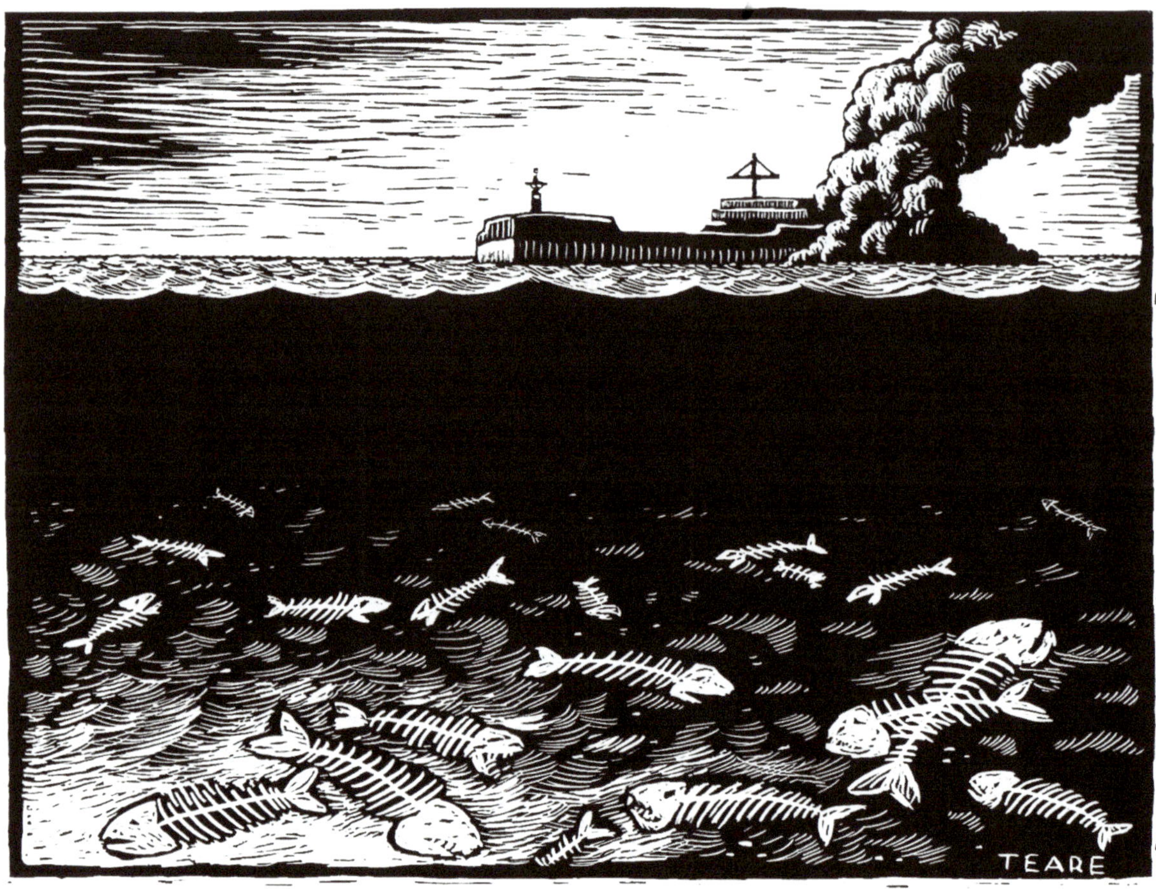

Brad Teare • Cost of Oil Spills • Scratchboard

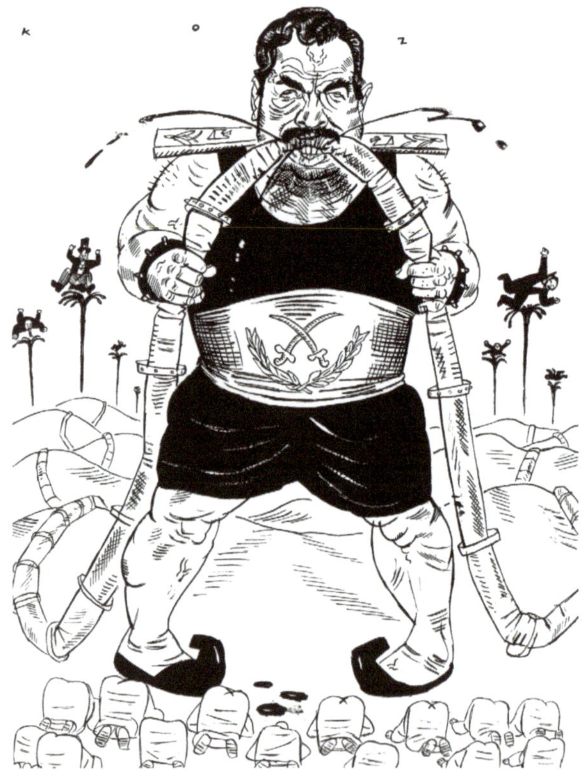

Martin Kozlowski • Saddam Hussein • Pen & Ink

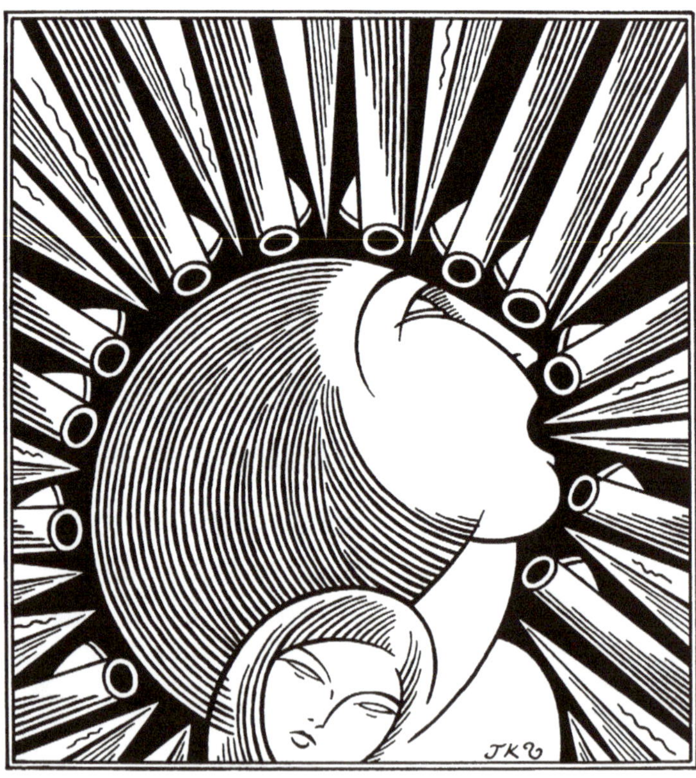

Jill Karla Schwarz • Gun Control • Pen & Ink

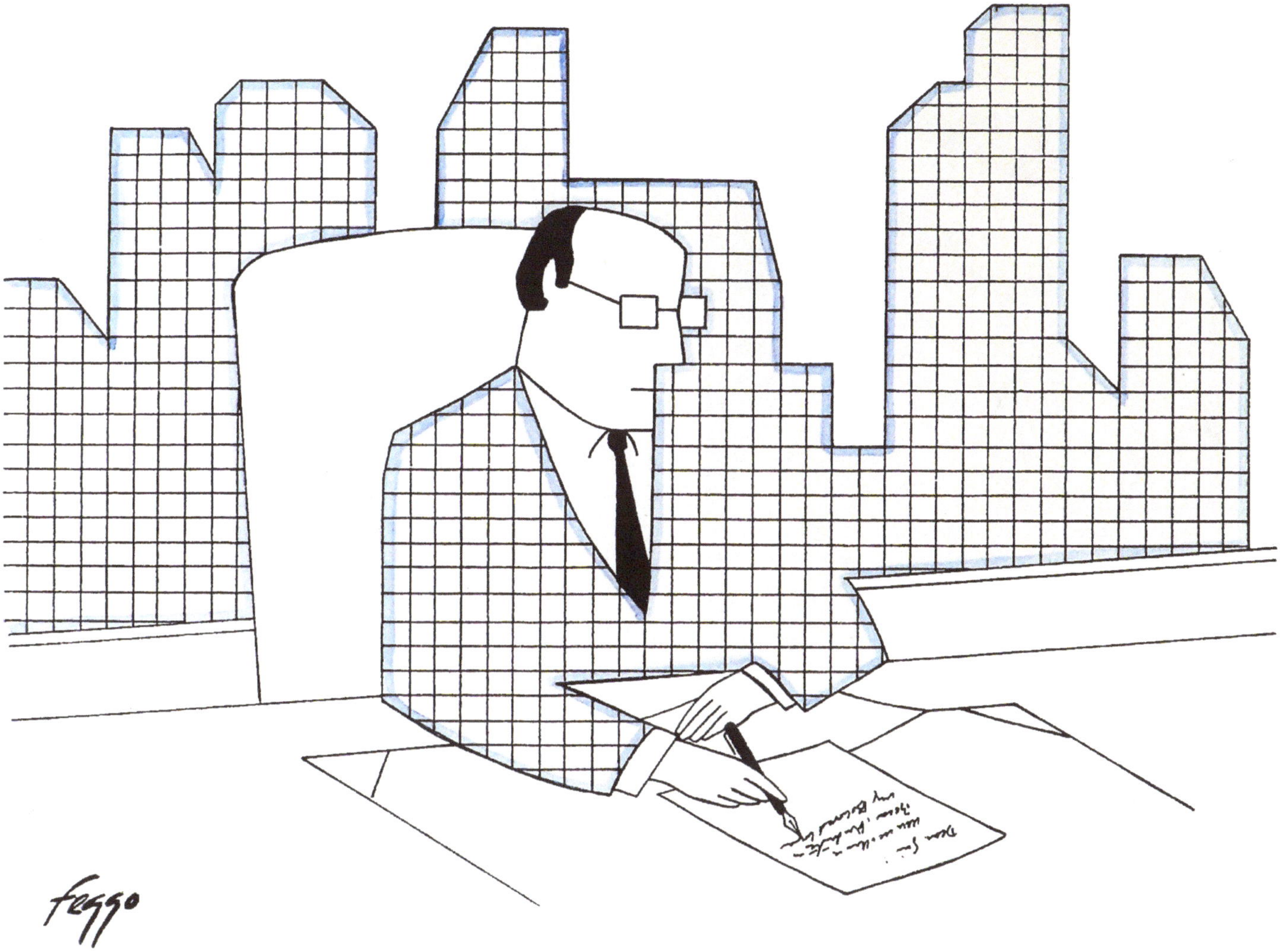

Felipe Galindo • Urban Chameleon • Pen, Ink & Wash

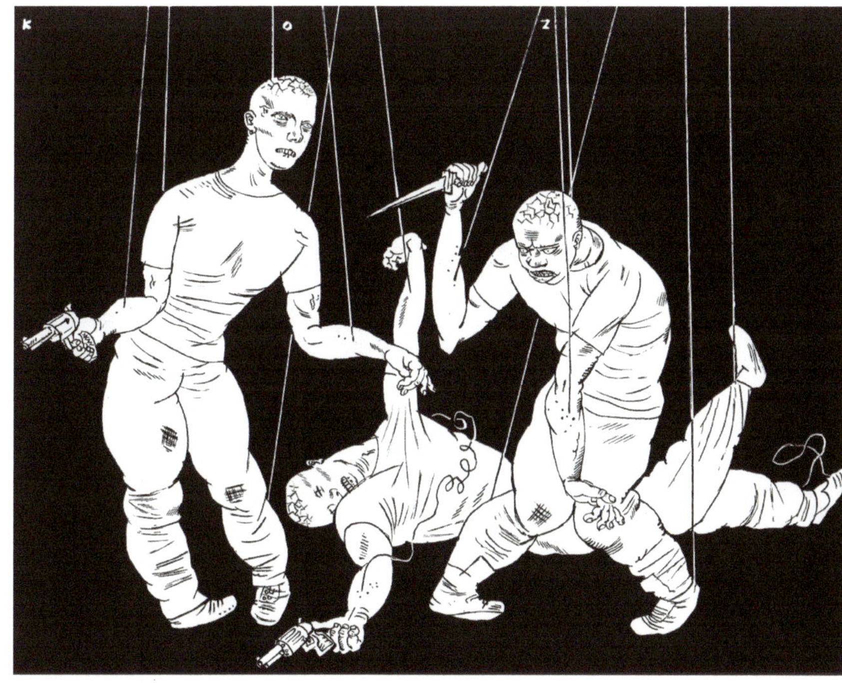

Martin Kozlowski • Crackheads • Pen & Ink

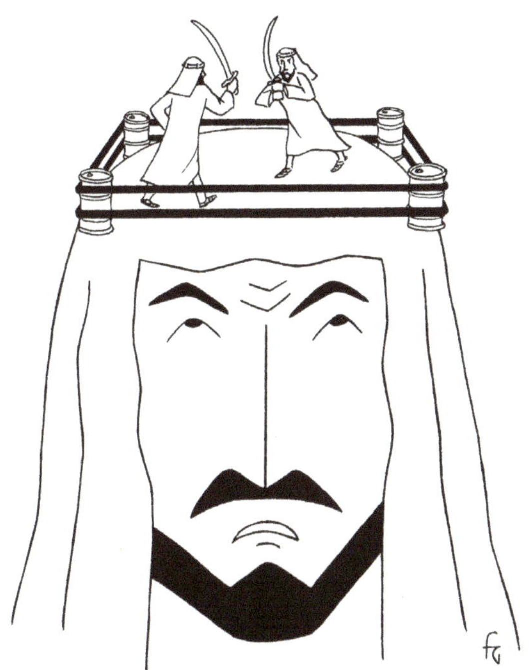

Felipe Galindo • Oil Price Wars • Pen & Ink

1991

The Gulf War ends. Soviet Union dissolves, Boris Yeltsin first President of Russian Federation. Clarence Thomas confirmed to Supreme Court despite Anita Hill's sexual harassment charges.

Although most work was still physically mailed or shipped, a new age dawned as fax machines allowed for the electronic delivery of line art, even though the resolution was low, the reproduction muddy, and the toner constantly running out.

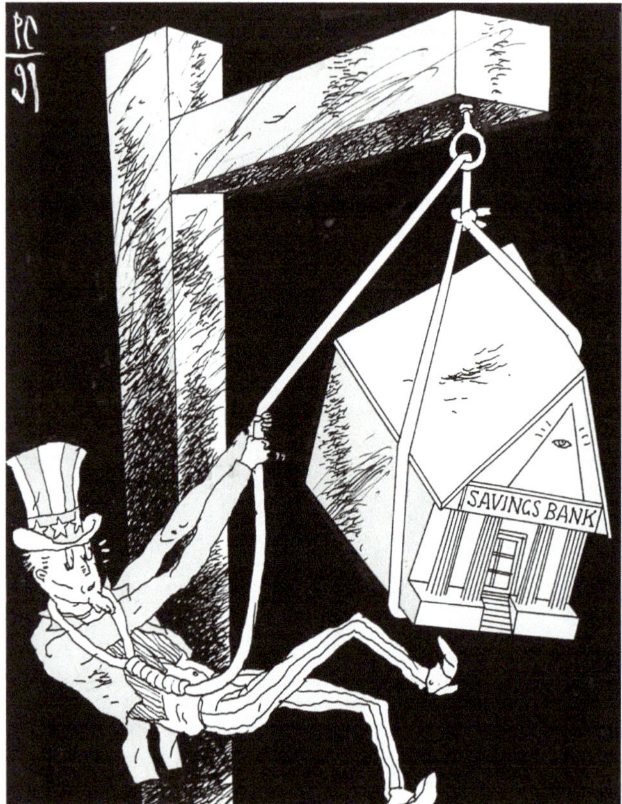

Paul Corio • Bank Failures • Pen & Ink

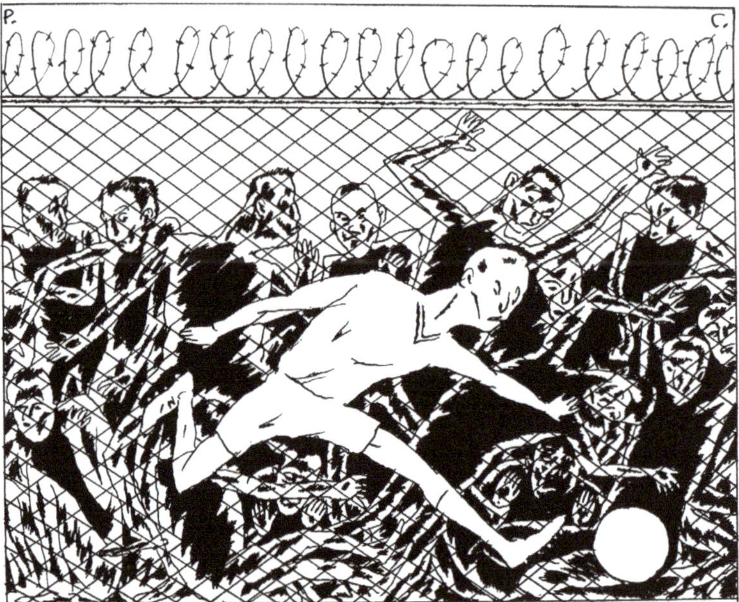

Paul Corio • Soccer Violence • Pen & Ink

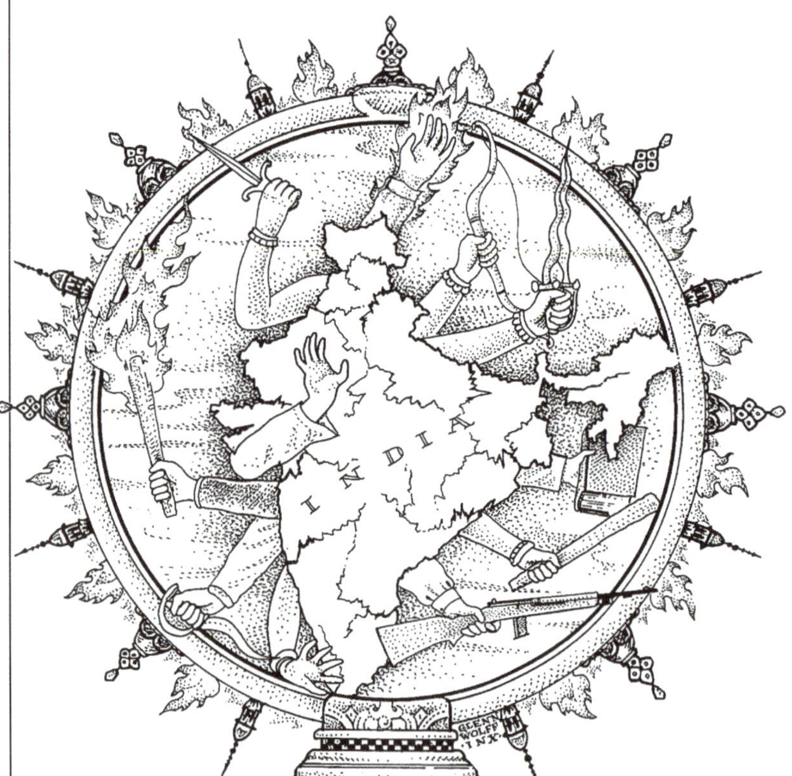

Glenn Wolff • India: Land of Conflict • Pen & Ink

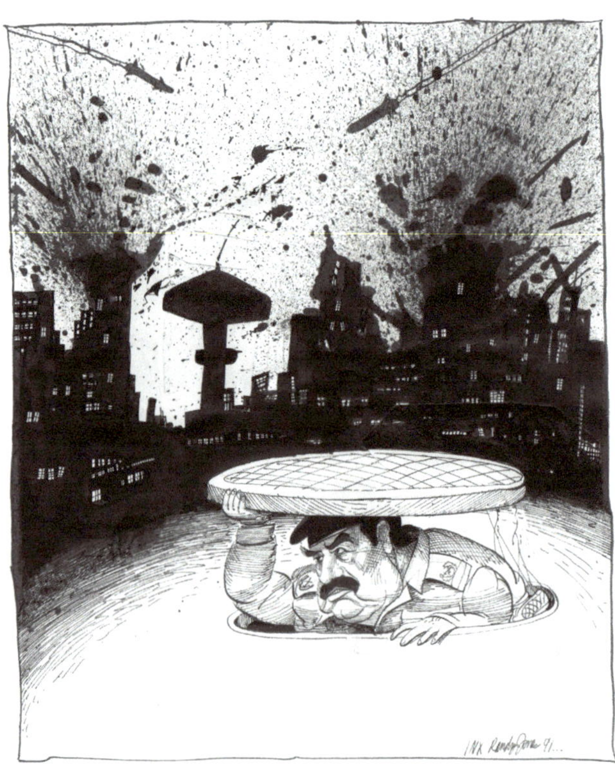

Randy Jones • Saddam Hides • Pen & Ink

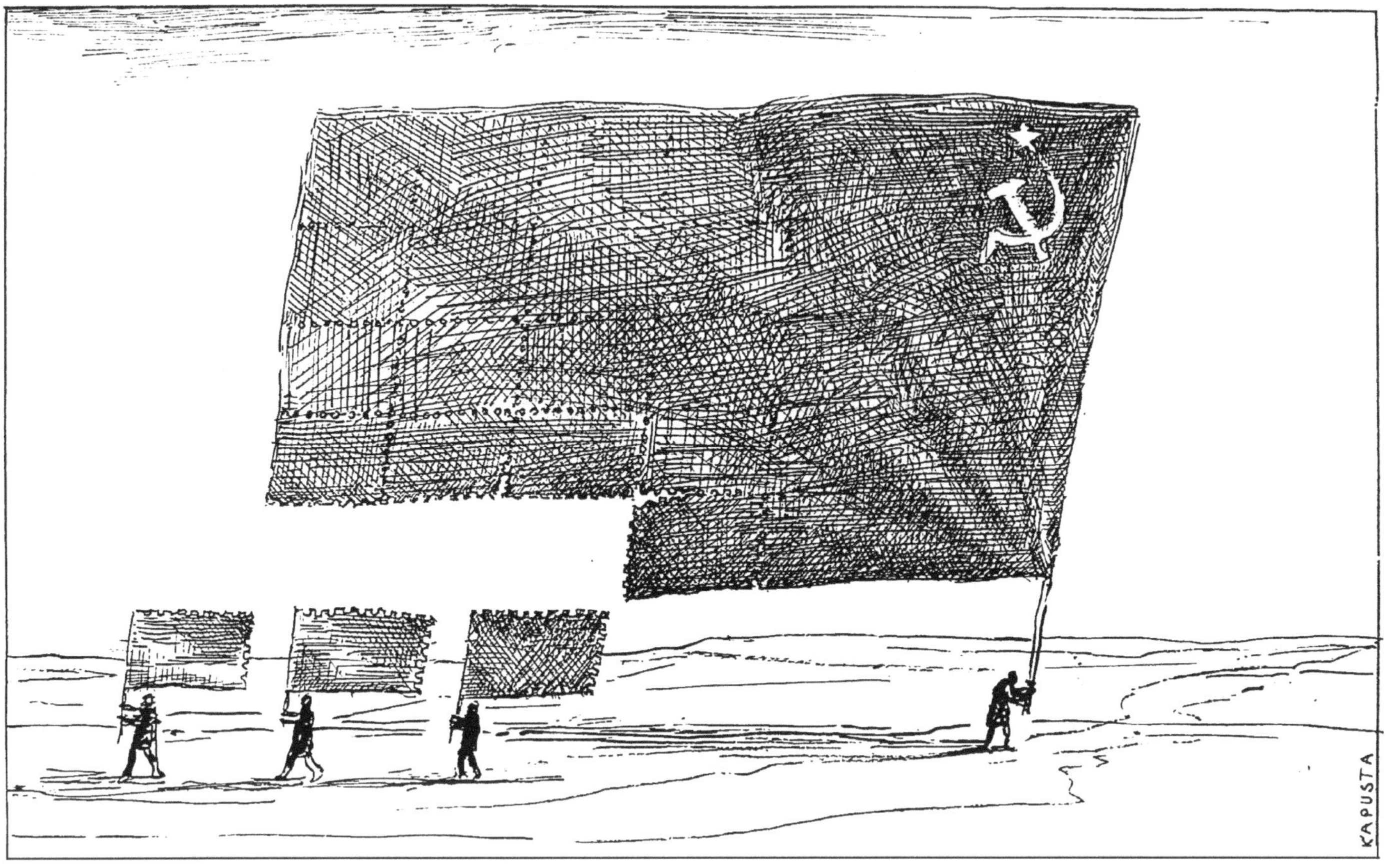

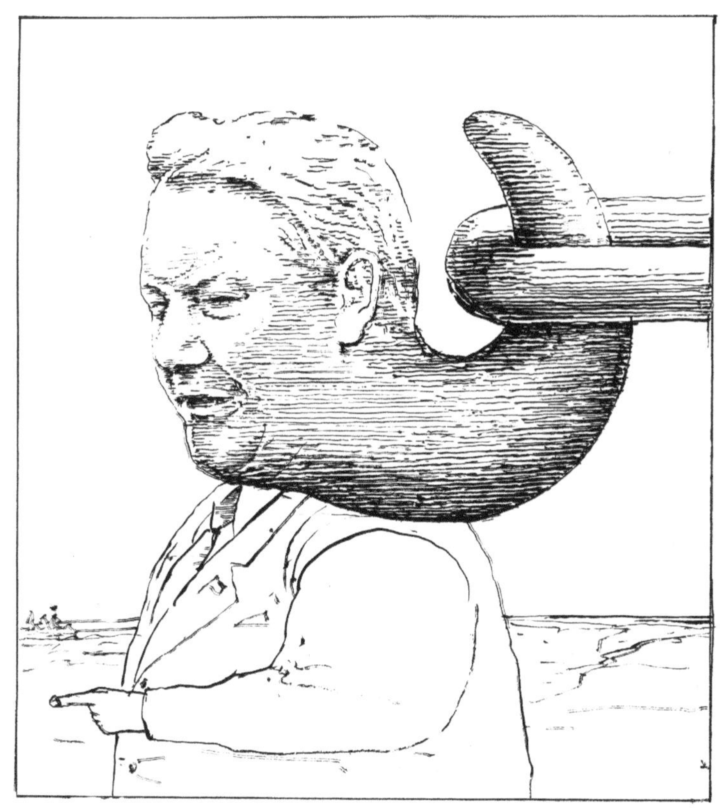

Janusz Kapusta • Breakup of U.S.S.R. • Pen & Ink

LEADER

Janusz Kapusta • Boris Yeltsin • Pen & Ink

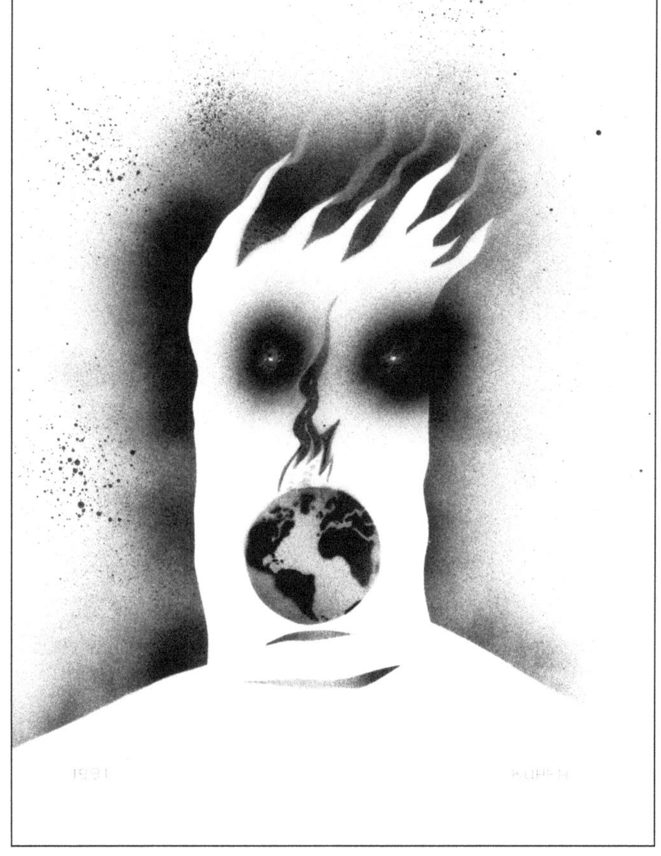

Peter Kuper • Global Warming • Spray Enamel

1992

European Union created. Bill Clinton defeats George H.W. Bush. Dictatorship ends in South Korea. Civil War ends in El Salvador. LA riots result in 53 deaths and $1 billion in damage.

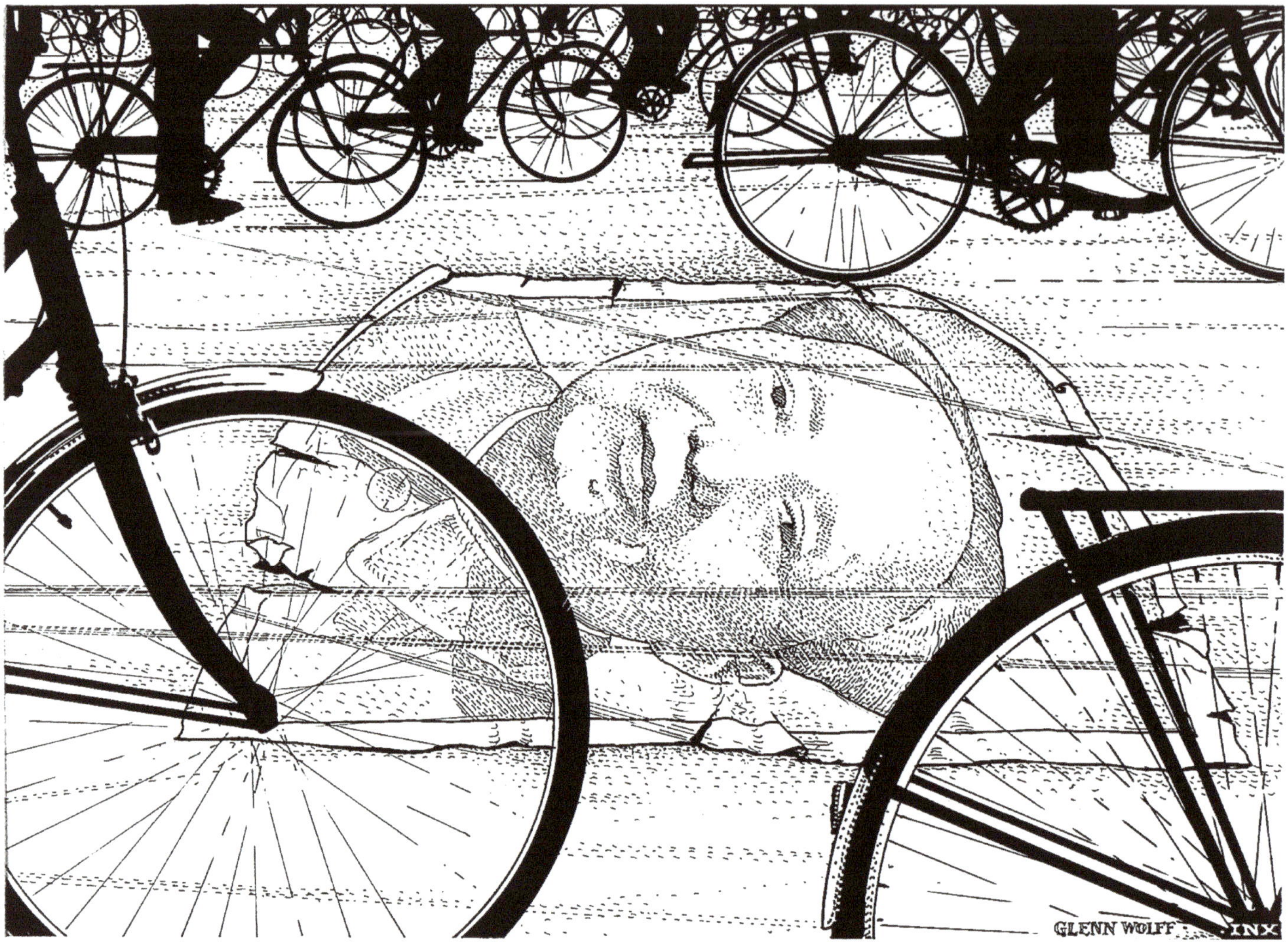

Glenn Wolff • China After Mao • Pen & Ink

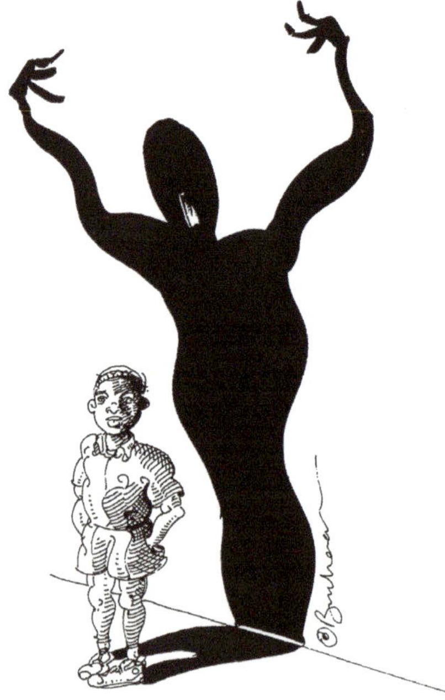

Yvonne Buchanan • Fear of Blacks • Pen & Ink

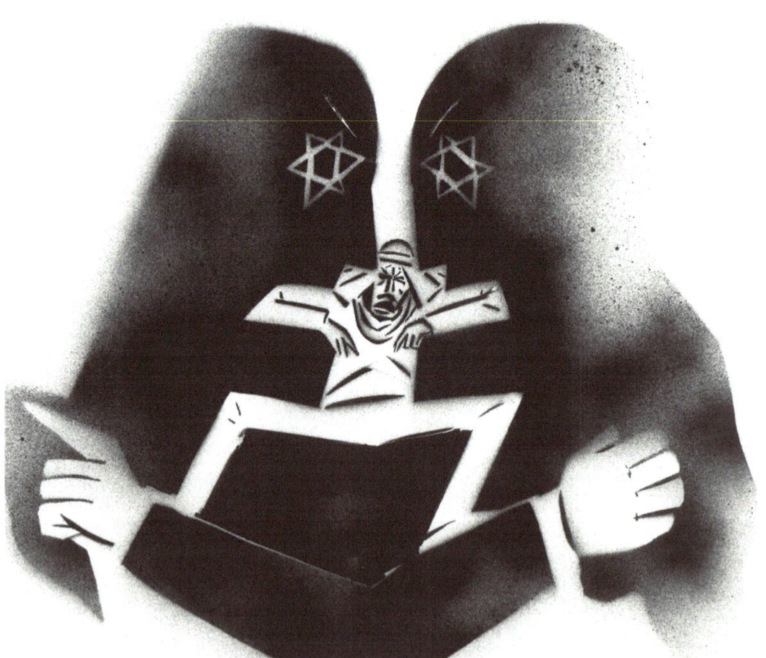

Peter Kuper • Israel Debates PLO Issue • Spray Enamel

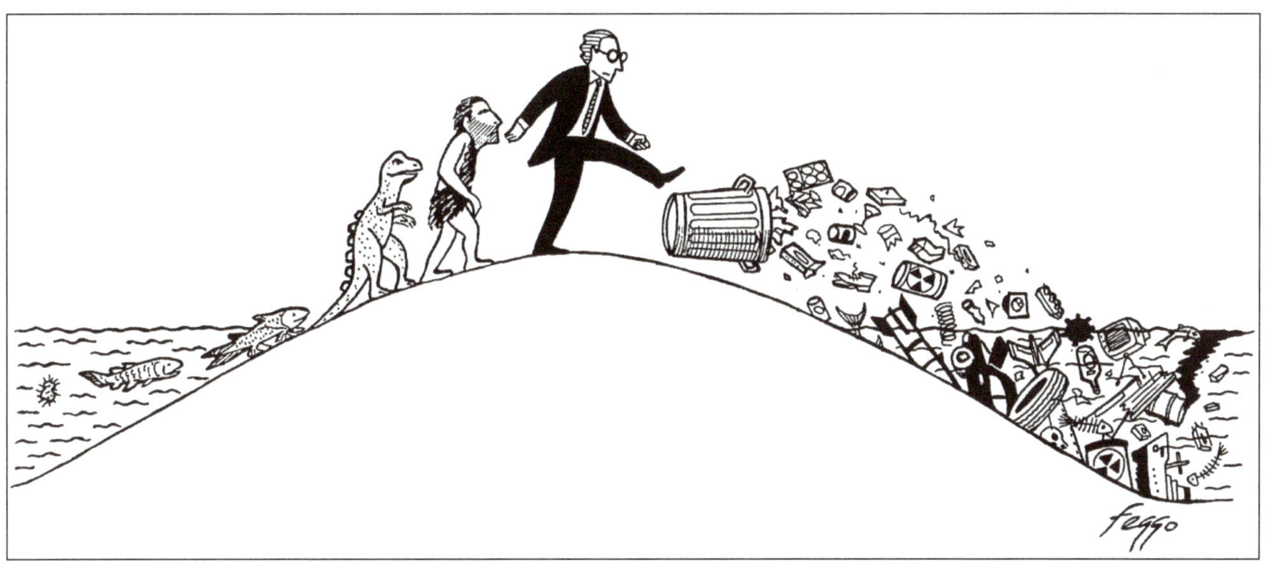

Felipe Galindo • Pollution Evolution • Pen & Ink

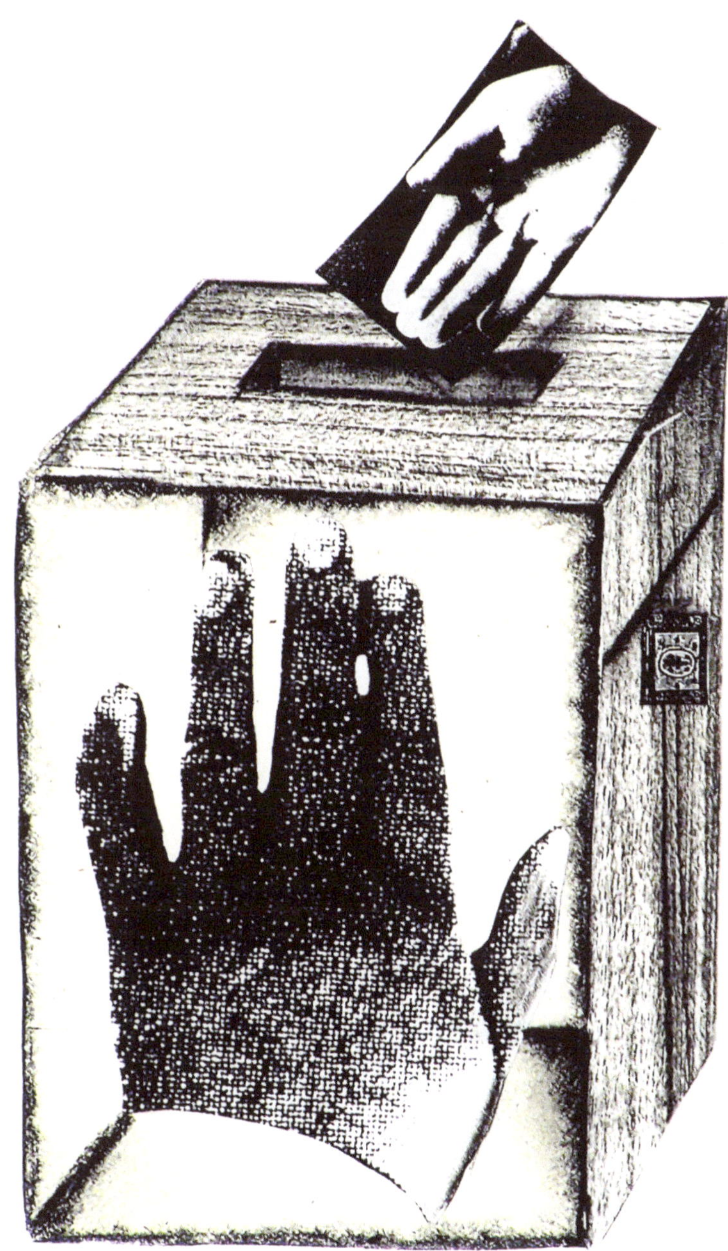

Ellen Weinstein • Race and Voting • Collage

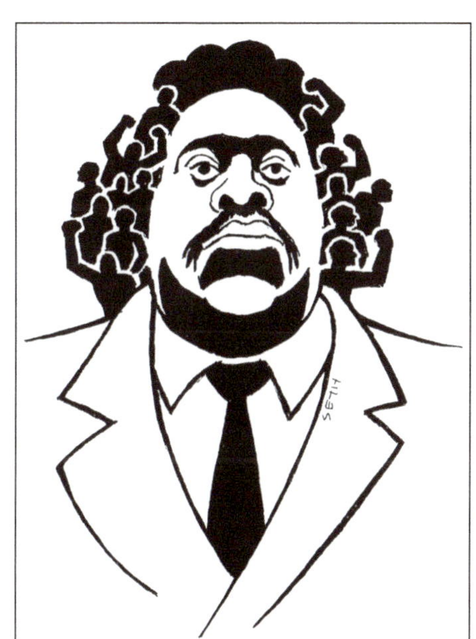

Seth Tobocman • Al Sharpton • Pen & Ink

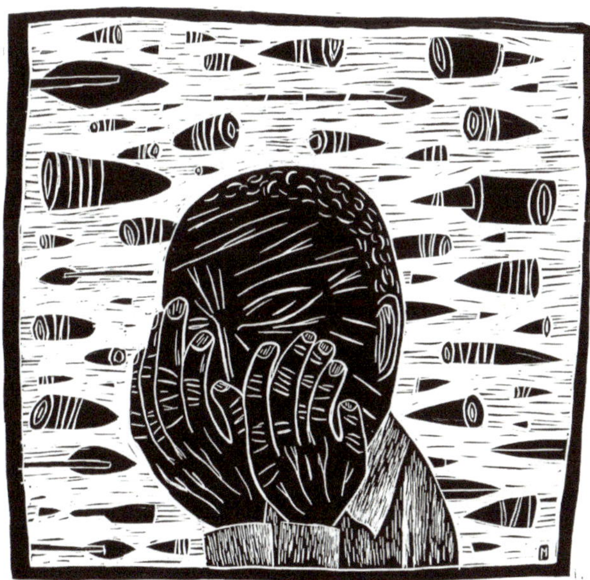

Melinda Beck • War in Africa • Scratchboard

Truck bomb beneath the World Trade Center kills 6, injures thousands. Branch Davidians standoff and fire in Waco, Texas. 'Don't ask, don't tell' becomes law for gays in military.

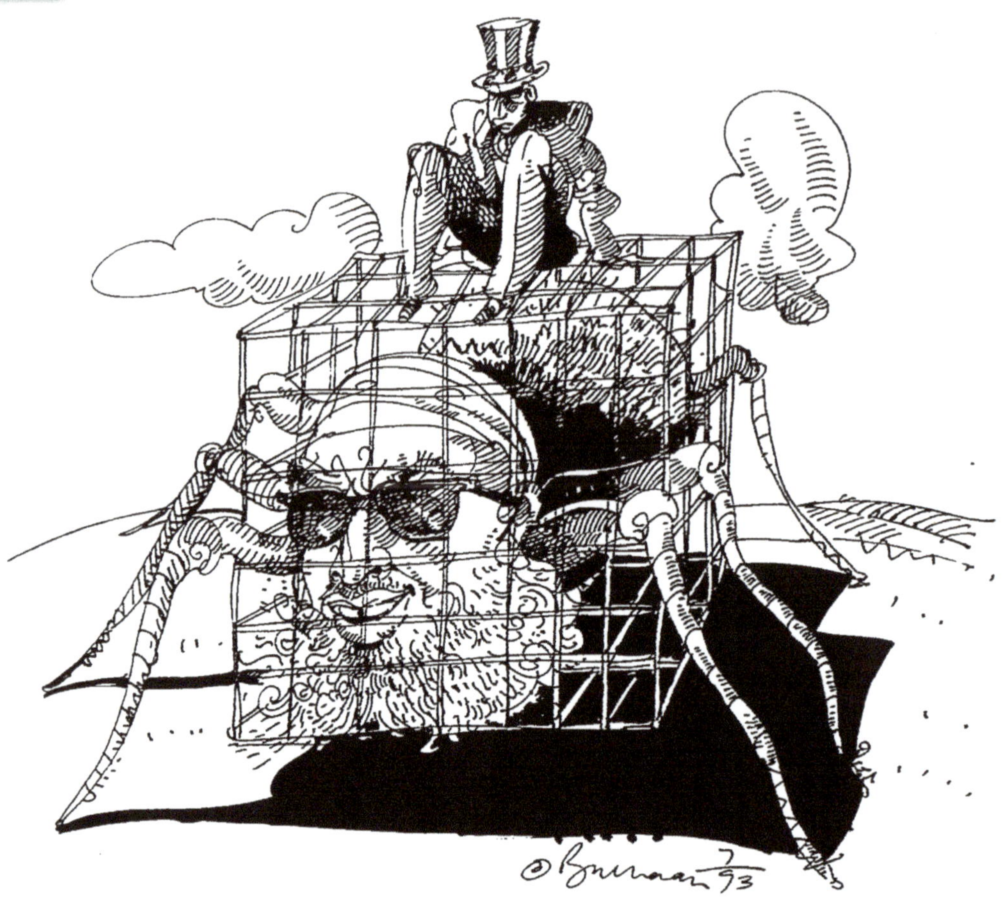

Yvonne Buchanan • Caging Sheikh Rahman • Pen & Ink

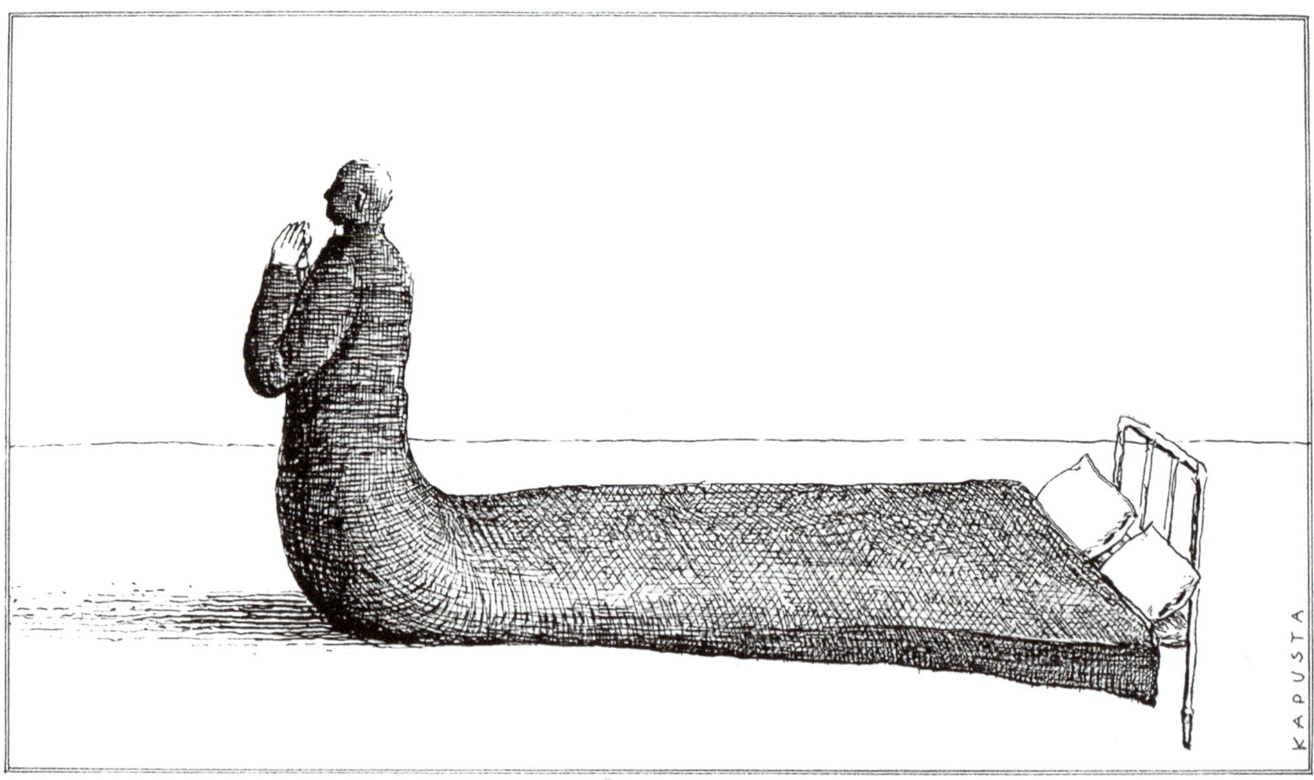

Janusz Kapusta • Sex & Religion • Pen & Ink

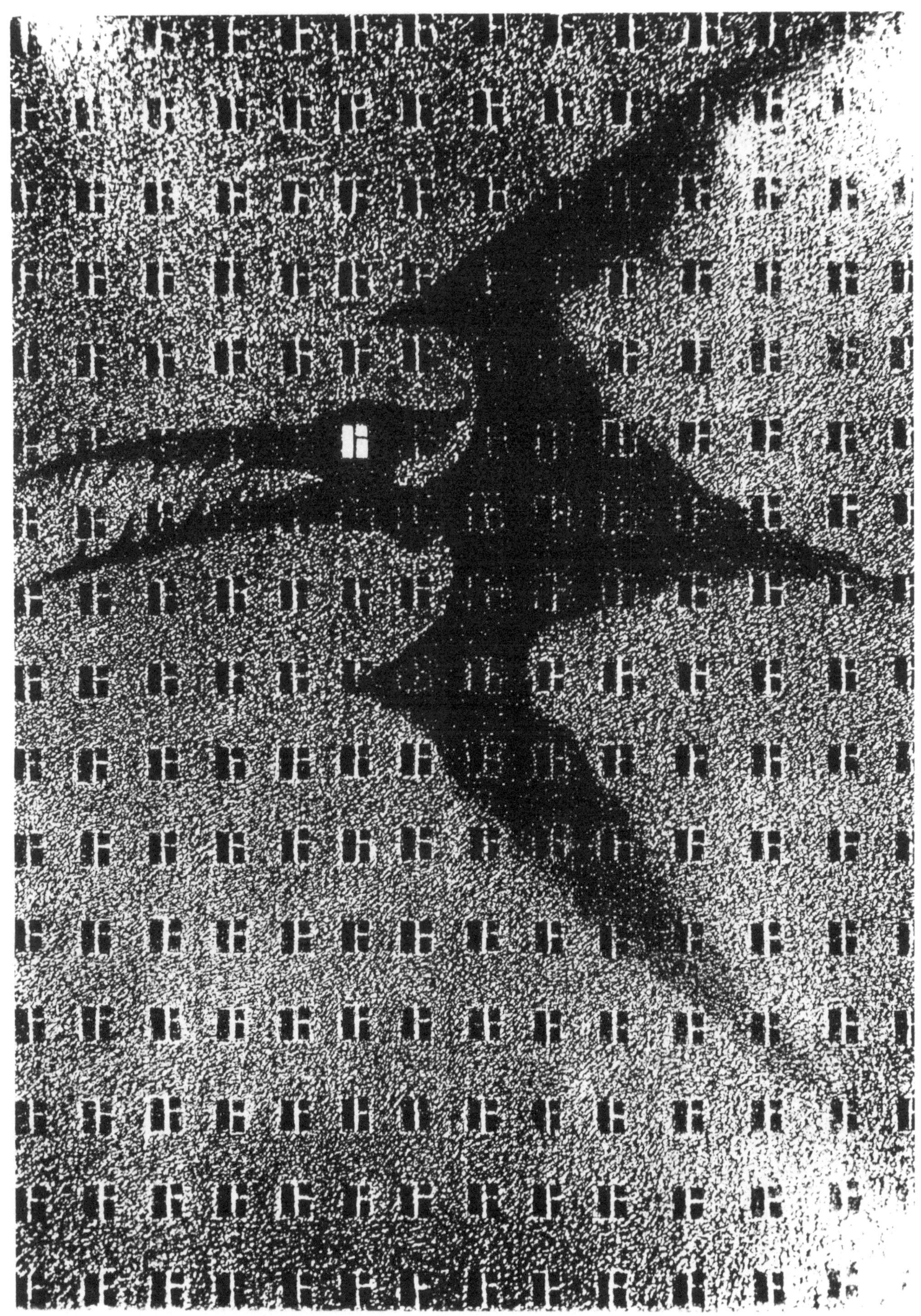

Igor Kopelnitsky • Urban Anxiety • Digital Media

Apartheid ends in South Africa, Nelson Mandela elected president. NAFTA established. First Chechen War begins. Genocide in Rwanda. Northridge earthquake kills 72, injures 9,000.

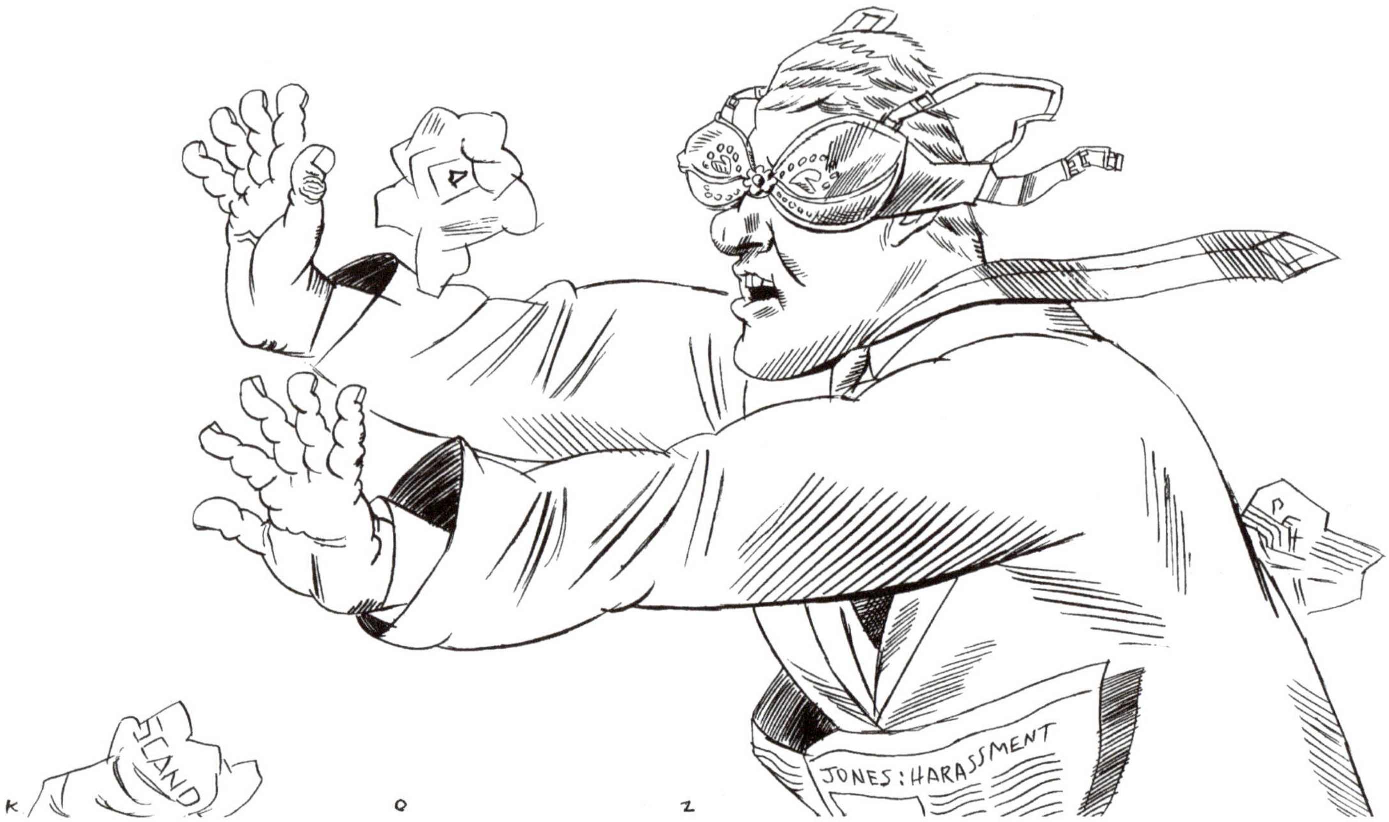

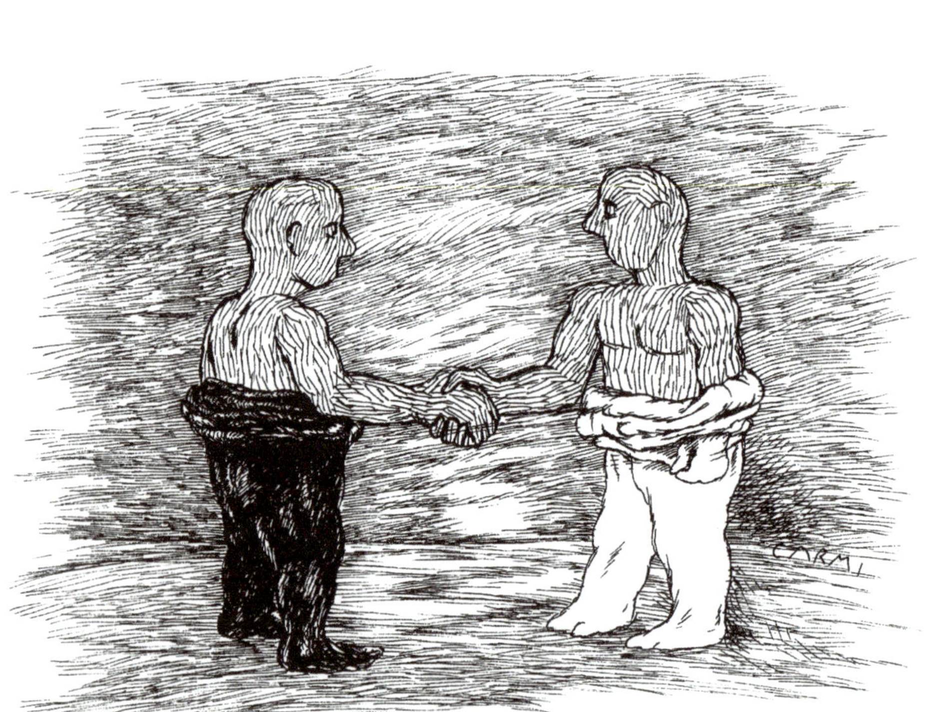

Martin Kozlowski • Clinton's Scandals • Pen & Ink

Giora Carmi • Black Vote in South Africa • Pen & Ink

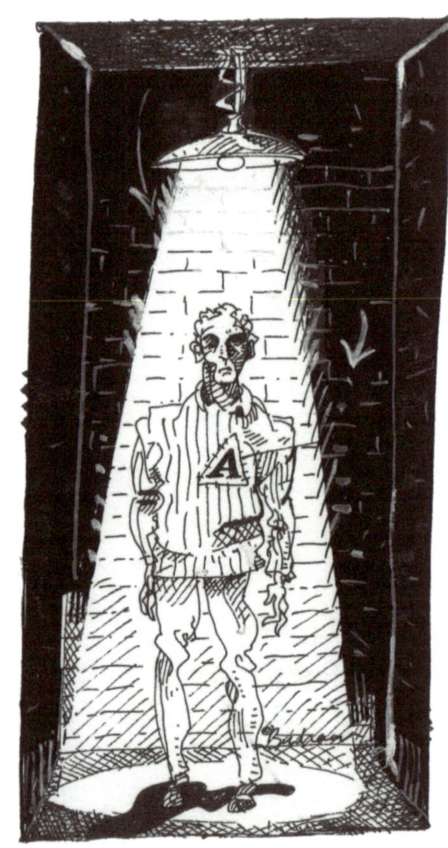

Yvonne Buchanan • AIDS • Pen & Ink

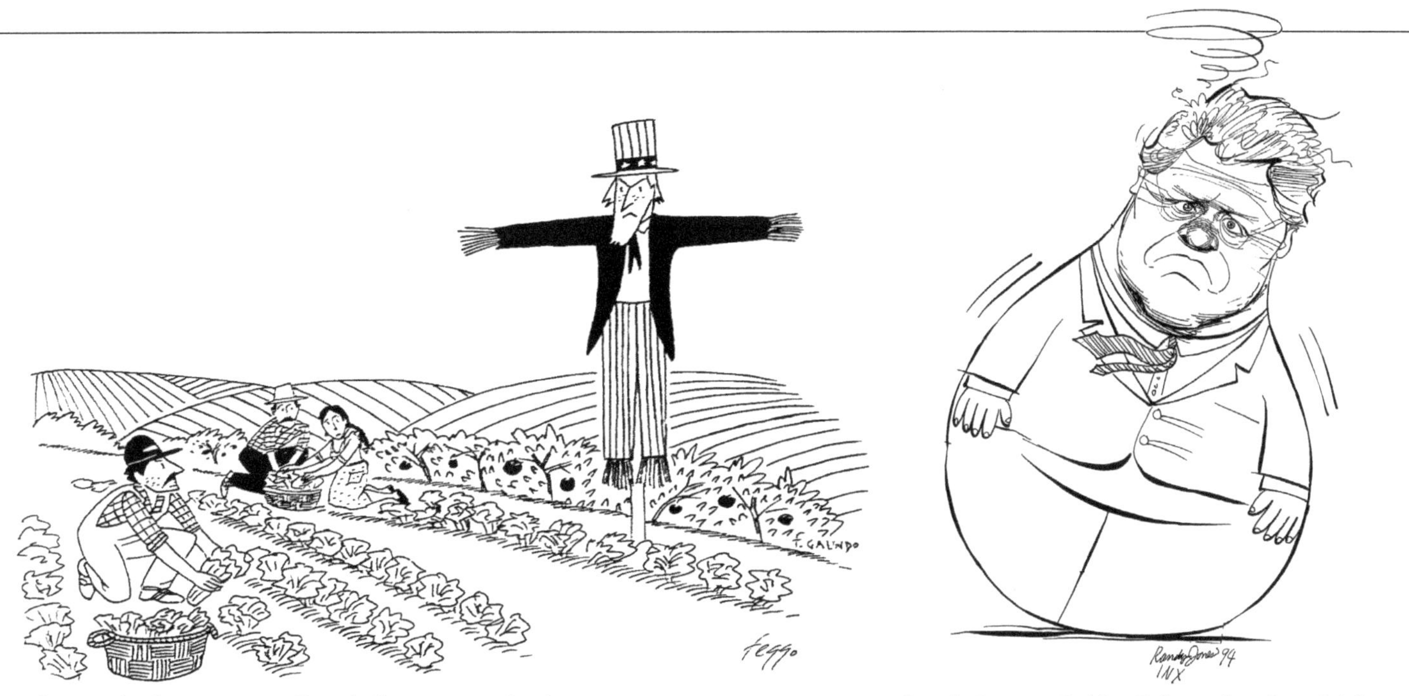

Felipe Galindo • Scaring Illegal Aliens • Pen & Ink

Randy Jones • Bubba Rebounds • Pen & Ink

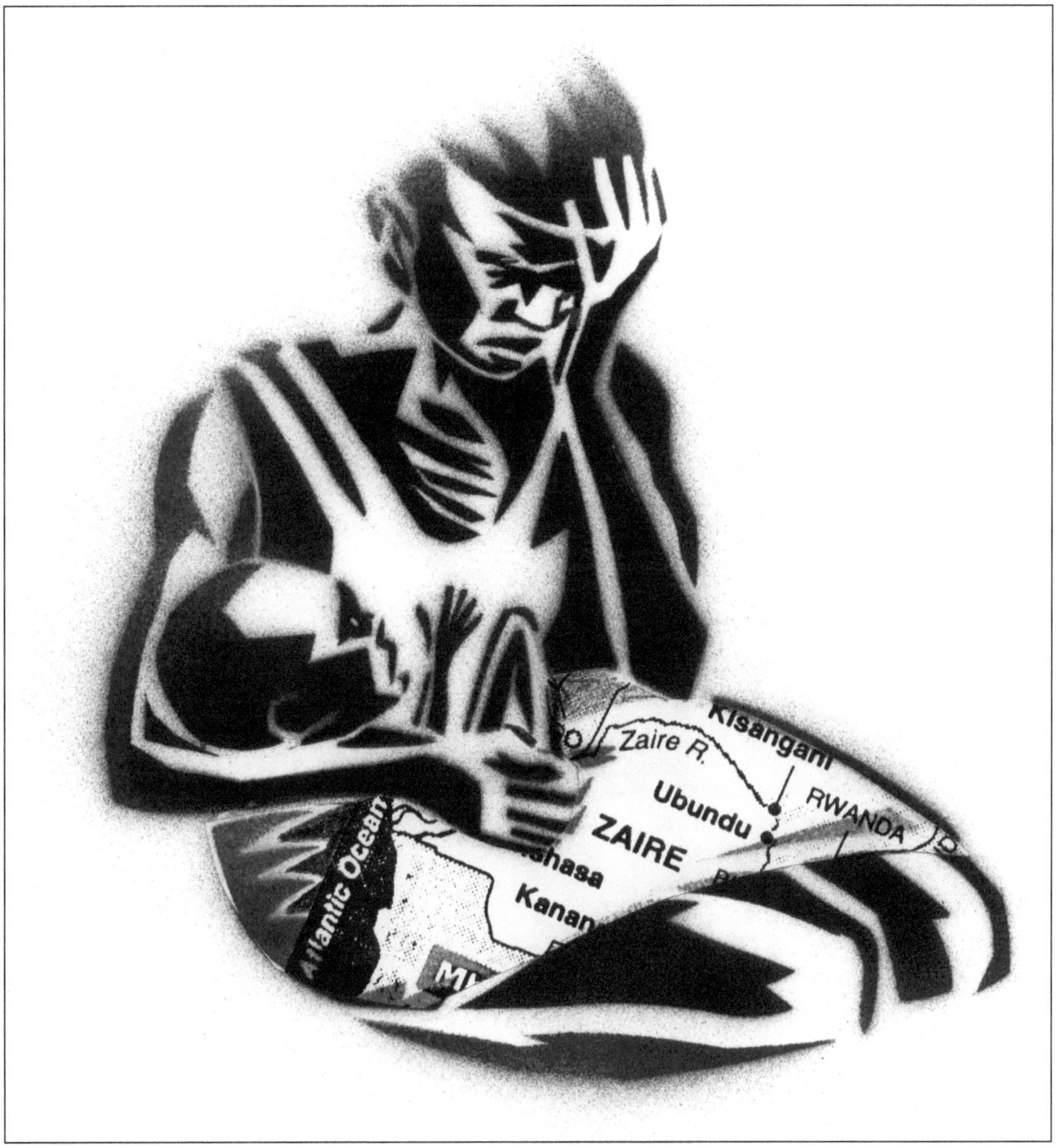

Peter Kuper • Rwandan Civil War • Spray Enamel & Collage

Republicans gain control of both the House and Senate. Oklahoma City bombing kills 168 and wounds 800. World Trade Organization established. NATO bombing raids in Bosnia.

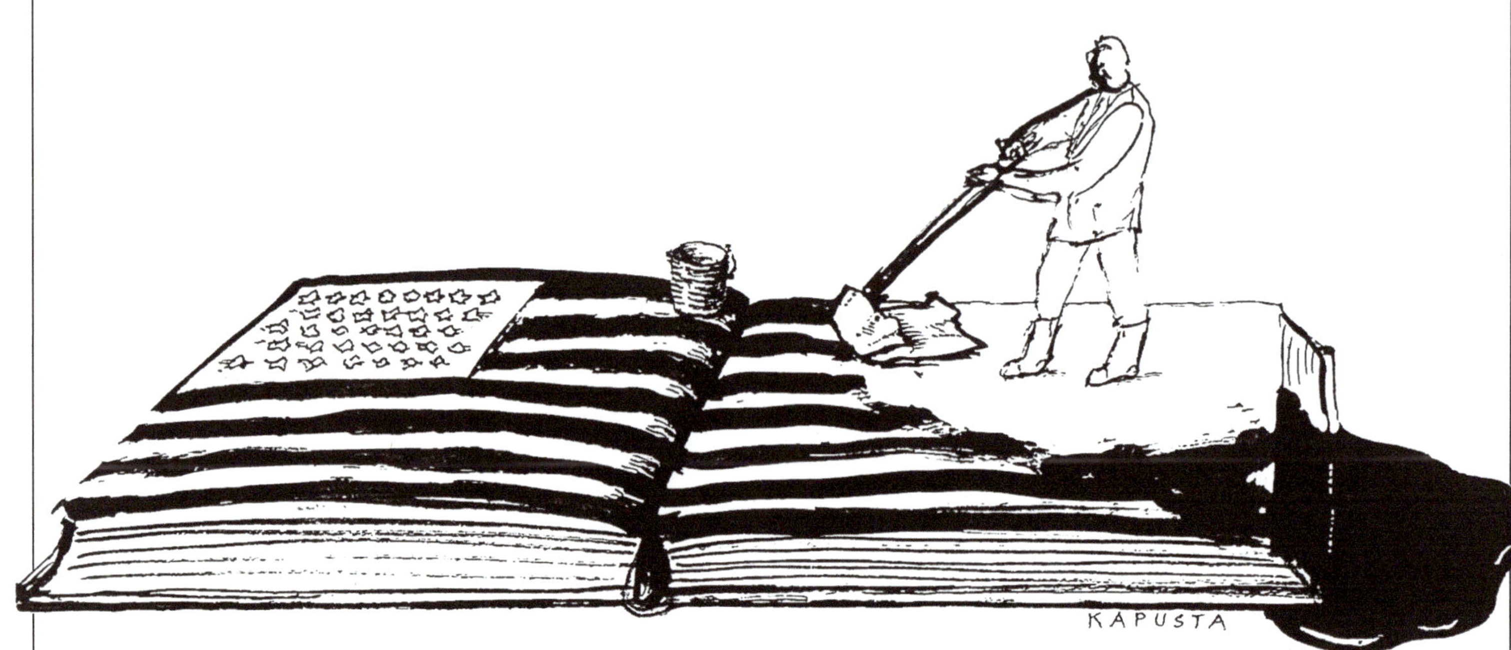

Janusz Kapusta • Censoring U.S. History • Pen & Ink

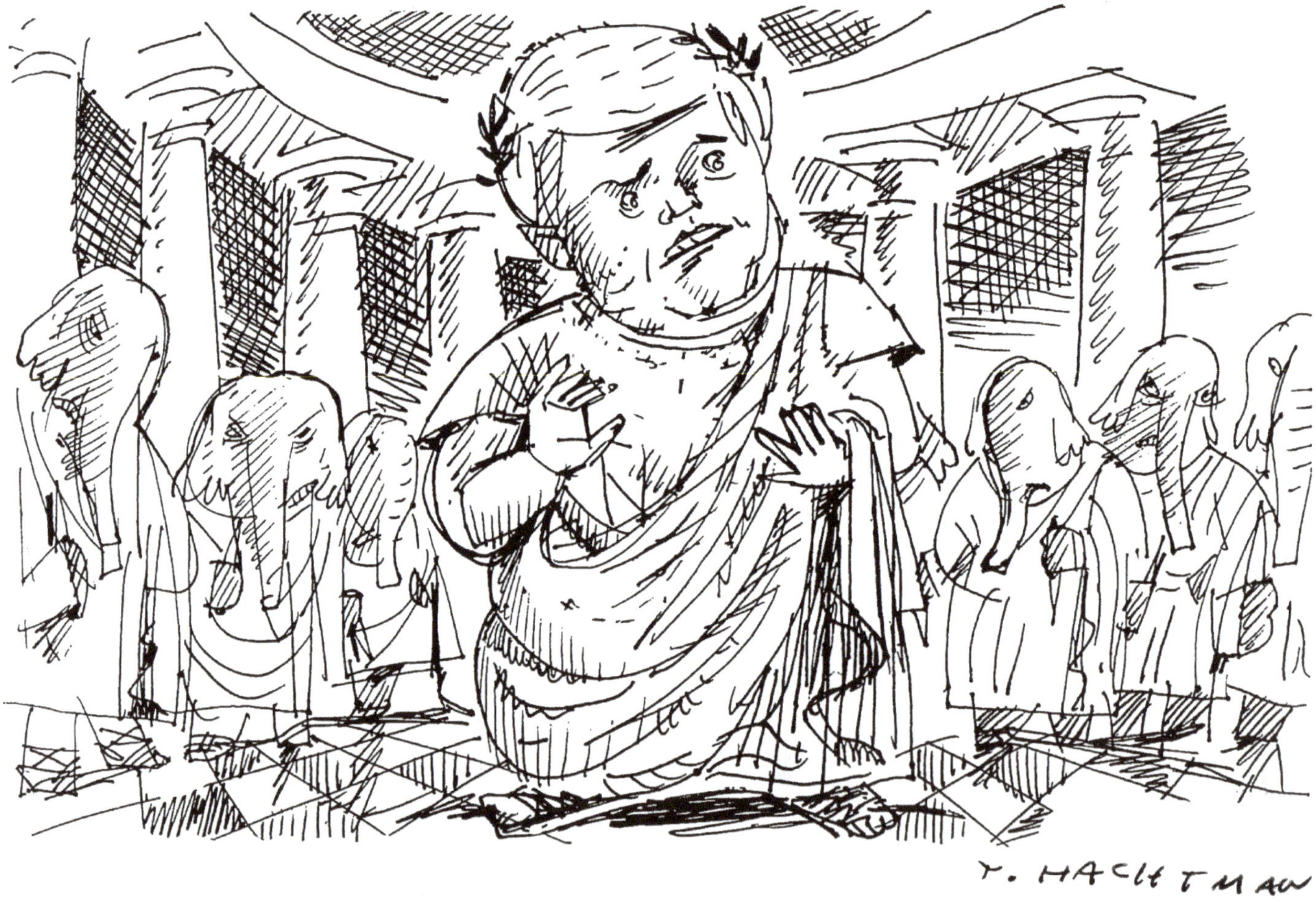

Tom Hachtman • Et Tu, Newt? • Pen & Ink

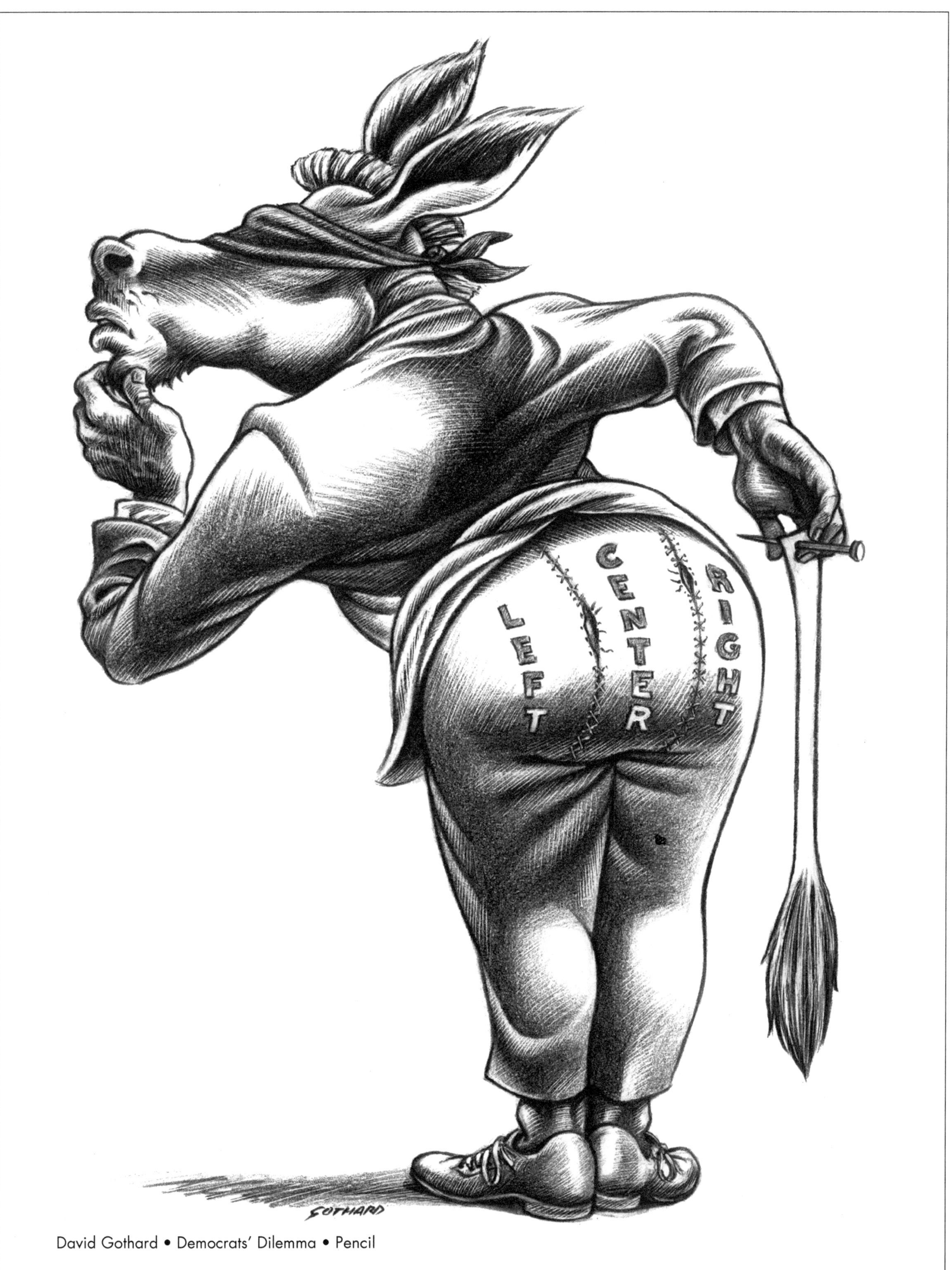

David Gothard • Democrats' Dilemma • Pencil

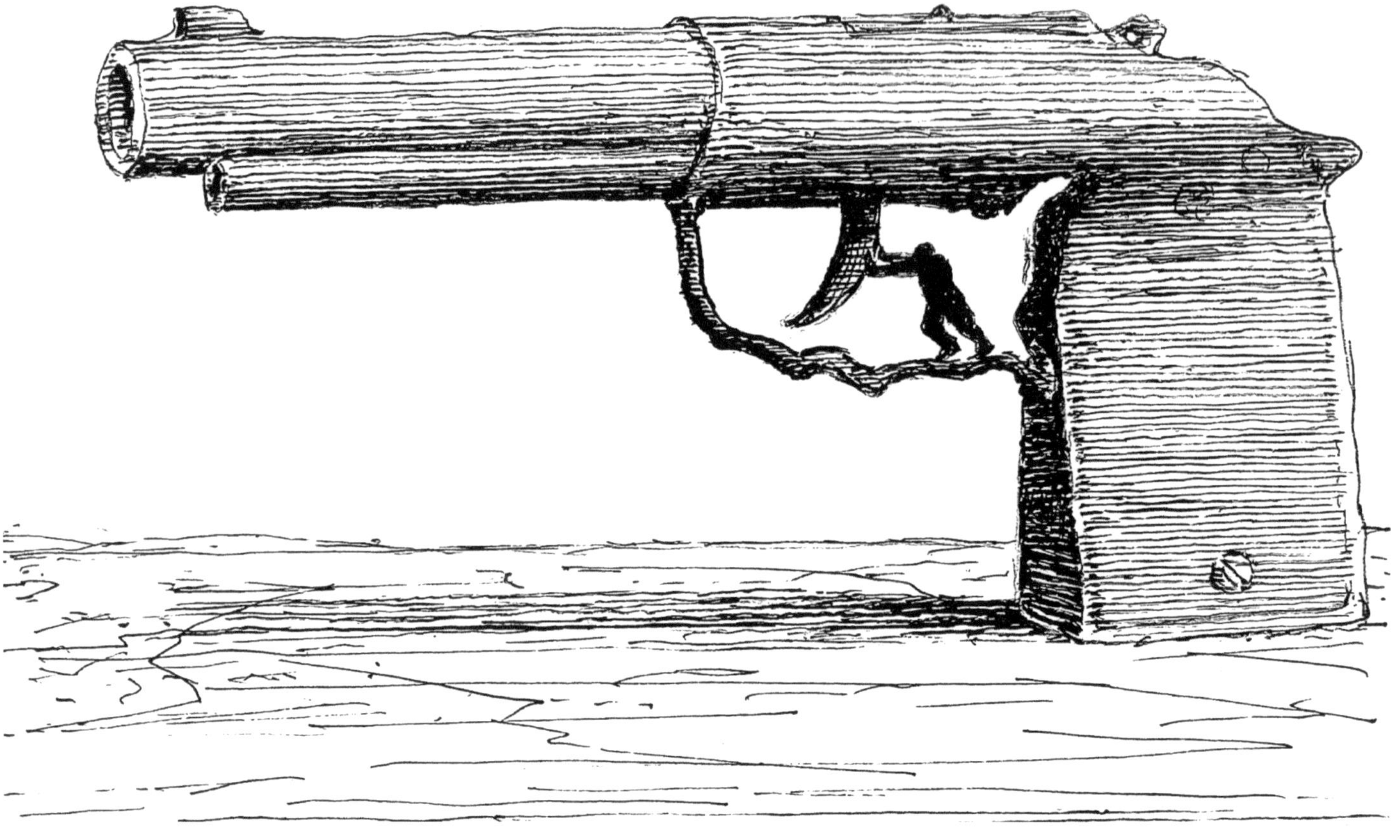

Janusz Kapusta • Gun Control • Pen & Ink

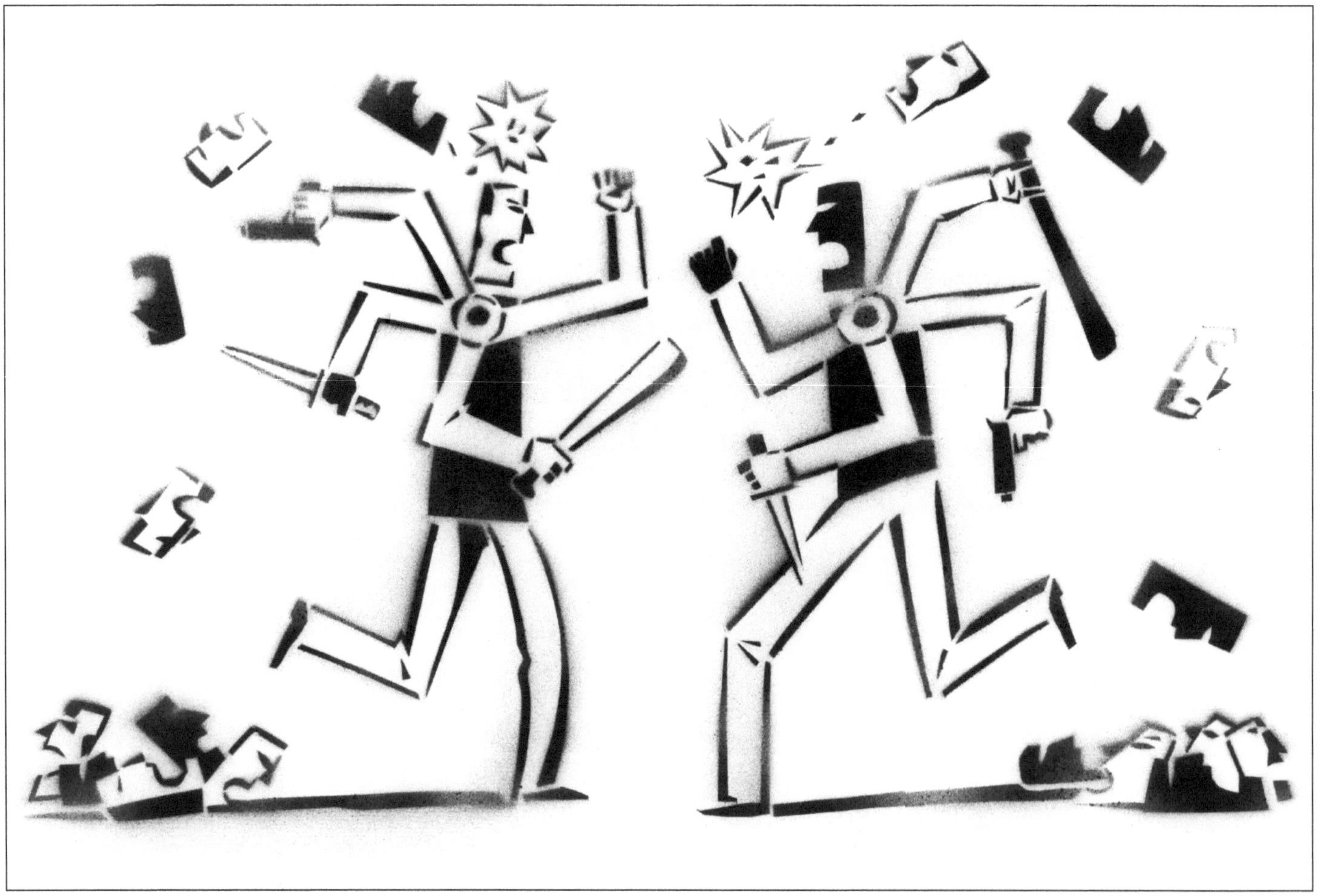

Peter Kuper • Cycles of Hatred • Spray Enamel & Ink

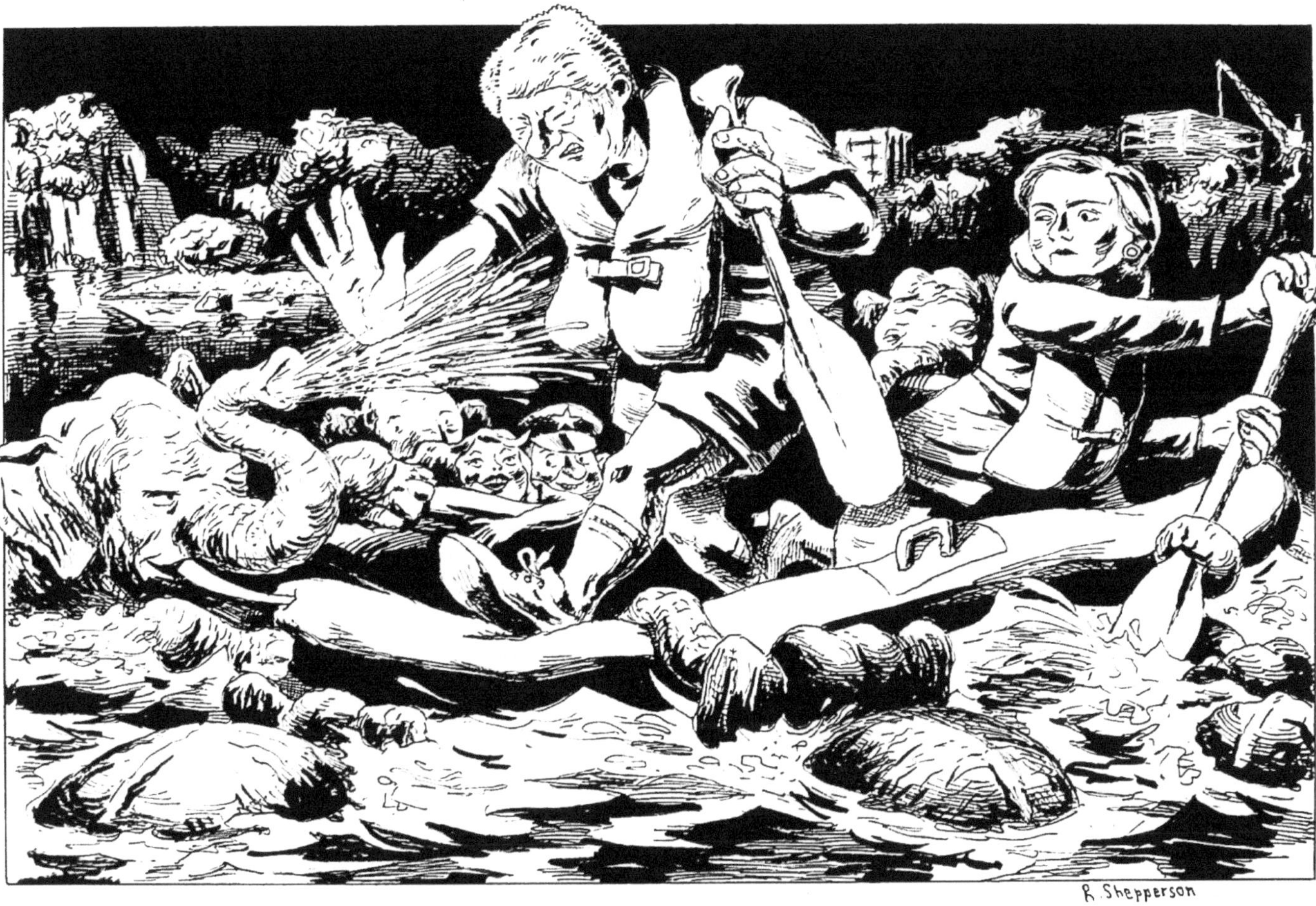

Rob Shepperson • Clinton & Whitewater • Pen & Ink

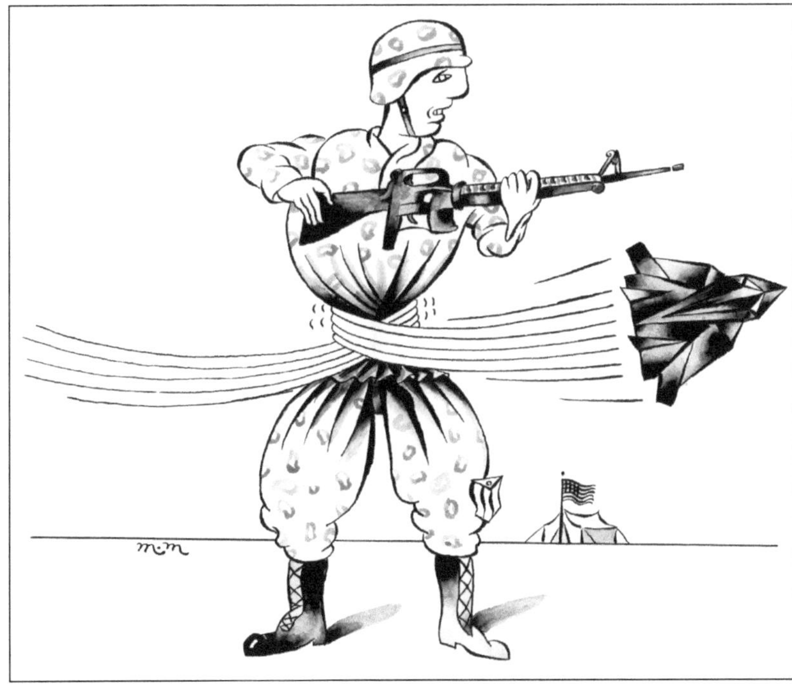

Matthew Martin • High-priced Military Technology • Brush & Ink

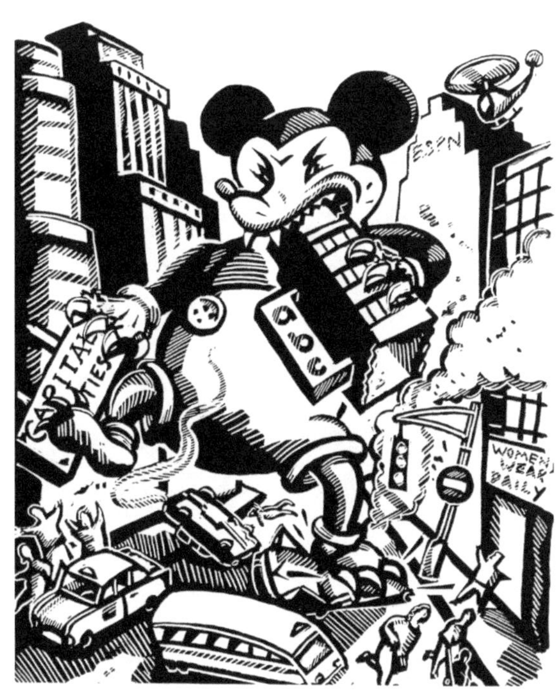

Rupert Howard • Disney New York • Scratchboard

Bombing kills 19 U.S. servicemen in Saudi Arabia. Bill Clinton reelected, beating Bob Dole. Dolly the sheep successfully cloned. The Taliban take control of Afghanistan's government.

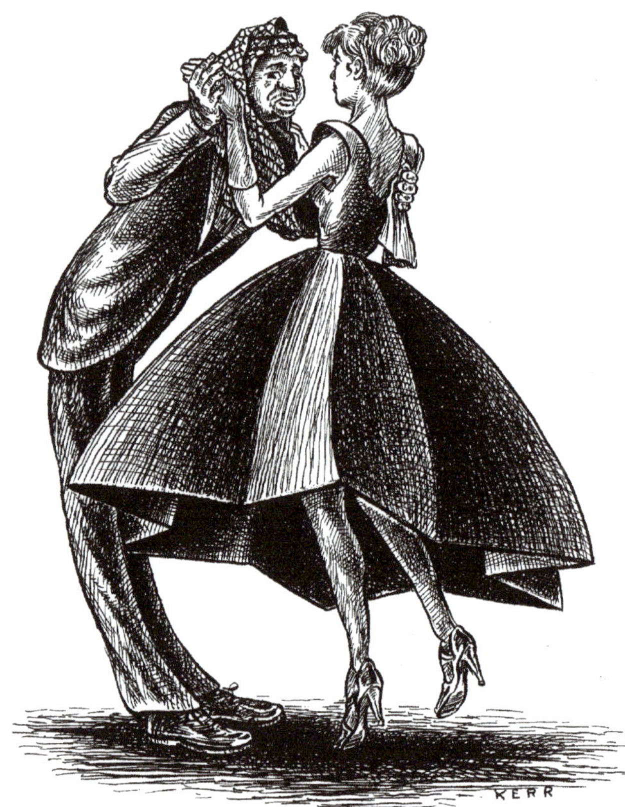

Thomas Kerr • Arafat's Nimble Dance • Pen & Ink

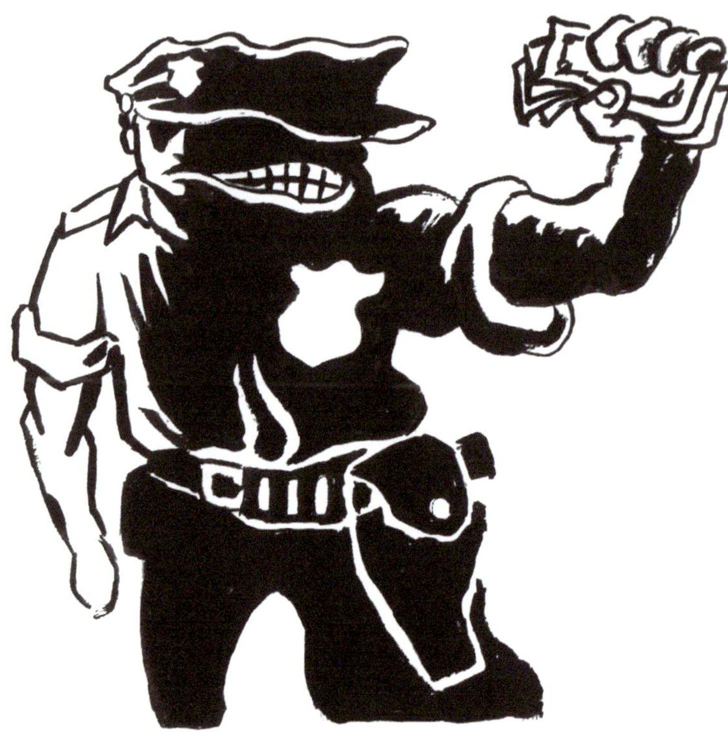

Seth Tobocman • Corrupt Cops • Brush & Ink

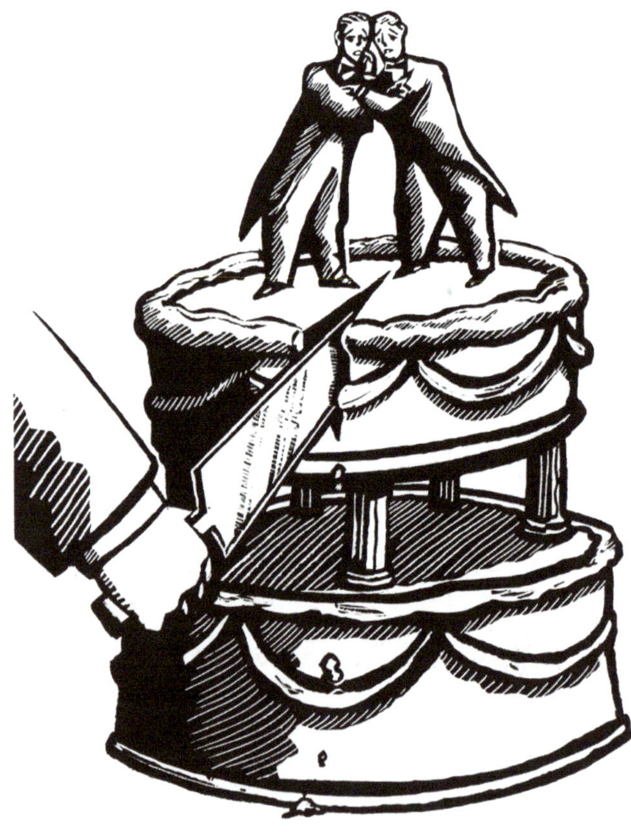

Rupert Howard • Gay Weddings • Scratchboard

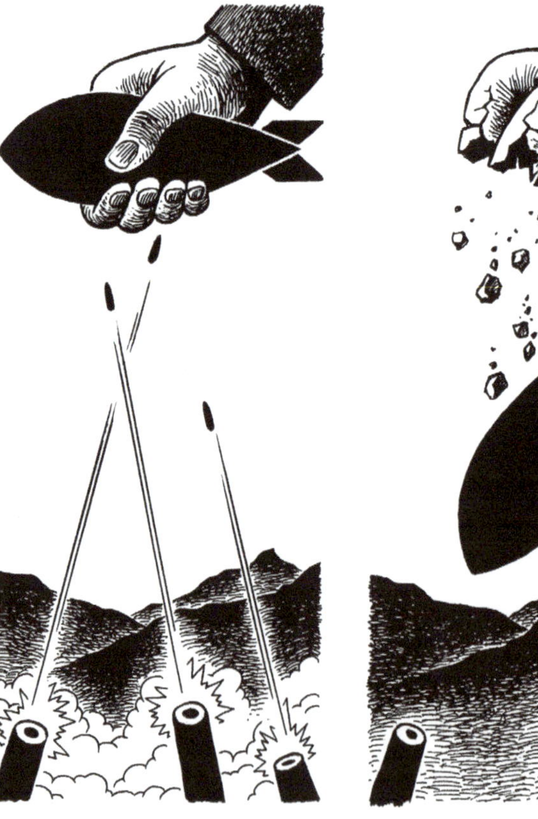

Christophe Vorlet • Air Strike in Yugoslavia • Pen & Ink

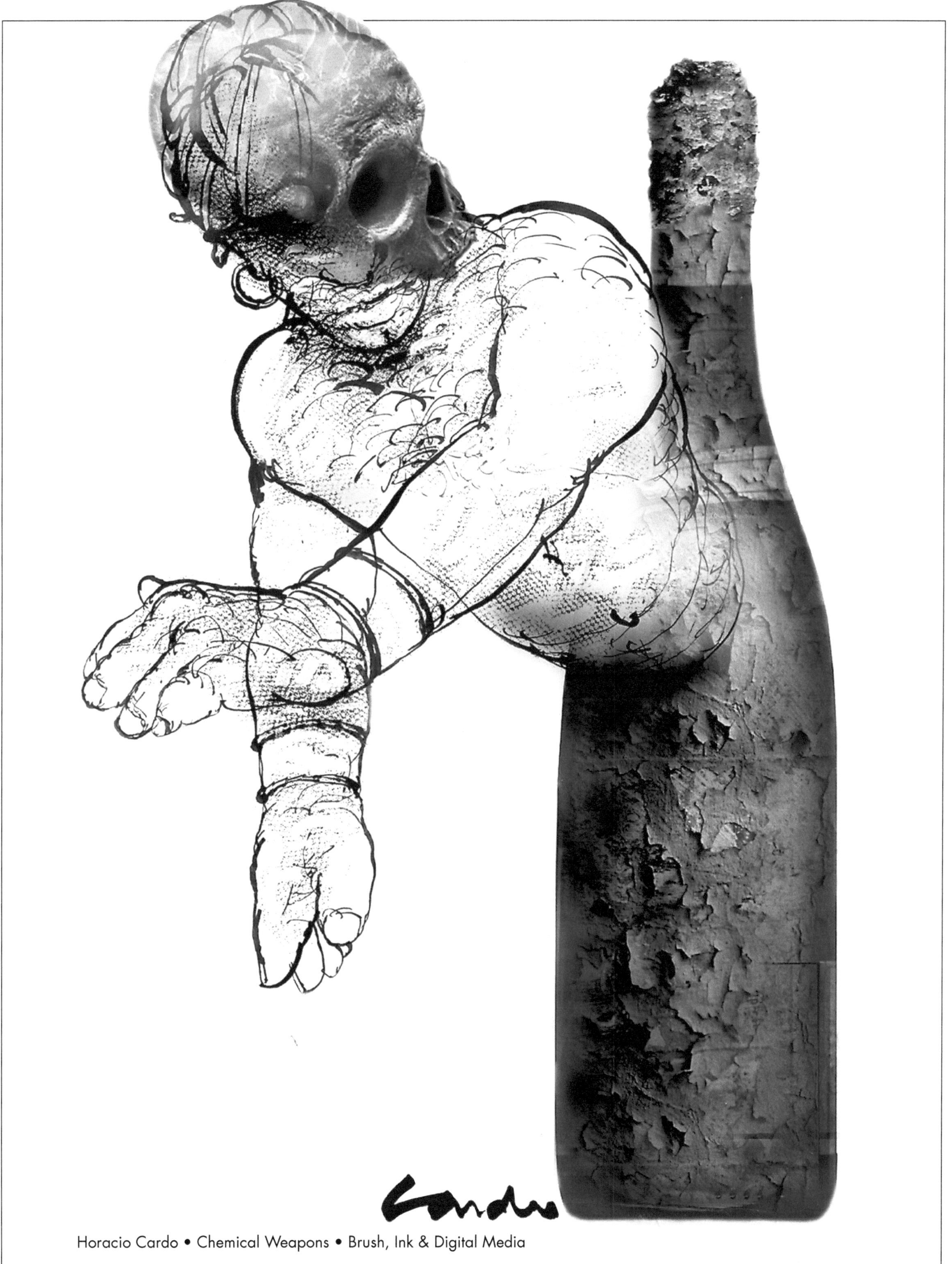

Horacio Cardo • Chemical Weapons • Brush, Ink & Digital Media

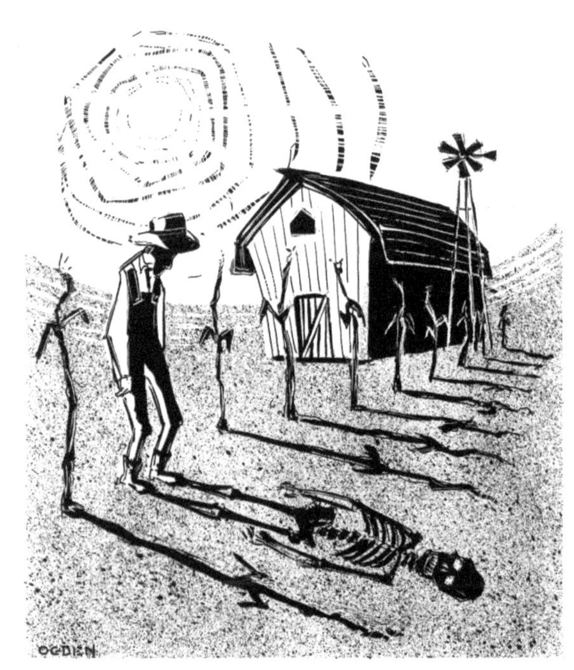

Laird Ogden • Drought • Pen & Ink

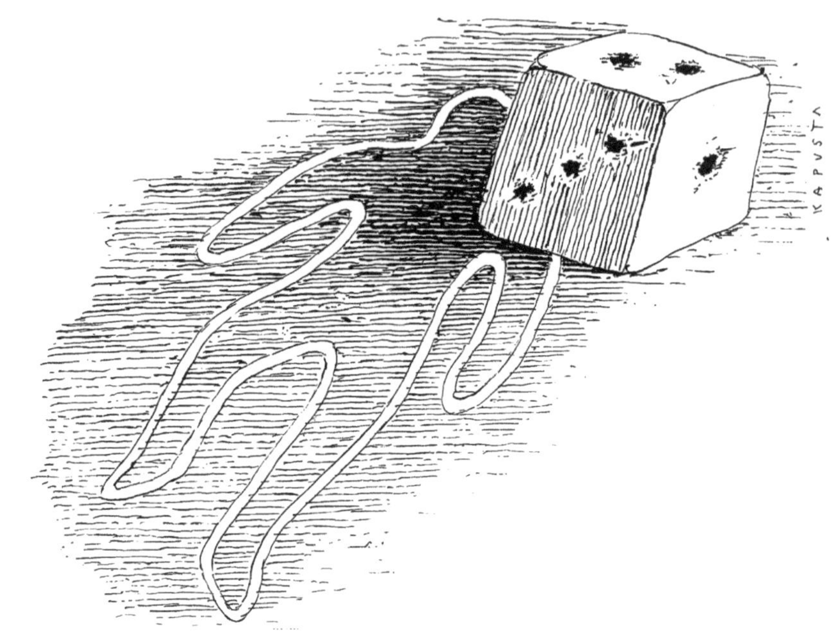

Janusz Kapusta • Accidental Killings • Pen & Ink

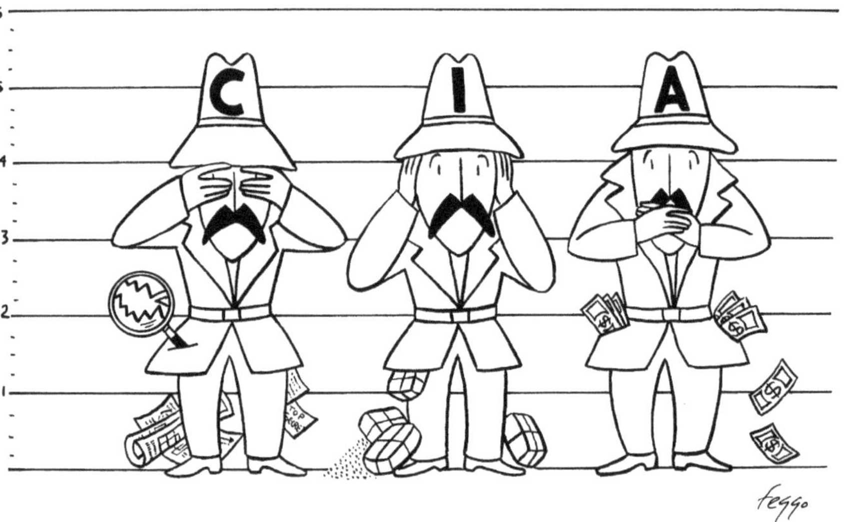

Felipe Galindo • CIA Hijinx • Pen & Ink

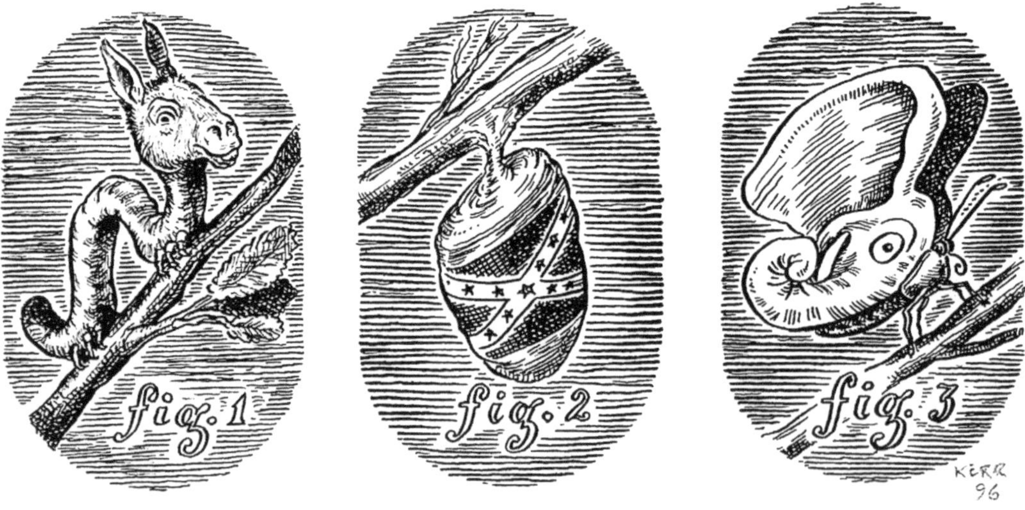

Thomas Kerr • Dixiecrat to Republican • Pen & Ink

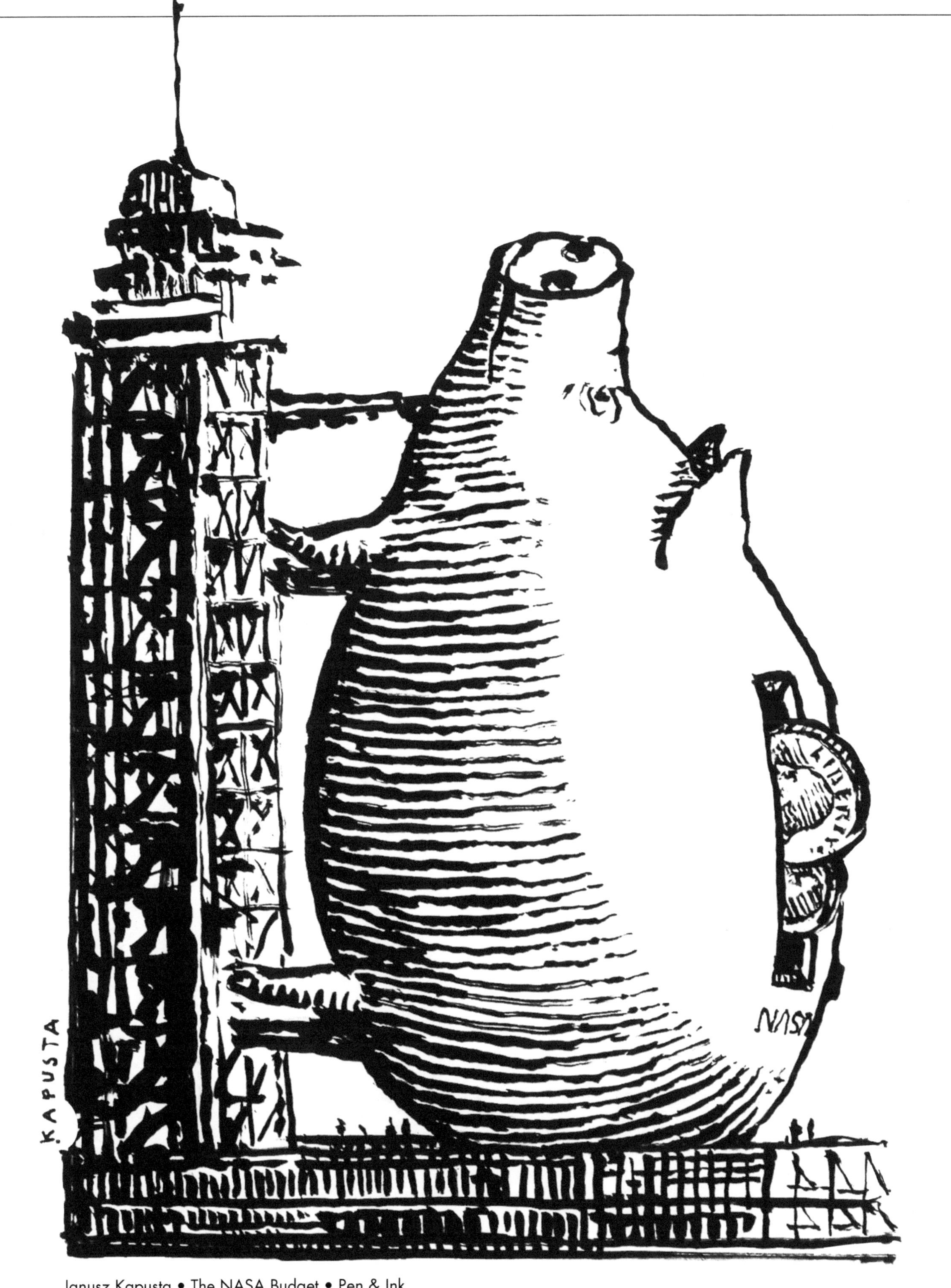

Janusz Kapusta • The NASA Budget • Pen & Ink

1997

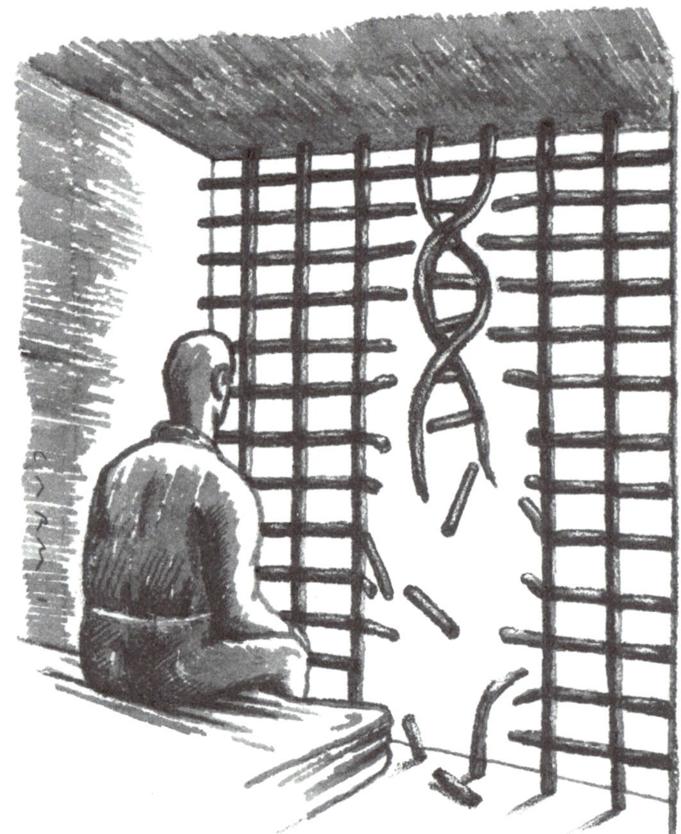

Giora Carmi • DNA Evidence • Pen, Brush & Ink

Peter Kuper • Breast Cancer • Spray Enamel & Ink

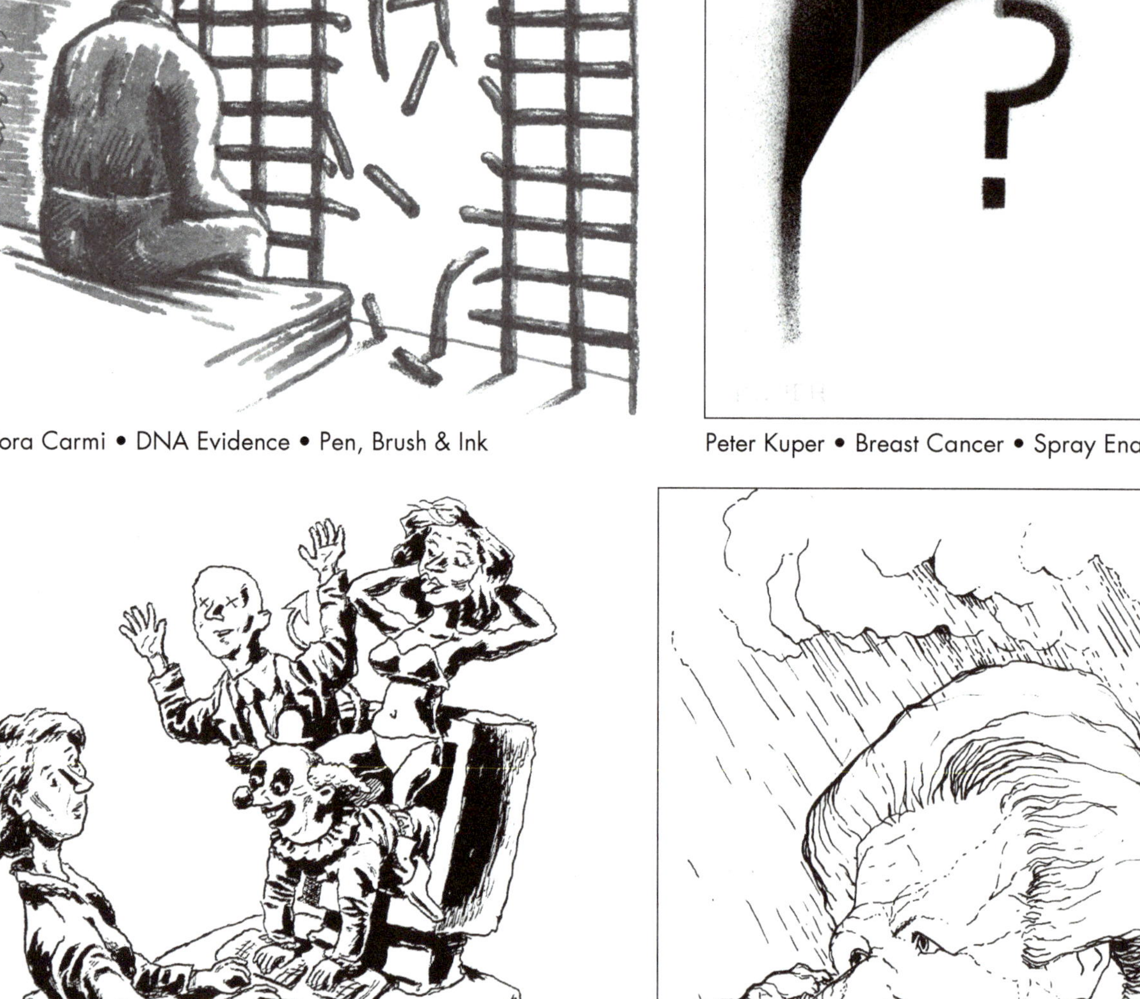

Rob Shepperson • Internet • Pen & Ink

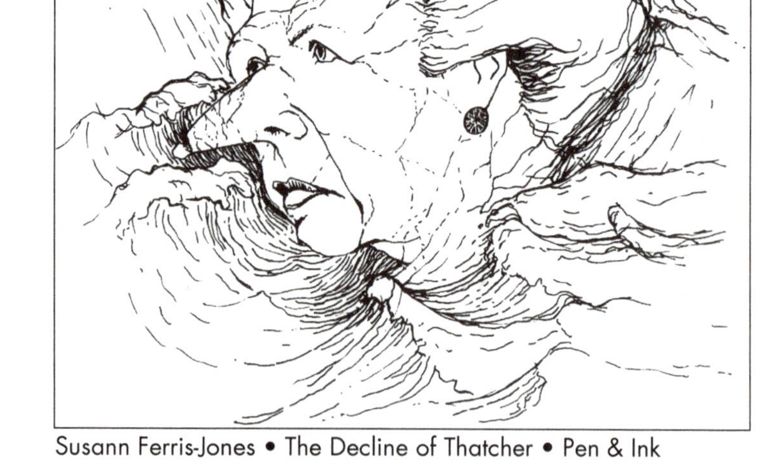

Susann Ferris-Jones • The Decline of Thatcher • Pen & Ink

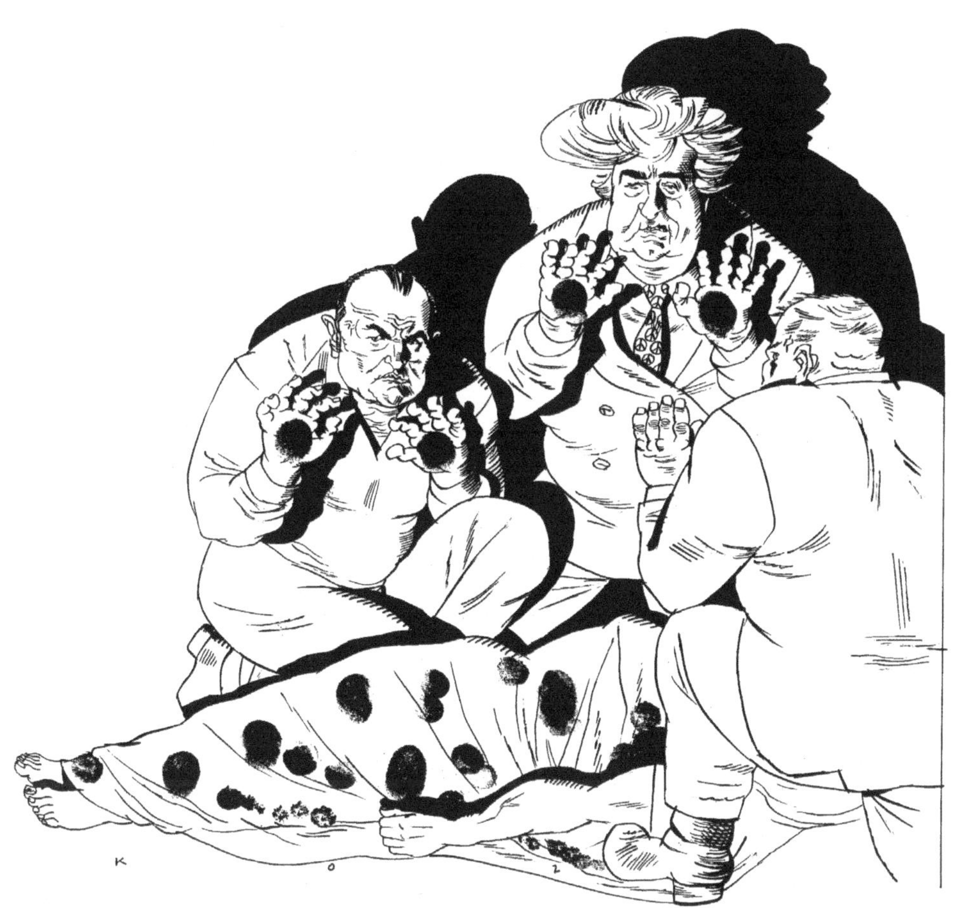

Martin Kozlowski • Serb War Crimes • Pen & Ink

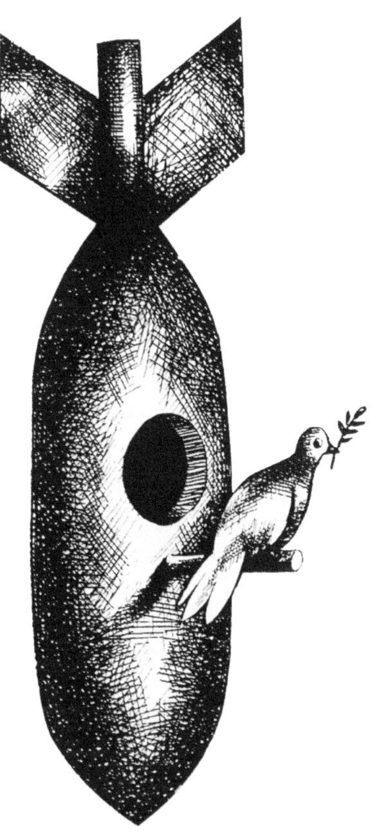

Igor Kopelnitsky
Bombs For Bosnia
Pen & Ink

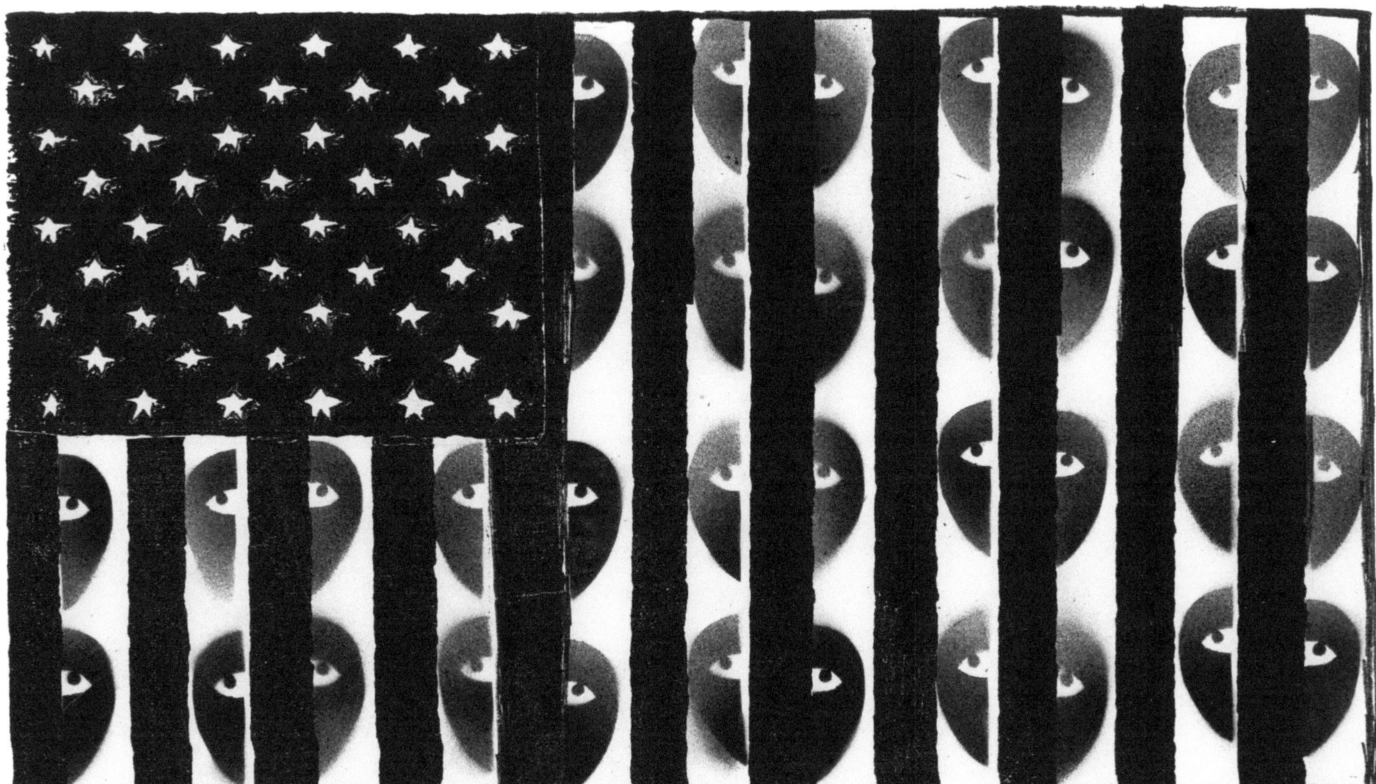

Scott Cunningham • Prison Overcrowding • Spray Enamel & Ink

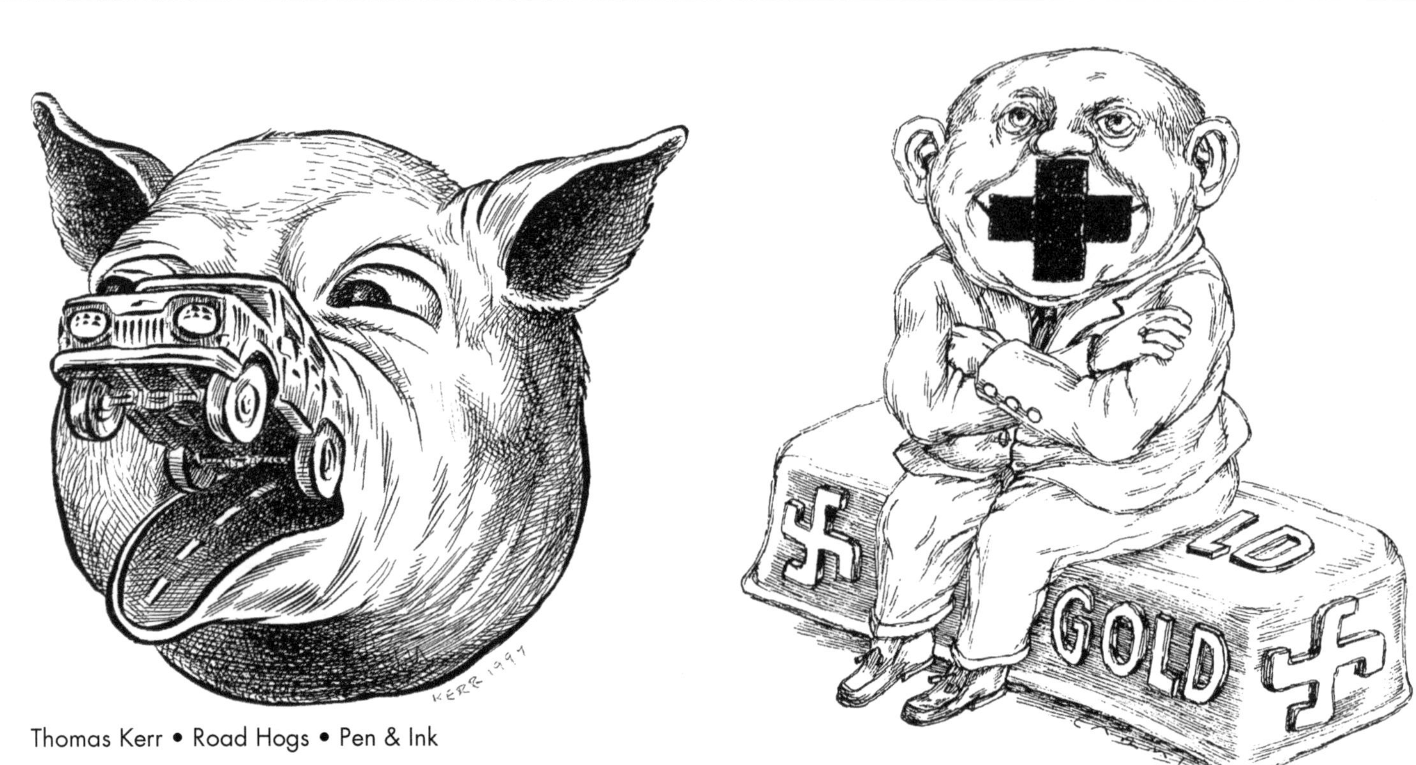

Thomas Kerr • Road Hogs • Pen & Ink

Giora Carmi • Nazi Gold • Pen & Ink

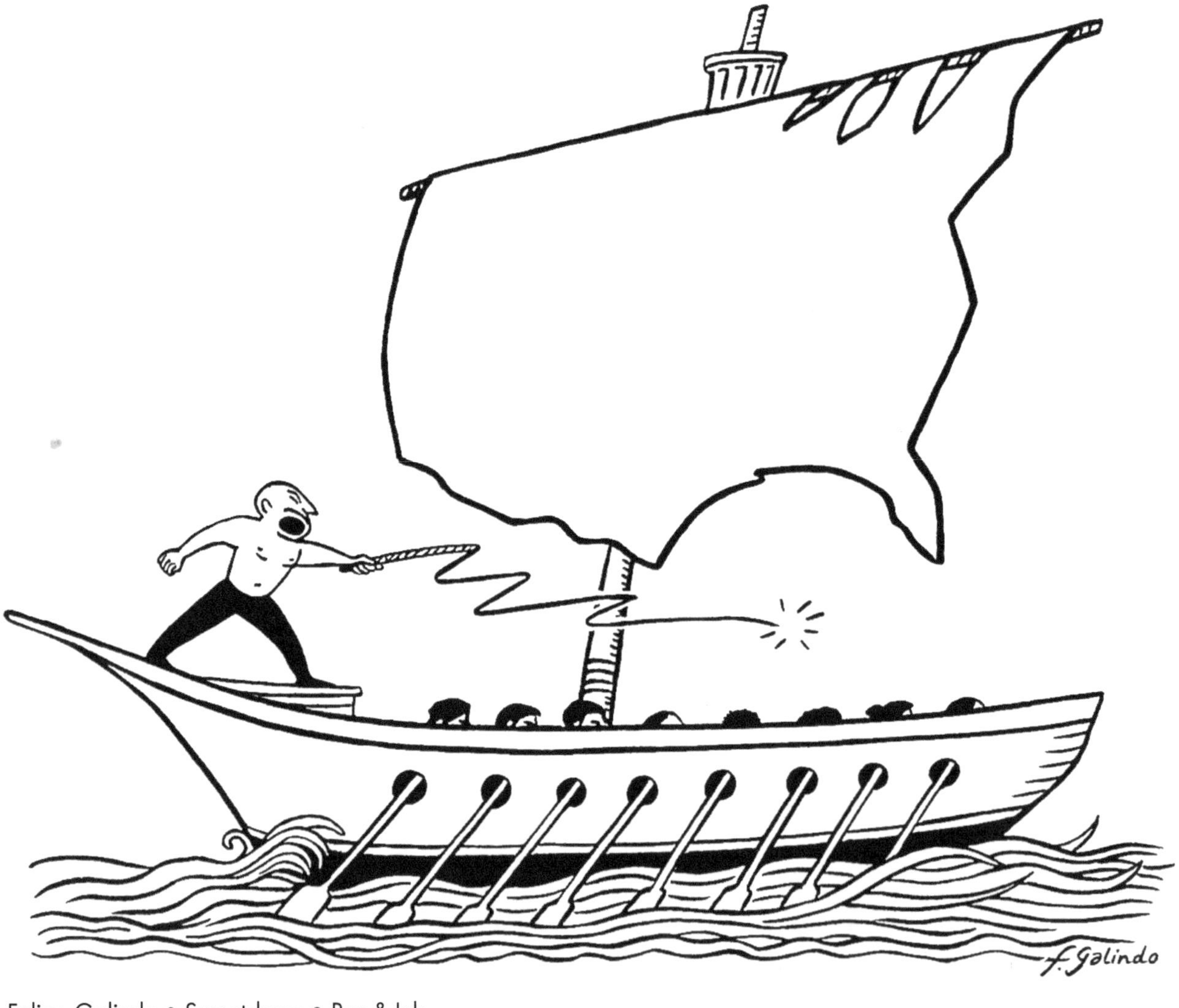

Felipe Galindo • Sweatshops • Pen & Ink

1998

Clinton accused of having sex with intern Monica Lewinsky. Good Friday Agreement ends The Troubles in Northern Ireland. 224 killed in U.S. embassy bombings in Tanzania and Kenya.

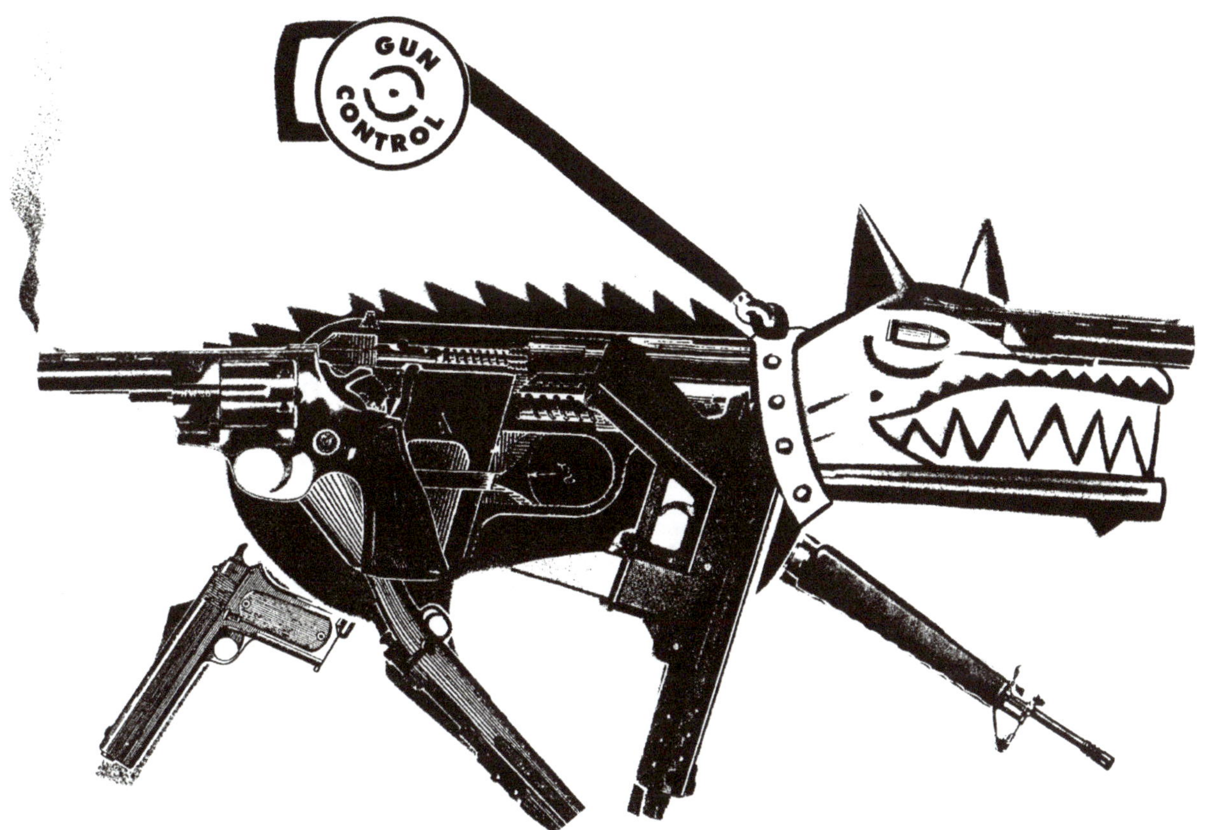

Peter Kuper • Gun Control • Spray Enamel & Collage

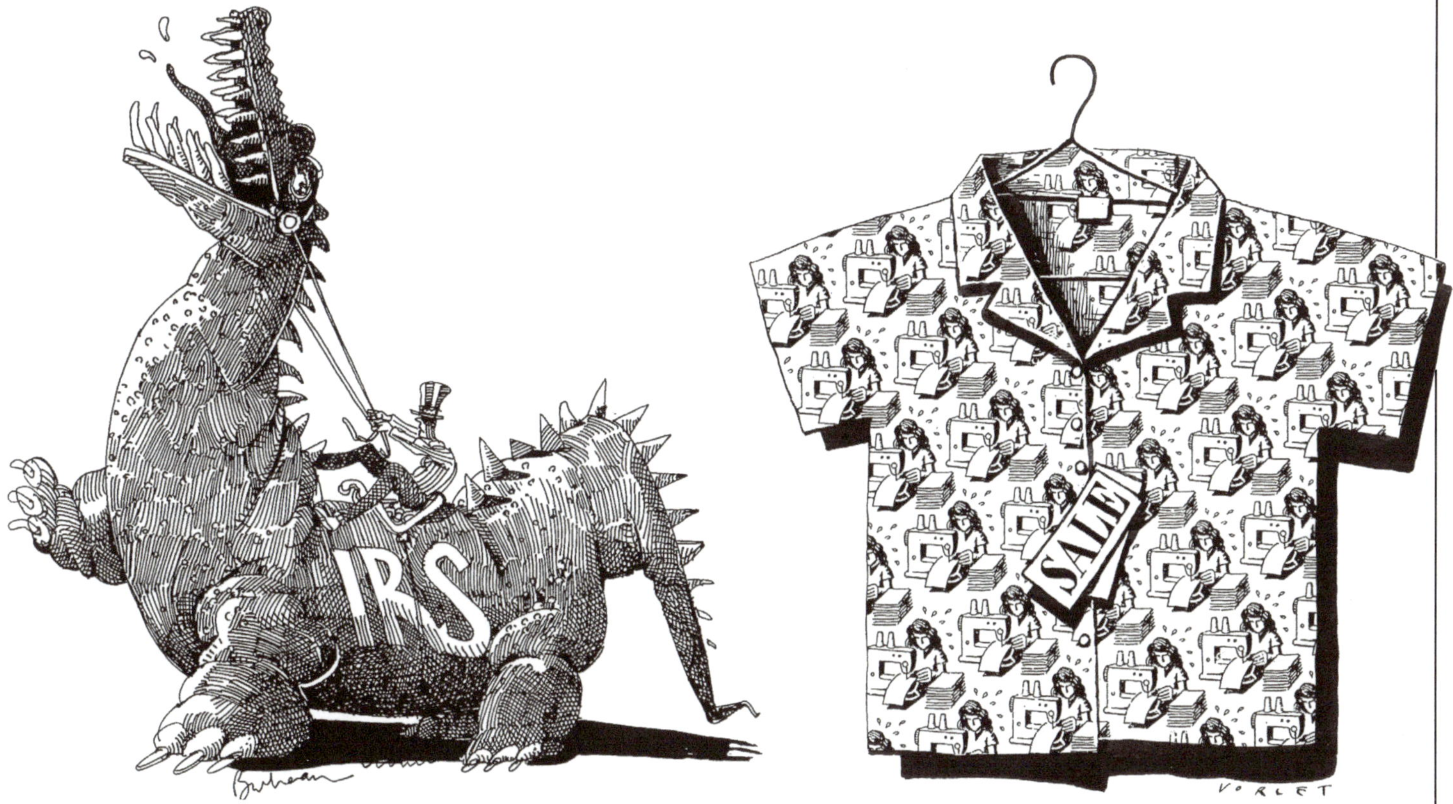

Yvonne Buchanan • IRS • Pen & Ink

Christophe Vorlet • Exploited Labor • Pen & Ink

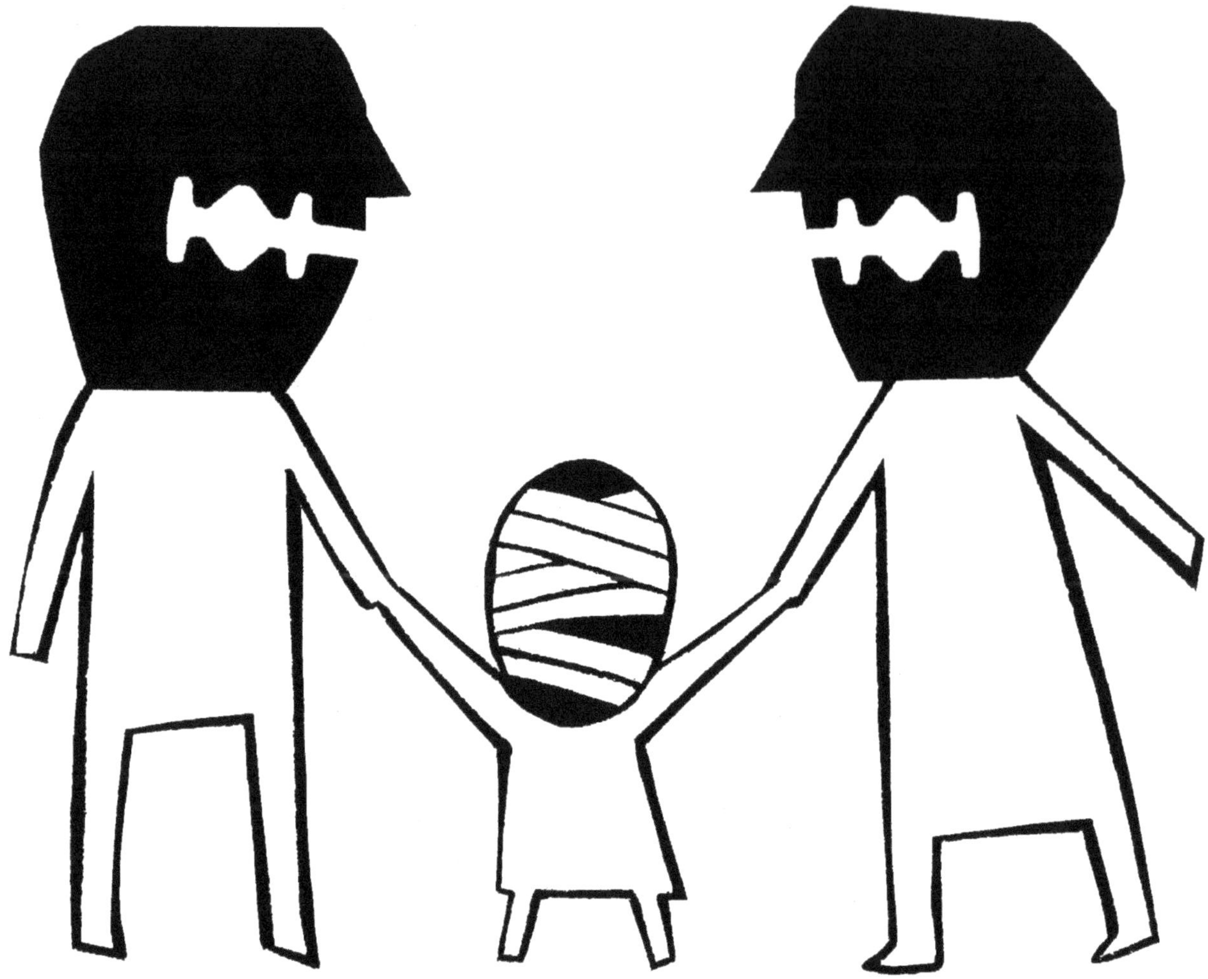

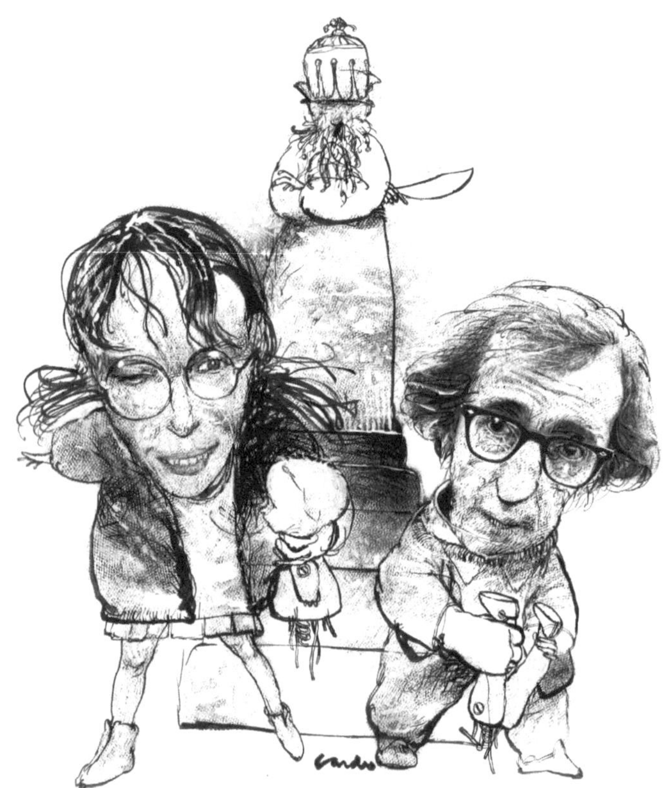

Igor Kopelnitsky • Domestic Violence • Digital Media

Horacio Cardo • Woody & Mia • Brush & Ink

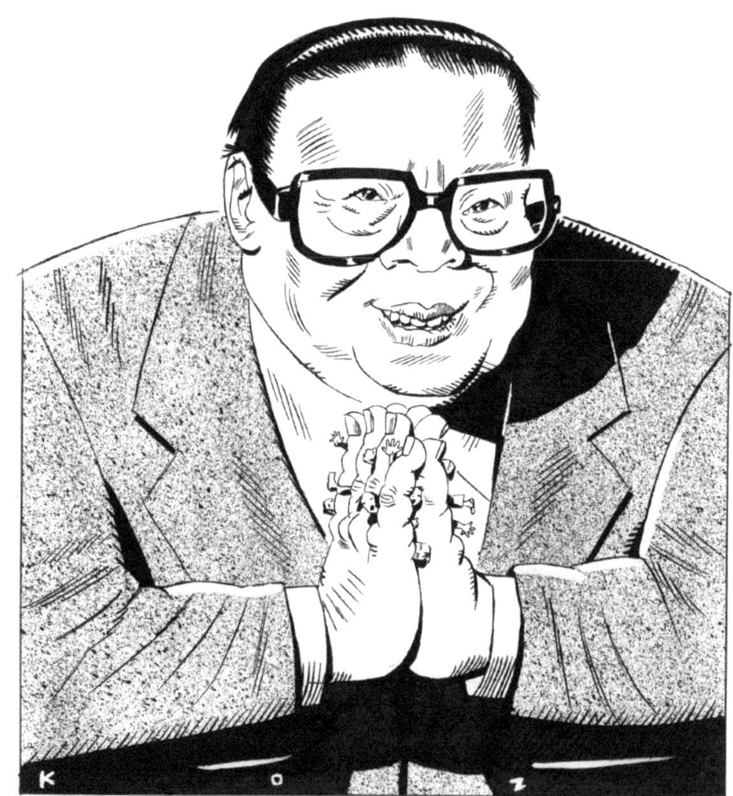

Martin Kozlowski • Jiang Zemin • Pen & Ink

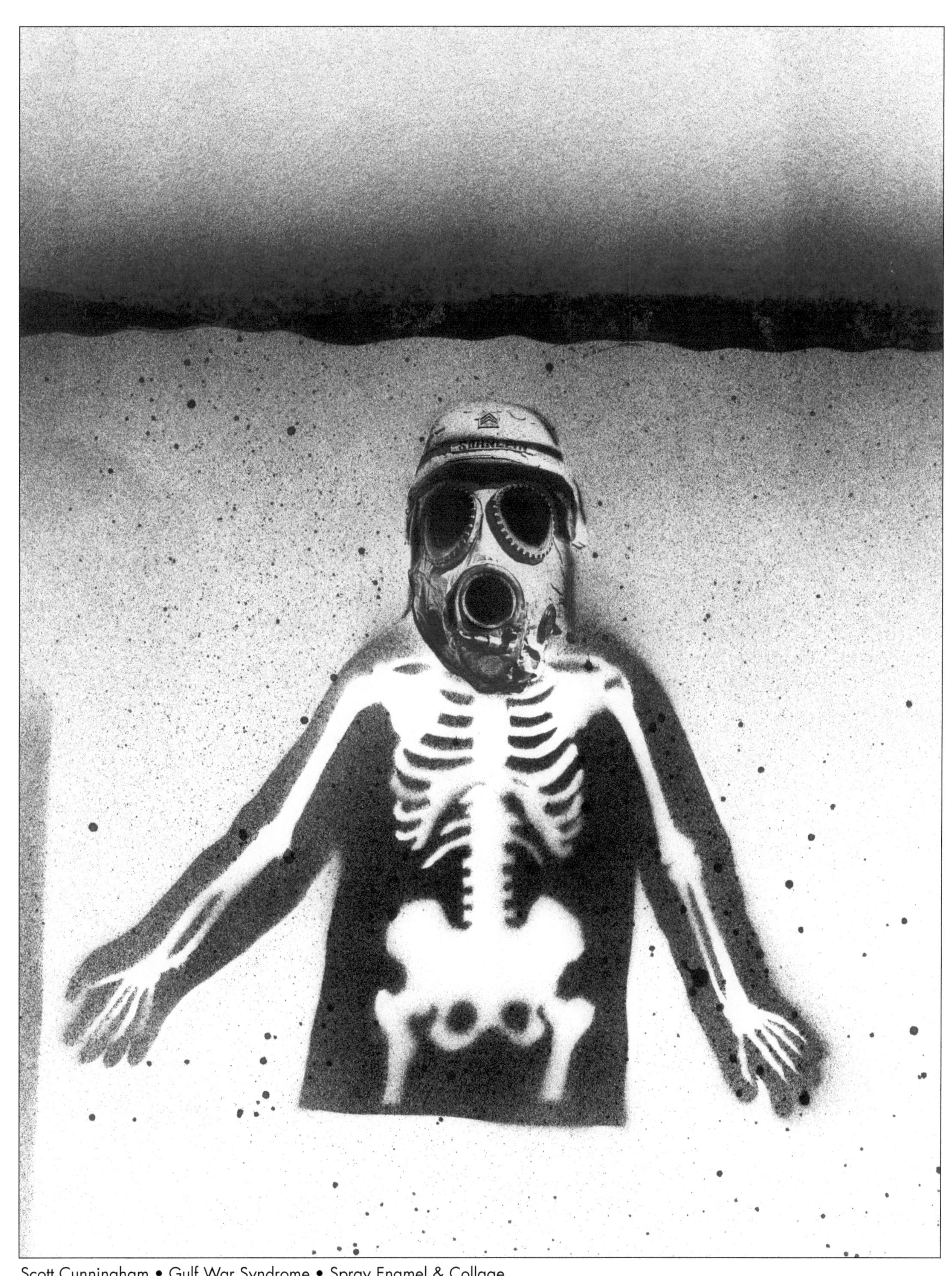

Scott Cunningham • Gulf War Syndrome • Spray Enamel & Collage

Massacre at Columbine High School. Clinton survives impeachment. Euro is introduced. Kosovo War ends the wars in Yugoslavia. Hugo Chavez elected President of Venezuela.

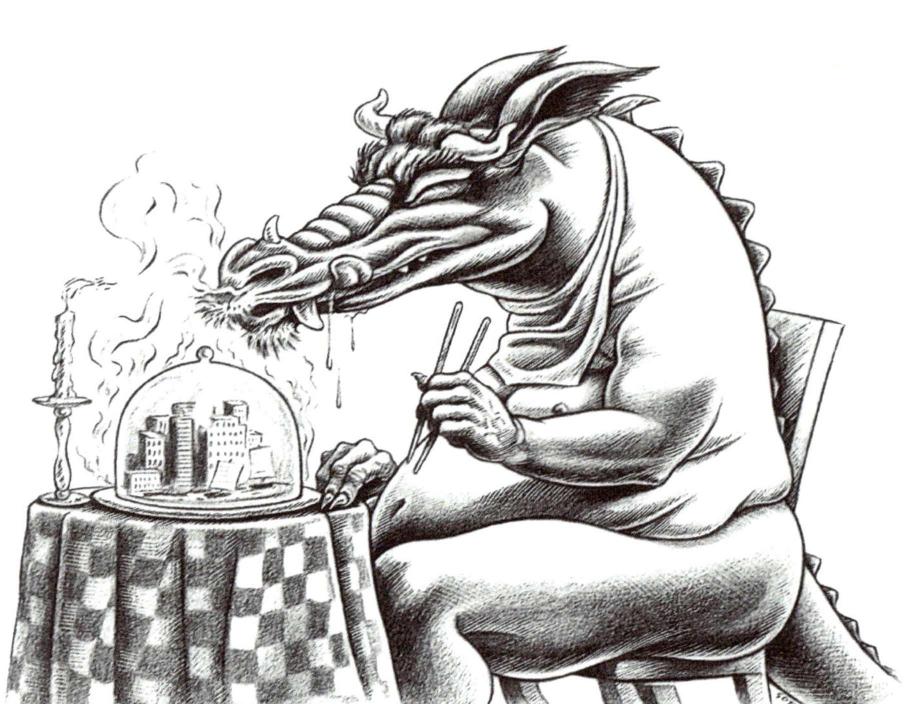

David Gothard • China Swallows Hong Kong • Pencil

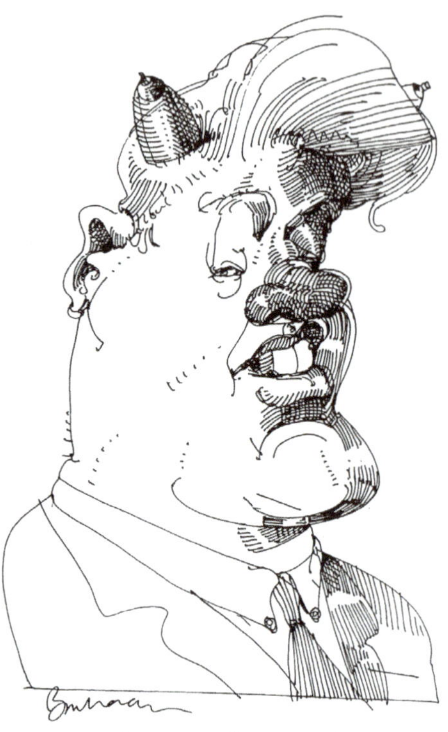

Yvonne Buchanan • Clinton & Women
Pen & Ink

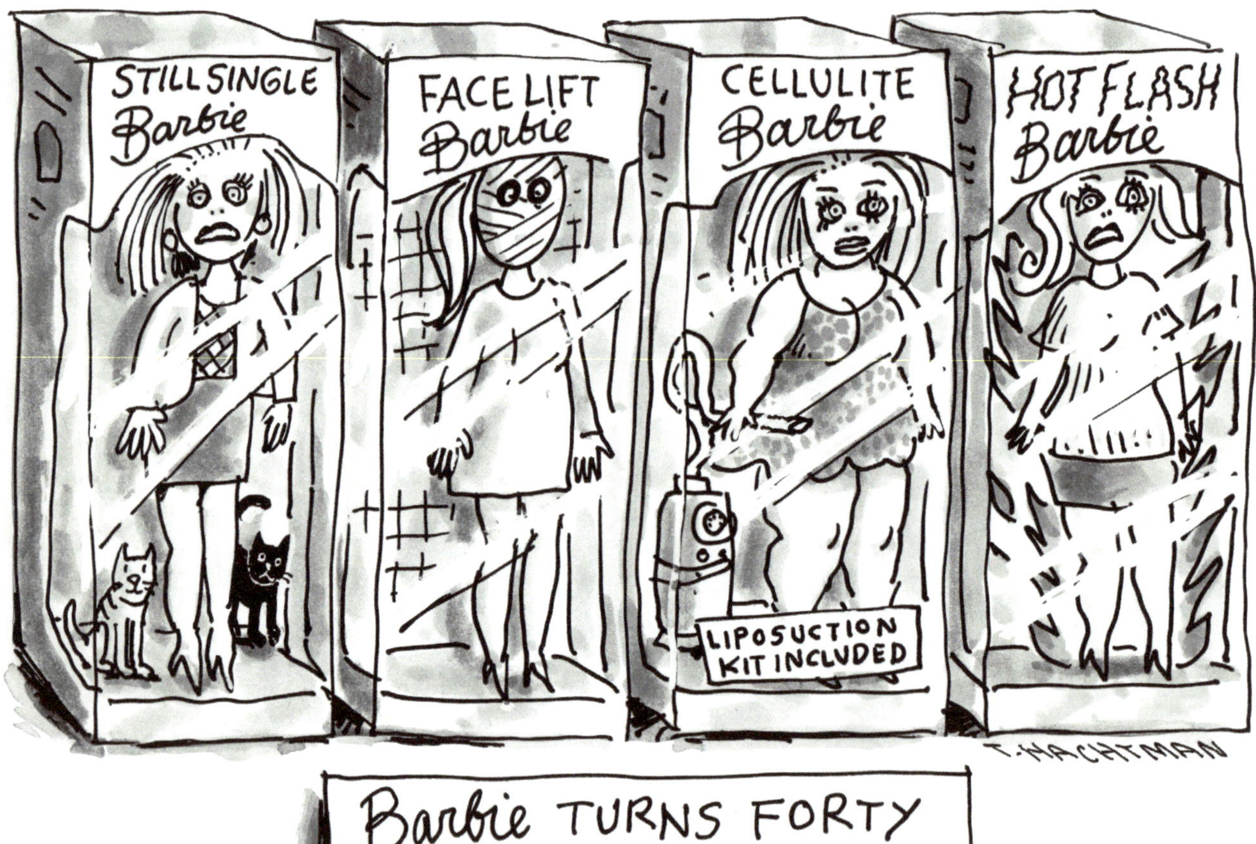

Tom Hachtman • Barbie Turns 40 • Pen, Brush & Ink

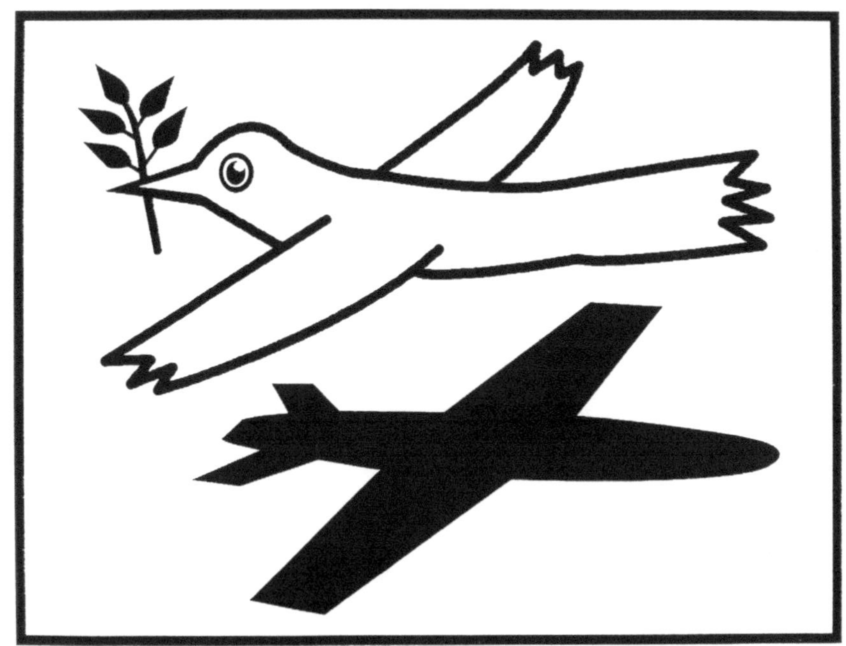

Igor Kopelnitsky • Peace • Pen & Ink

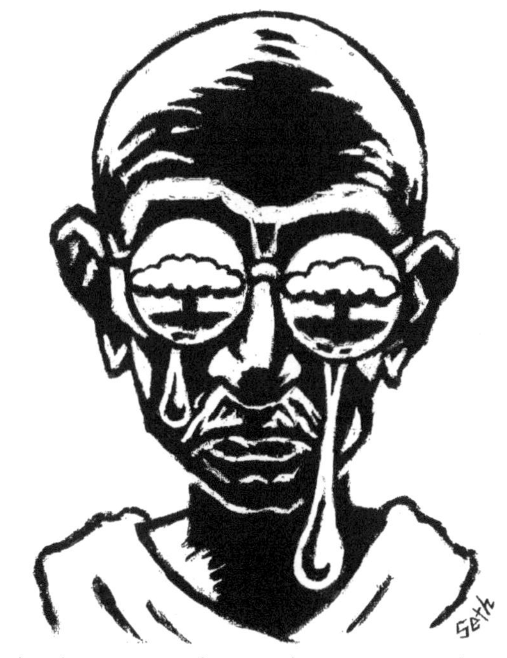

Seth Tobocman • Indian Nuclear Tests • Brush & Ink

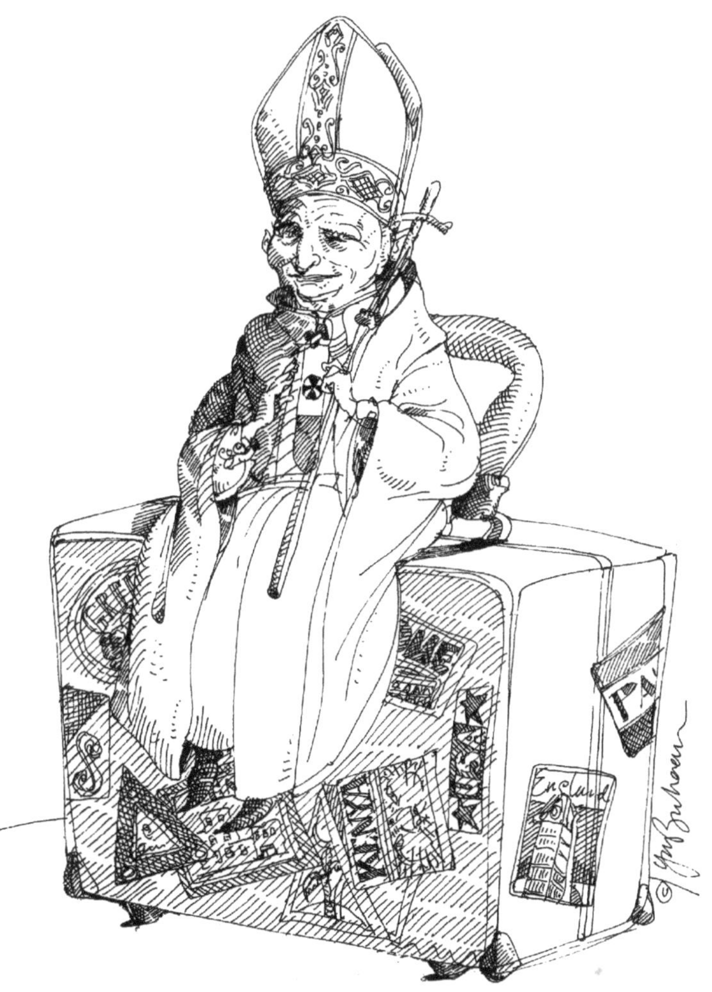

Yvonne Buchanan • Well-traveled Pope • Pen & Ink

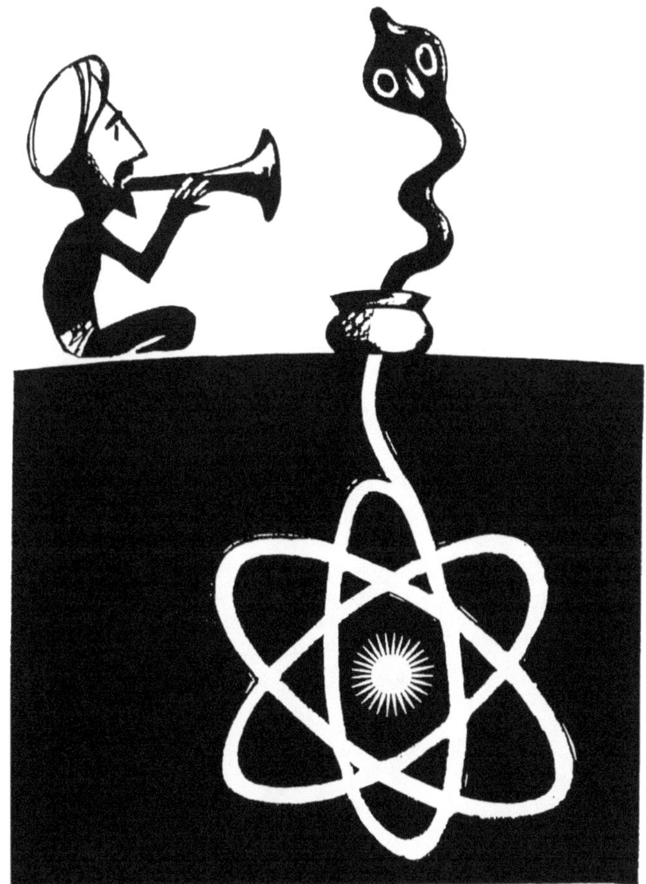

Igor Kopelnitsky • India's Nuclear Viper • Brush & Ink

As the millenium drew to a close, digital technology was transforming how artists created and delivered their work, with the computer scanner and the e-mail account becoming as commonplace as the pencil and the postage stamp.

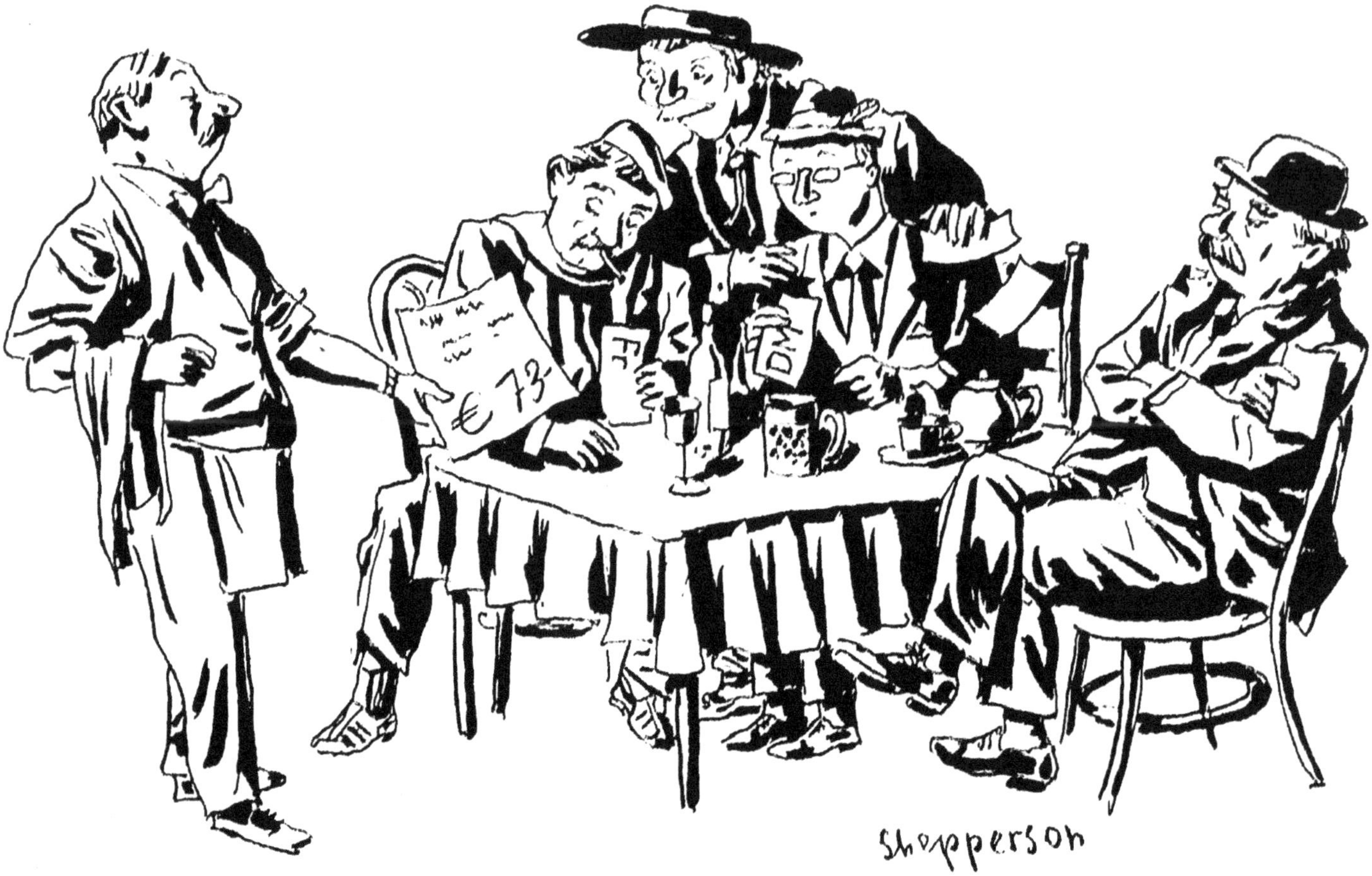

Rob Shepperson • The Euro • Pen & Ink

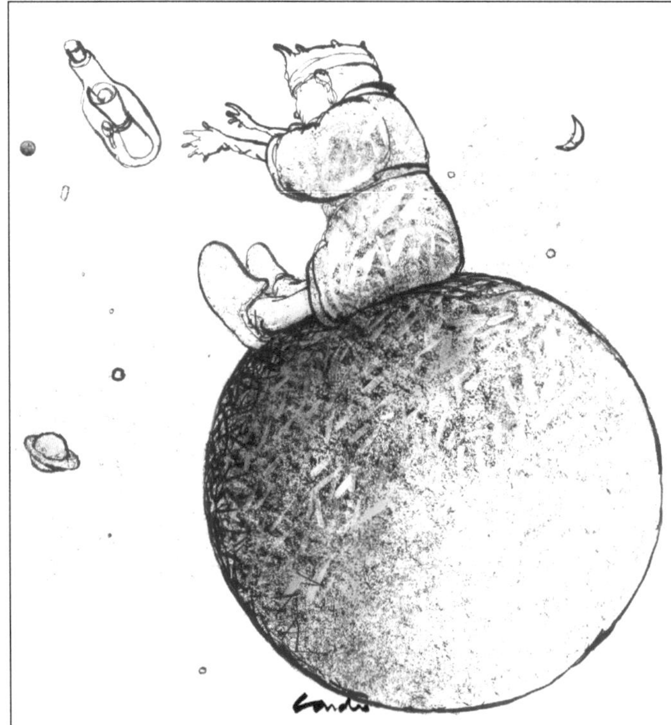

Horacio Cardo • Life on Mars • Brush & Ink

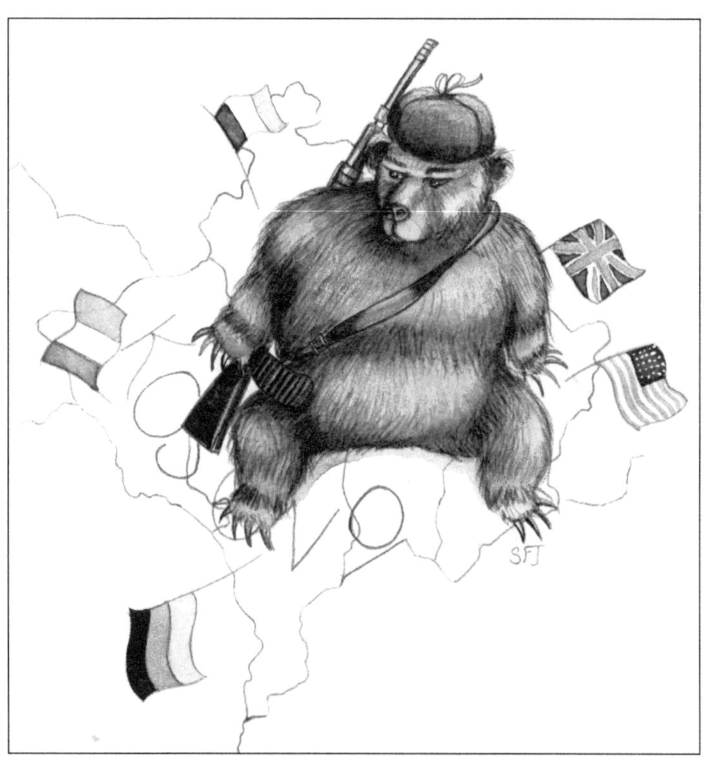

Susann Ferris-Jones • Russia & Kosovo • Pencil

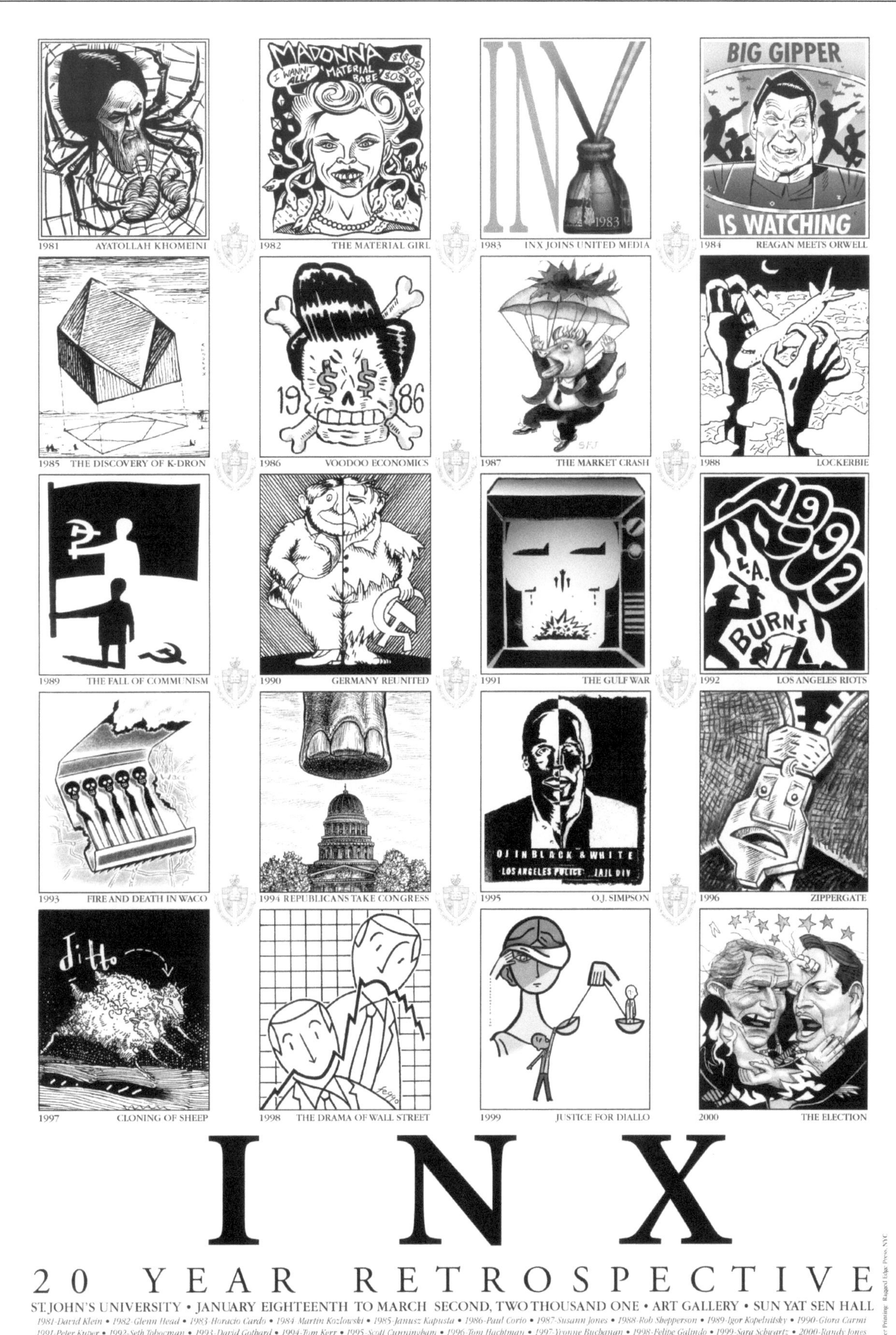

Poster for the 20 Year INX Retrospective at St. John's University in 2001 featuring images by 20 INX artists.

George W. Bush wins disputed election with Al Gore. Suicide bombing of the USS Cole by al-Qaeda. End of Israeli occupation of Lebanon. Second Intifada begins. Vladimir Putin elected President of Russia.

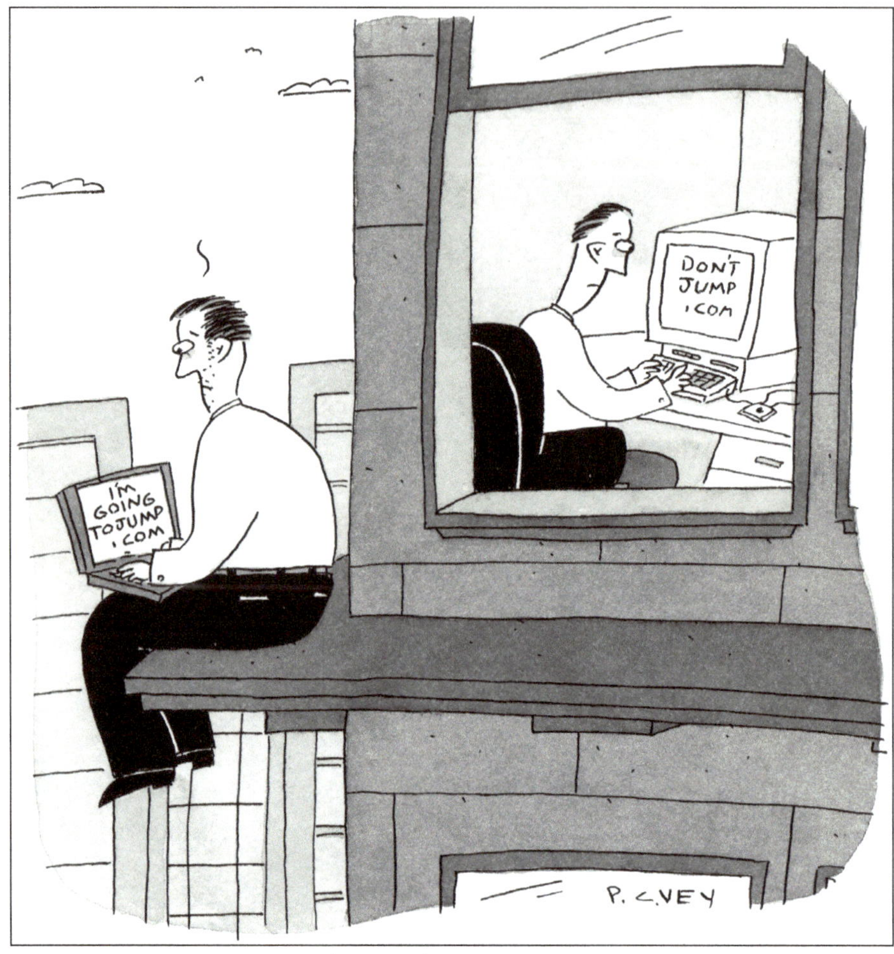

P.C. Vey • jump.com • Pen, Ink & Wash

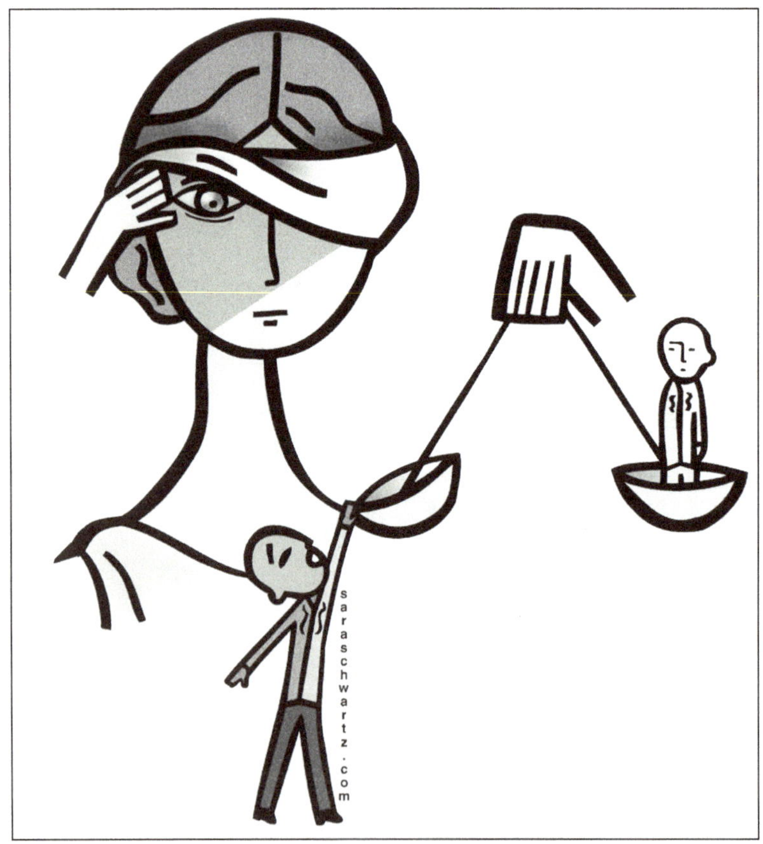

Sara Schwartz • Racial Injustice •Digital Media

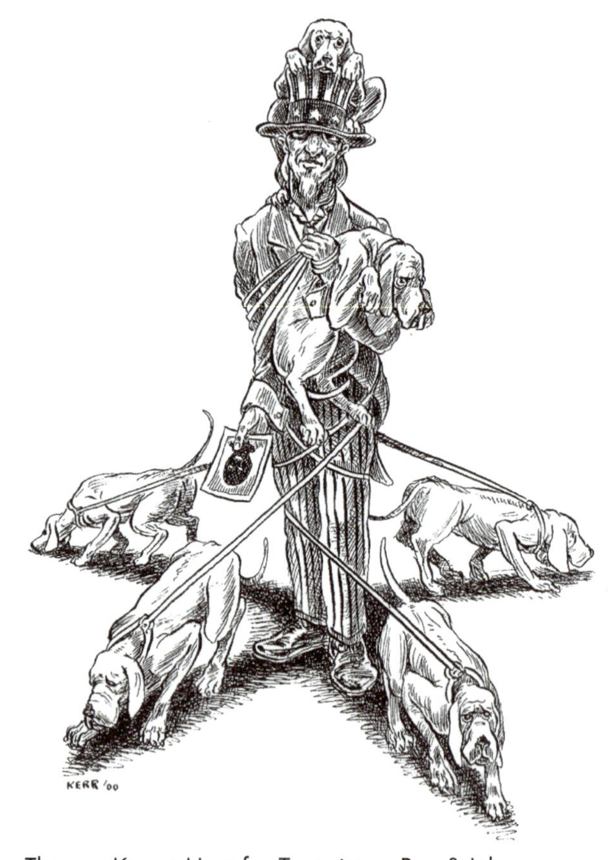

Thomas Kerr • Hunt for Terrorists • Pen & Ink

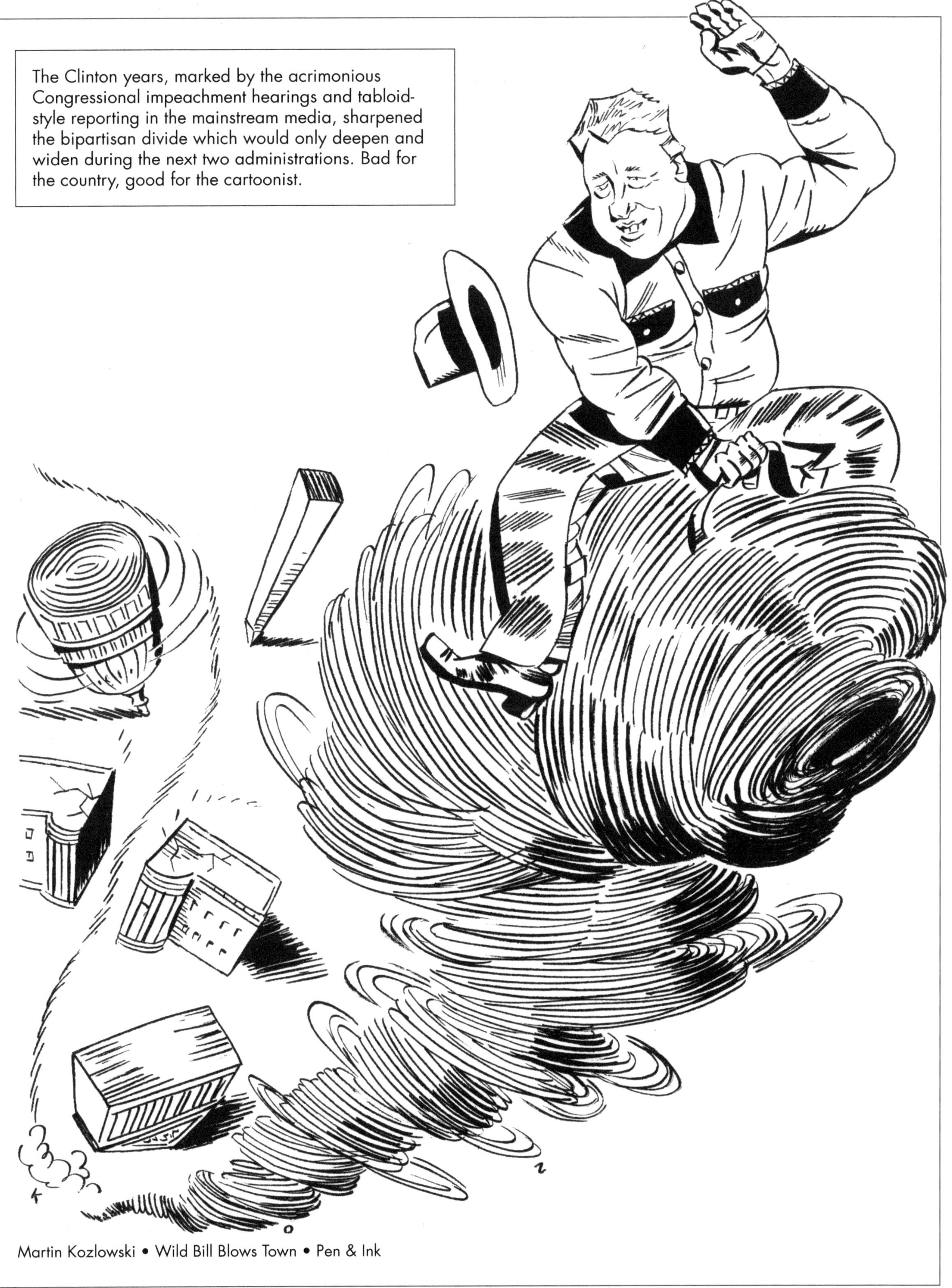

Martin Kozlowski • Wild Bill Blows Town • Pen & Ink

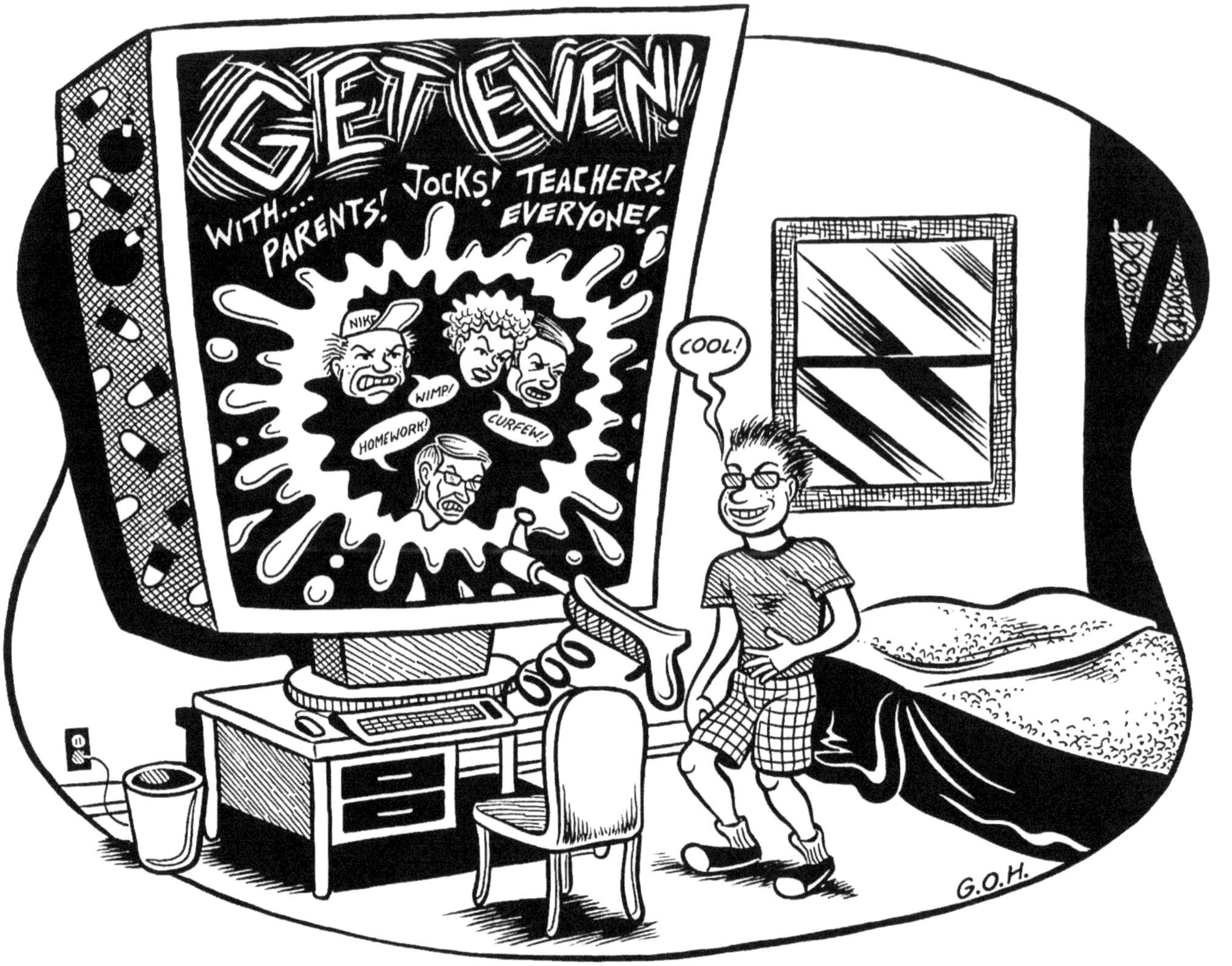

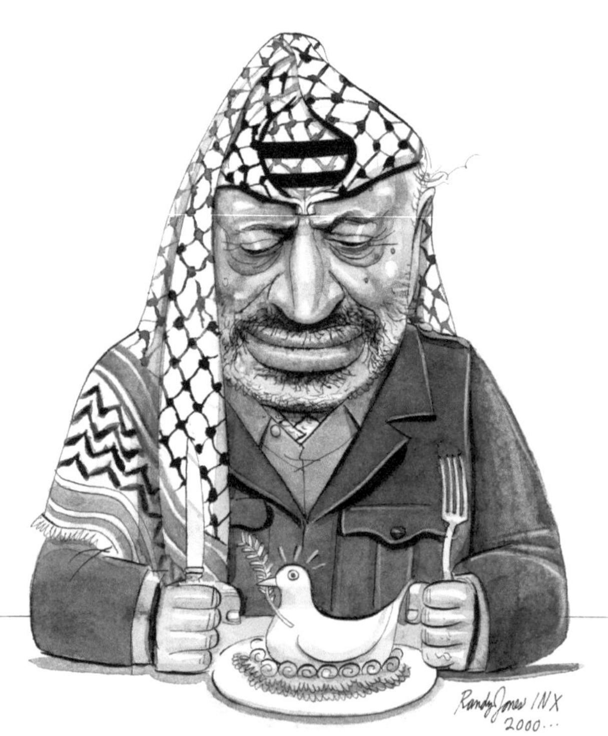

Glenn Head • Violent Video Games • Pen & Ink

Randy Jones • Arafat Samples Peace • Pen, Ink & Wash

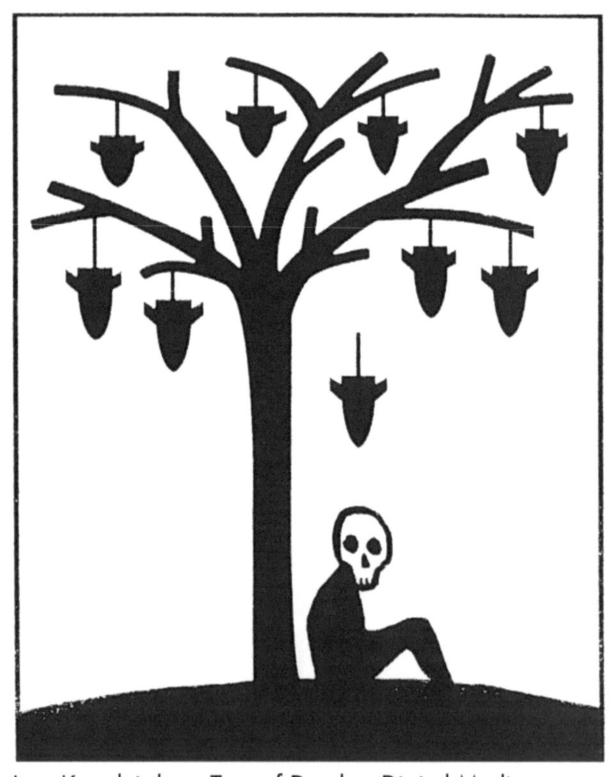

Igor Kopelnitsky • Tree of Death • Digital Media

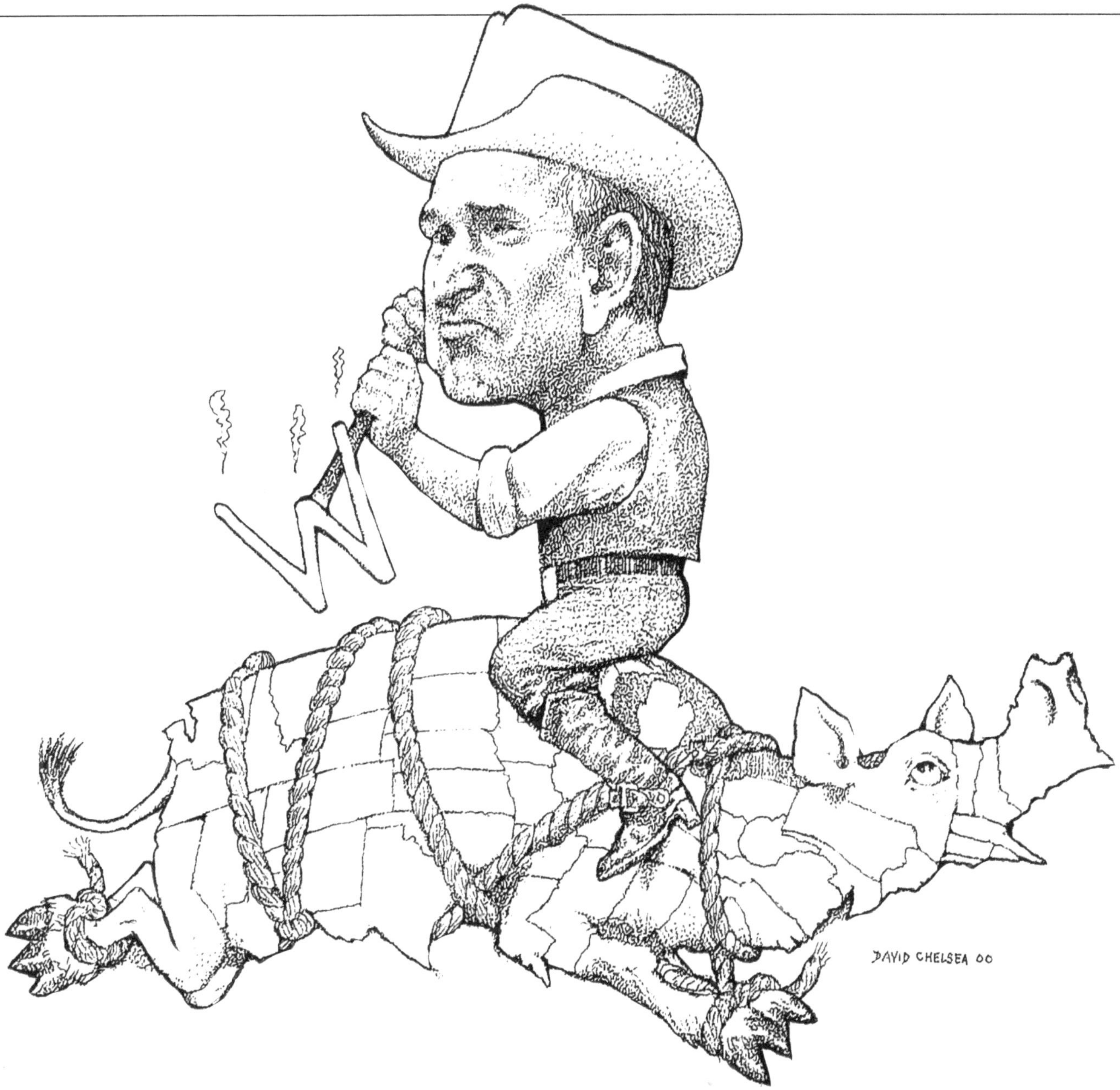

David Chelsea • Bush Brands U.S.A. • Pen & Ink

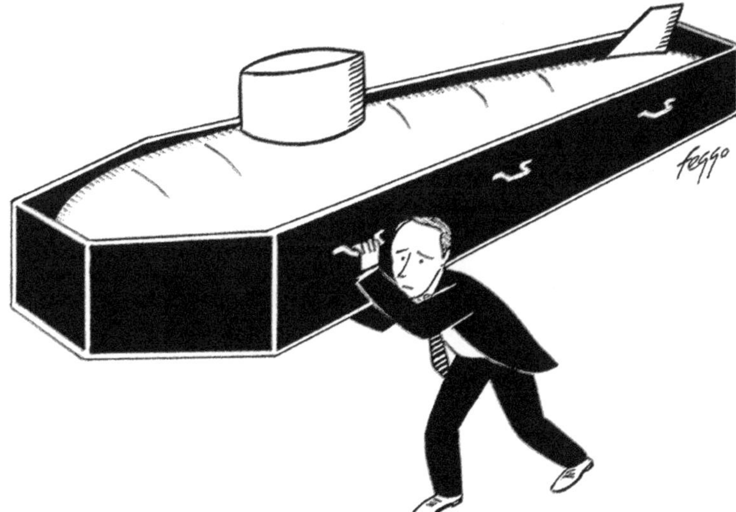

Felipe Galindo • The Kursk: Russian Tragedy • Pen & Ink

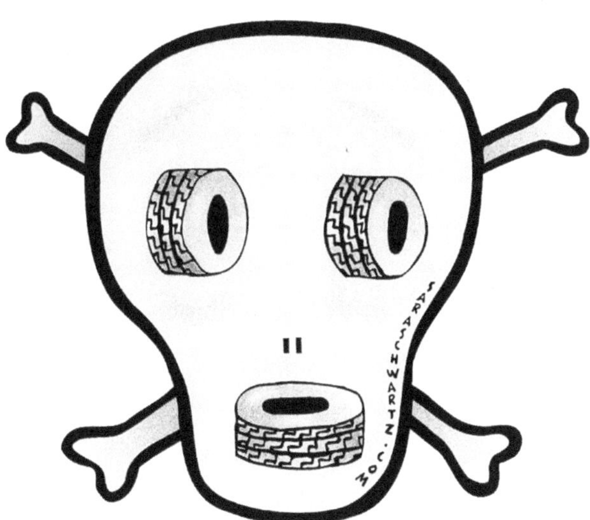

Sara Schwartz • Firestone Tire Recall • Digital Media

September 11 terror attacks on World Trade Center and Pentagon. U.S. launches invasion of Afghanistan. Anti-terror Patriot Act enacted. No Child Left Behind education bill passed.

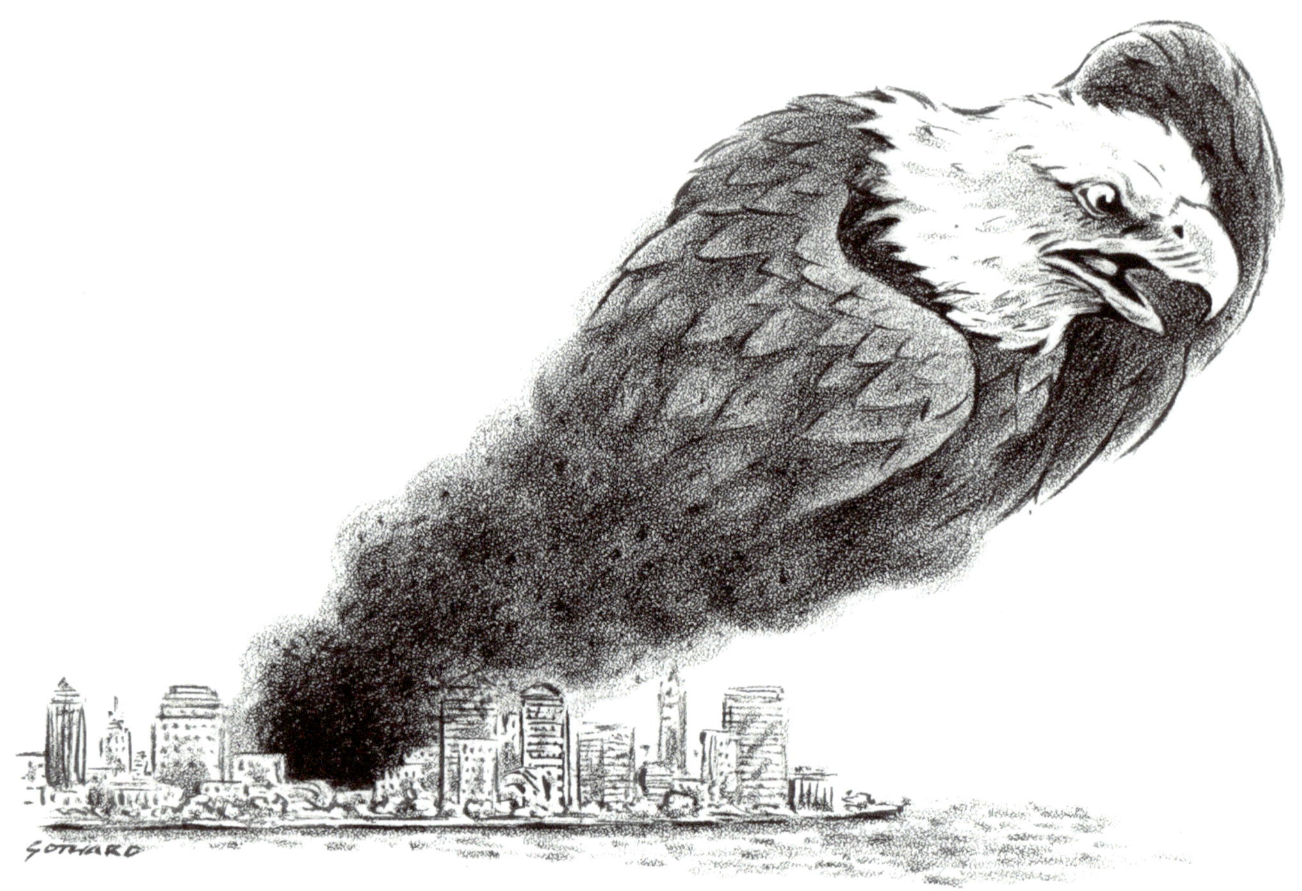

David Gothard • American Phoenix • Pencil & Ink

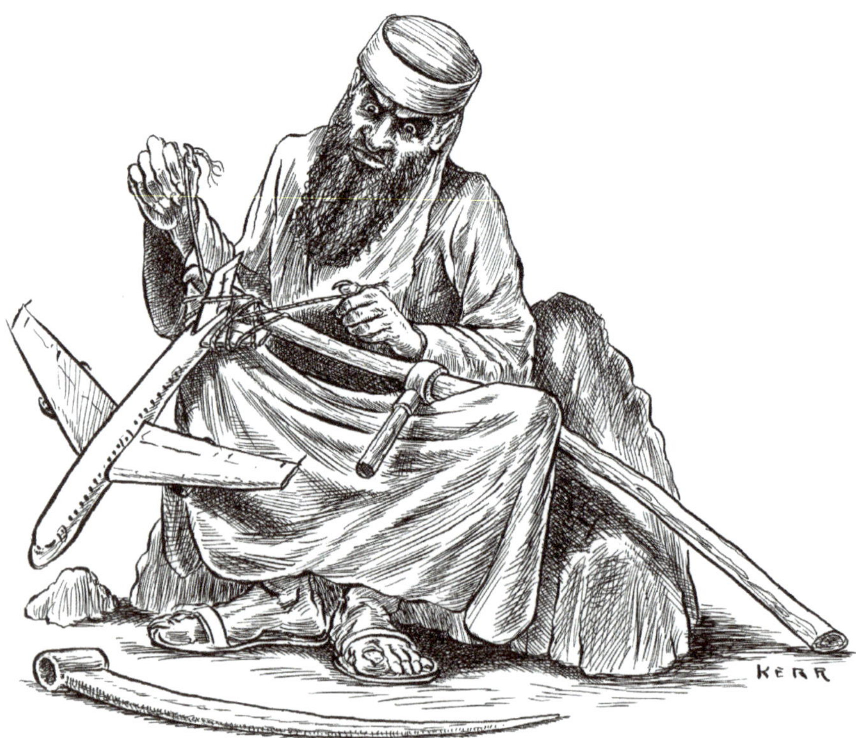

Thomas Kerr • Osama bin Laden • Pen & Ink

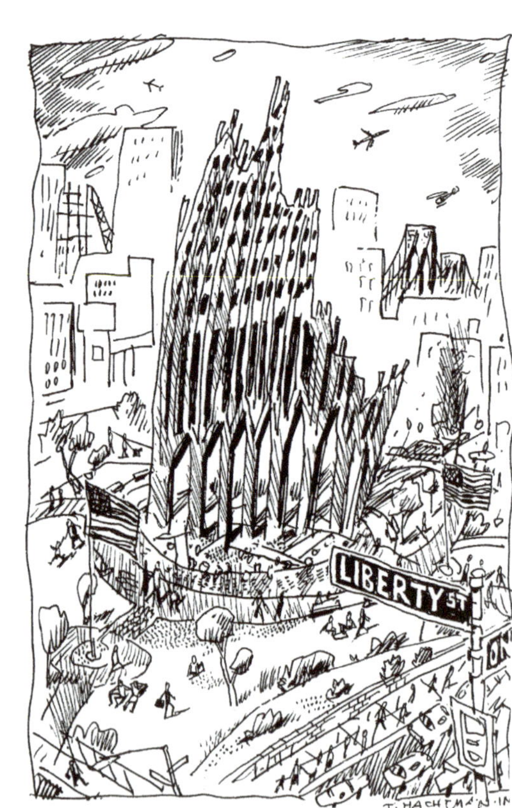

Tom Hachtman • 9/11 Memorial • Pen & Ink

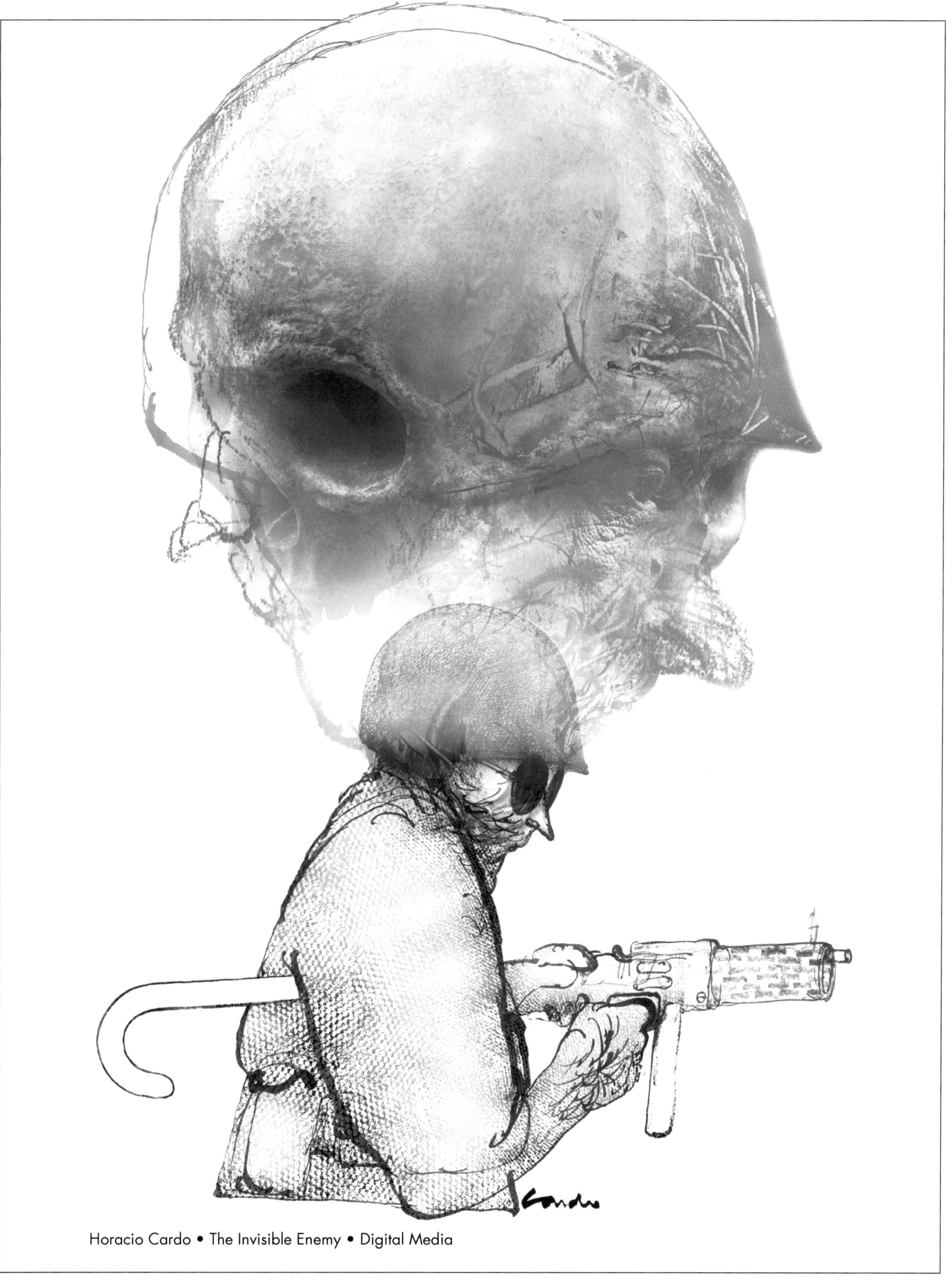

Horacio Cardo • The Invisible Enemy • Digital Media

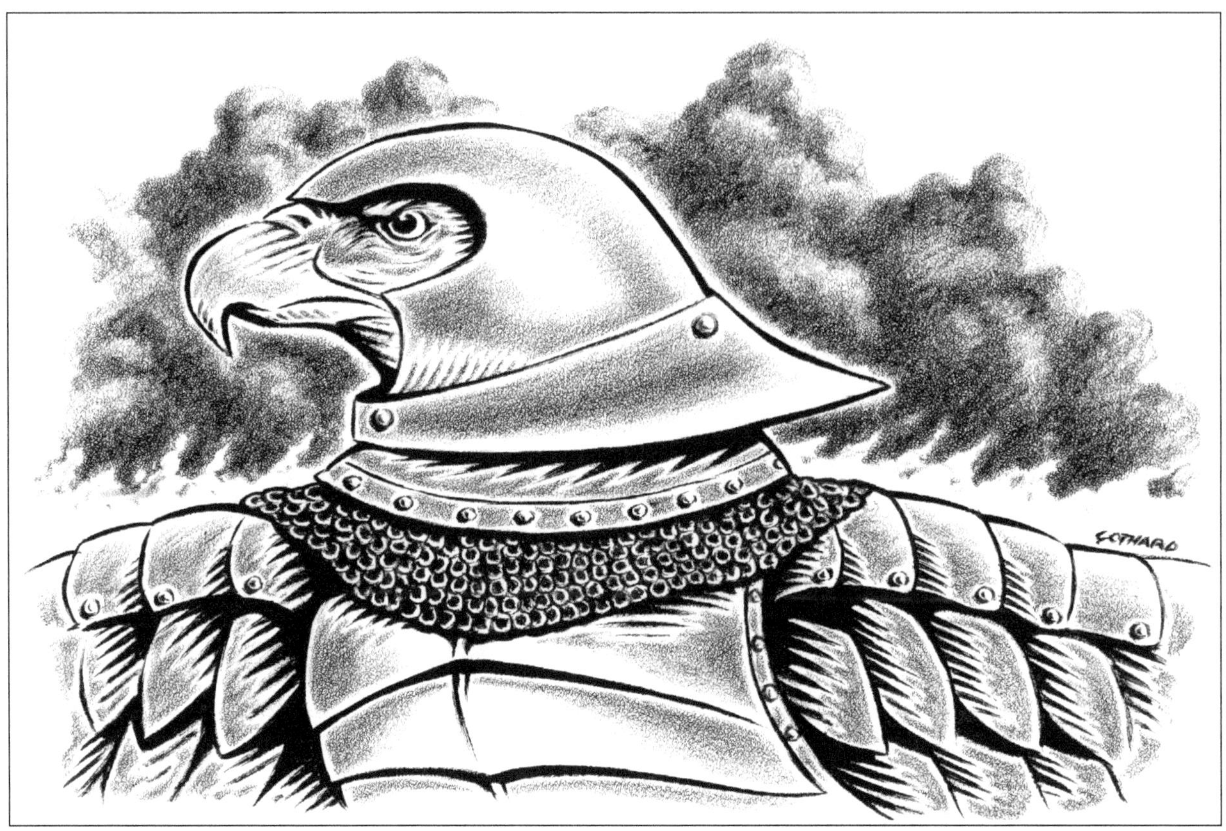

David Gothard • U.S.A. at War • Pencil & Ink

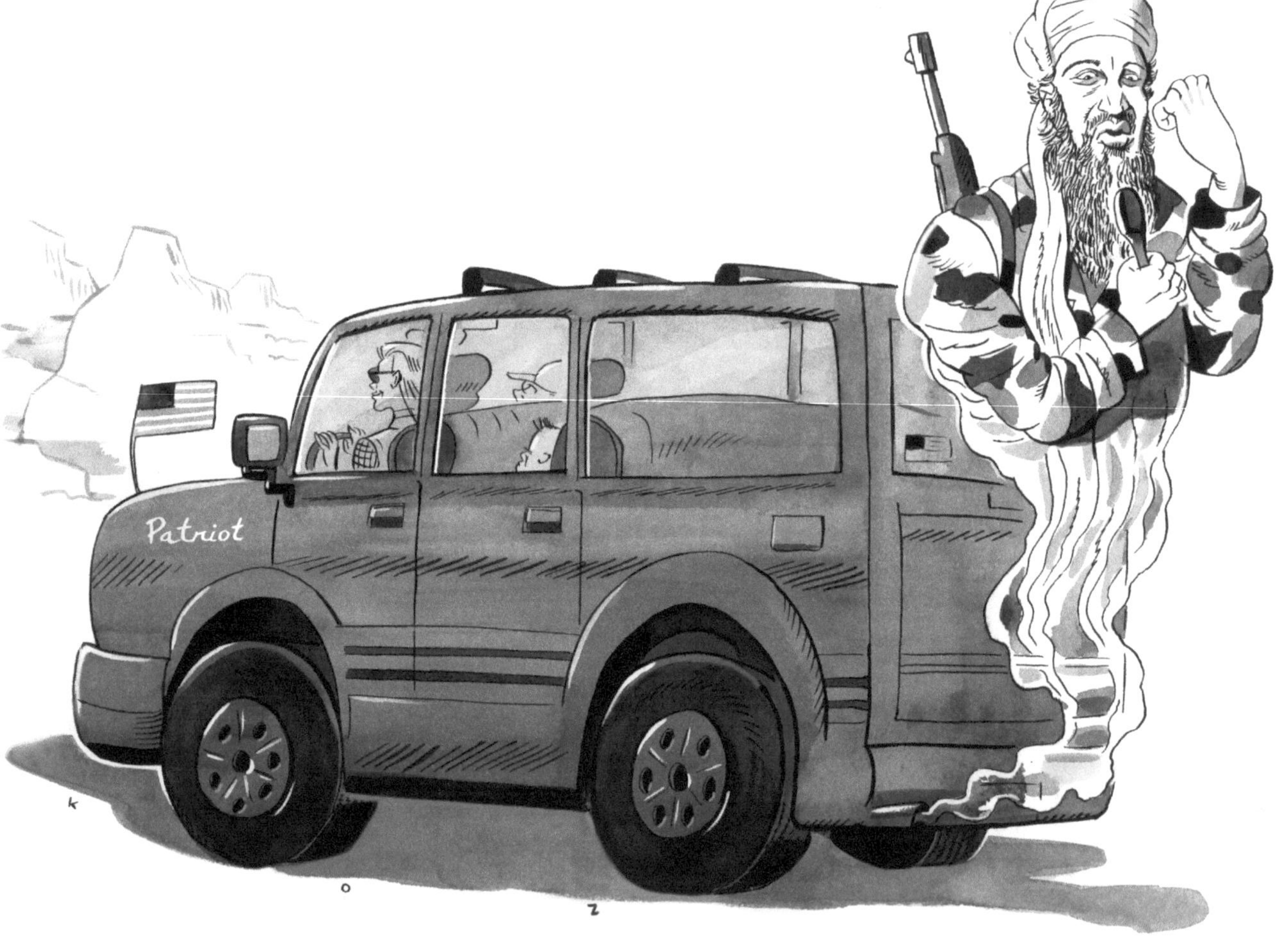

Martin Kozlowski • Fueling Terror • Pen, Brush & Ink

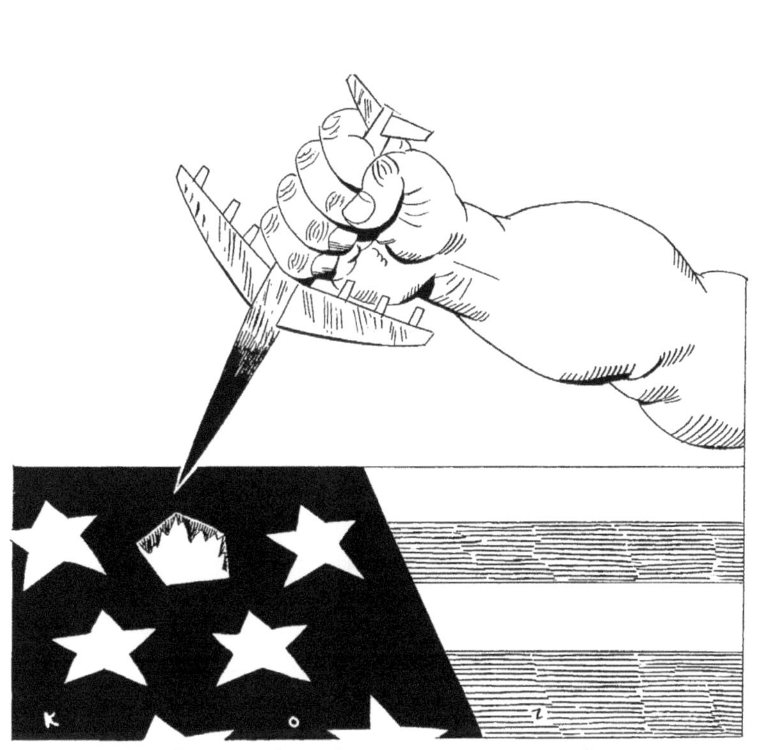

Martin Kozlowski • Attack on the Pentagon • Pen & Ink

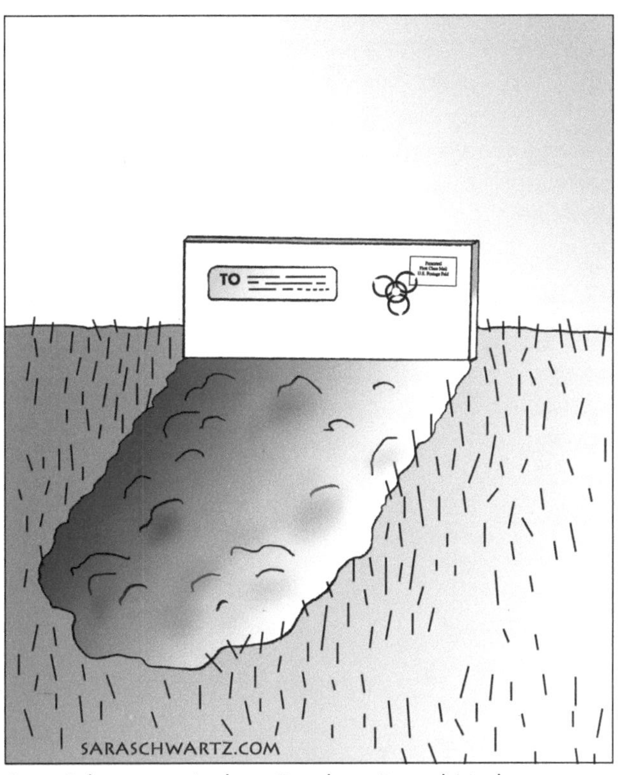

Sara Schwartz • Anthrax Deaths • Digital Media

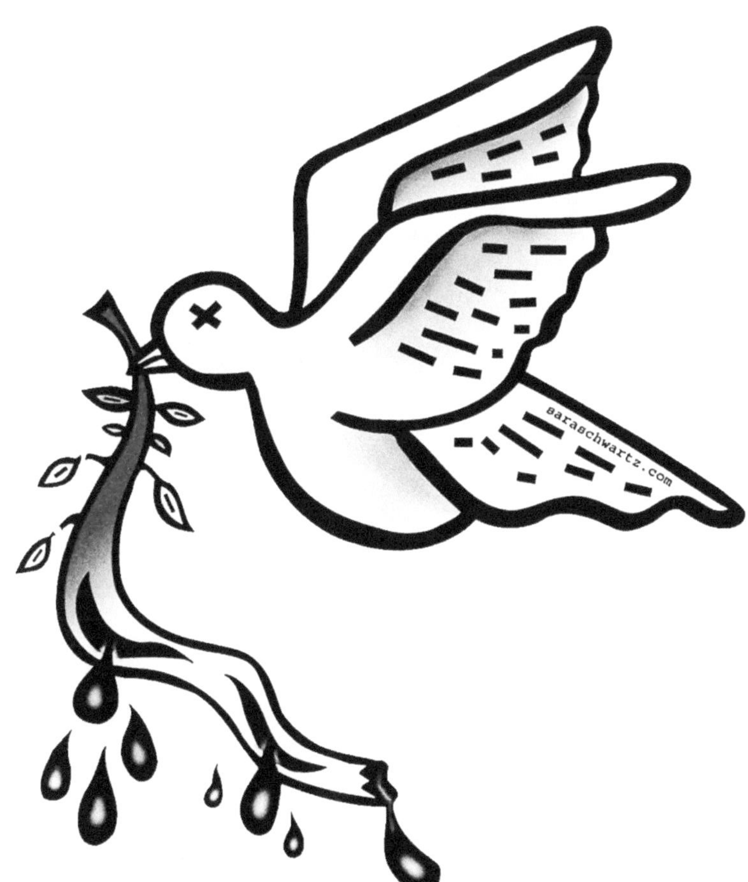

Sara Schwartz • Mideast Strife • Digital Media

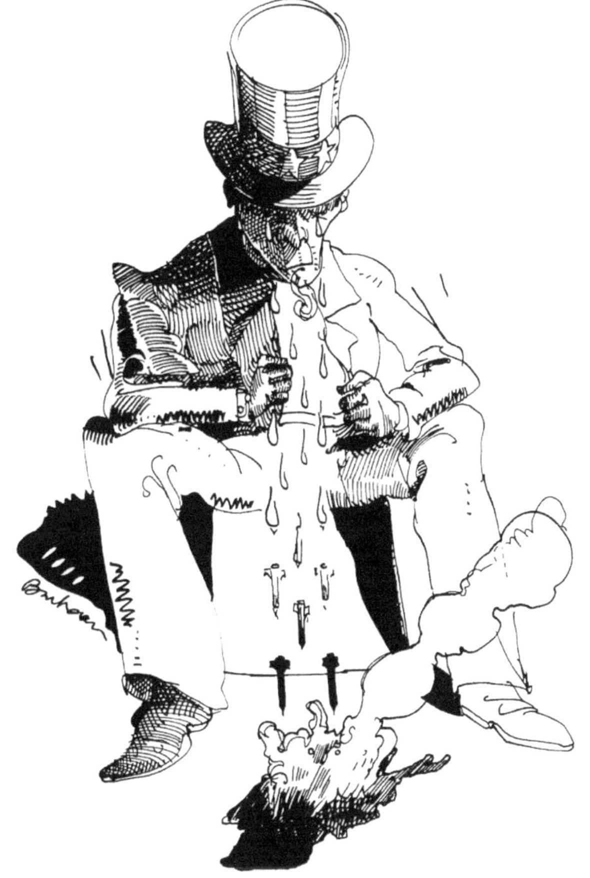

Yvonne Buchanan • From Grief to Rage • Pen & Ink

The Department of Homeland Security created. Guantanamo Bay detention camp established. Chechen rebels seize theatre in Moscow. U.S. demands Iraq allow full access to weapons inspectors. U.S. withdraws from Anti-Ballistic Missile Treaty.

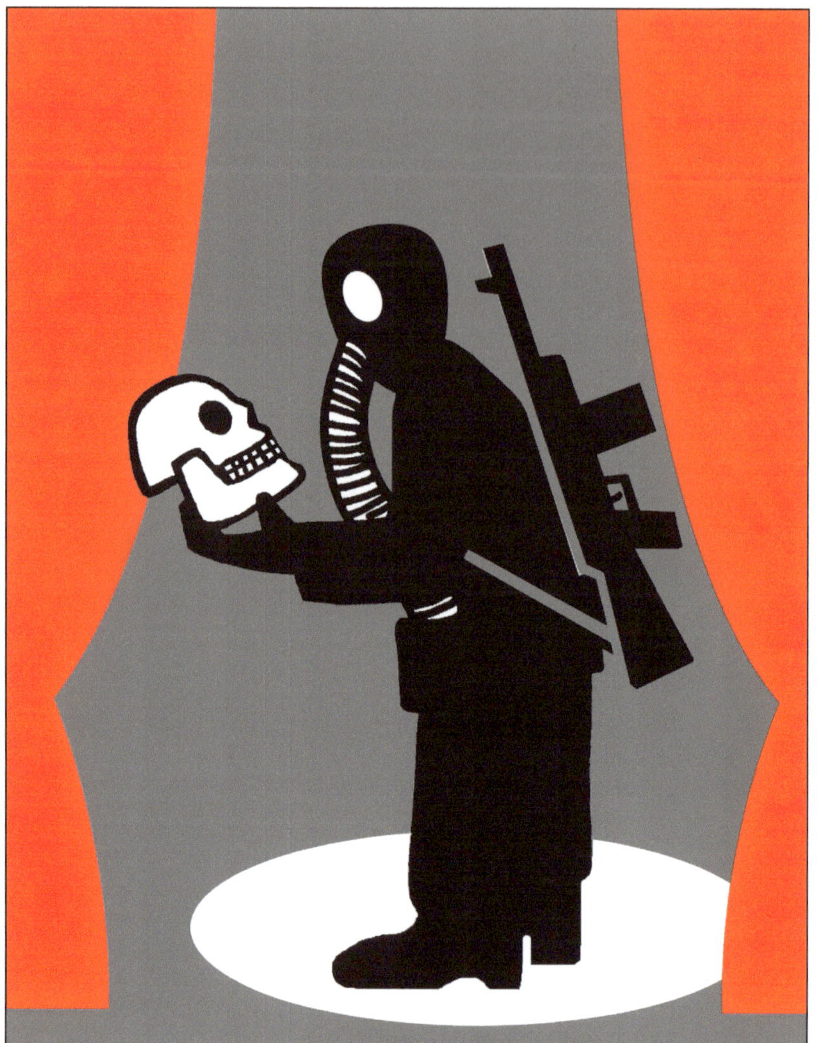

Igor Kopelnitsky • Moscow's Act of Terror • Digital Media

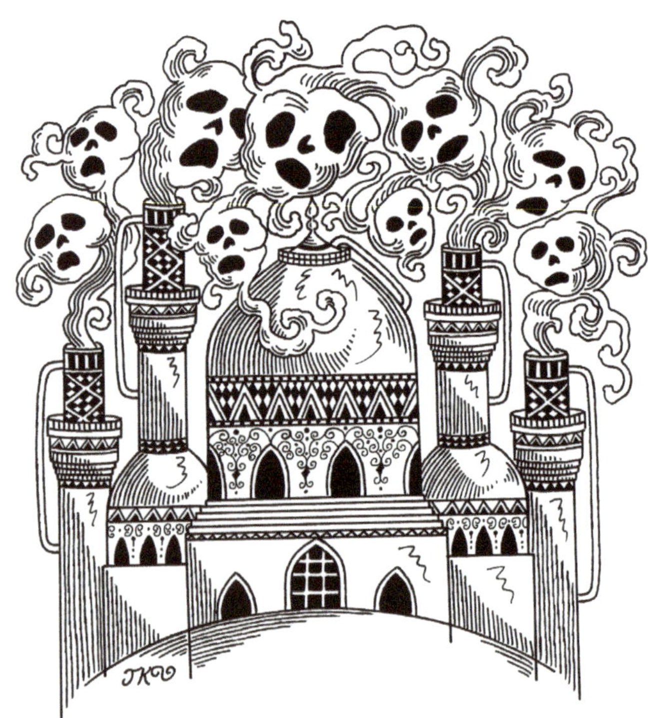

Jill Karla Schwarz • Saddam's Poisonous Secrets • Pen & Ink

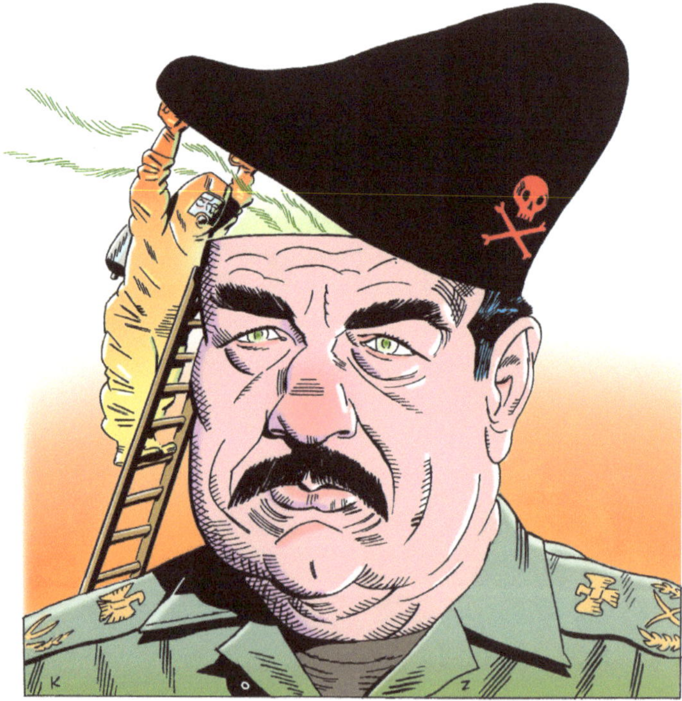

Martin Kozlowski • Saddam & UN Inspectors
Pen, Ink & Digital Color

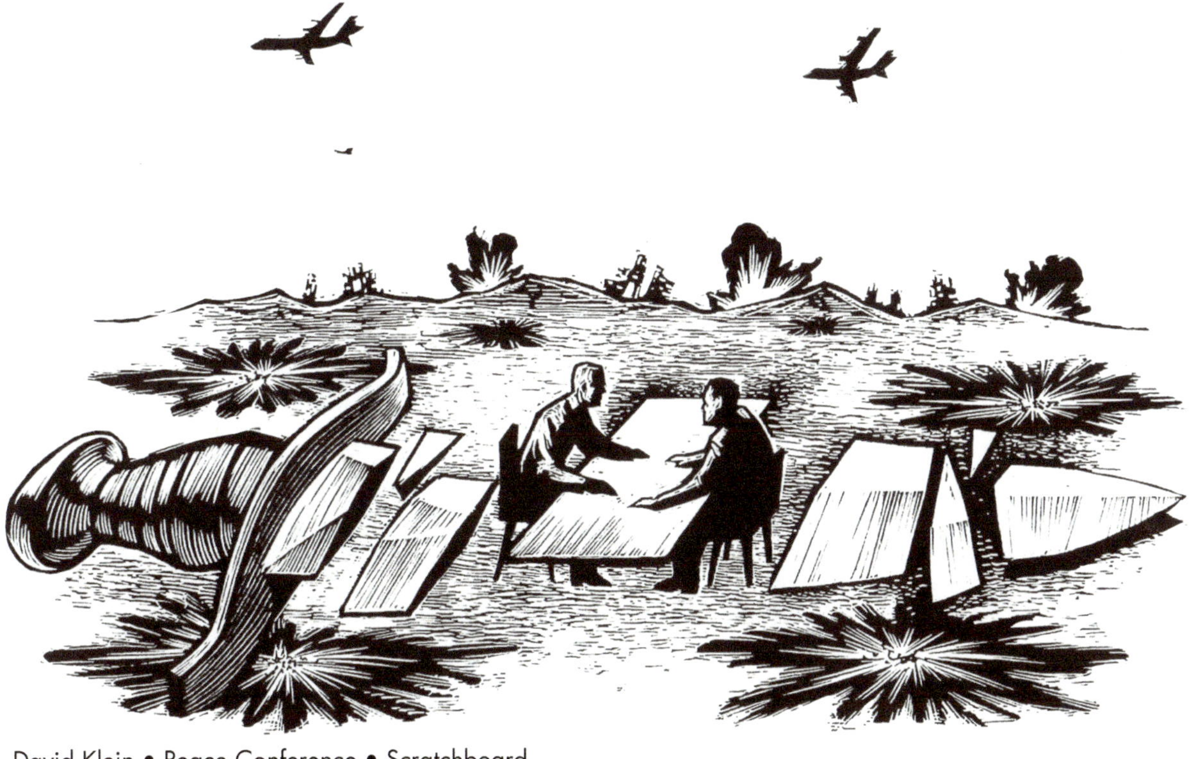

David Klein • Peace Conference • Scratchboard

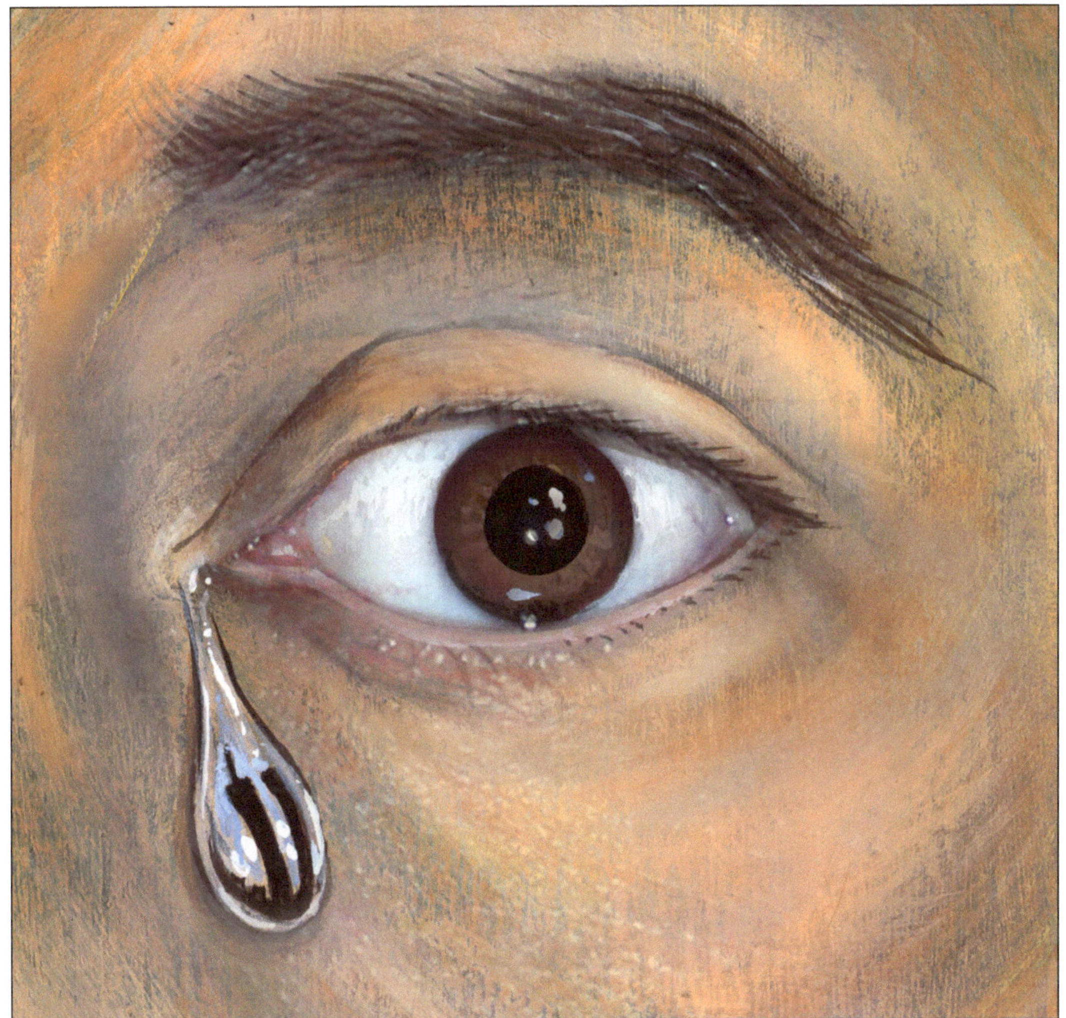

Thomas Kerr • Reflections on 9/11 • Acrylics

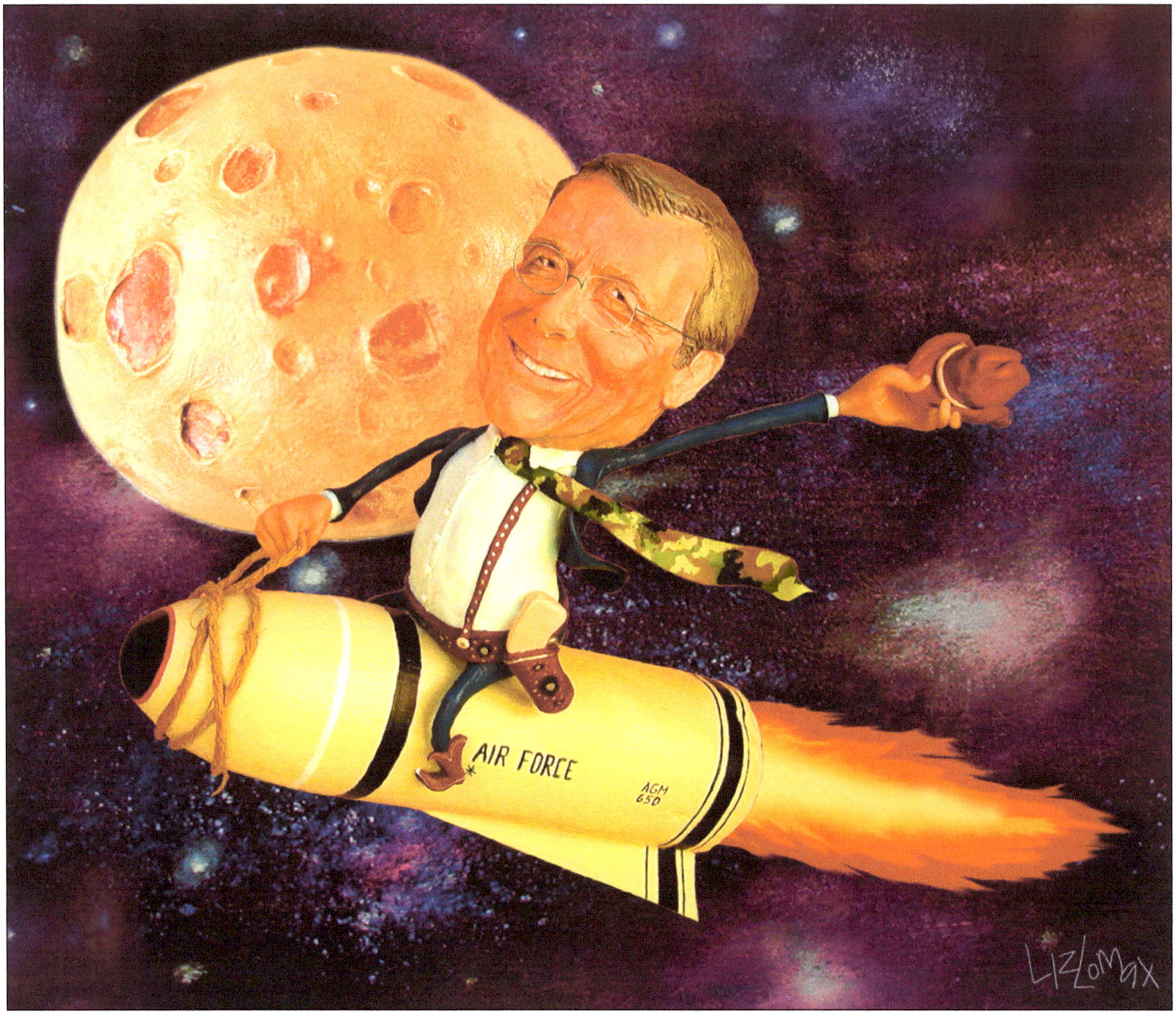

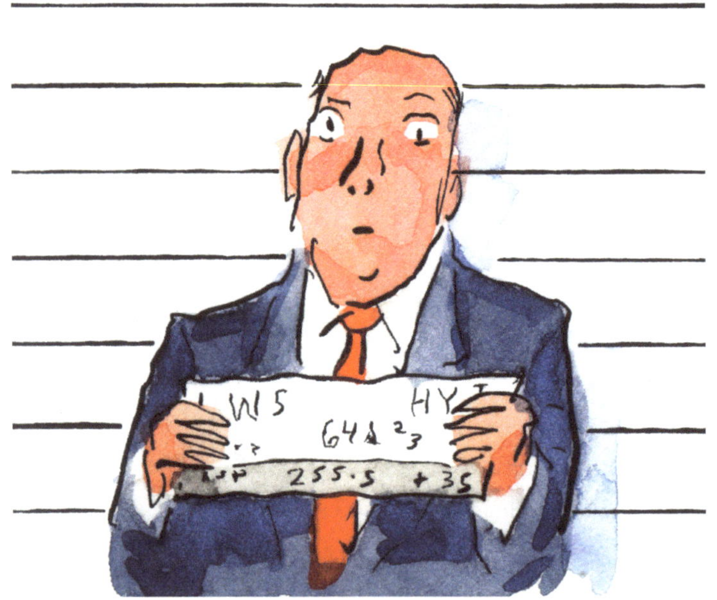

Liz Lomax • Rumsfeld Shoots the Moon • Sculpture & Collage

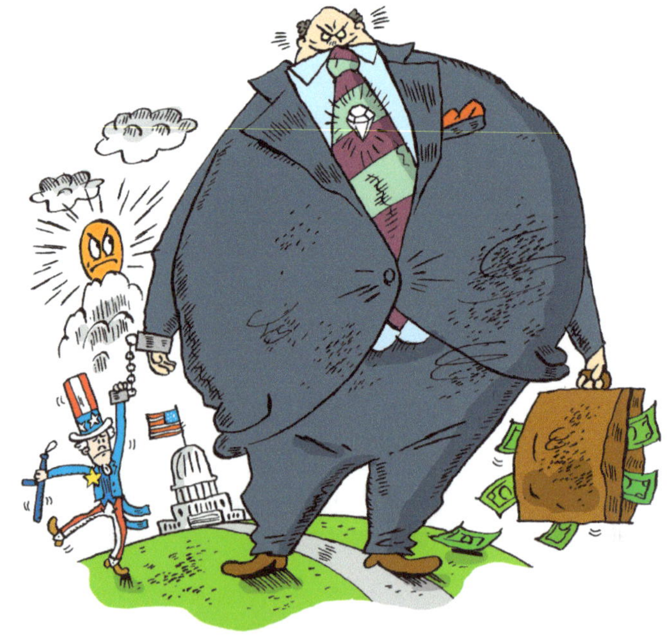

Rob Shepperson • Corporate Perps
Pen, Ink & Watercolor

Paul Corio • U.S. Polices Big Business
Pen, Ink & Digital Color

2003

U.S. and its Coalition of the Willing launch Operation Iraqi Freedom beginning eight years of war. War in Darfur begins. Human Genome Project completed. Saddam Hussein captured.

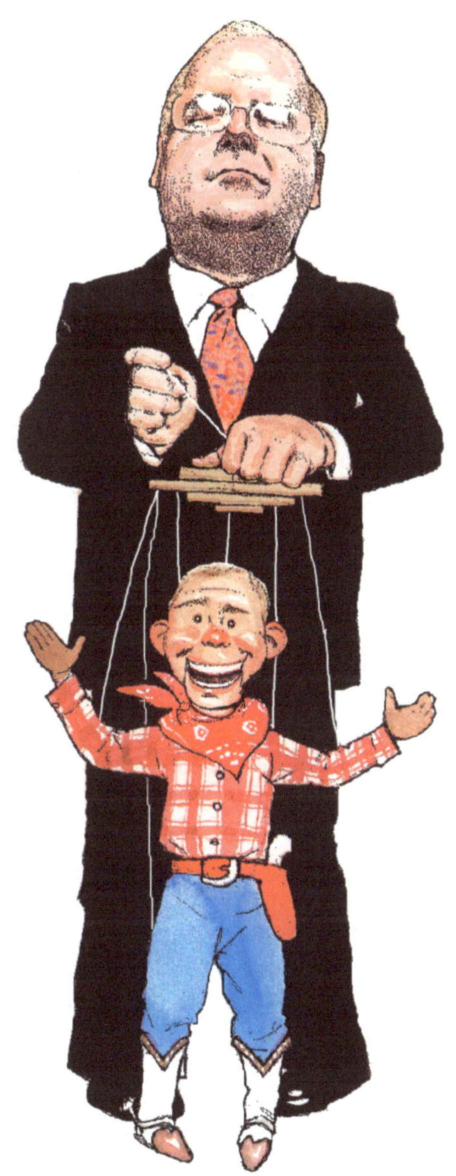

David Chelsea • Rove: Bush Puppeteer
Pen, Ink & Watercolor

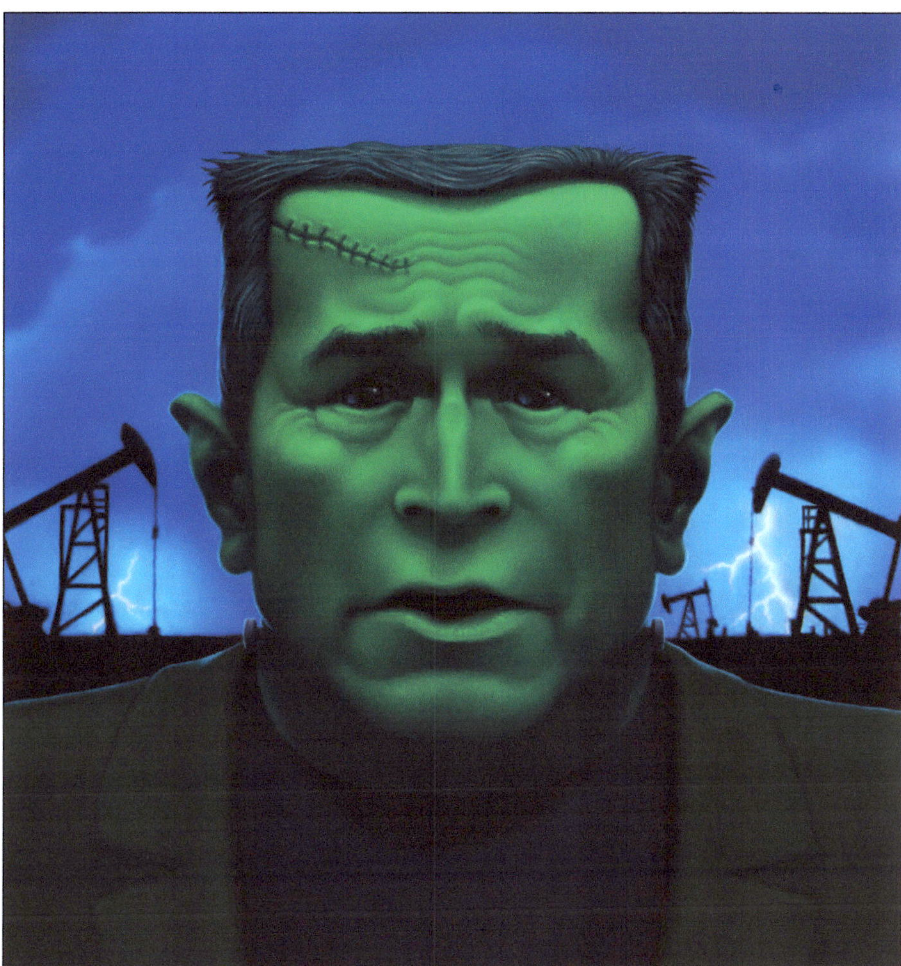

James Williamson • Bush's Scary Energy Policy • Digital Media

The fact that newspapers began using color on their editorial pages and then transferred vast amounts of the content that they had paid for onto the web to be accessed for free — a strategy which would eventually cripple the industry — meant that the artists on inxart.com began working in full color. The effect on them was liberating and the results were visually exciting.

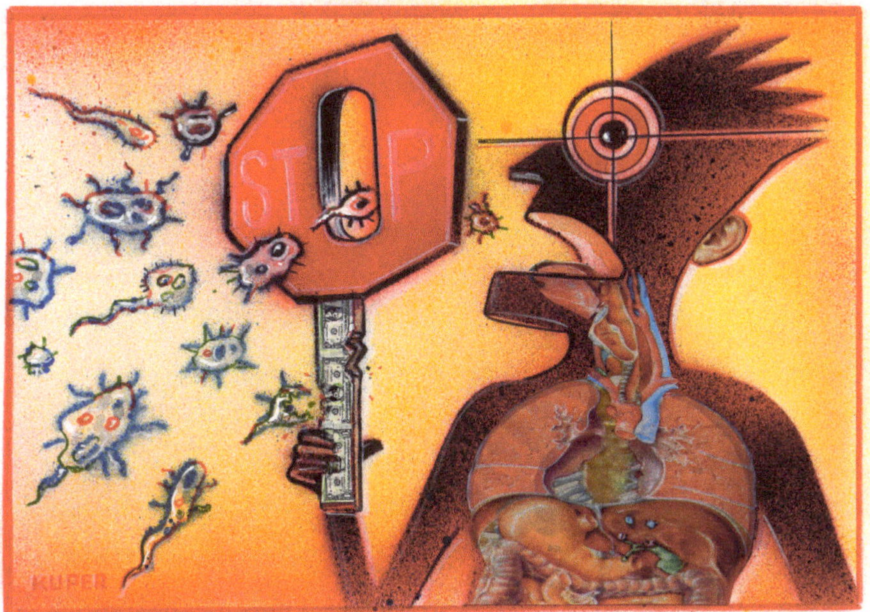

Peter Kuper • Fear of Infection • Mixed Media

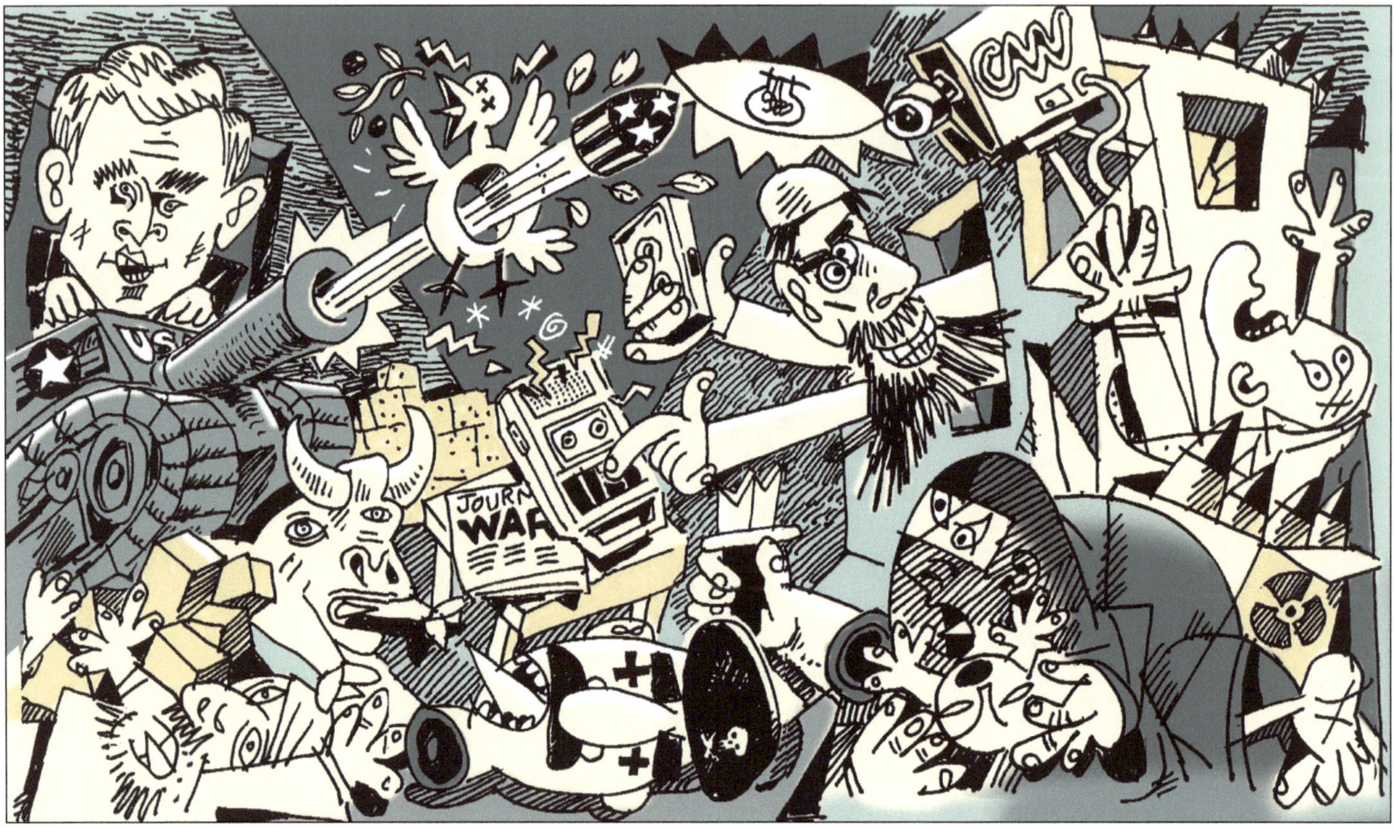

Tom Hachtman • Iraq: Guernica 2003 • Pen, Ink & Digital Color

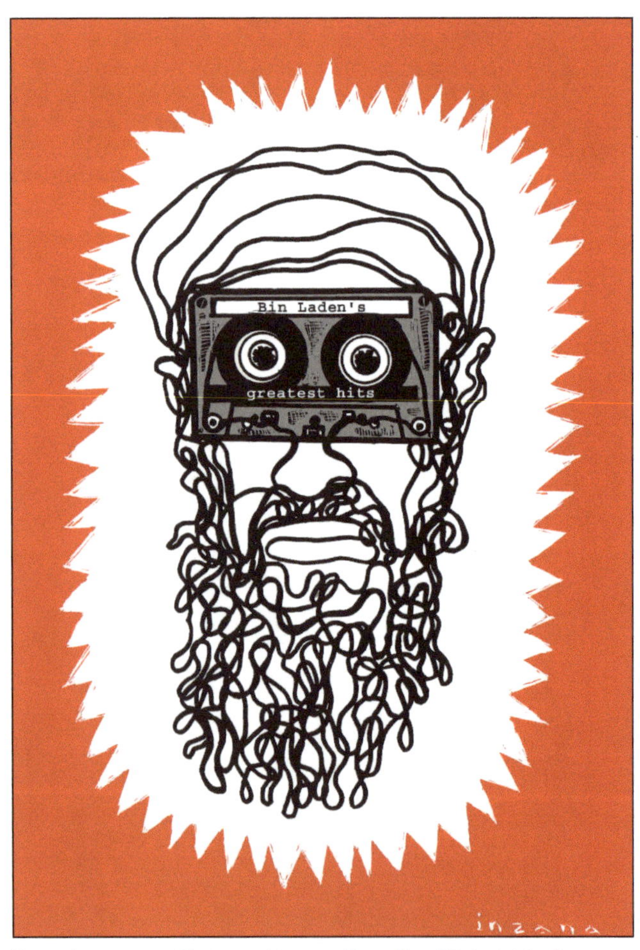

Ryan Inzana • Osama: Live on Tape? • Digital Media

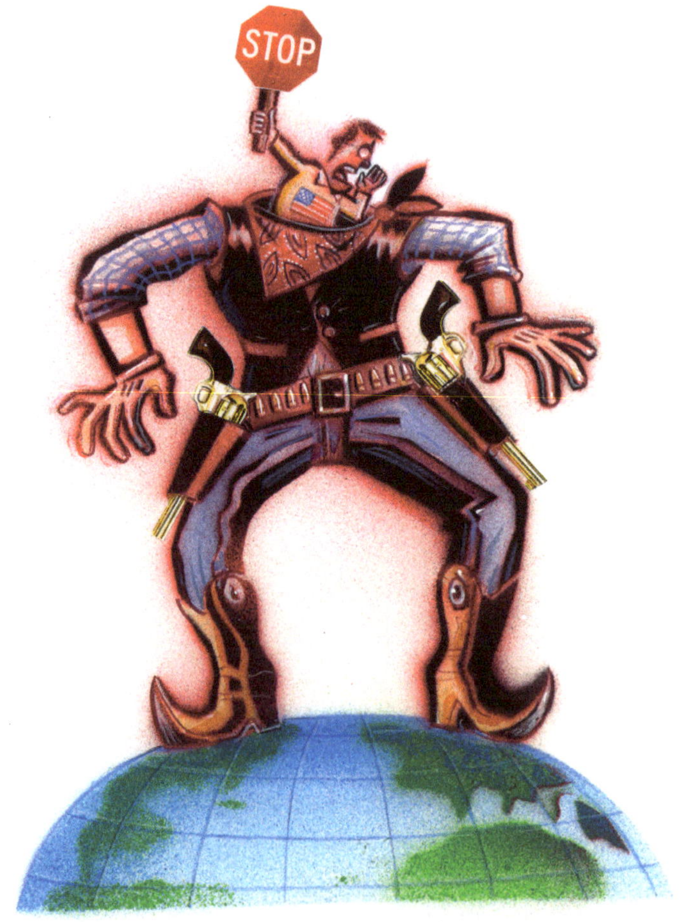

Peter Kuper • Anti-War Protests • Mixed Media

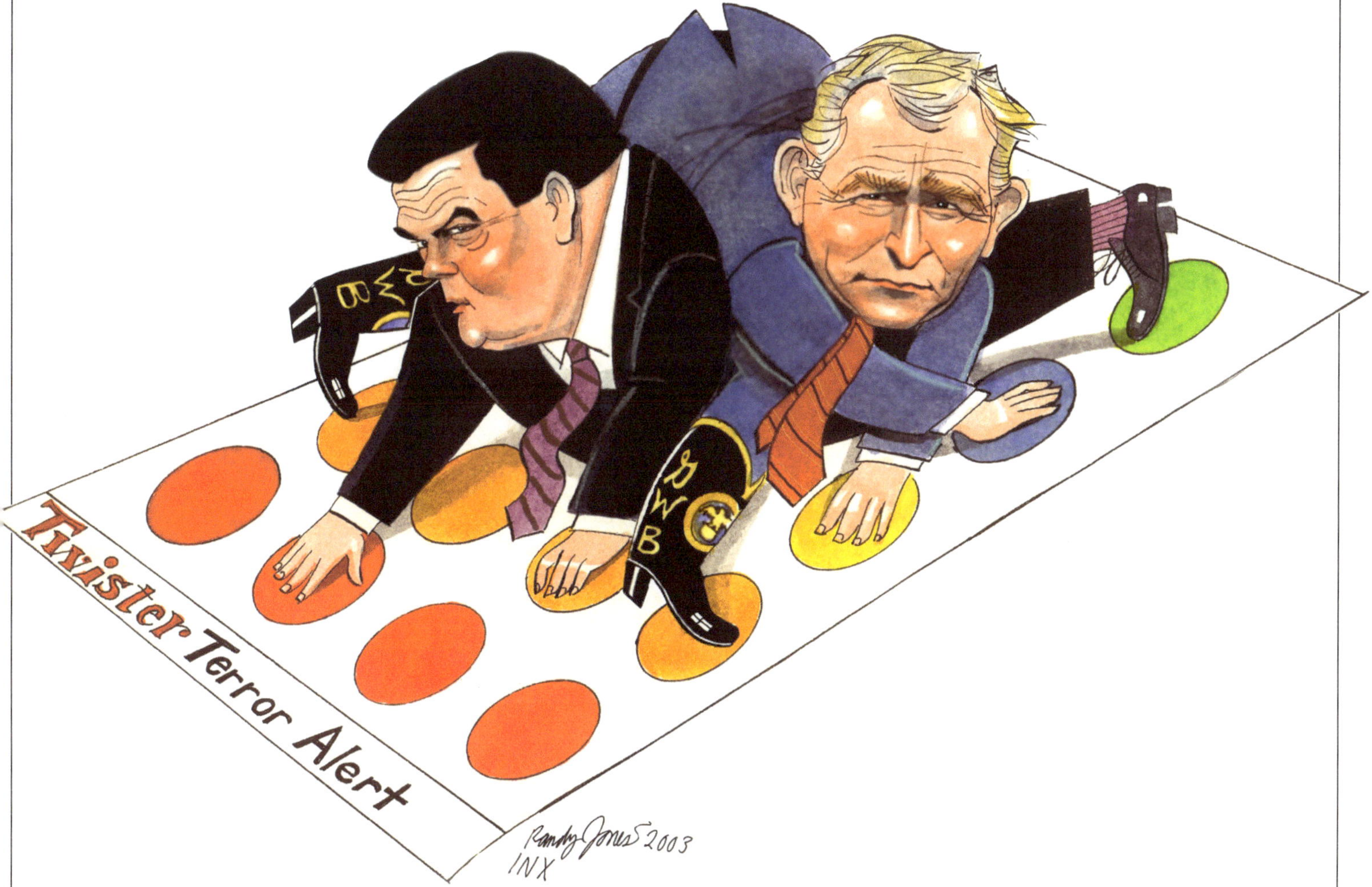

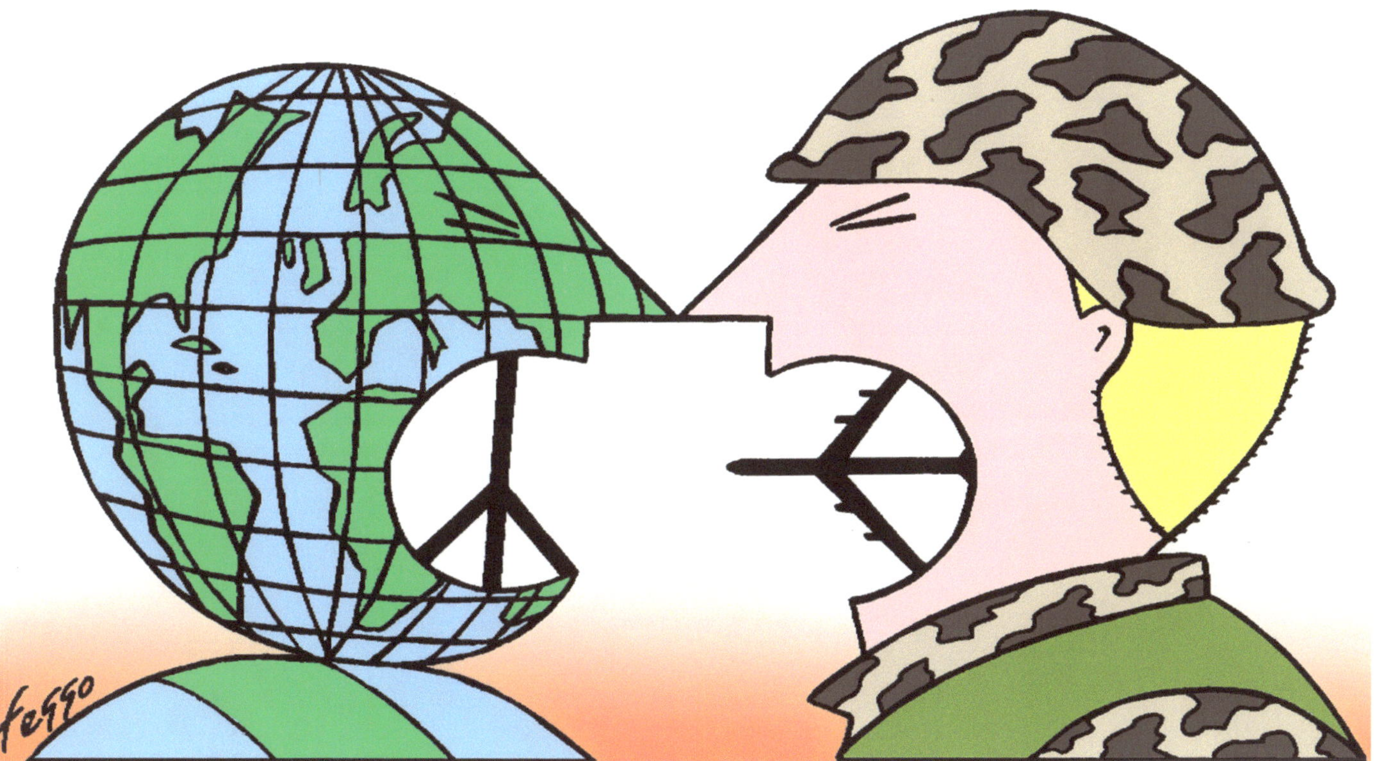

Randy Jones • Terror Alert Twister • Pen, Ink & Watercolor

Felipe Galindo • Debating War • Pen, Ink & Digital Color

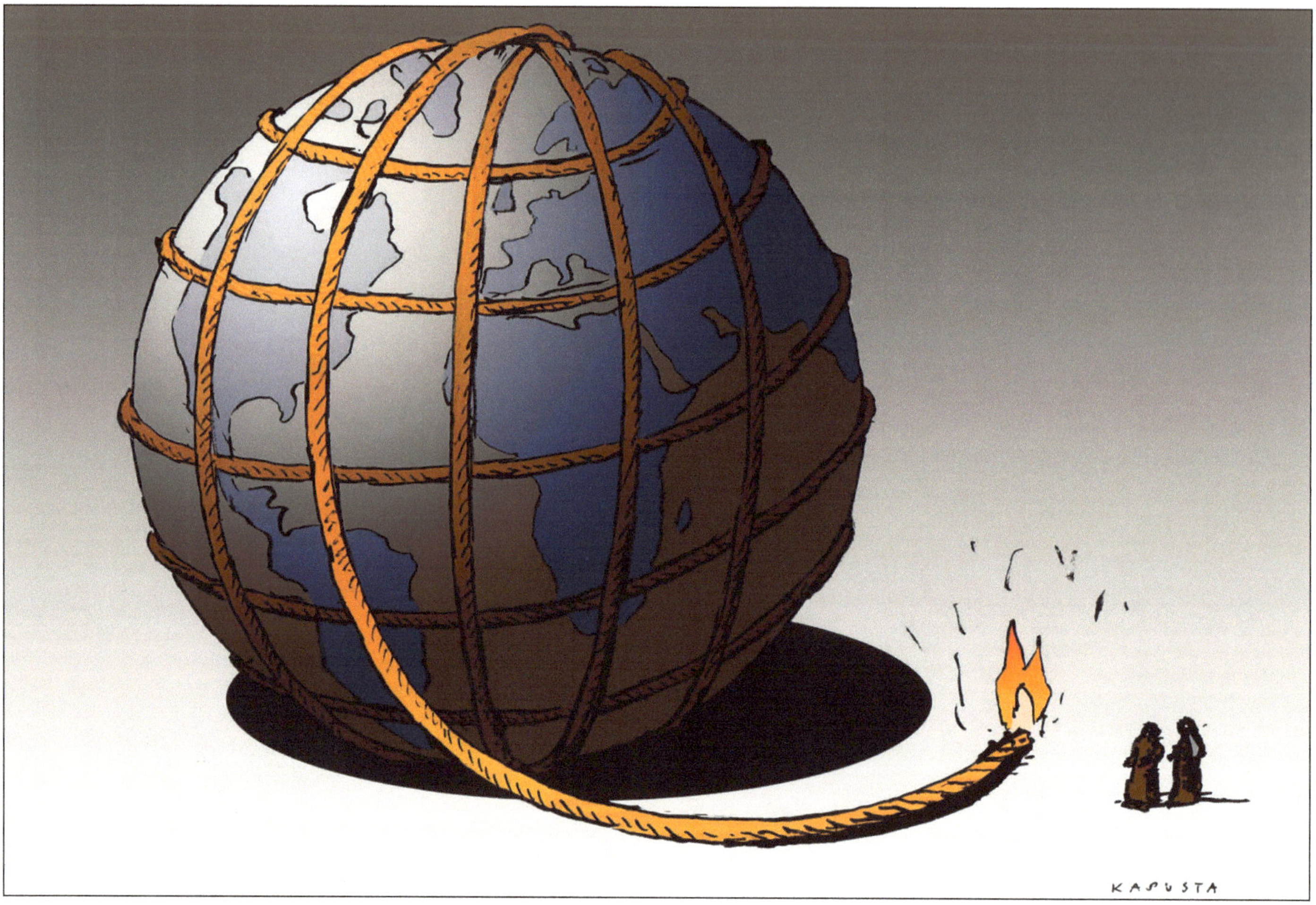

Janusz Kapusta • Worldwide Terror Threat • Brush, Ink & Digital Color

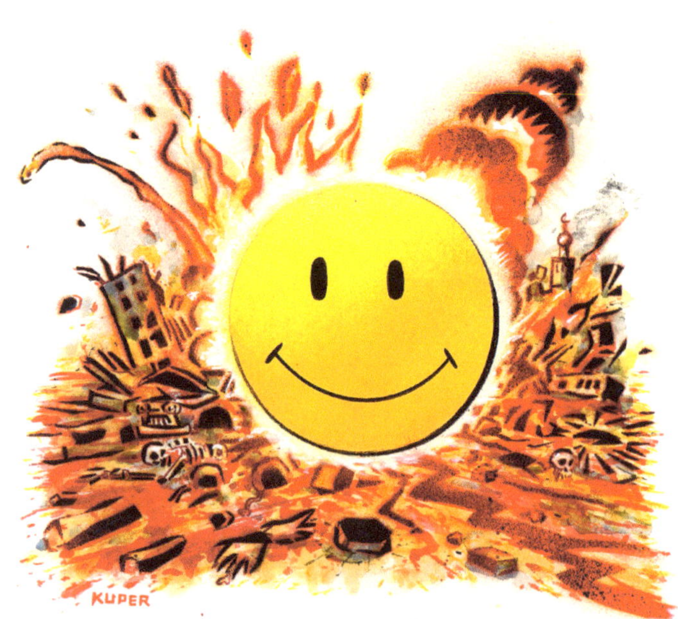

Peter Kuper • Happy Face on Iraq • Ink & Watercolor

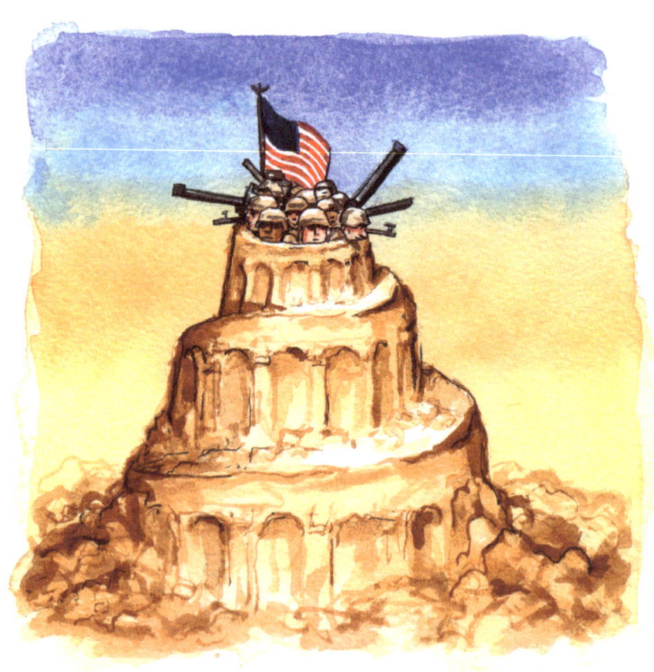

Rob Shepperson • Iraq's Tower of Babel • Watercolor

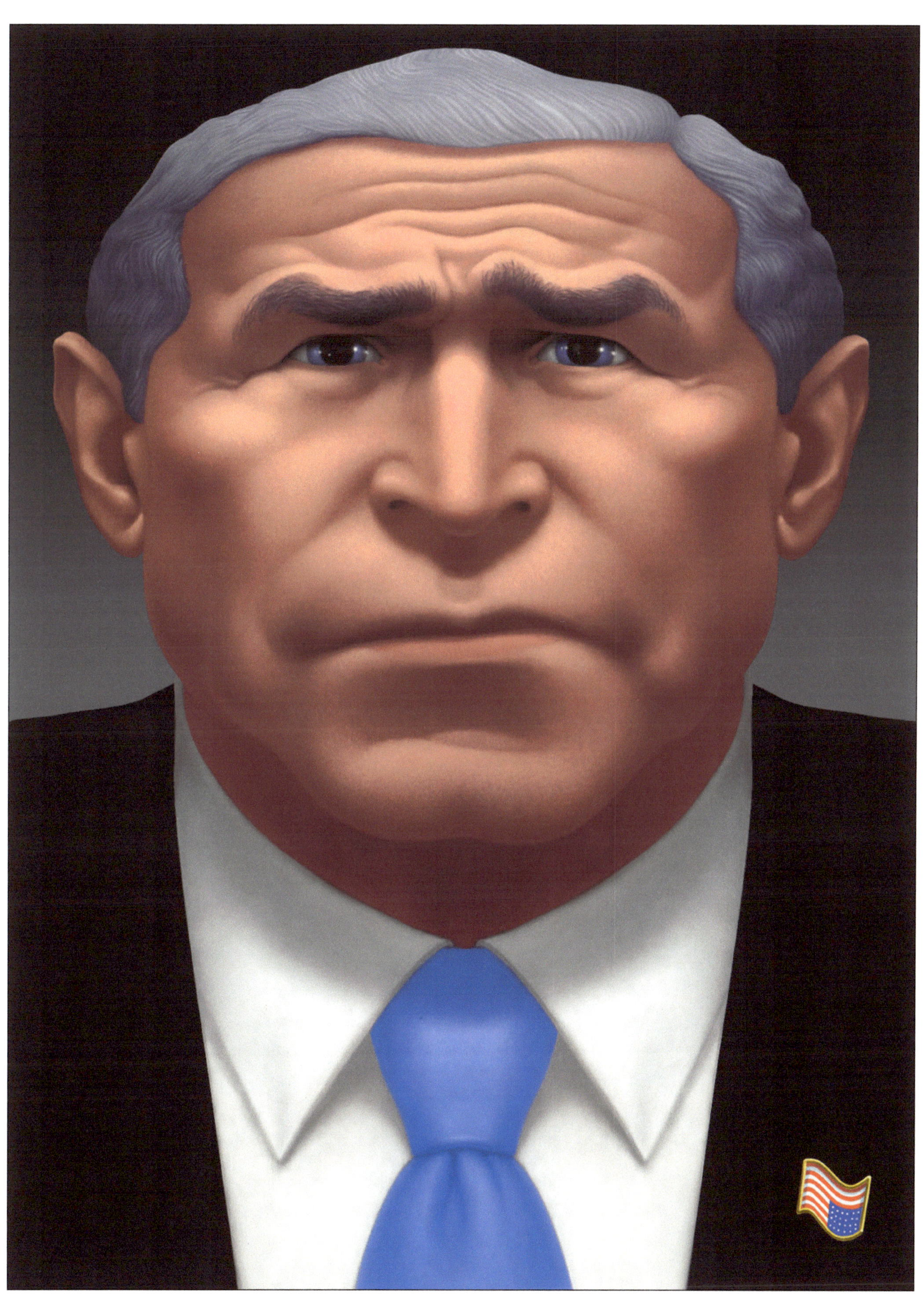

James Williamson • President George W. Bush • Digital Media

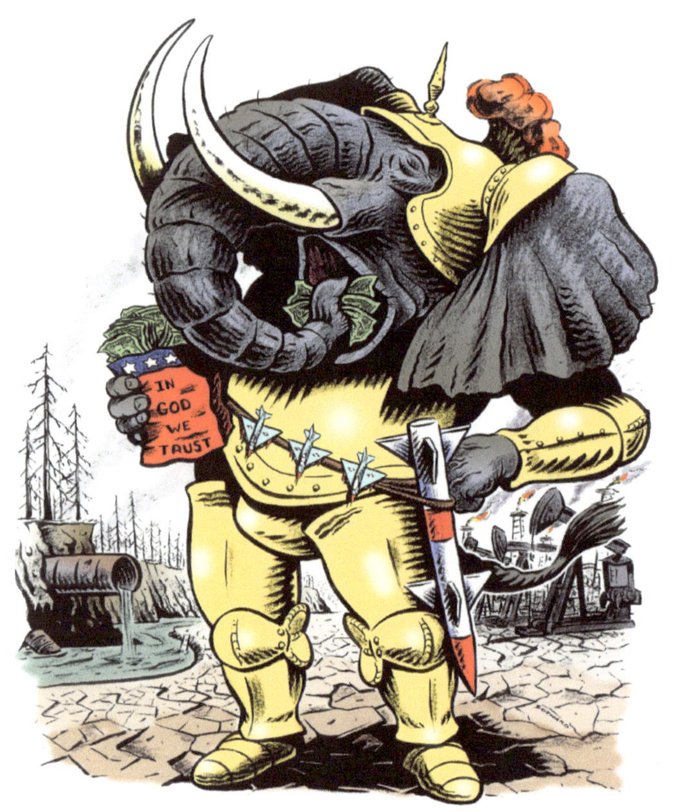

David Gothard • Girded for Battle • Brush, Ink & Watercolor

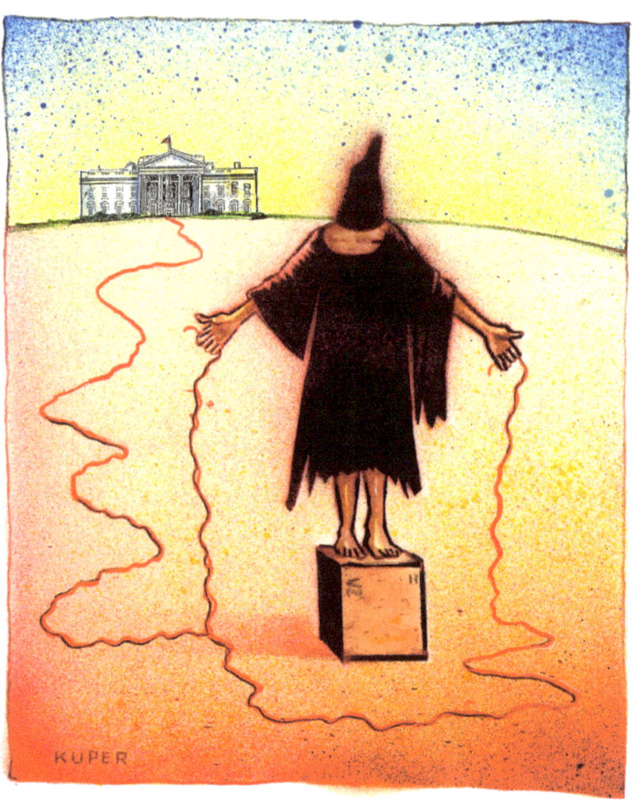

Peter Kuper • The Trail of Abu Ghraib • Ink & Watercolor

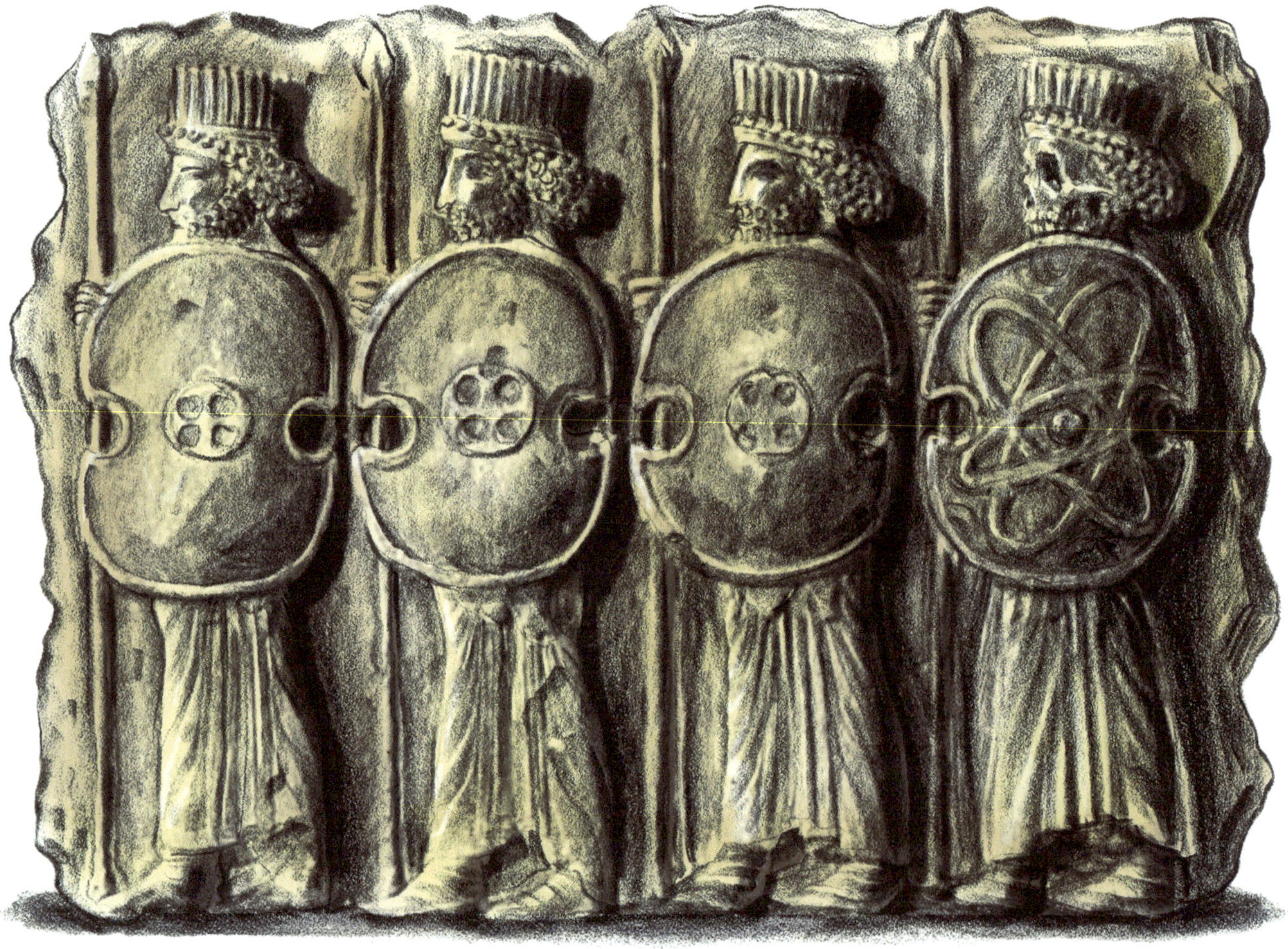

Thomas Kerr • Iran's March to Nuclear Weapons • Pencil & Digital Color

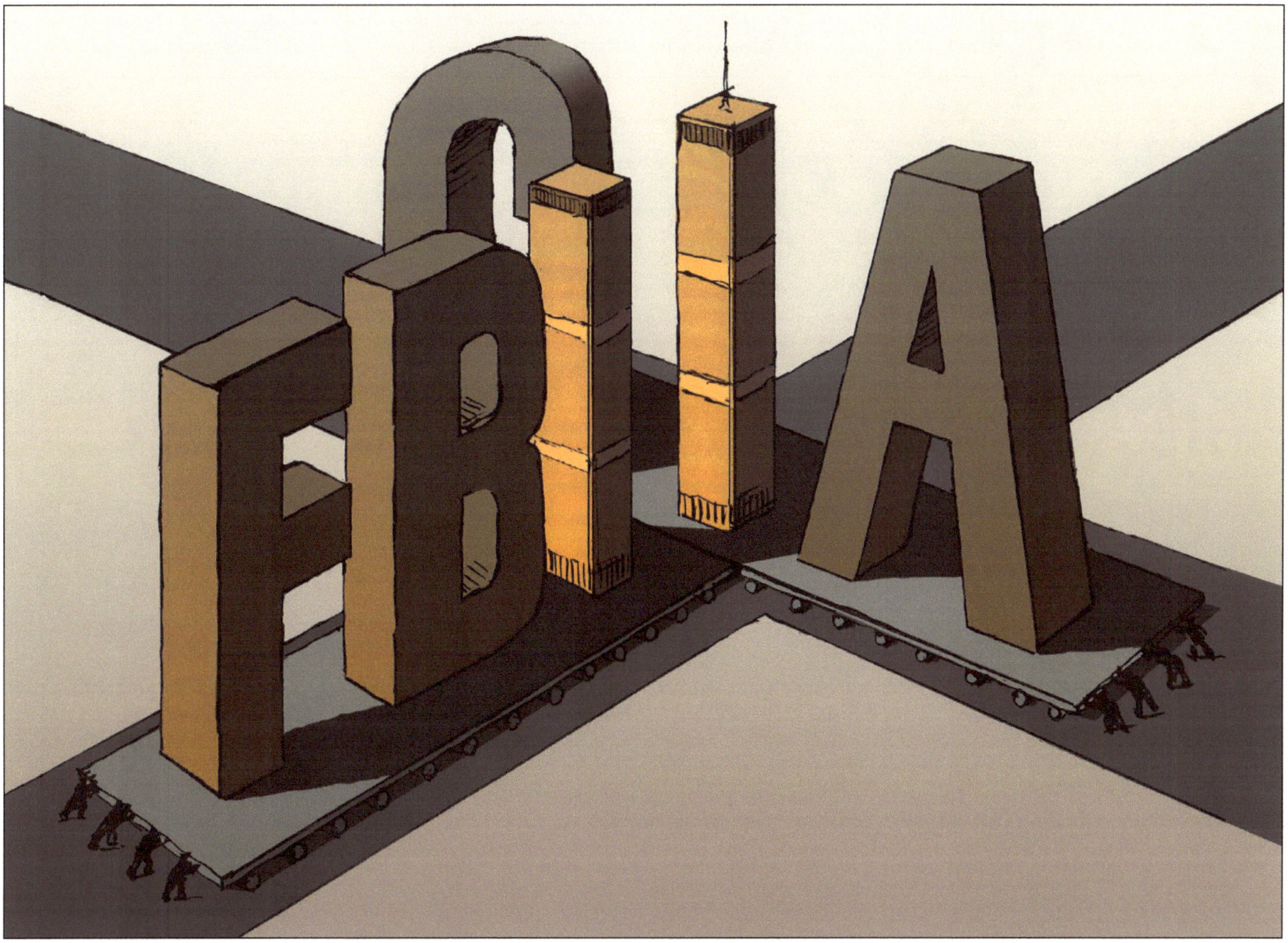

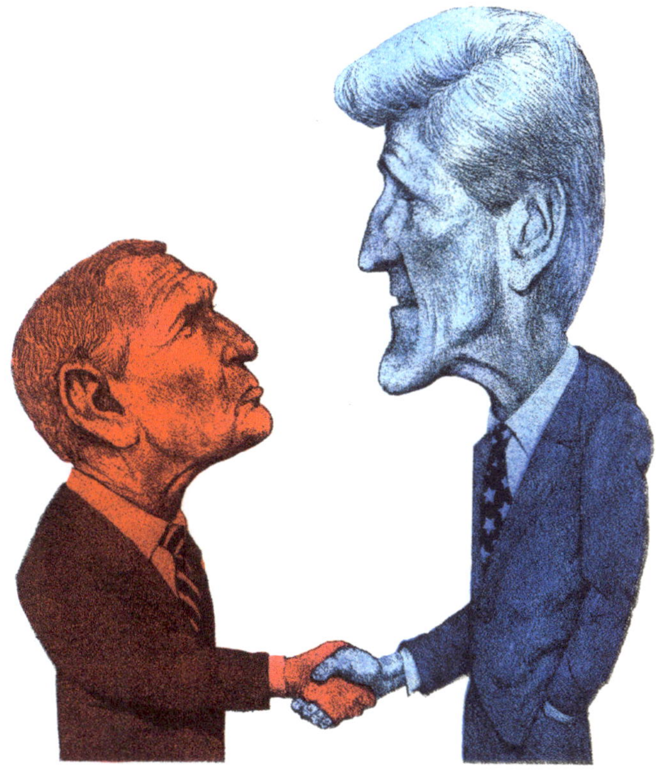

Janusz Kapusta • 9/11 Intelligence Cross Up • Brush, Ink & Digital Color

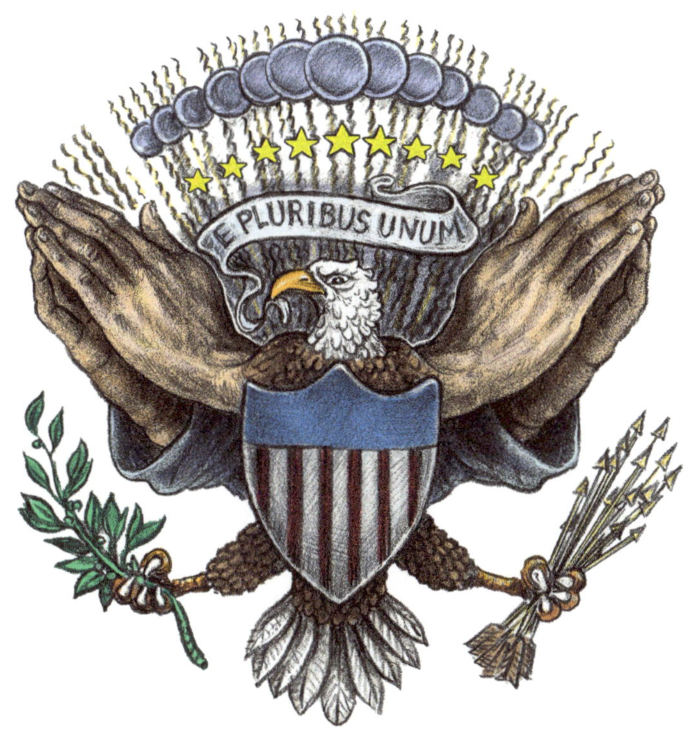

David Chelsea • Bush vs. Kerry • Pen, Ink & Watercolor

Thomas Kerr • U.S. Bird of Pray • Pencil & Digital Color

Hurricane Katrina ravages Gulf of Mexico coastline. Terror attacks on London Underground. Abu Ghraib prisoner abuse trials end in convictions. Cedar Revolution begins in Lebanon.

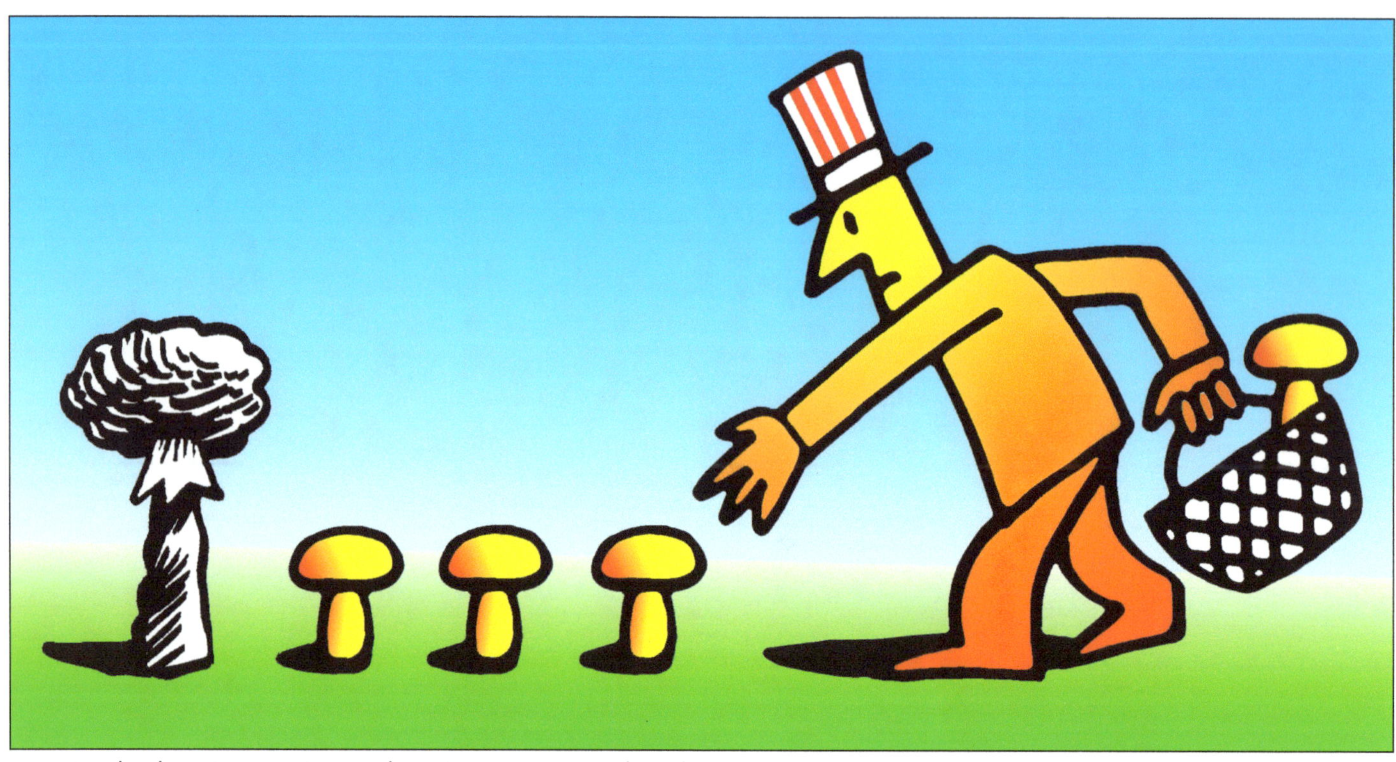

Igor Kopelnitsky • Rooting Out Nuclear Weapons • Digital Media

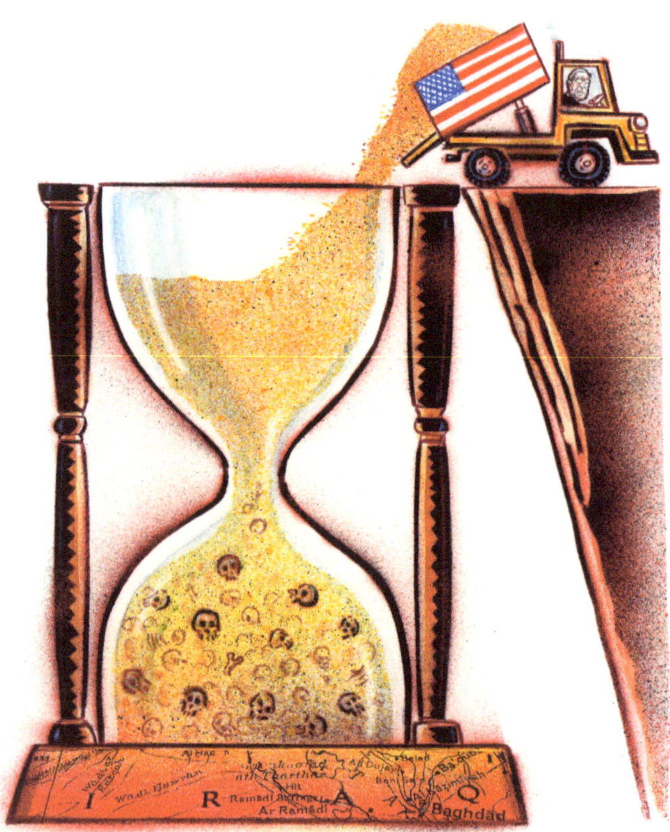

Peter Kuper • Timetable For Iraq • Ink & Watercolor

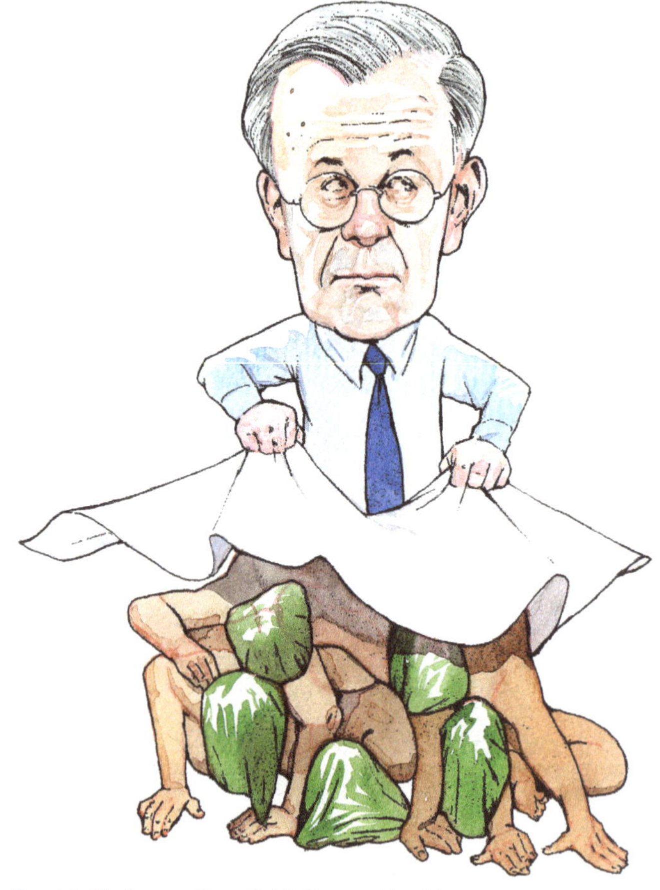

David Chelsea • Rumsfeld Covers Up Abuse
Pencil & Watercolor

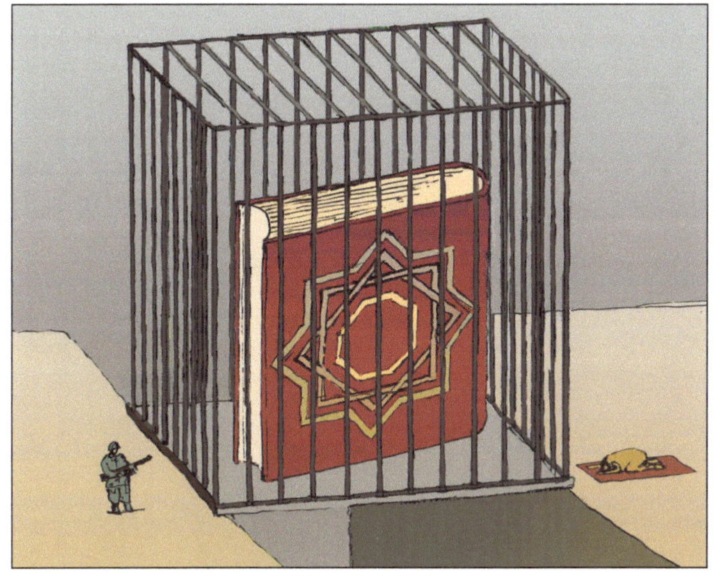

Janusz Kapusta • Dispute Over the Qu'ran
Brush, Ink & Digital Color

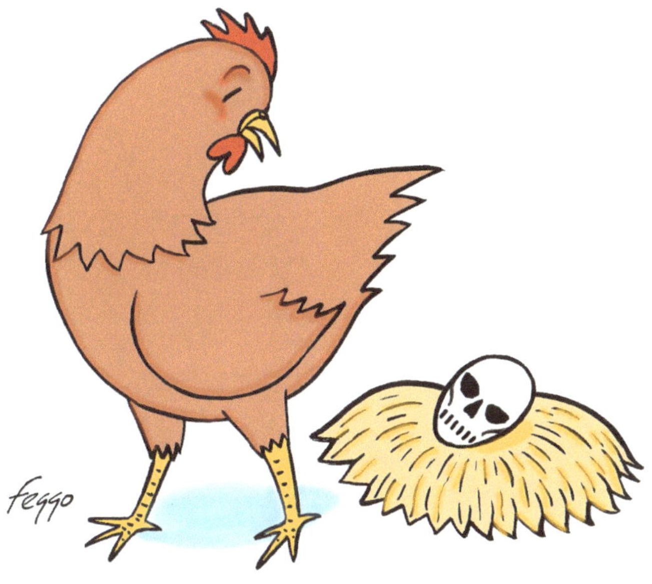

Felipe Galindo • Deadly Avian Flu • Pen, Ink & Digital Color

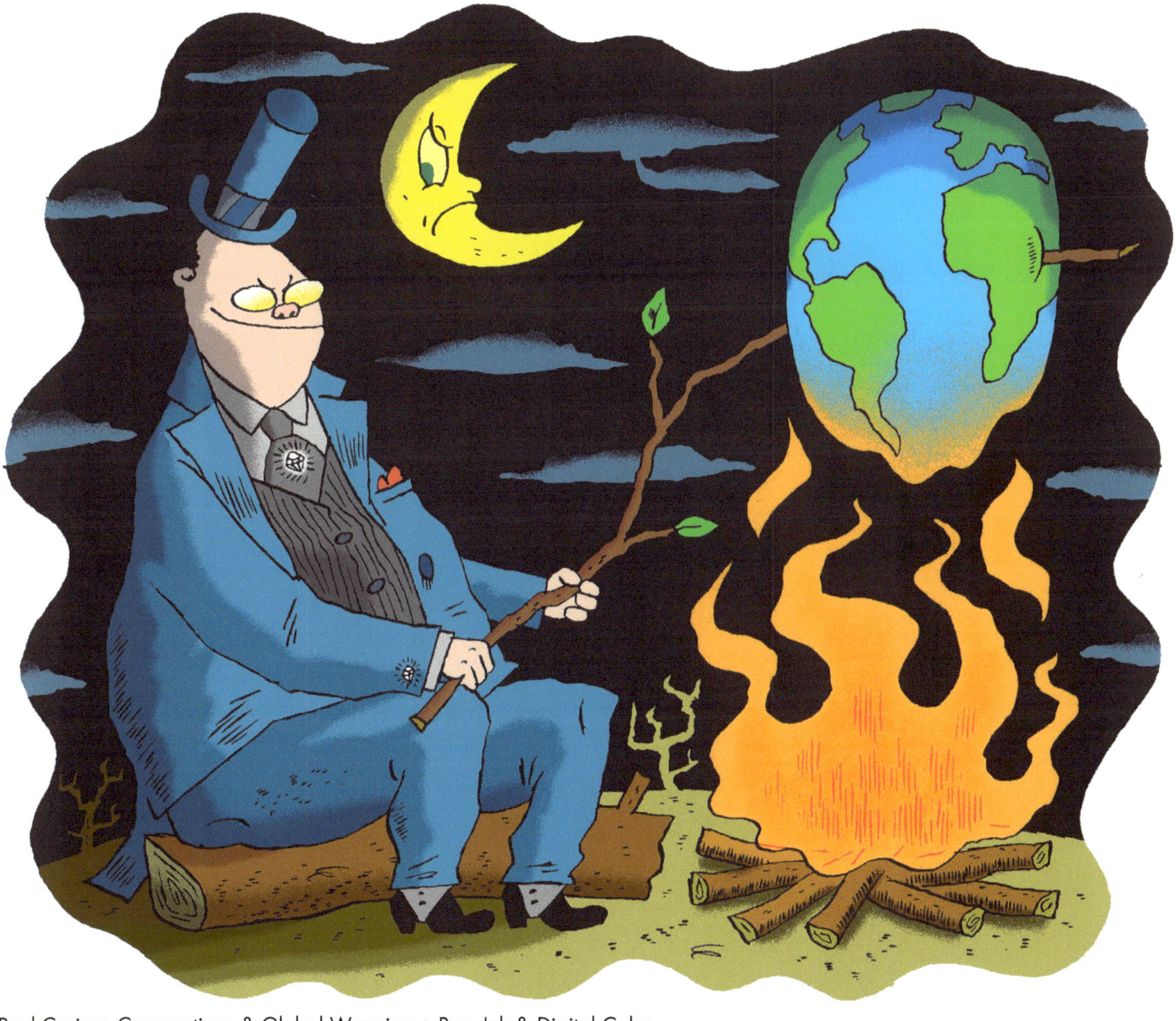

Paul Corio • Corporations & Global Warming • Pen, Ink & Digital Color

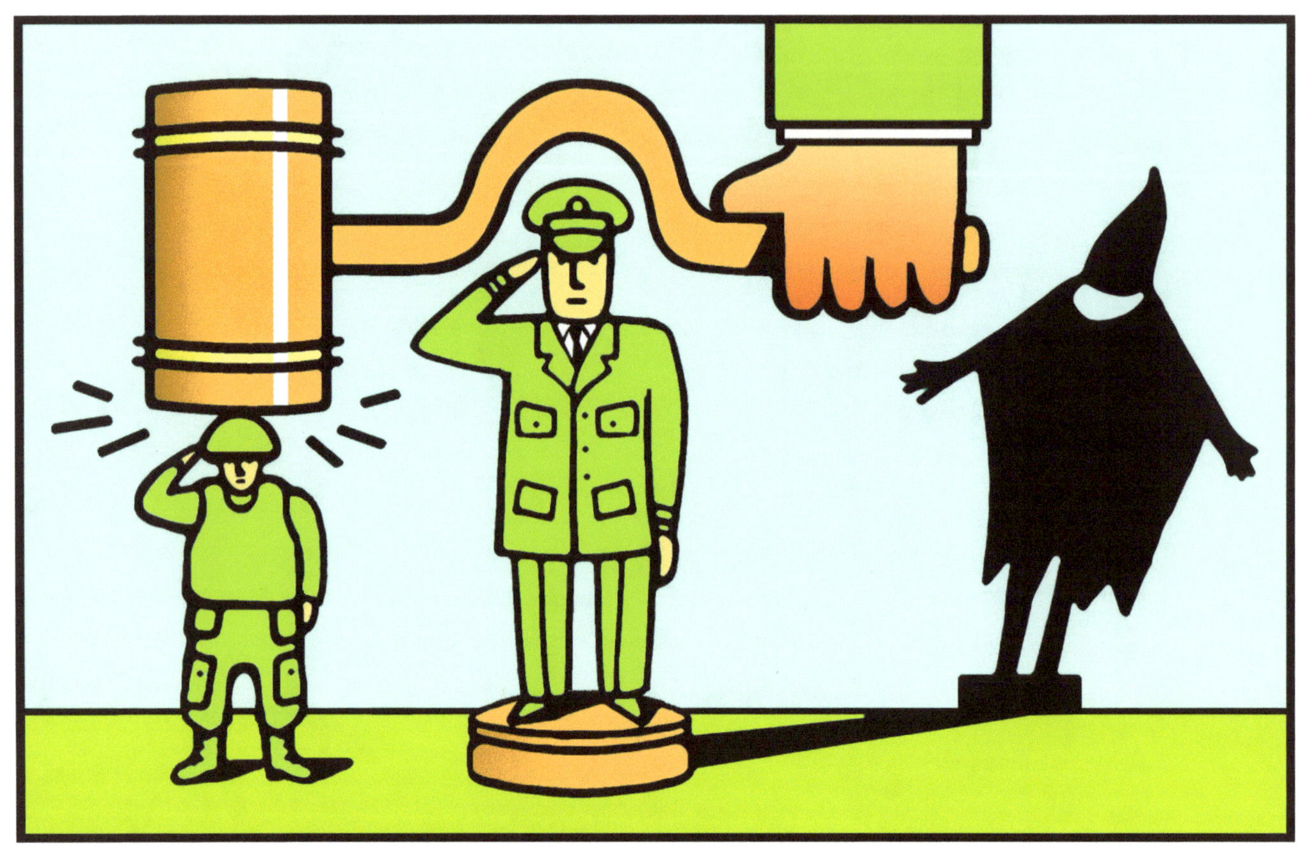

Igor Kopelnitsky • Punishment Over Abu Ghraib • Digital Media

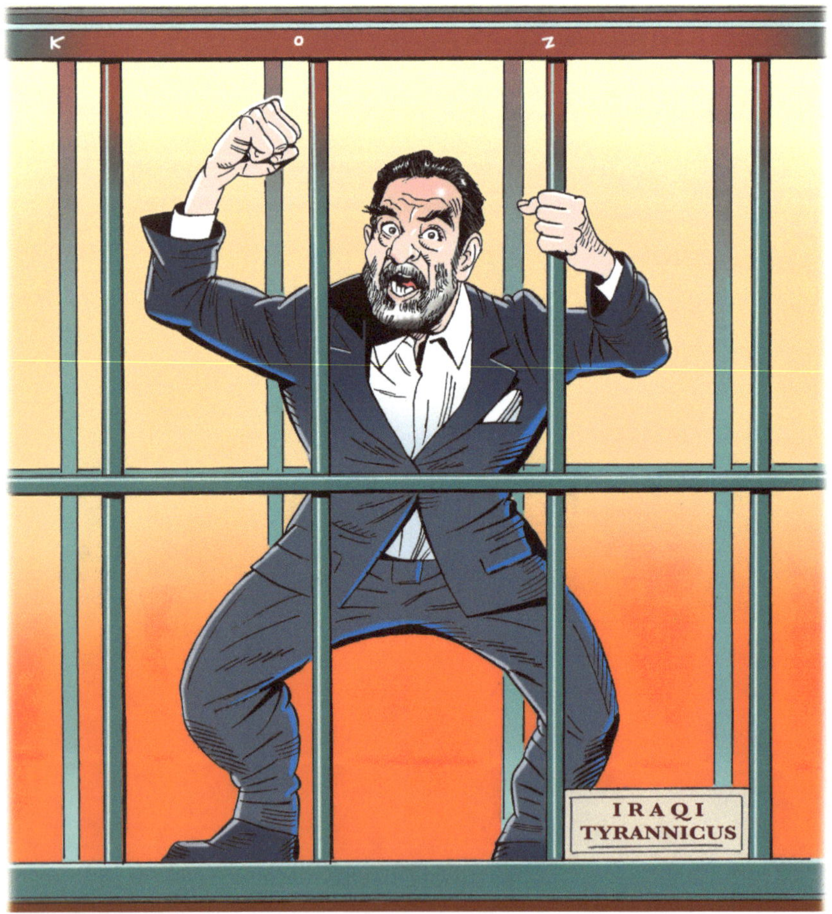

Martin Kozlowski • Saddam Hussein on Trial • Pen, Ink & Digital Color

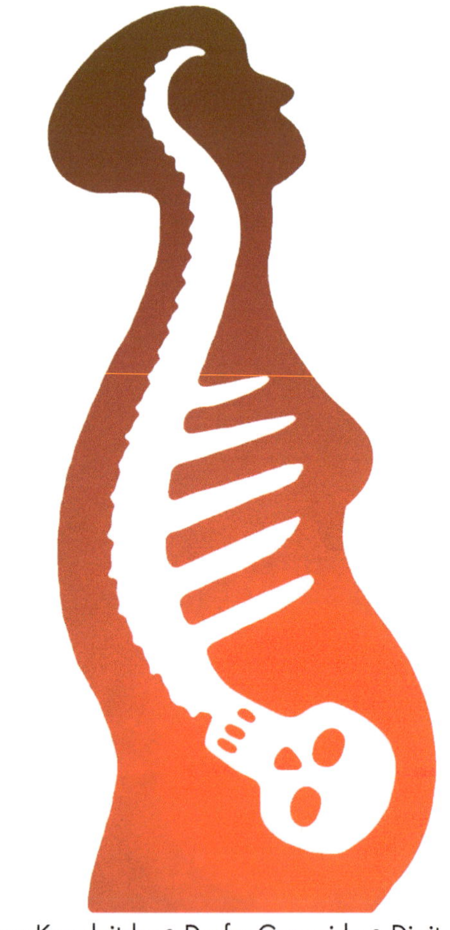

Igor Kopelnitsky • Darfur Genocide • Digital Media

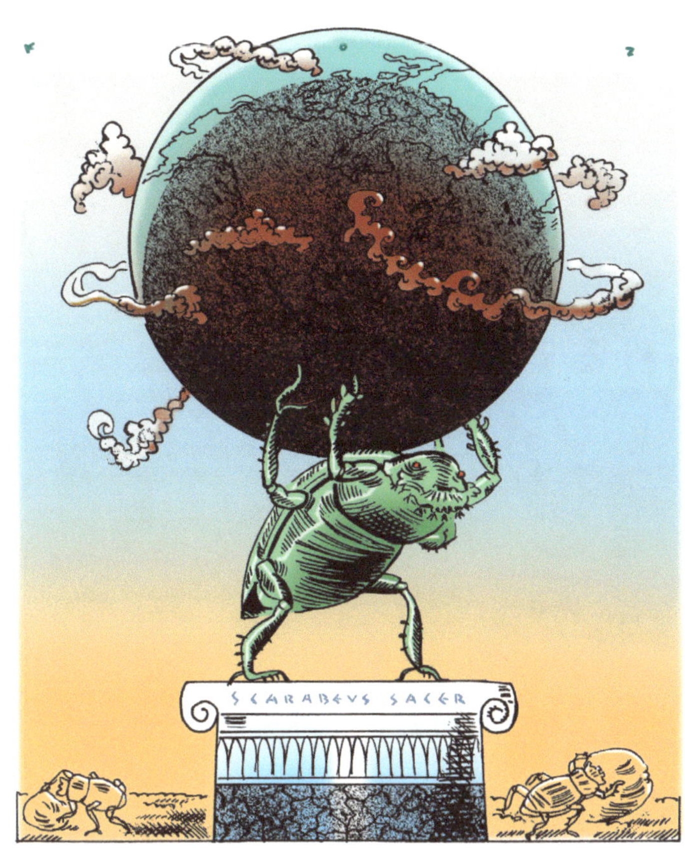

Martin Kozlowski • Global Warming Damage
Pen, Ink & Digital Color

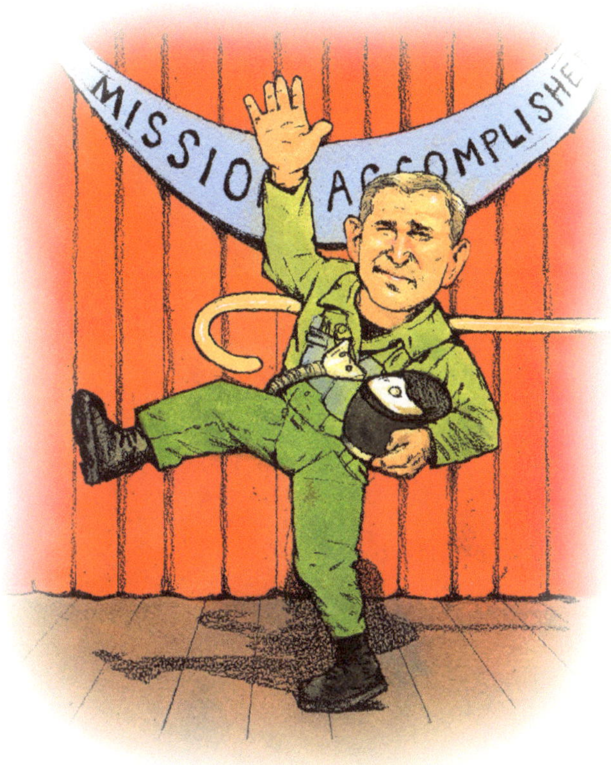

David Chelsea • Bush's Falling Approval Ratings
Pencil & Watercolor

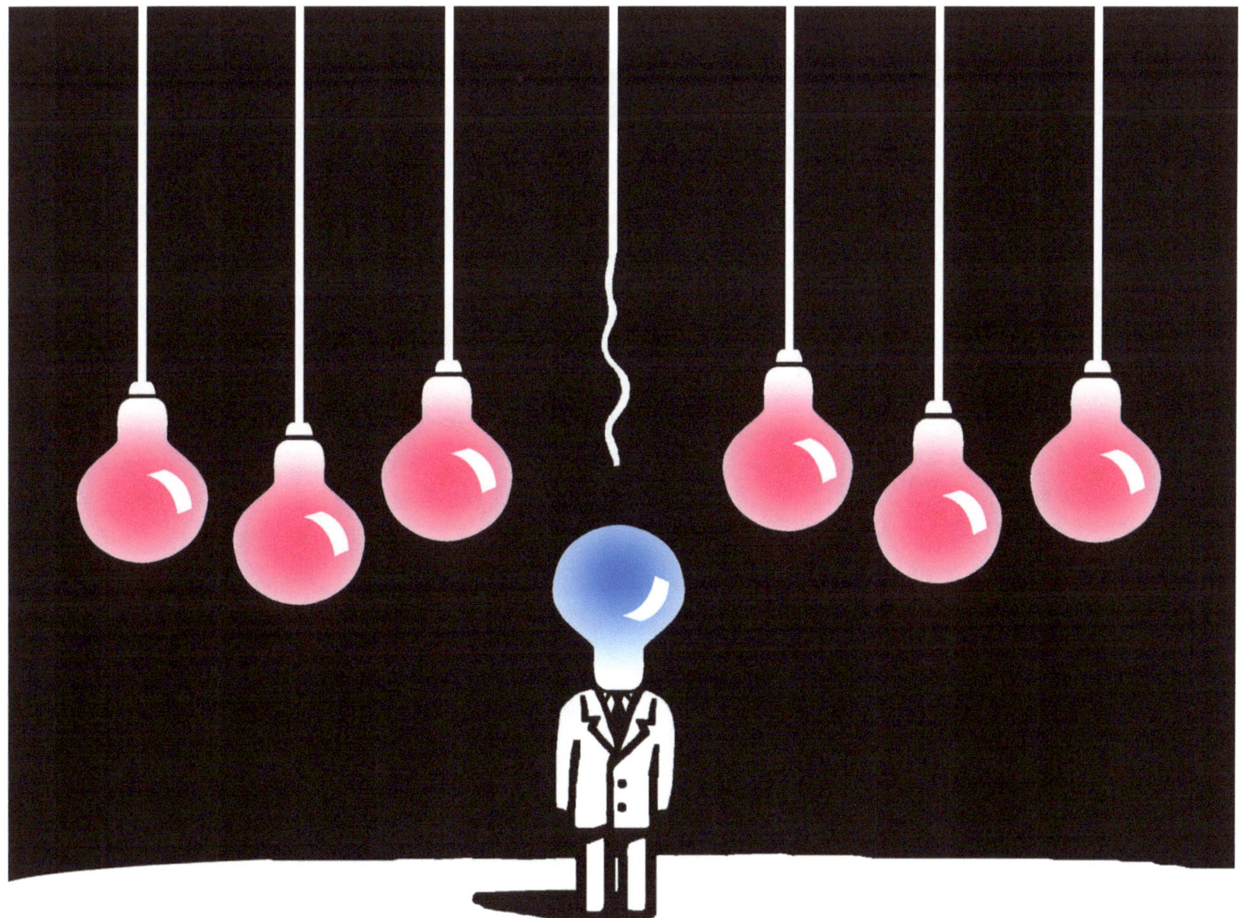

Igor Kopelnitsky • Intelligent Design? • Digital Media

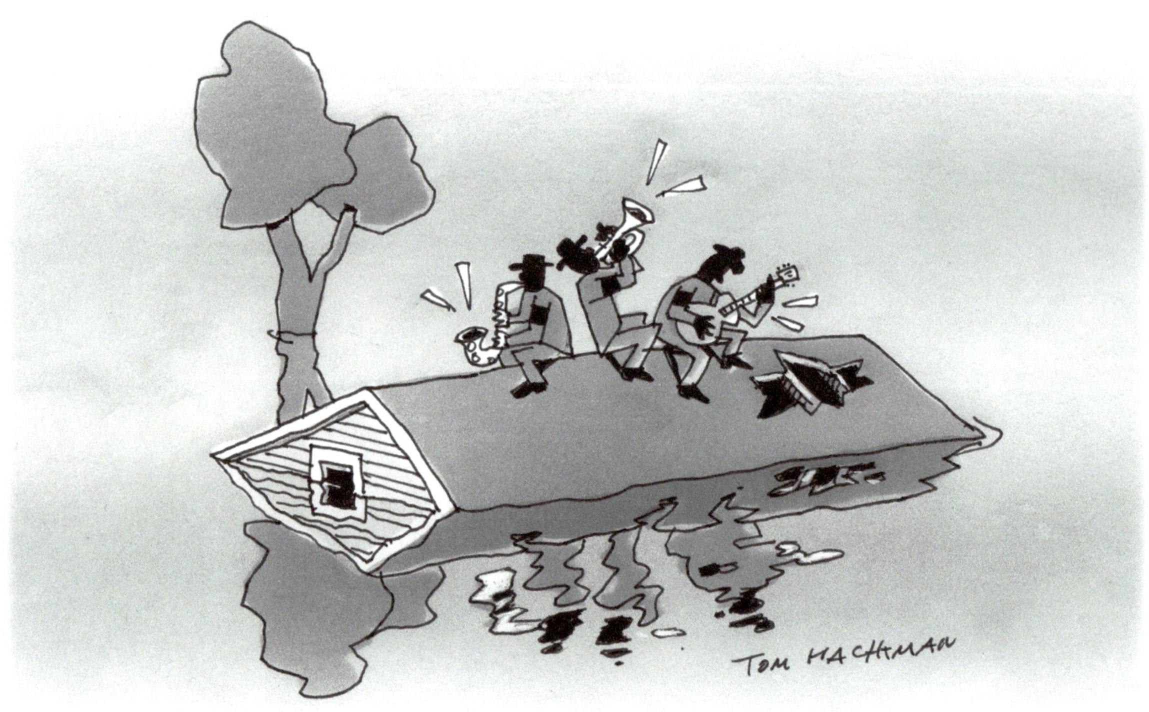

Tom Hachtman • New Orleans After Katrina • Watercolor

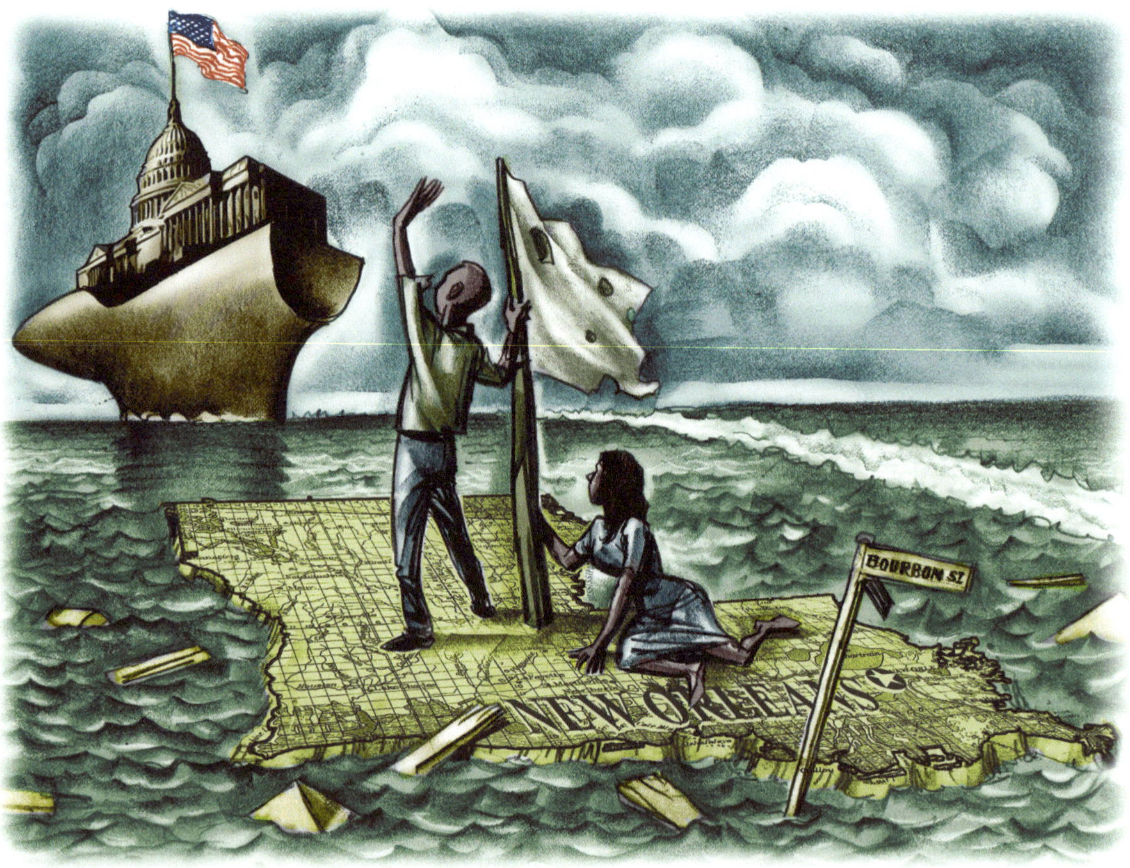

David Klein • Abandoning Katrina's Victims • Color Pencil & Digital Media

2006

Democratic Party retakes control of both the House and Senate. Israel confronts Hezbollah in Second Lebanon War. Terror bombings in Mumbai, India. Saddam Hussein executed in Baghdad.

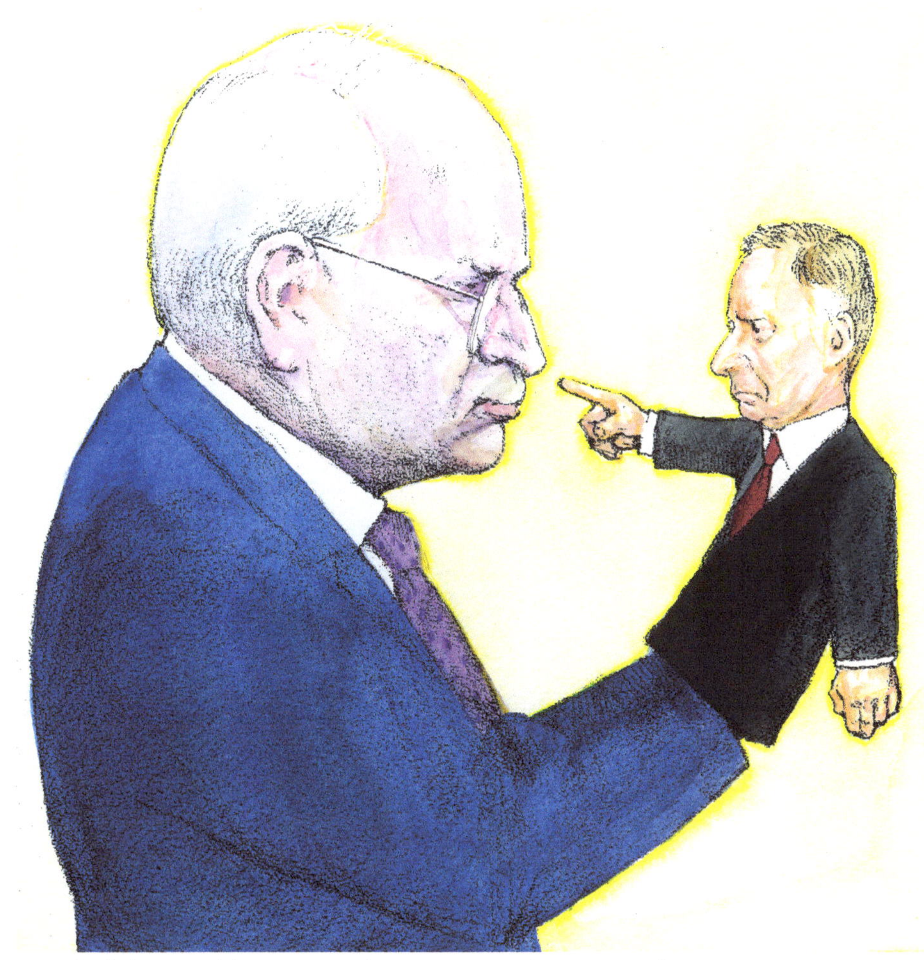

David Chelsea • Libby Fingers Cheney • Pen, Ink & Watercolor

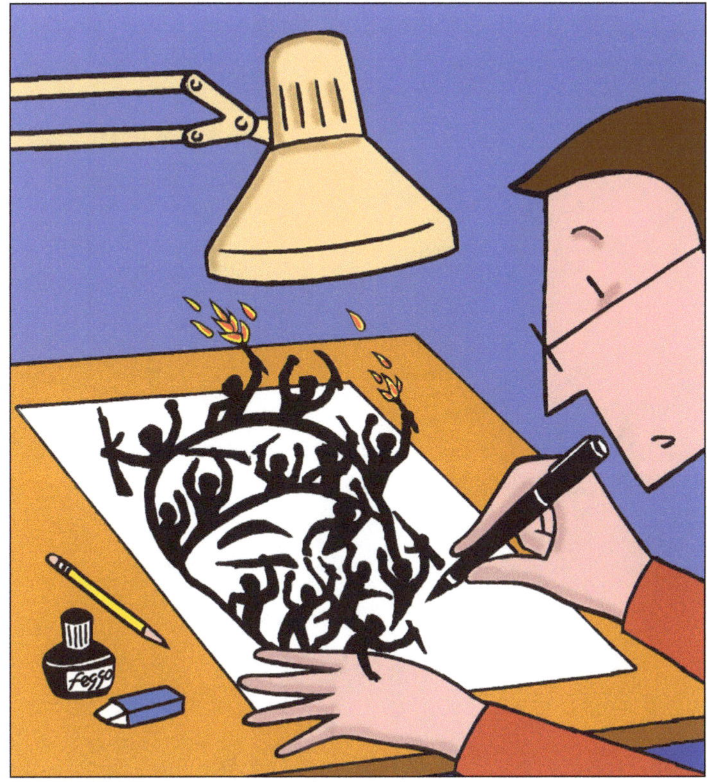

Felipe Galindo • Islamic Cartoon Uproar
Pen, Ink & Digital Color

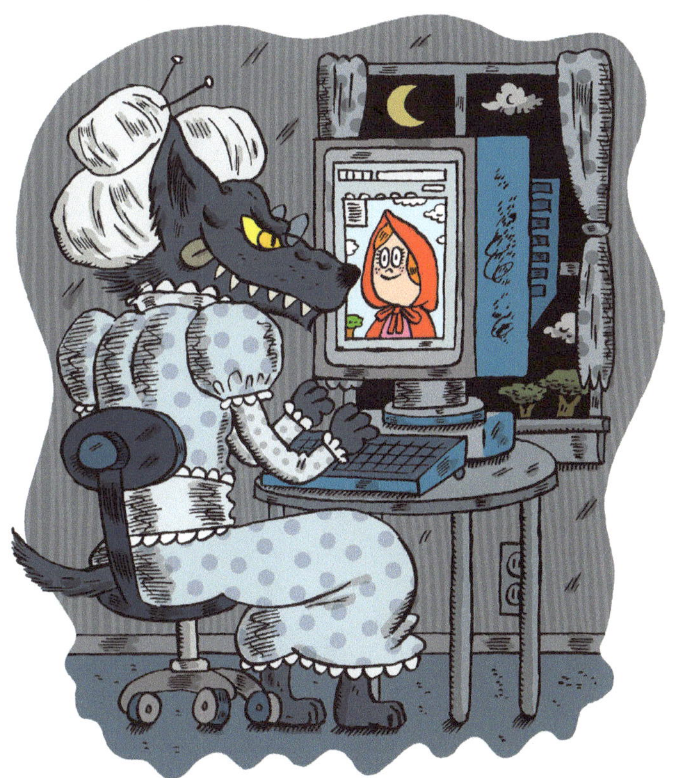

Paul Corio • Online Predators • Pen, Ink & Digital Color

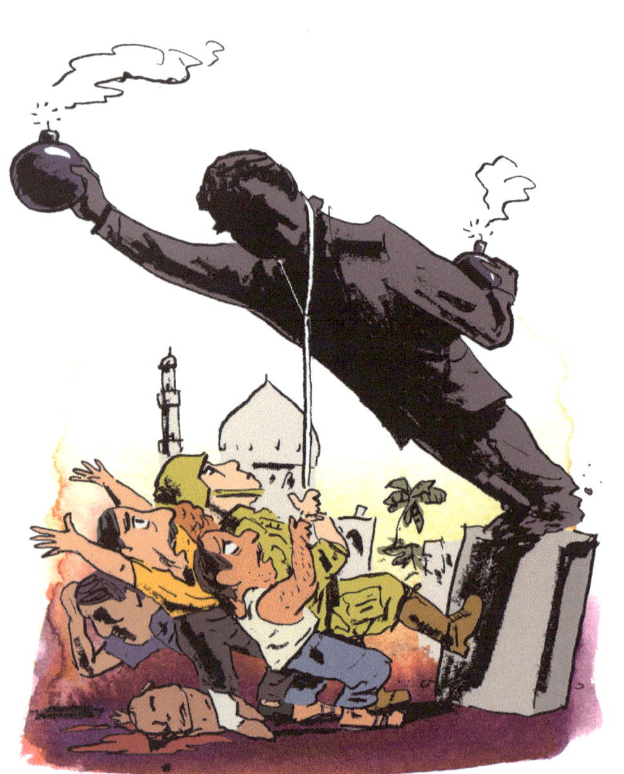

Rob Shepperson • Iraq Topples Into Chaos
Pen, Ink & Watercolor

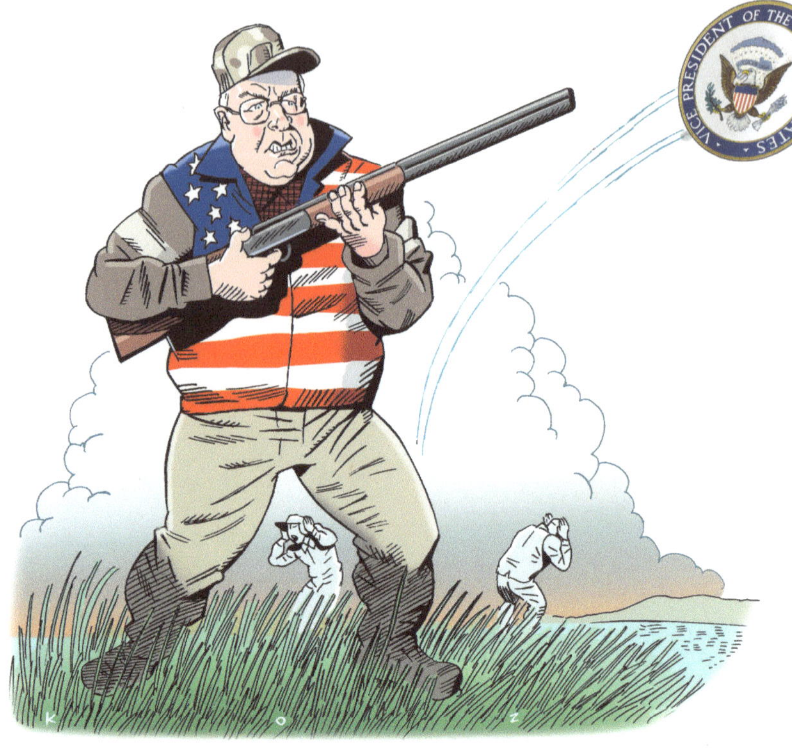

Martin Kozlowski • Cheney's Shot Reputation • Pen, Ink & Digital Color

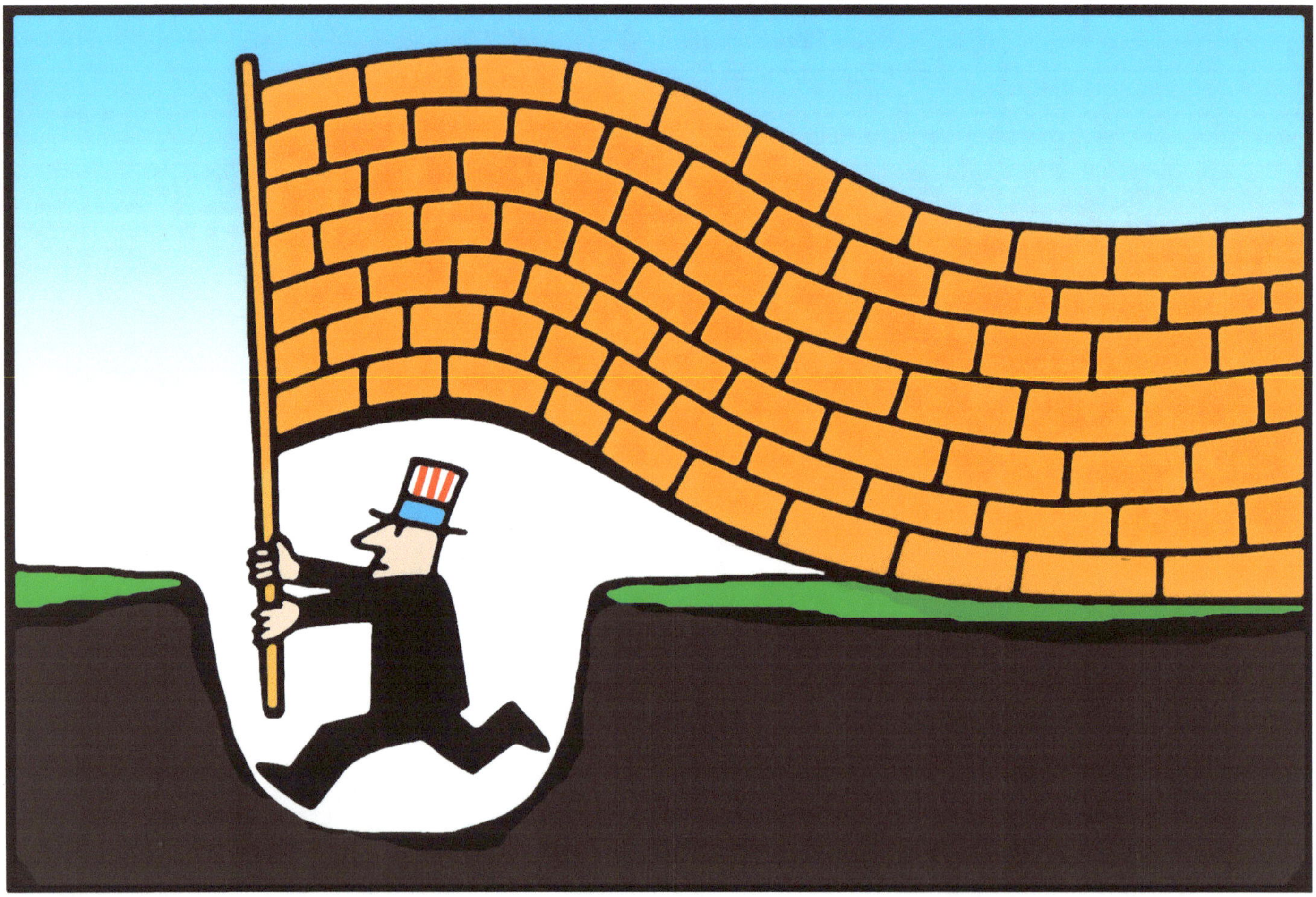

Igor Kopelnitsky • Will a U.S. Border Wall Work? • Digital Media

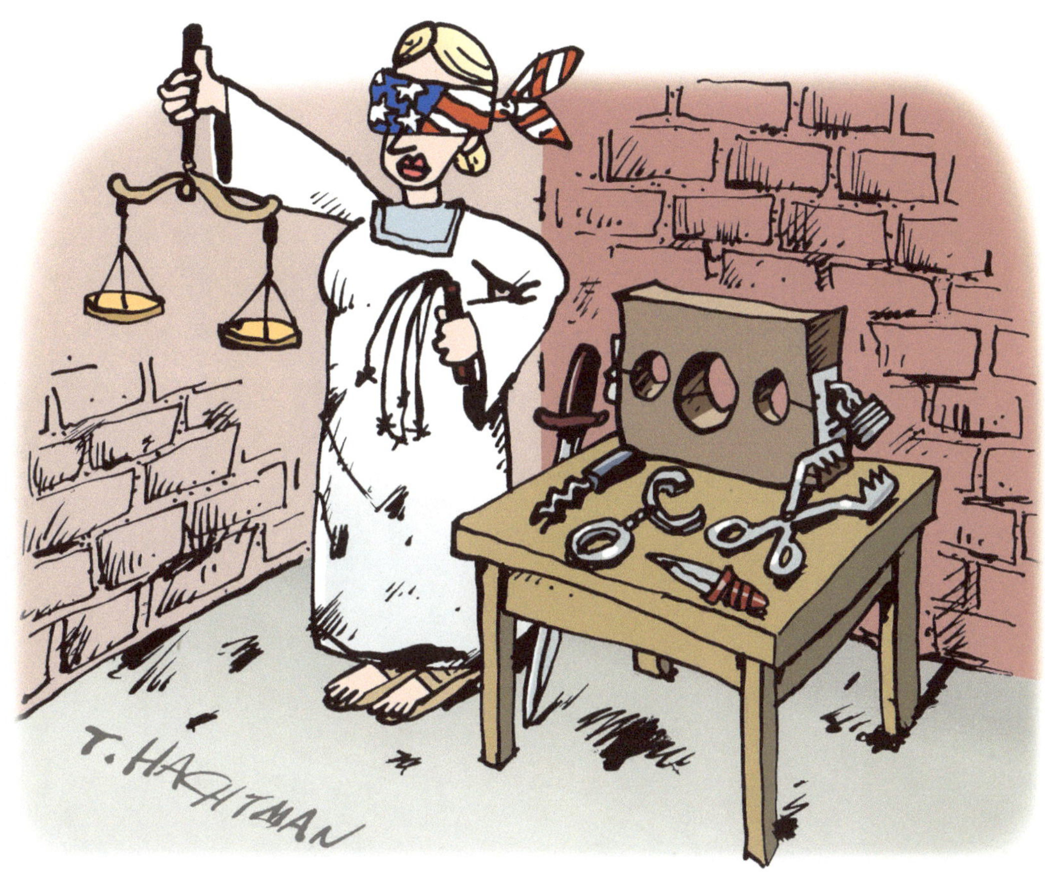

Tom Hachtman • U.S. Promotes "Alternative" Justice • Pen, Ink & Digital Color

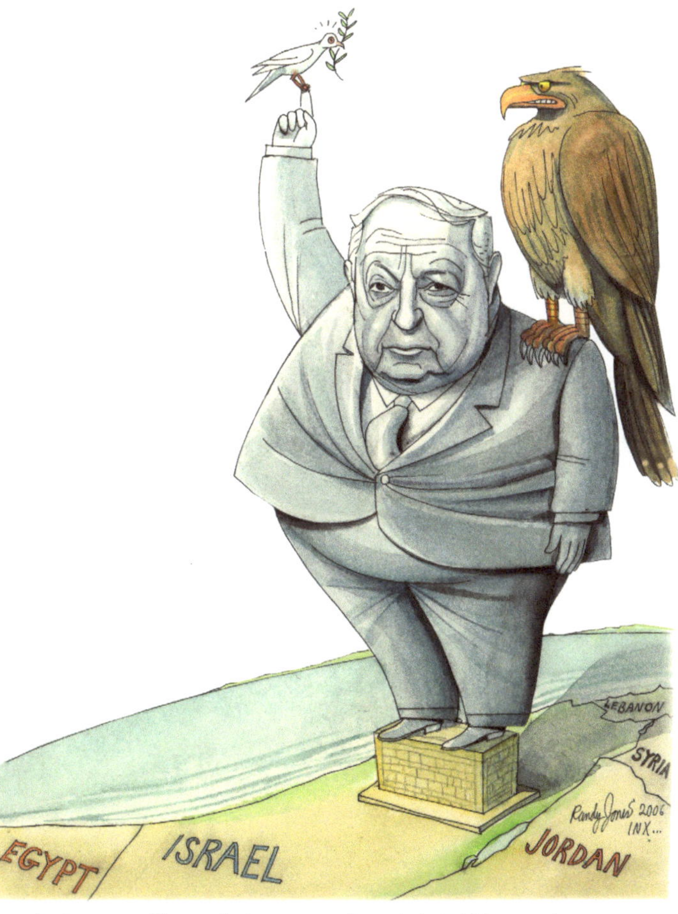

Randy Jones • Sharon's Legacy • Pen, Ink & Watercolor

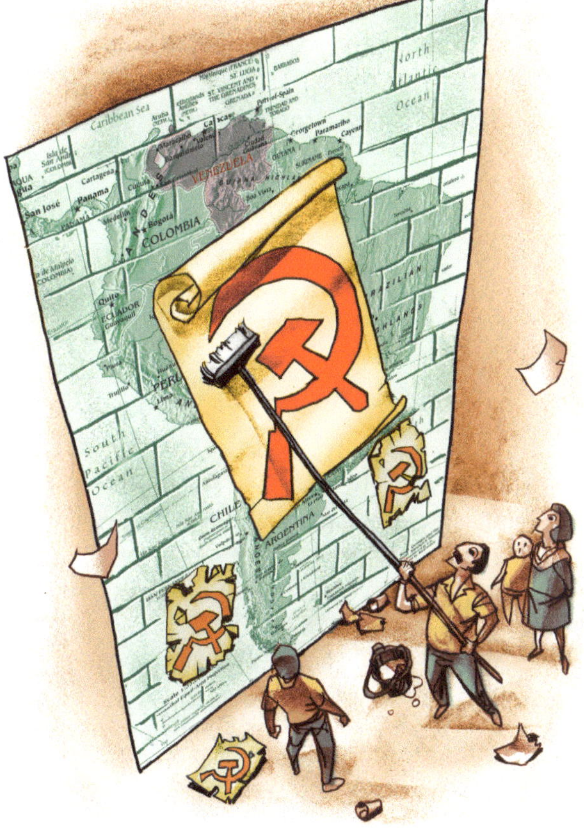

David Klein • South America Turns Towards the Left
Color Pencil & Digital Media

Bush orders a troop surge in Iraq. Sub-prime mortgage crisis helps trigger Great Recession. Nancy Pelosi becomes first female Speaker of the House. Anti-government protests in Myanmar.

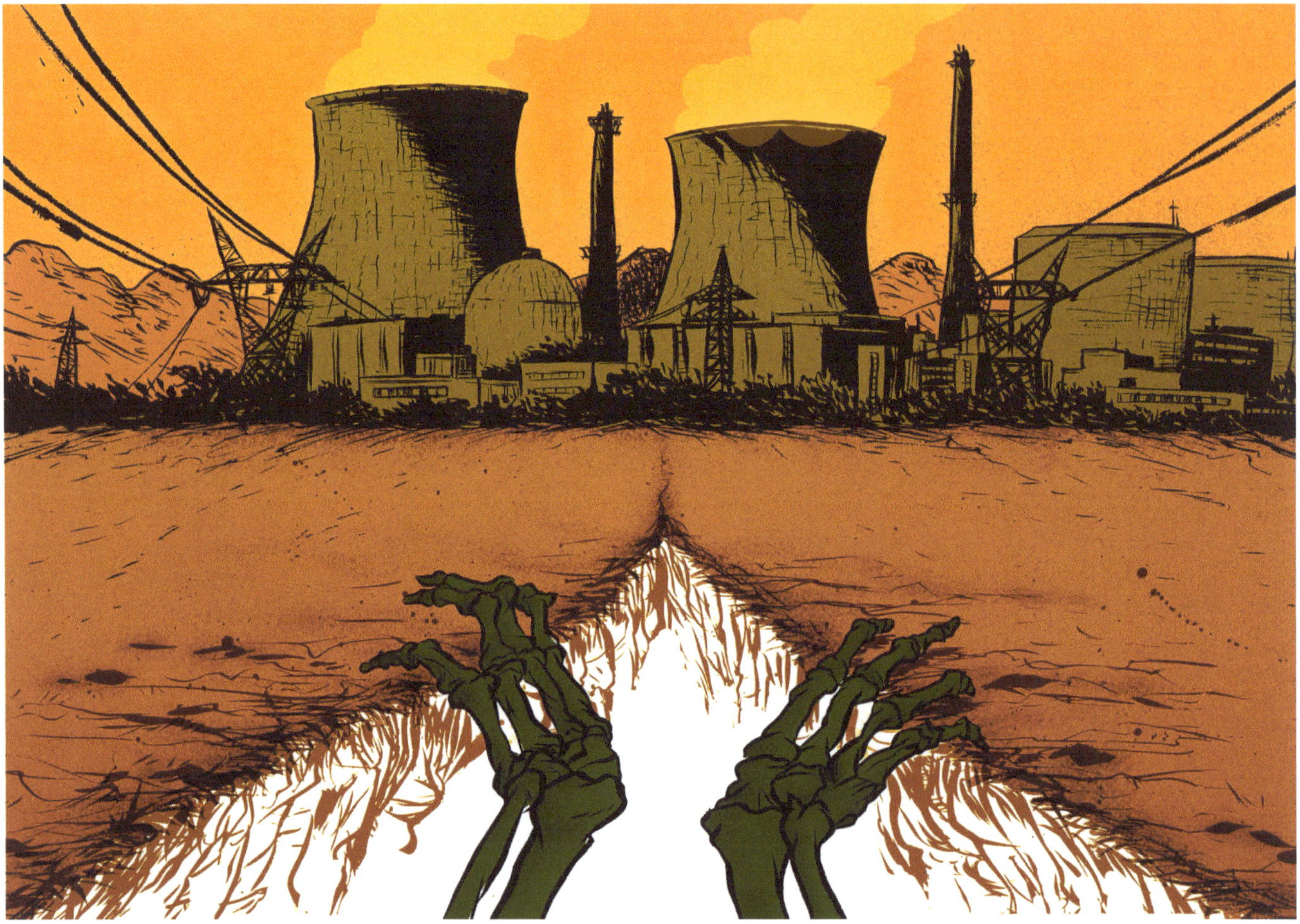

Ryan Inzana • Nuclear Accident Threat • Pen, Ink & Digital Color

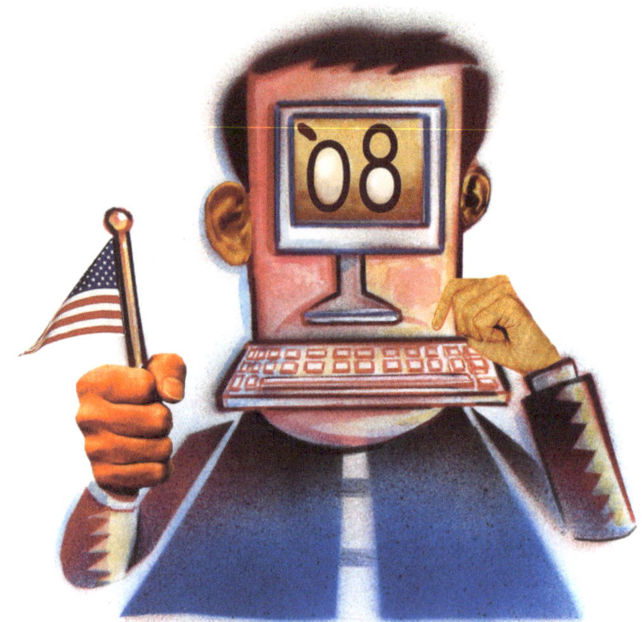

Peter Kuper • The Internet Campaign
Spray Enamel, Watercolor & Collage

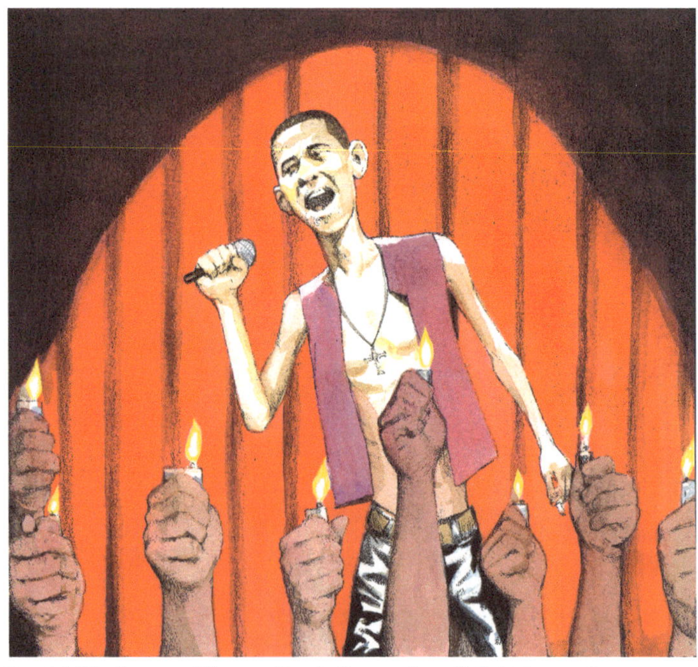

David Chelsea • Obama Rock Star • Pencil & Watercolor

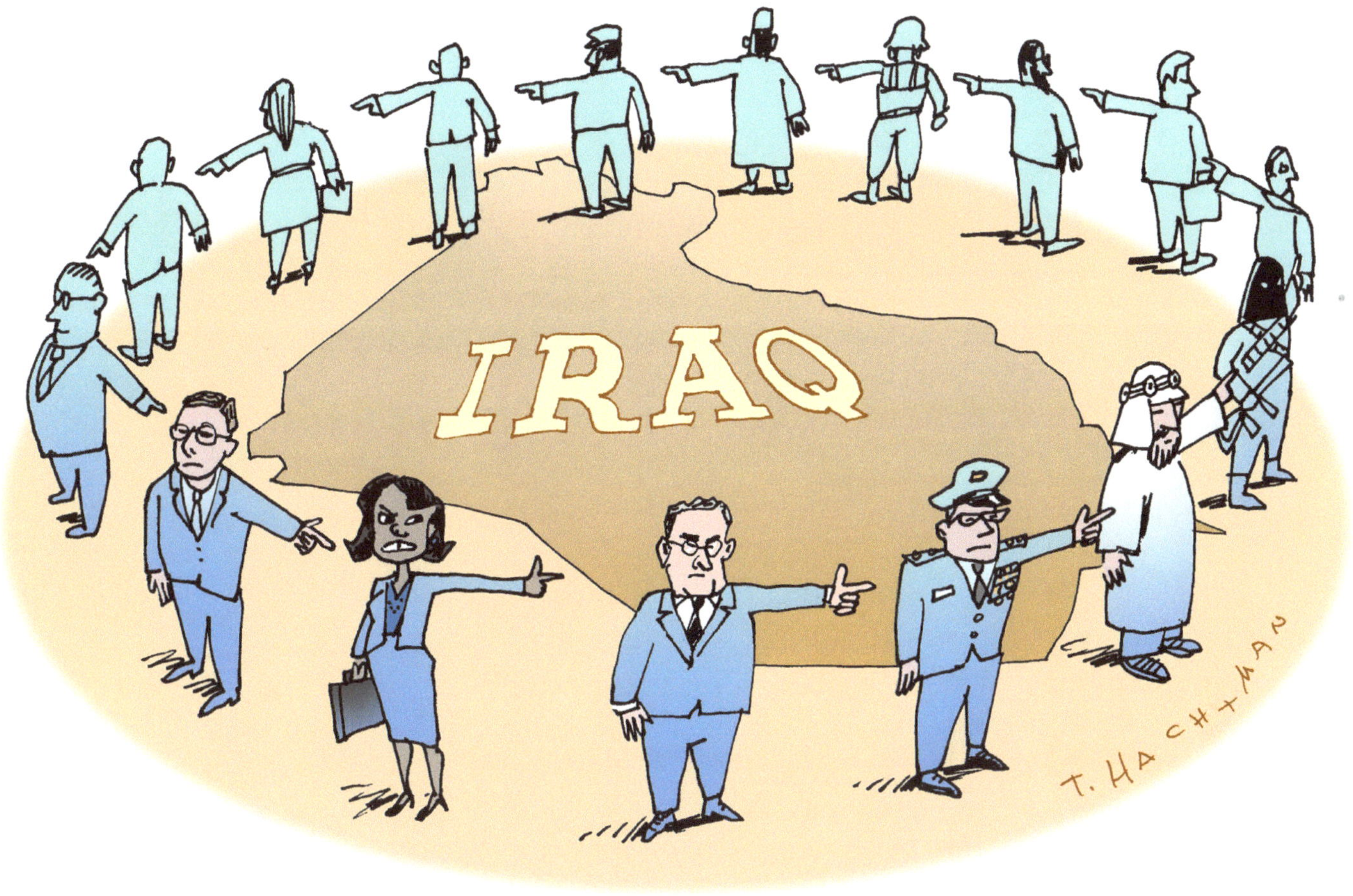

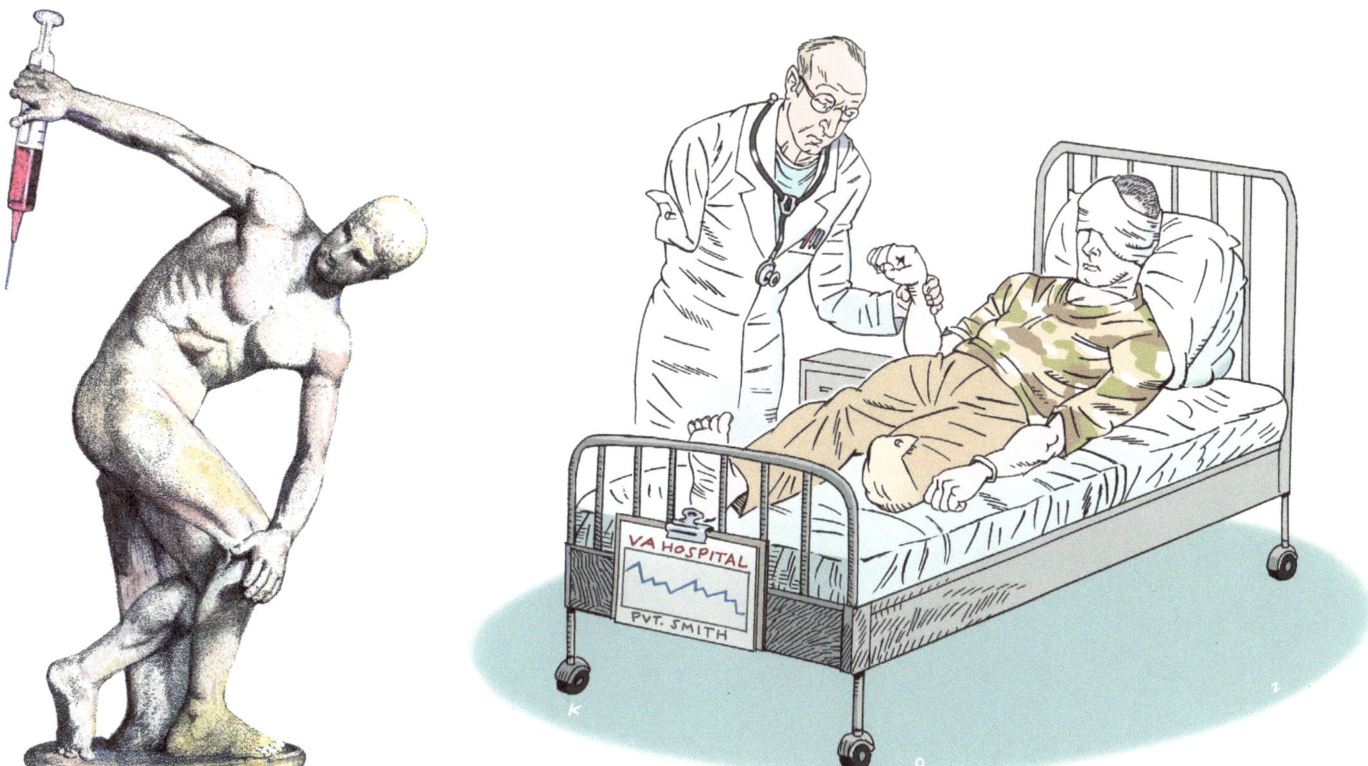

Tom Hachtman • Iraq Blame Game • Pen, Ink & Digital Color

David Chelsea • Sports Doping
Coquille Board & Watercolor

Martin Kozlowski • Poor Care for Iraq Wounded • Pen, Ink & Digital Color

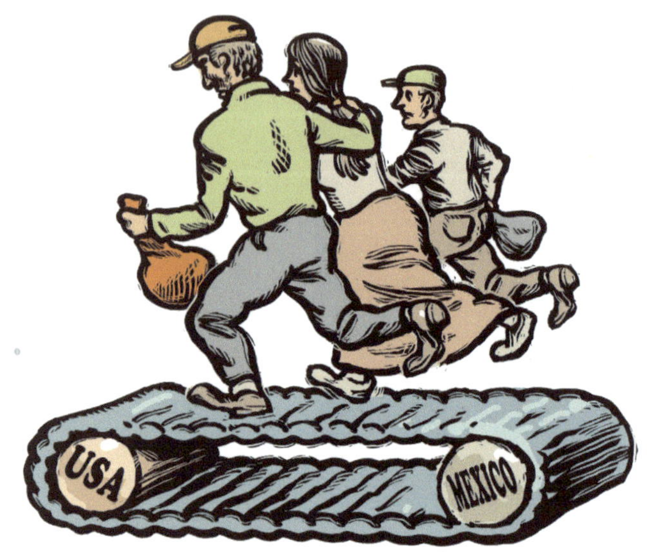

Bill Russell • Illegal Immigrant Treadmill • Linocut & Digital Color

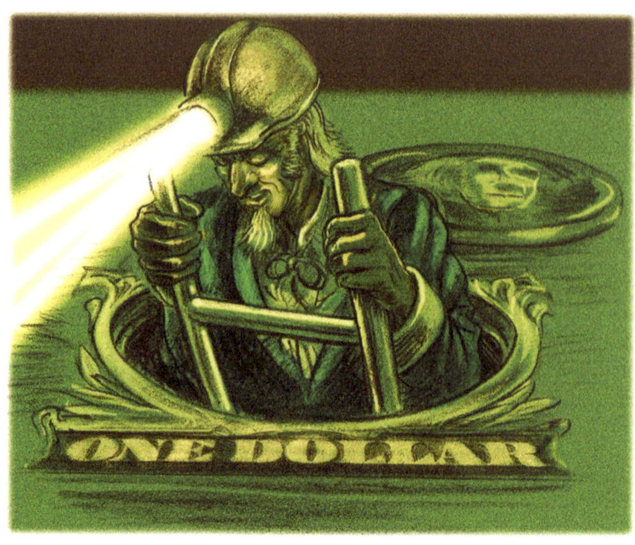

Thomas Kerr • Sinking Dollar • Pencil & Digital Color

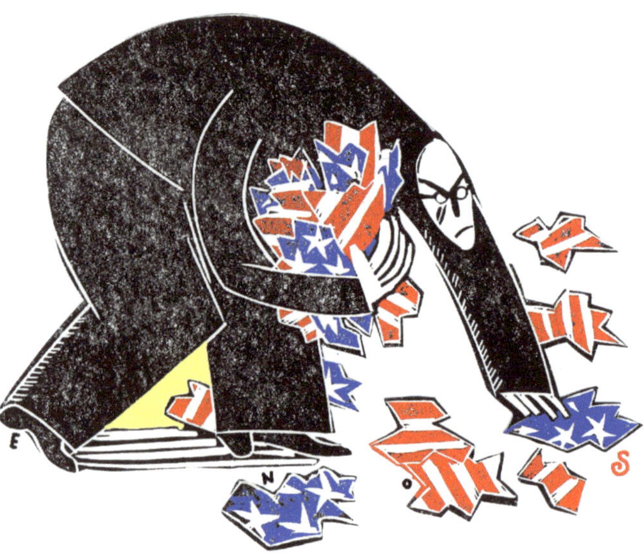

Randall Enos • America's Fractured Image
Linocut & Digital Color

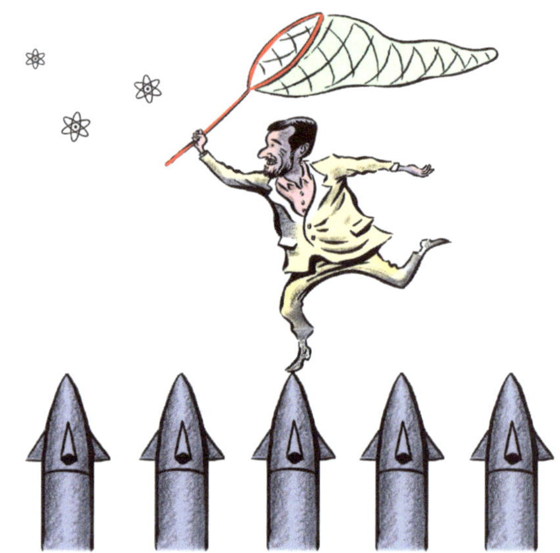

David Gothard • Iran's Nuclear Pursuit
Brush, Ink, Graphite & Digital Color

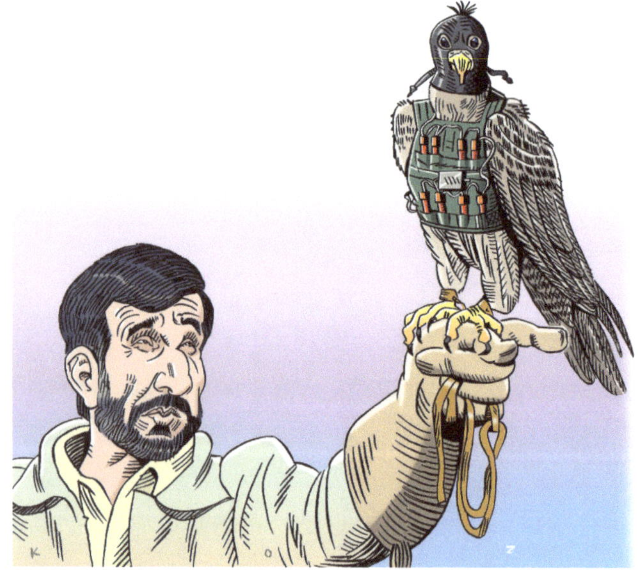

Martin Kozlowski • Ahmadinejad: Terror Master
Pen, Ink & Digital Color

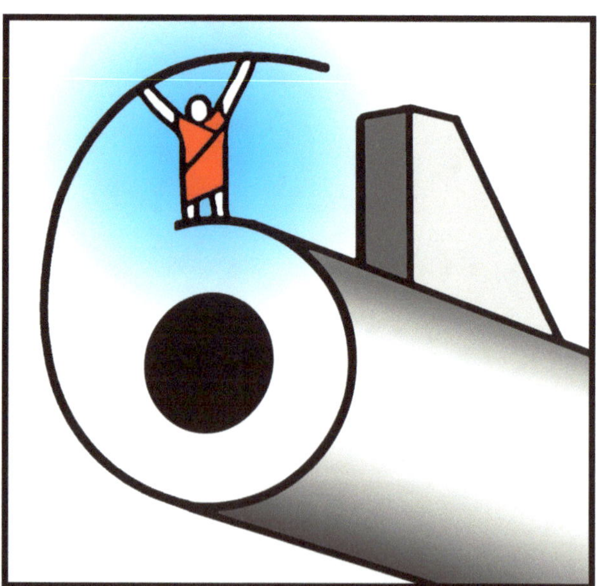

Igor Kopelnitsky • Monks Resist Myanmar Military
Digital Media

Great Recession intensifies. Stock market crashes. Dow loses 18% of its value in eight days. Government pumps $700 billion into troubled banks. U.S. oil prices hit a record $147 per barrel. Barack Obama defeats John McCain to become 44th U.S. President.

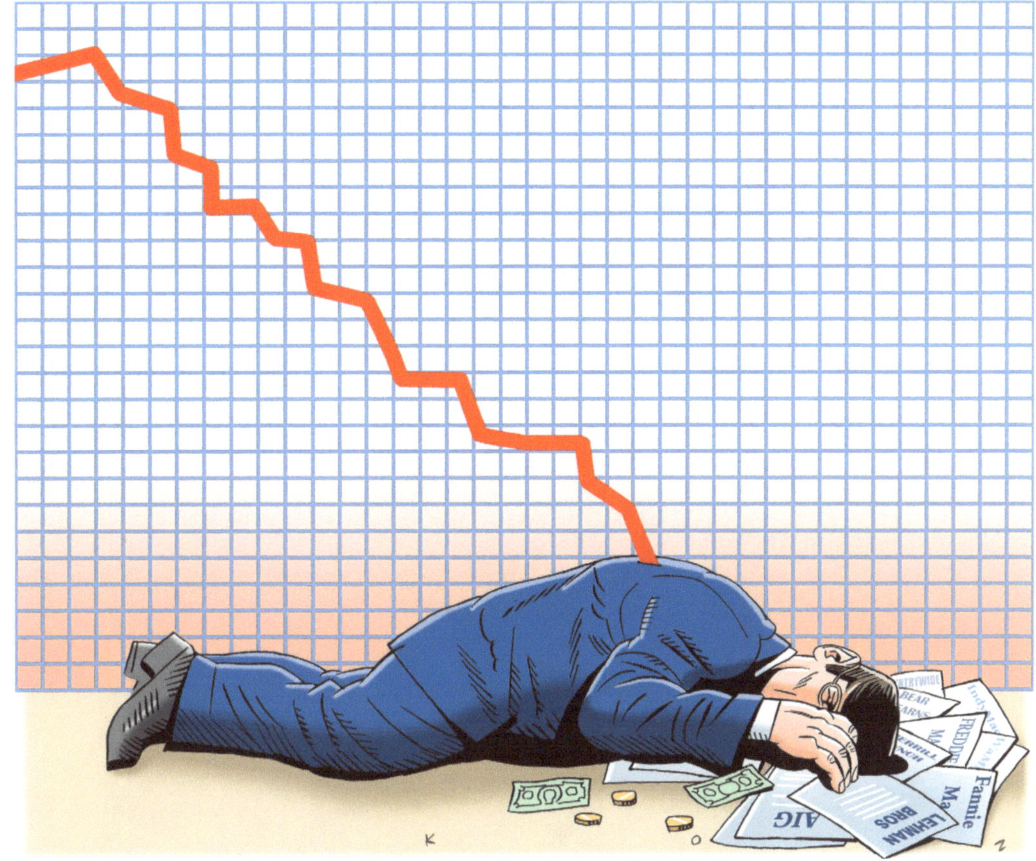

Martin Kozlowski • A Killing on Wall Street • Pen, Ink & Digital Color

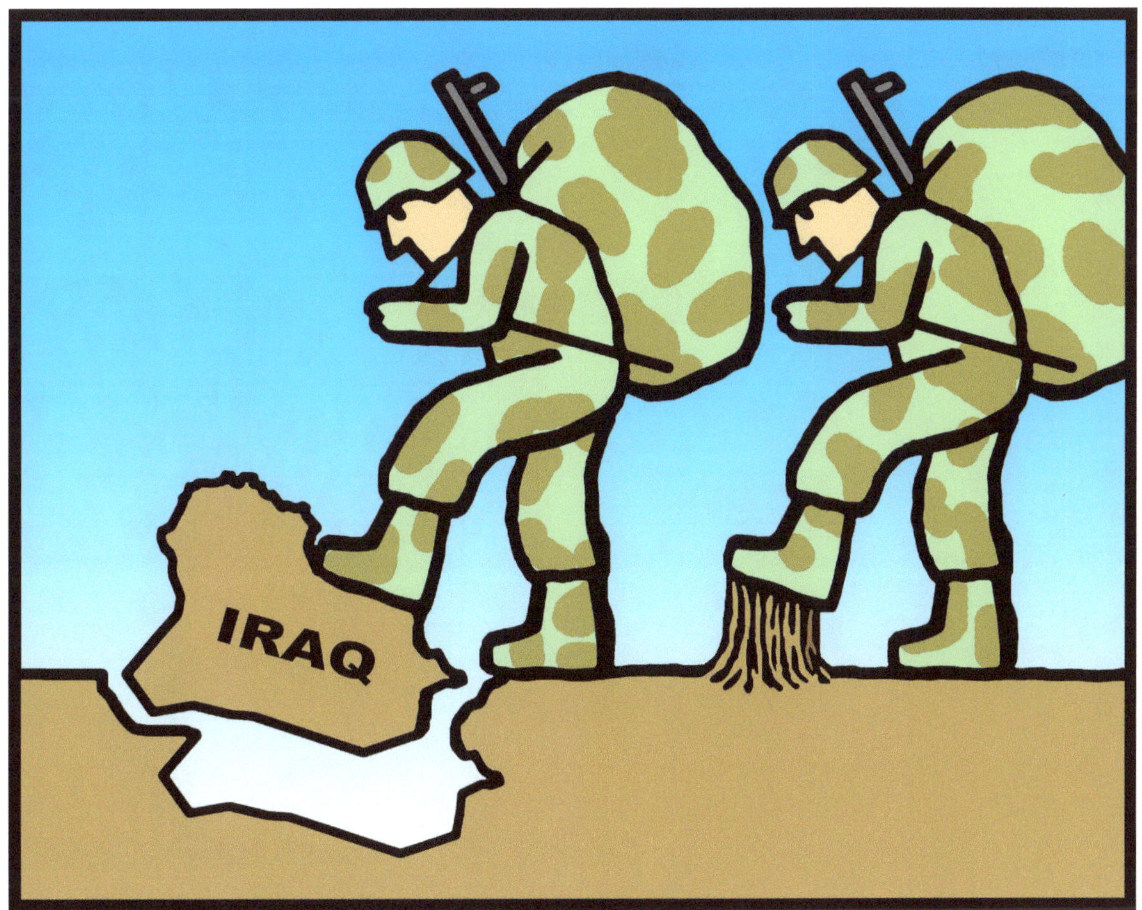

Igor Kopelnitsky • Reducing Troop Reductions • Digital Media

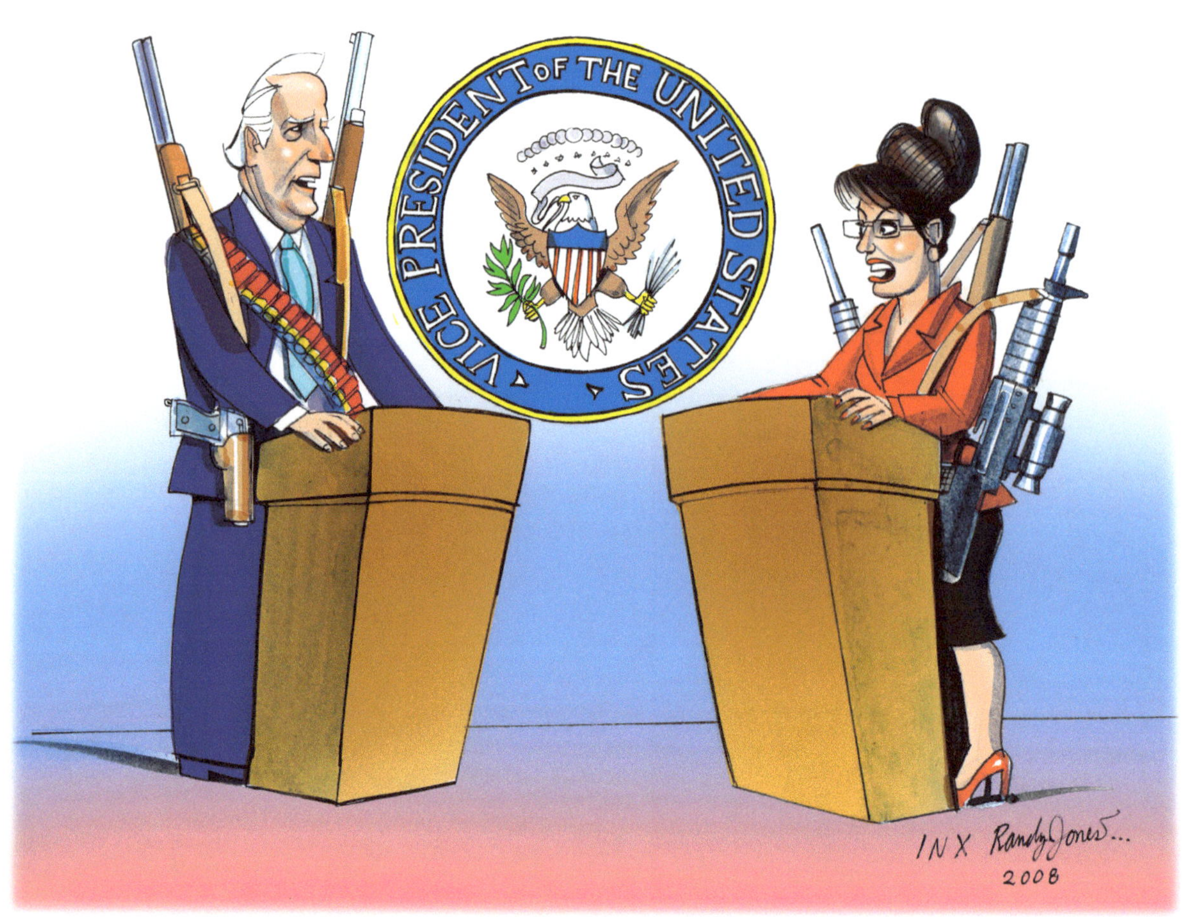

Randy Jones • Biden vs. Palin • Pen, Ink & Watercolor

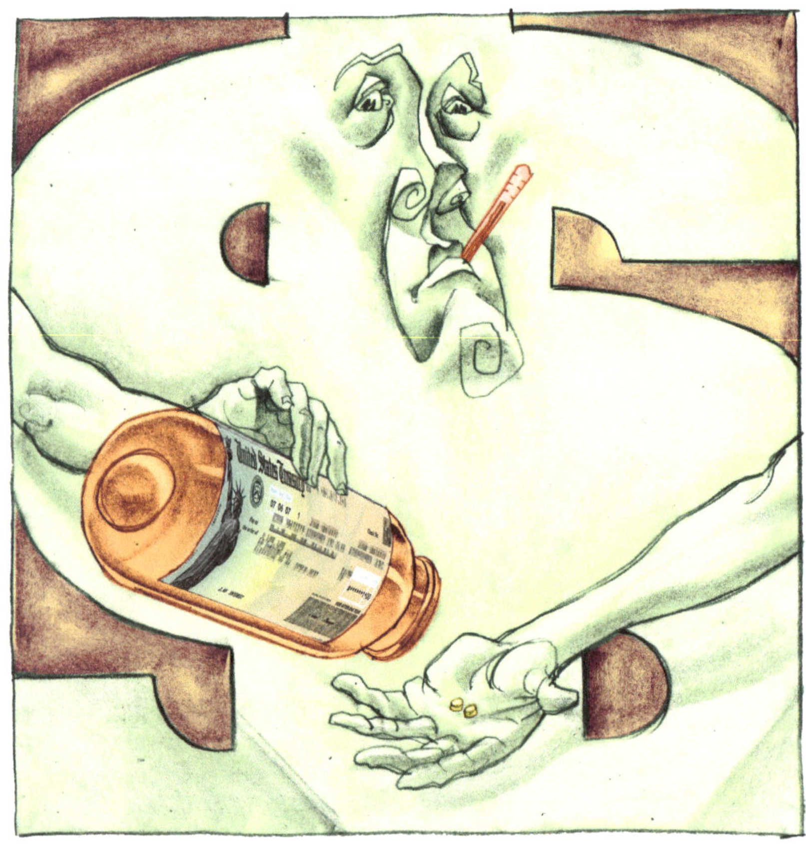

David Klein • Stimulus Prescriptions • Pencil, Watercolor & Digital Color

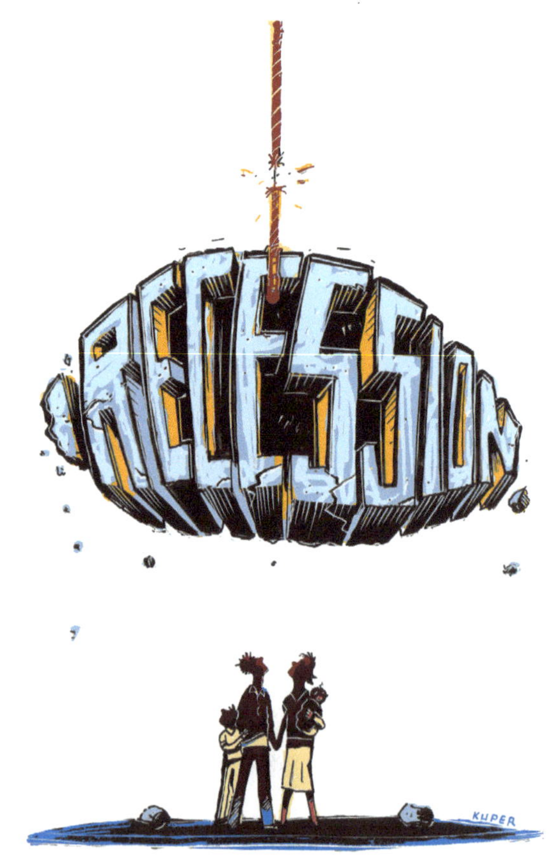

Peter Kuper • Recession Looms
Pen, Ink & Watercolor

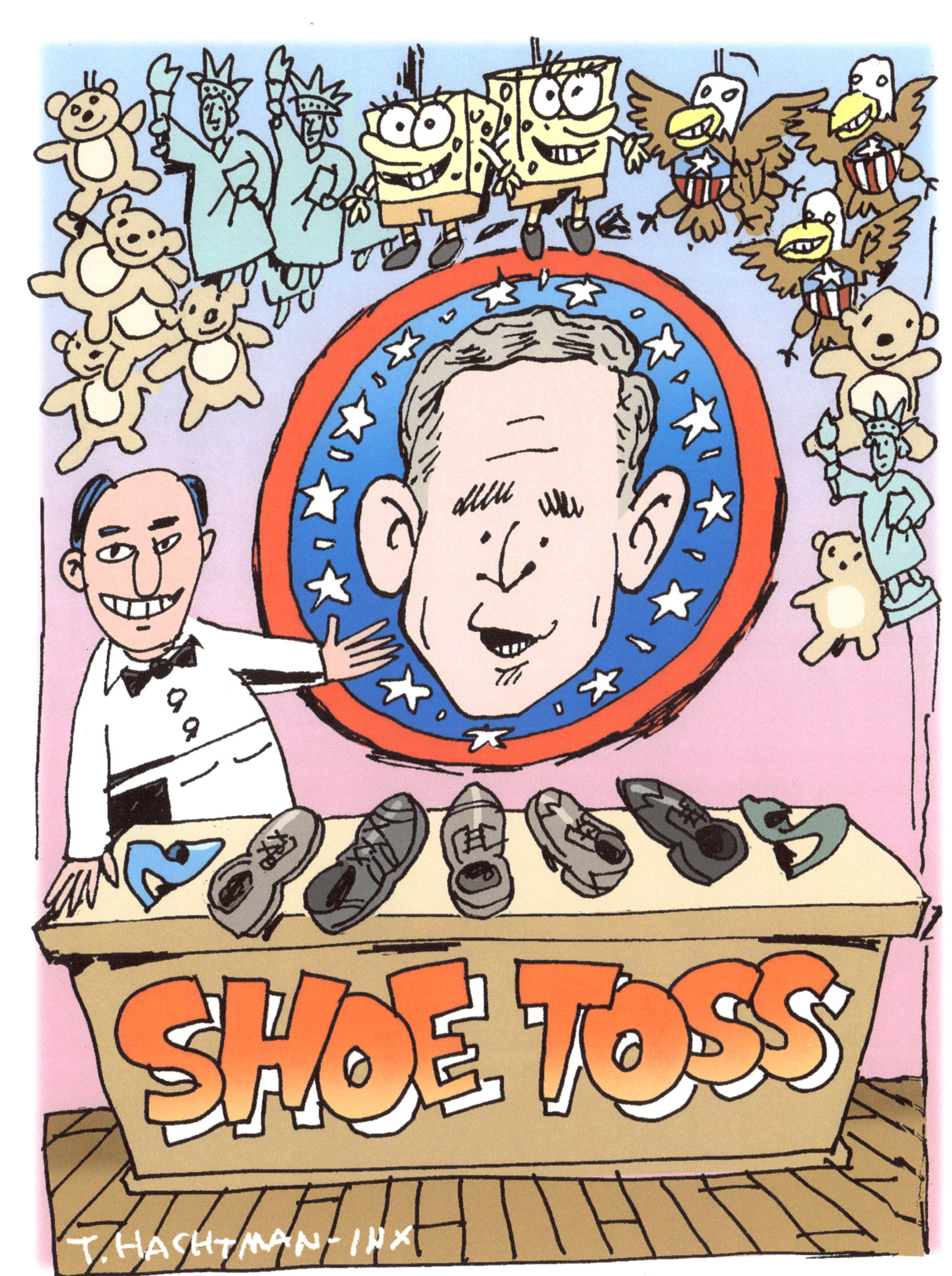

Tom Hachtman • Iraqis Take Aim at Bush • Pen, Ink & Digital Color

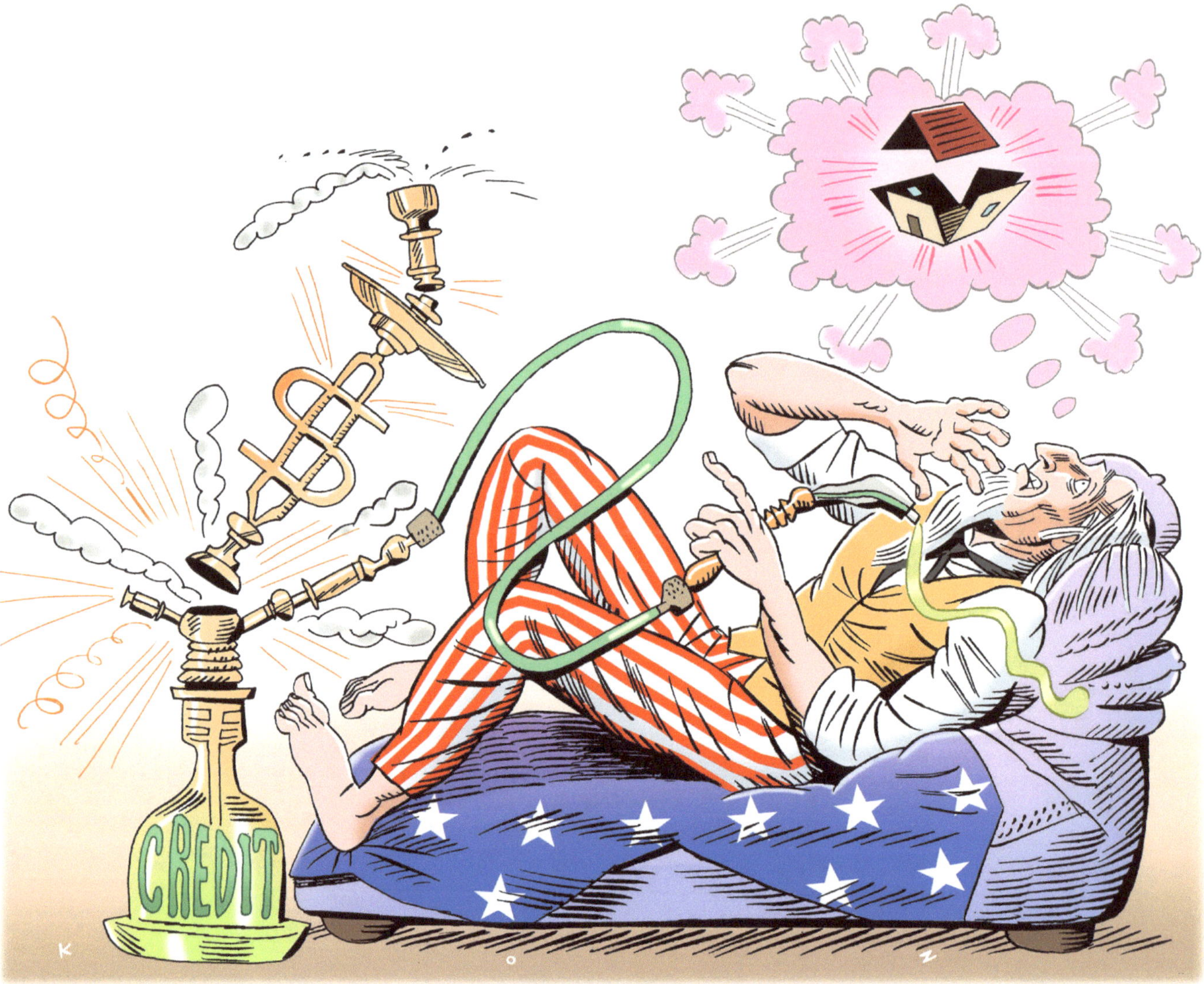

Martin Kozlowski • Burst American Dream • Pen, Ink & Digital Color

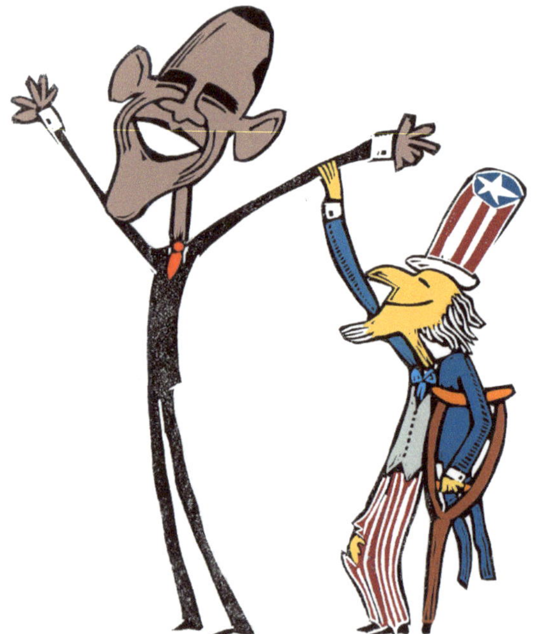

Randall Enos • Obama Elected
Linocut & Digital Color

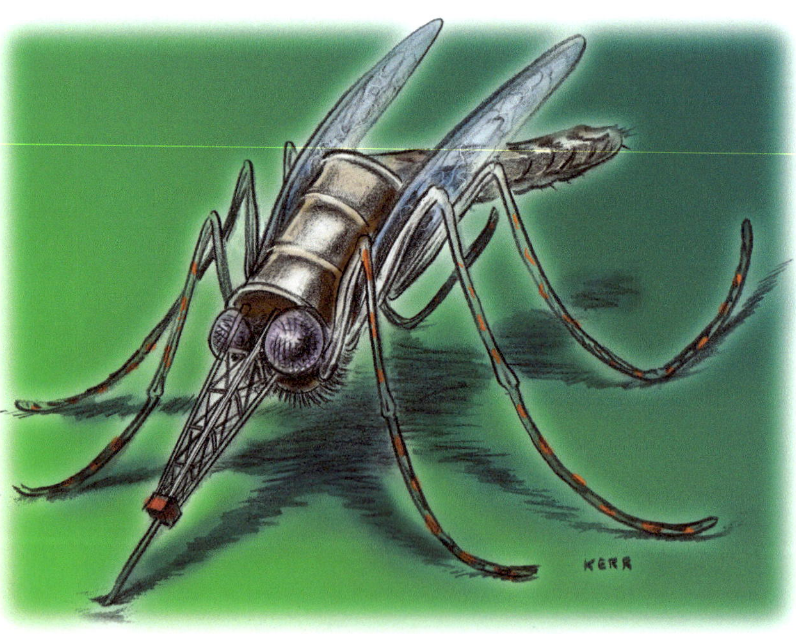

Thomas Kerr • Expanding Oil Exploration • Pencil & Digital Color

Tea Party protests begin. Congress approves $787 billion stimulus package. Twelve servicemen killed in Fort Hood shooting. Gaza War ends. Election protests begin in Iran. Drug wars grow deadlier in Mexico.

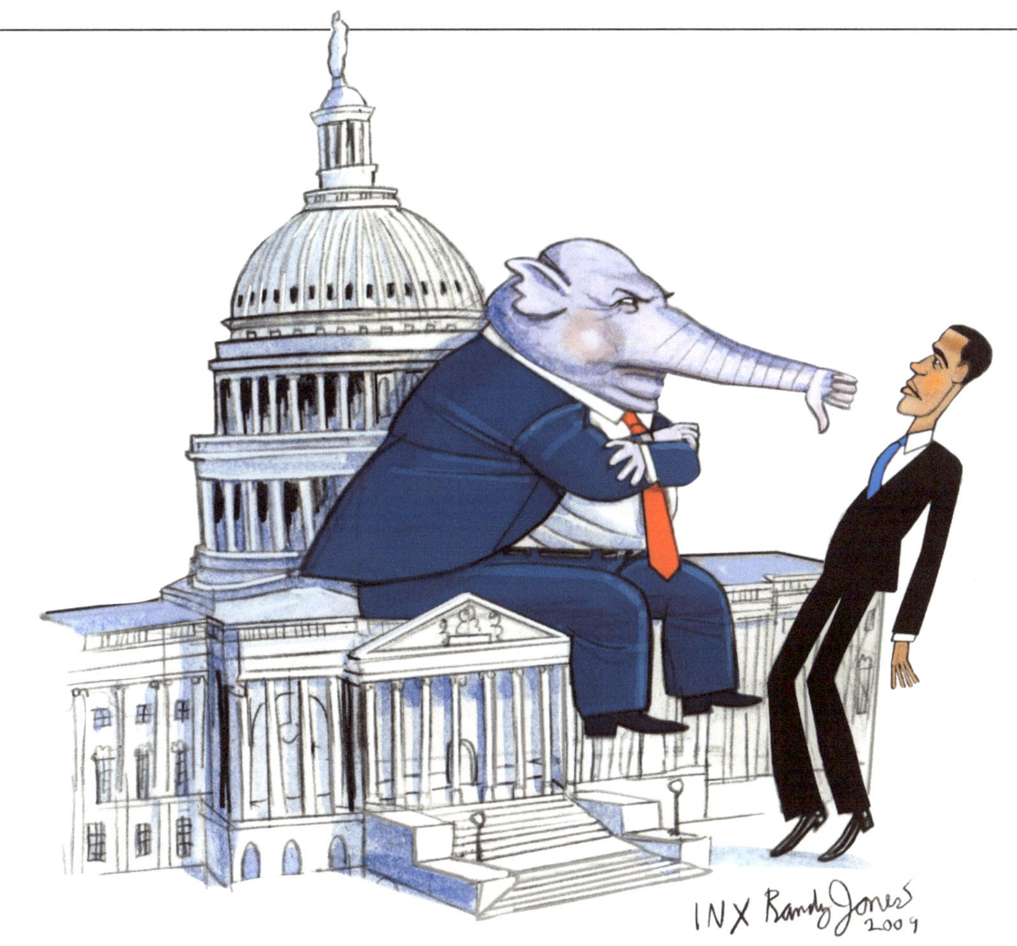

Randy Jones • Republicans Just Say No • Pen, Ink & Watercolor

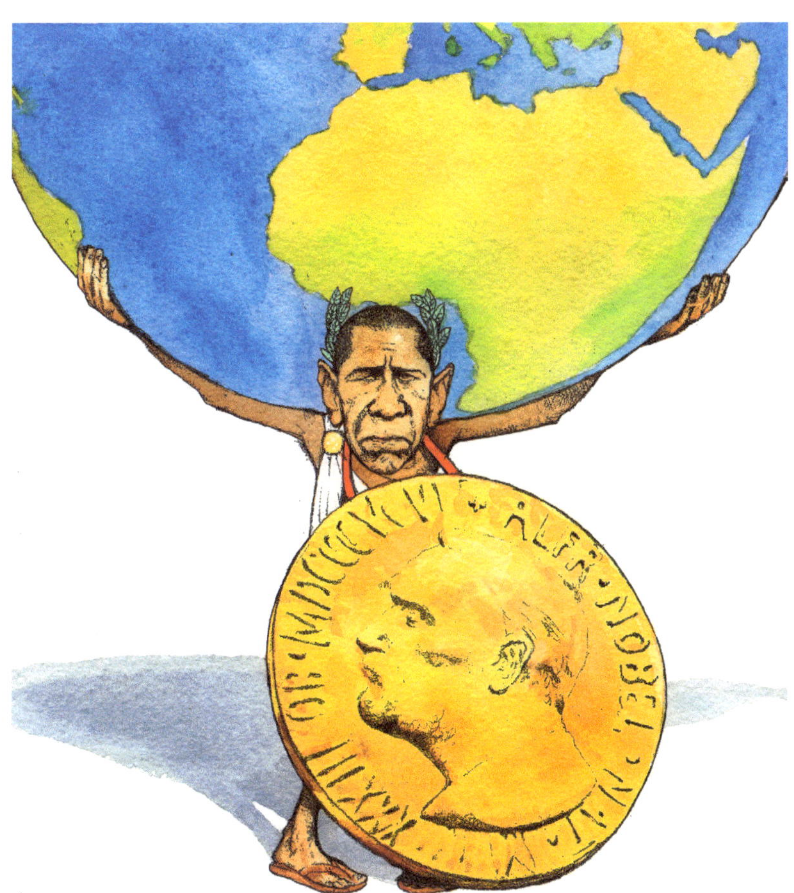

David Chelsea • Obama's Nobel Peace Prize • Pen, Ink & Watercolor

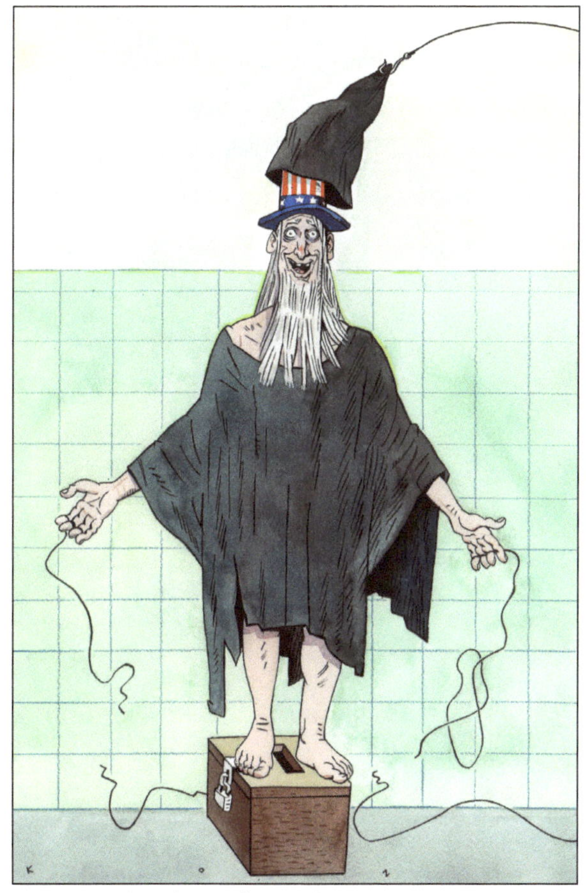

Martin Kozlowski • After Bush: No More Torture
Pen, Ink & Watercolor

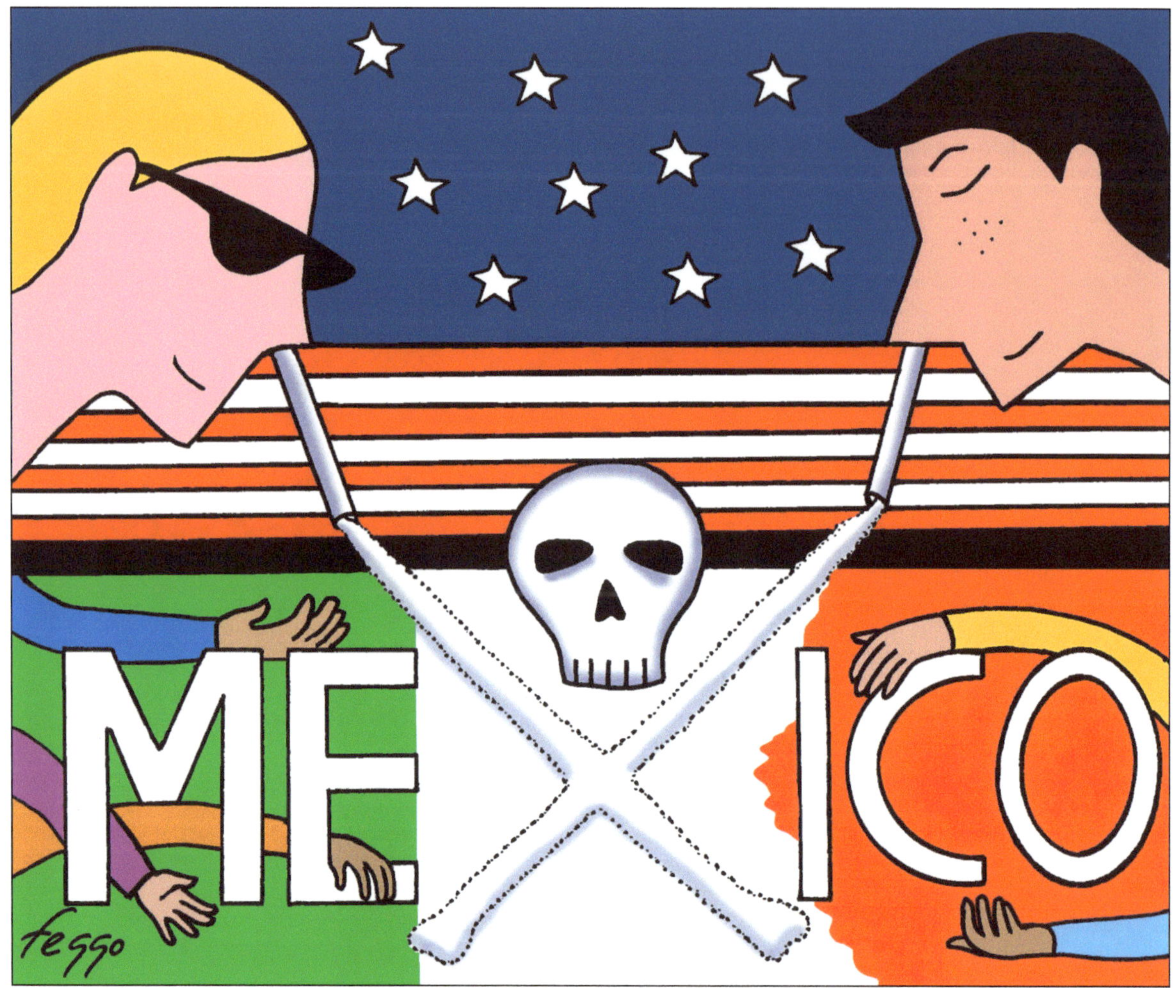

Felipe Galindo • U.S. Fuels Mexican Drug War • Pen, Ink & Digital Color

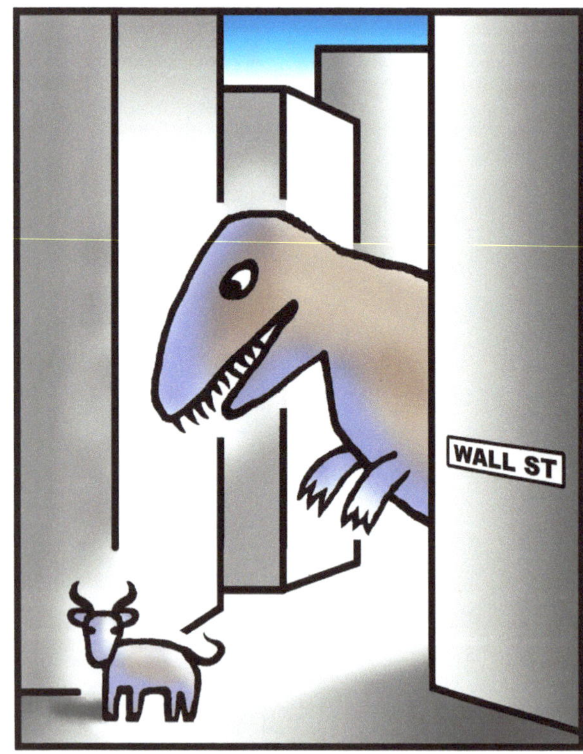

Igor Kopelnitsky • A Nightmare on Wall Street
Digital Media

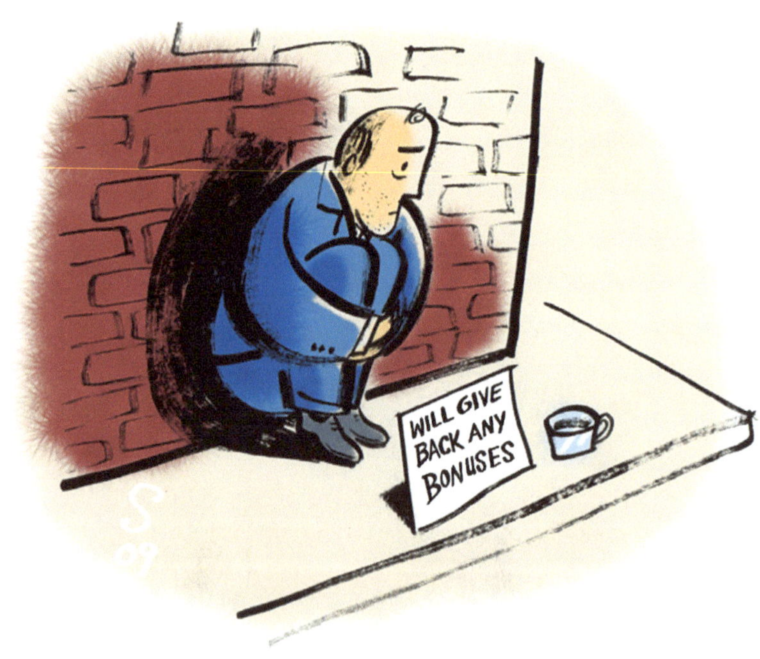

Steven Salerno • The New Unemployed • Brush, Ink & Watercolor

In the 1980s, the political cartoonist was forced to find fresh ways to depict nuclear weapons in order to accompany all the ballistic missile treaty stories that clogged editorial pages — make them new, and not offend the editorial watchdogs sniffing about for phallic imagery. By 2008, the epic economic downturn posed the challenge of manipulating fever lines and dollar signs to connote decay and decline in as original a fashion as possible.

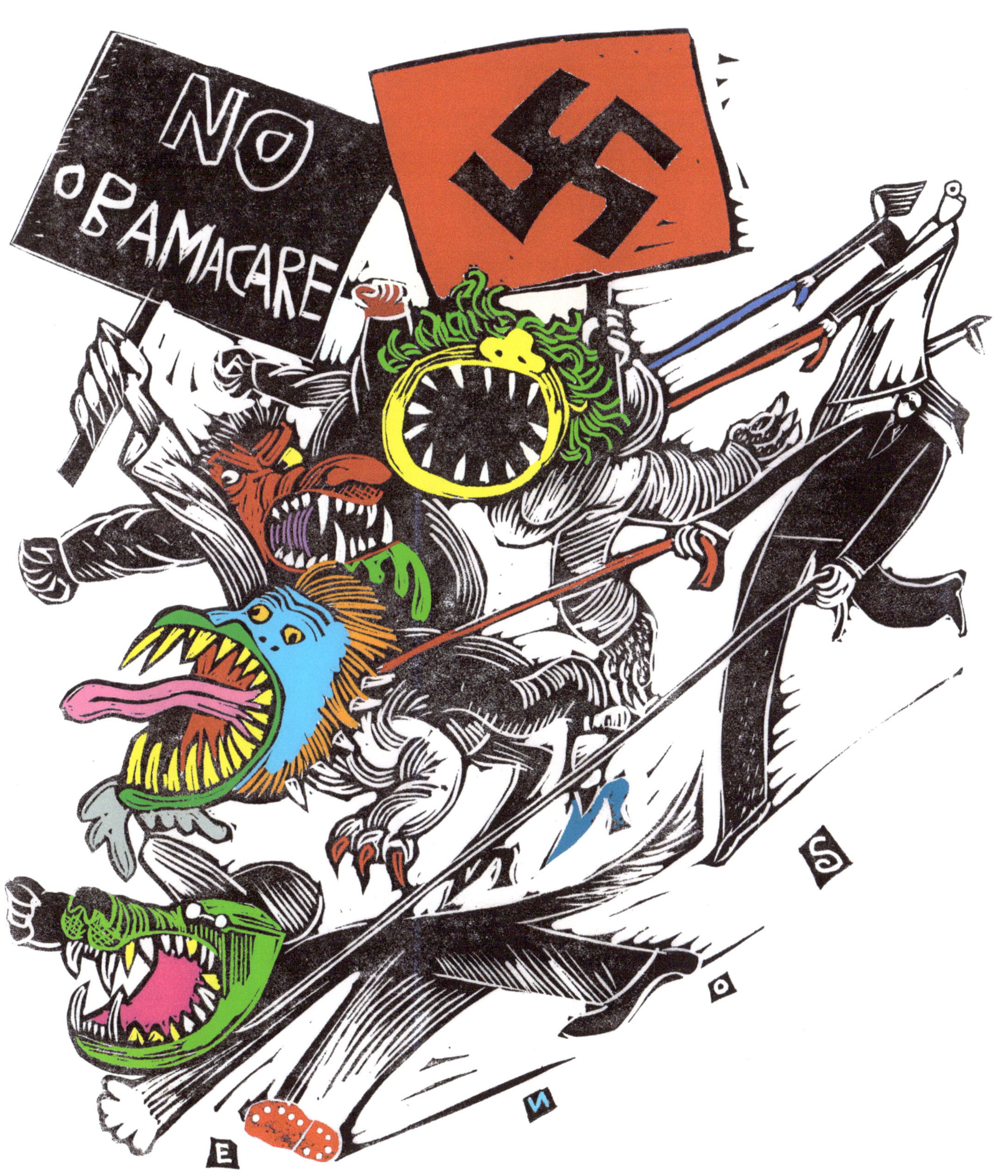

Randall Enos • Vicious Healthcare Protests • Linocut & Digital Color

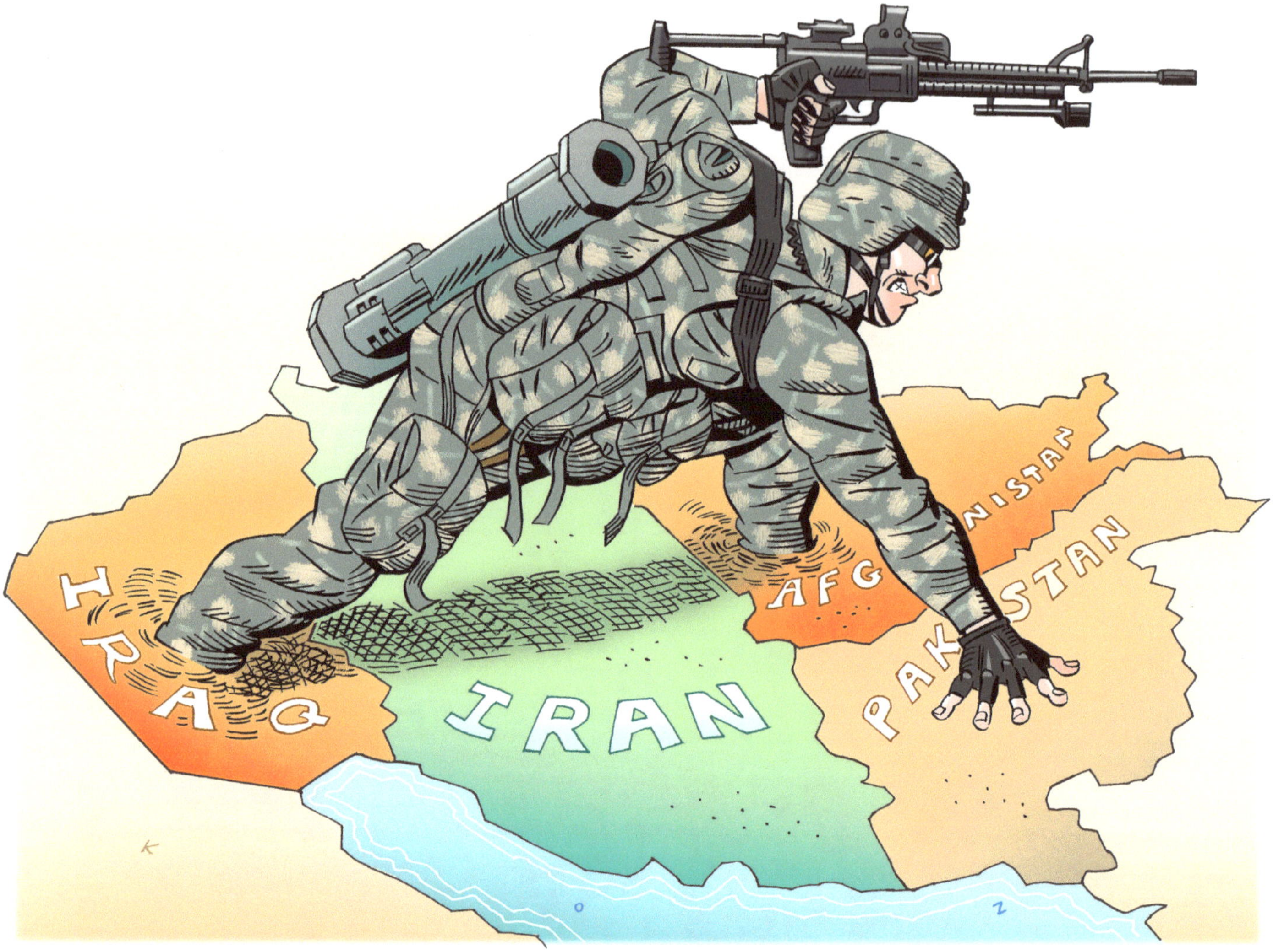

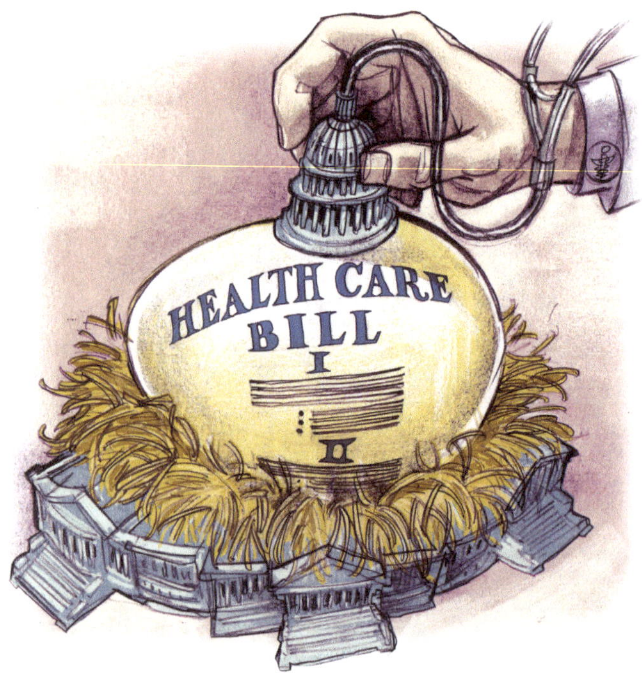

Martin Kozlowski • Overextended U.S. Troops • Pen, Ink & Digital Color

David Klein • Health of the Healthcare Bill
Pencil & Watercolor

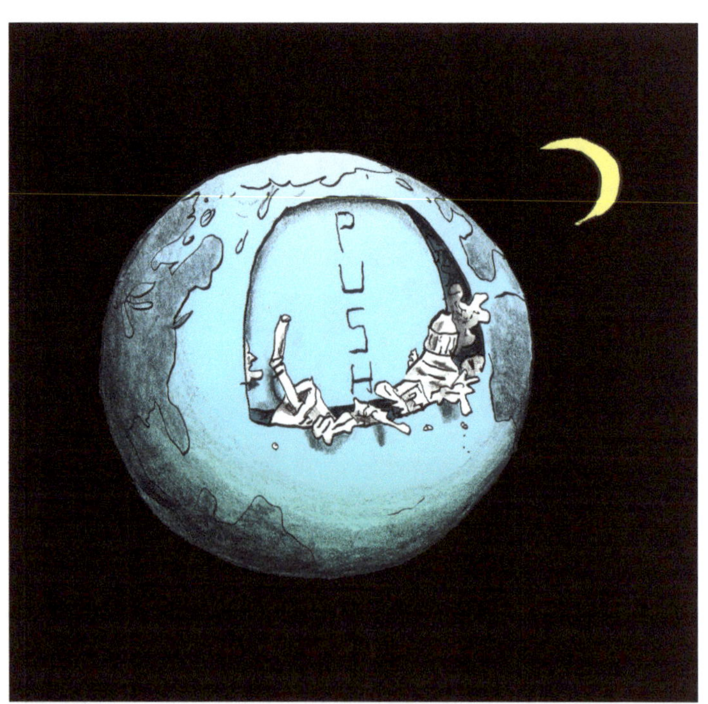

Rob Shepperson • Global Pollution • Pencil & Digital Color

Congress passes Obama's healthcare reform bill. BP oil spill in Gulf of Mexico. Wikileaks releases classified U.S. documents. Dodd–Frank Wall Street Reform Act signed into law.

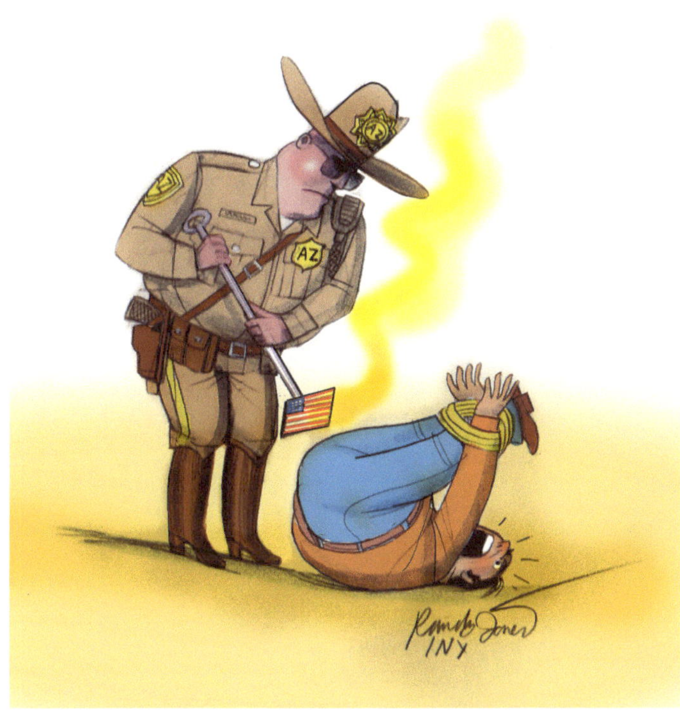

Randy Jones • Arizona Brand of Immigration Law
Pencil & Watercolor

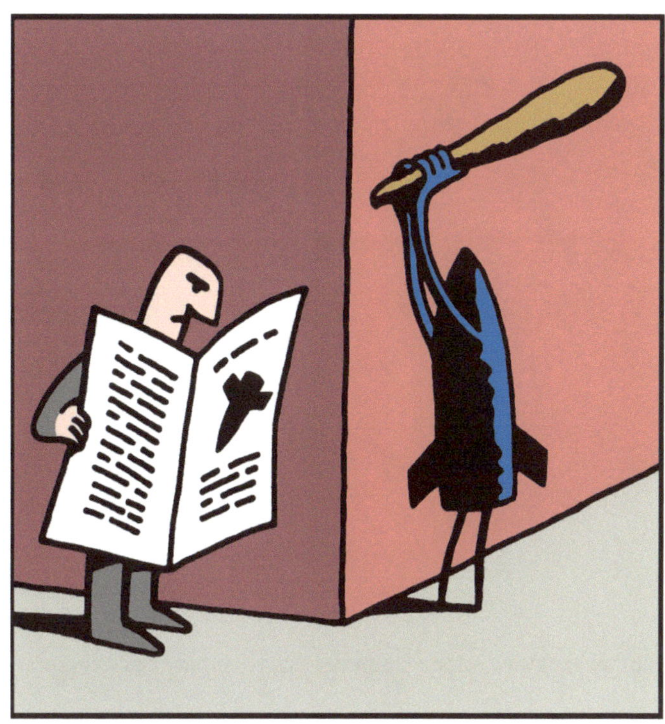

Igor Kopelnitsky • Nuclear Disarmament Worries
Digital Media

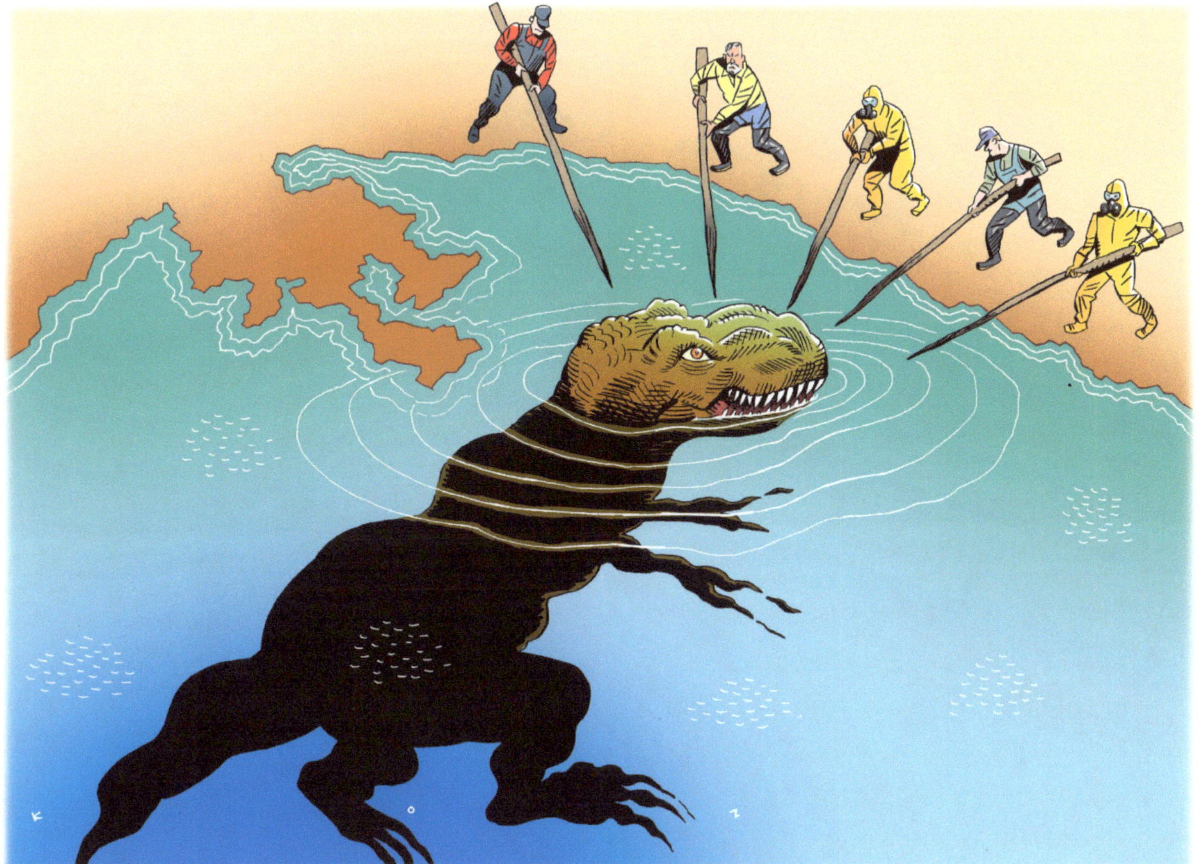

Martin Kozlowski • Gulf Spill's Primordial Threat • Pen, Ink & Digital Color

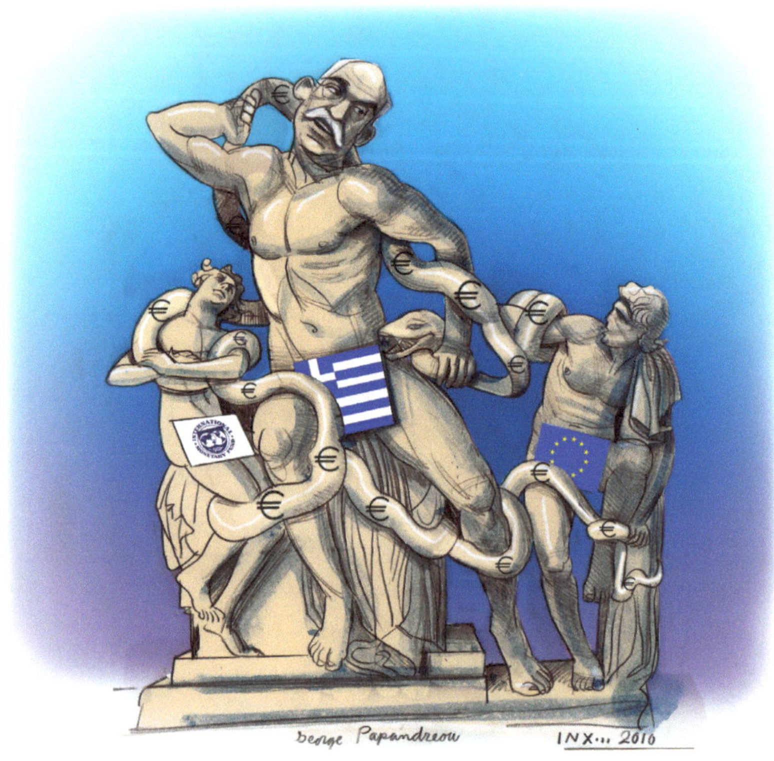

Randy Jones • Greece Entangles EU • Pen, Ink & Watercolor

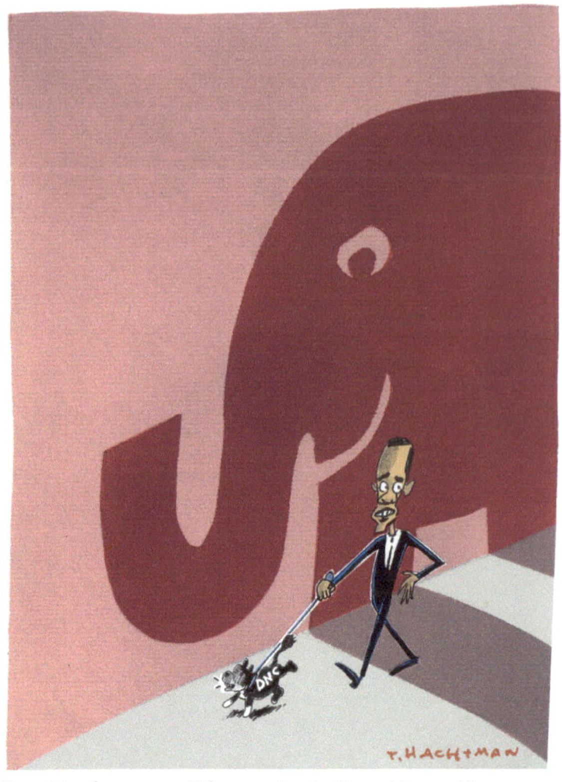

Tom Hachtman • Obama Feels Republican Threat
Pen, Ink & Watercolor

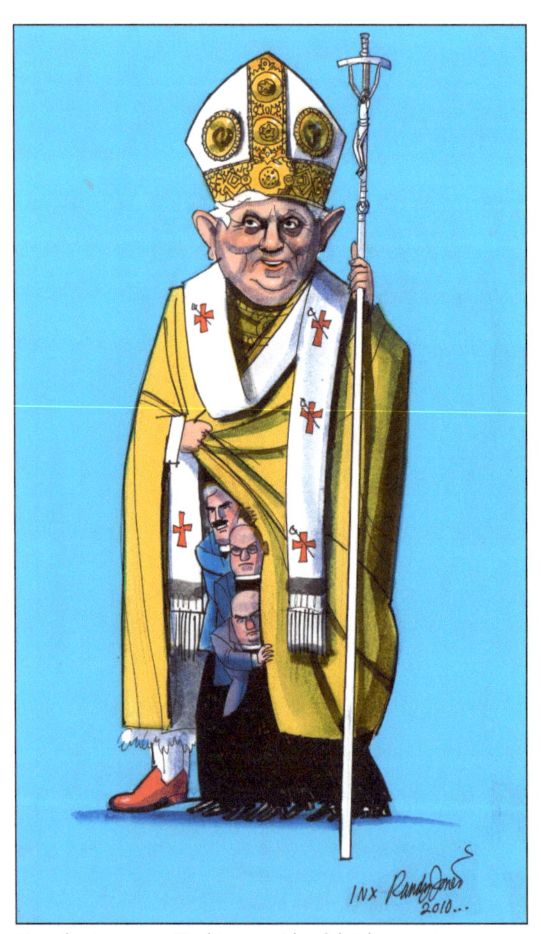

Randy Jones • Did Pope Shield Abusers?
Pen, Ink & Watercolor

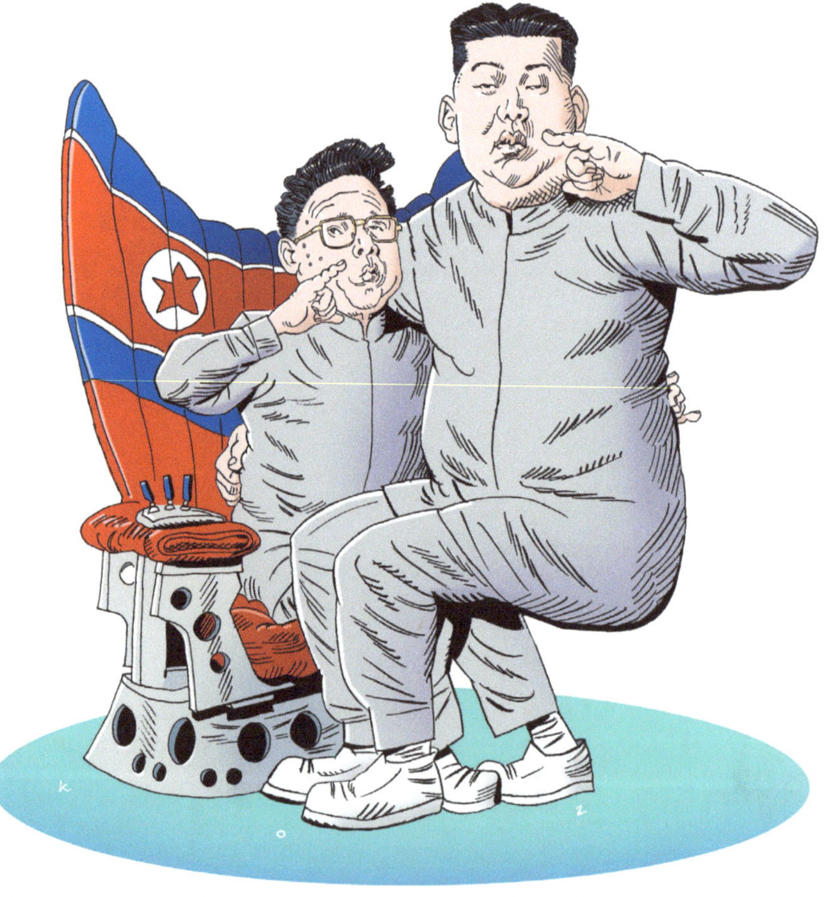

Martin Kozlowski • Kim Jong-il & Jong-un • Pen, Ink & Watercolor

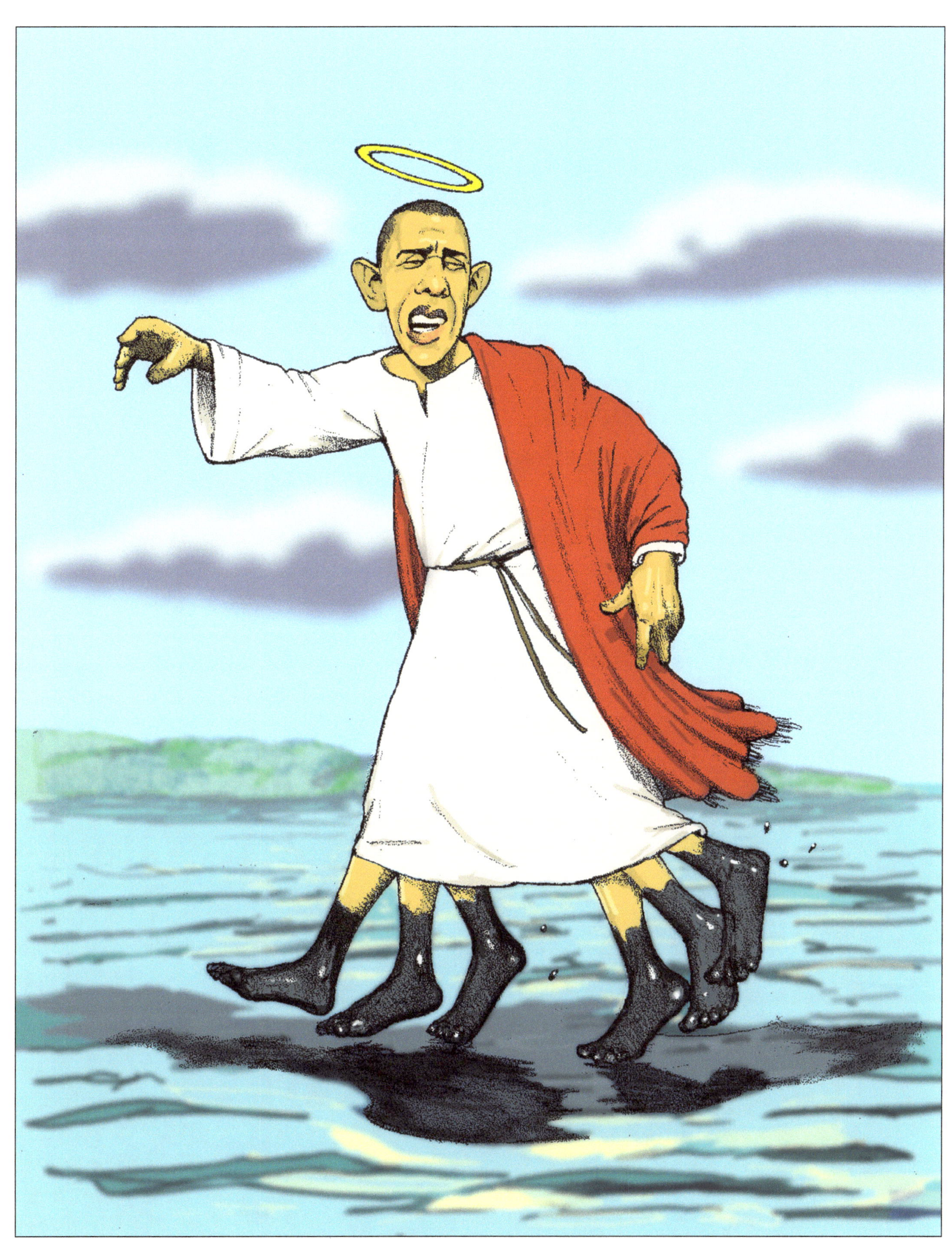

David Chelsea • Obama's Oil Spill Slip-up • Pencil & Digital Color

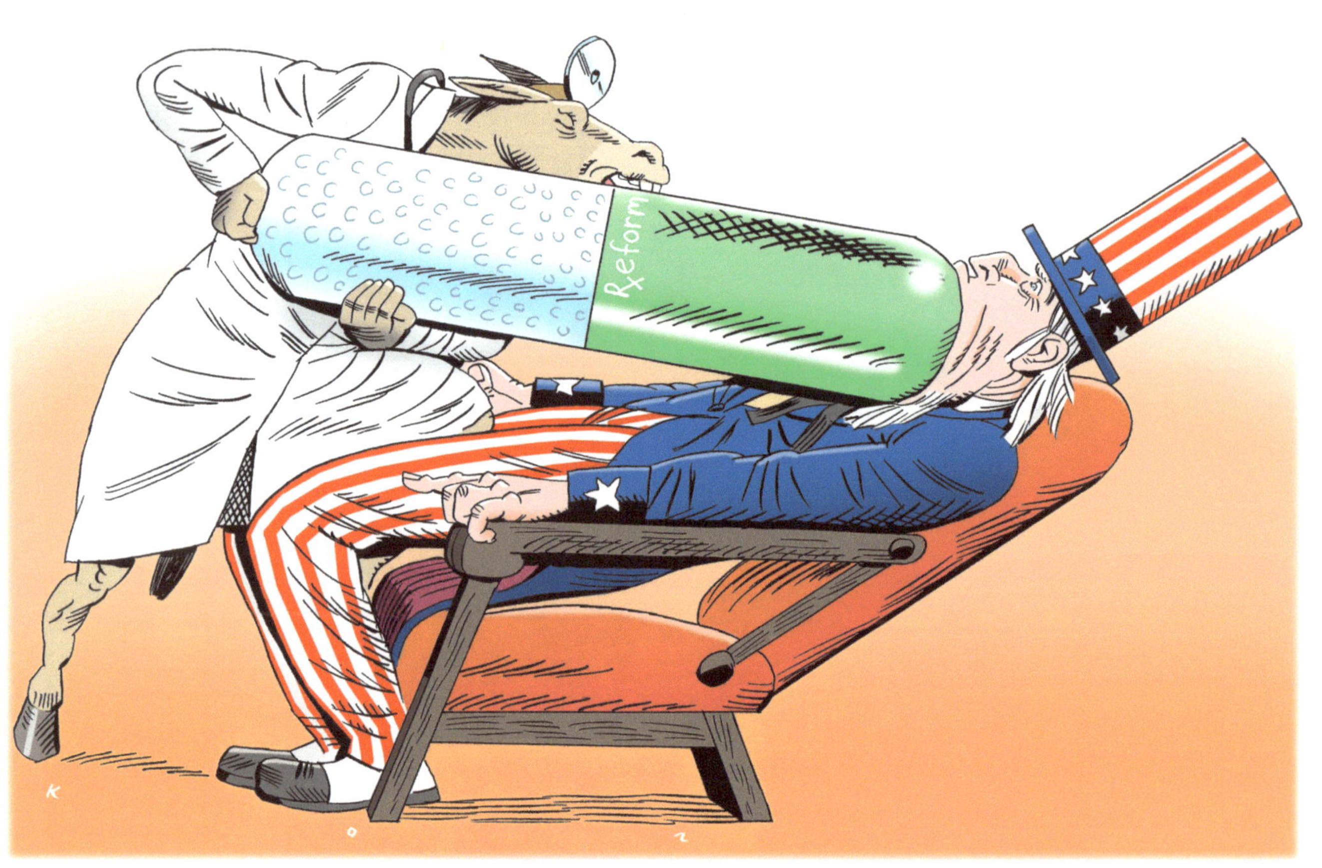

Martin Kozlowski • Democrats' Healthcare Medicine • Pen, Ink & Digital Color

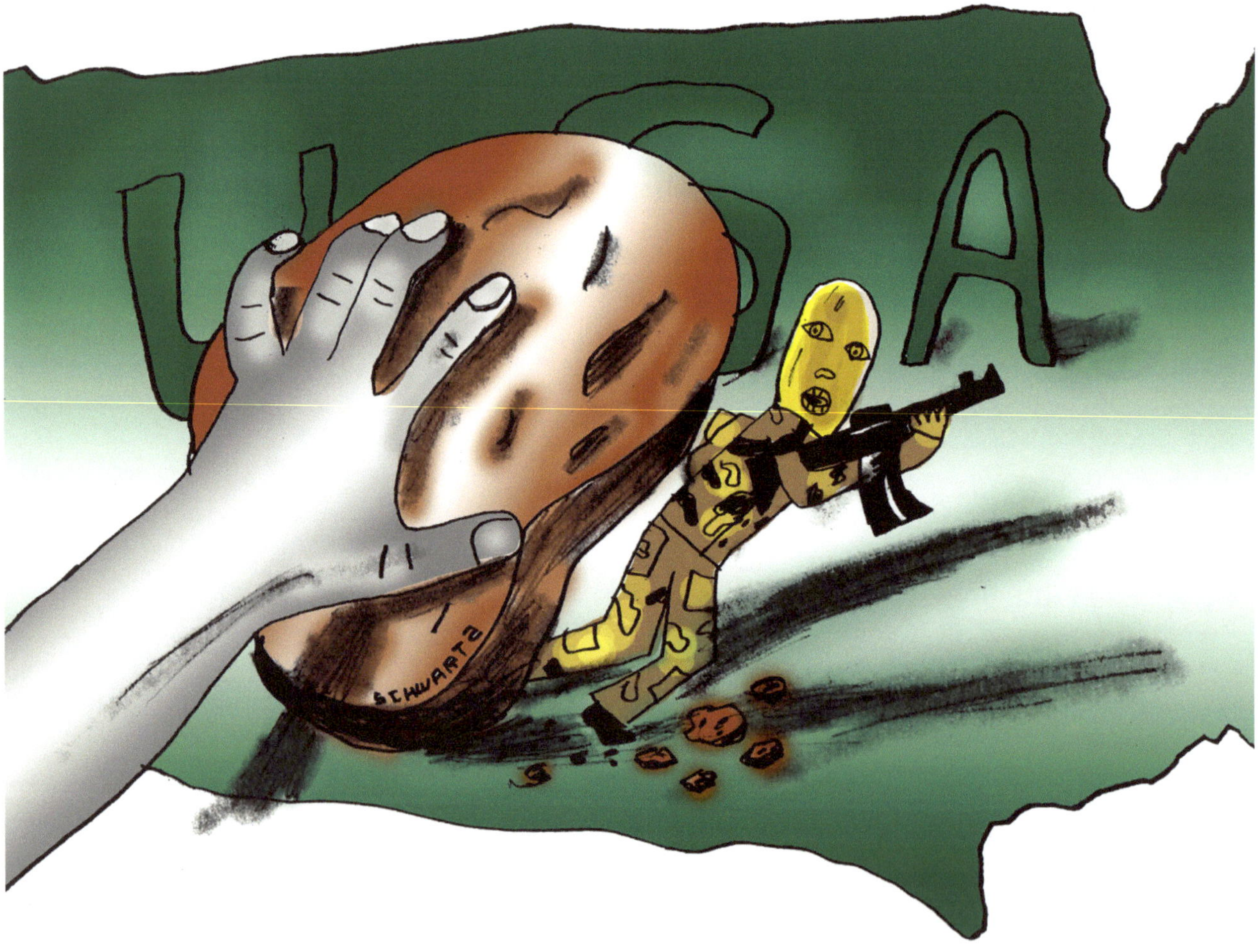

Sara Schwartz • Homegrown Far-right Militias • Pen, Ink & Digital Color

Arab Spring erupts with revolts in Tunisia, Egypt, Libya, and unrest across the region. 9.0 quake rocks Japan, tsunami causes nuclear reactor meltdown. Occupy movement spreads.

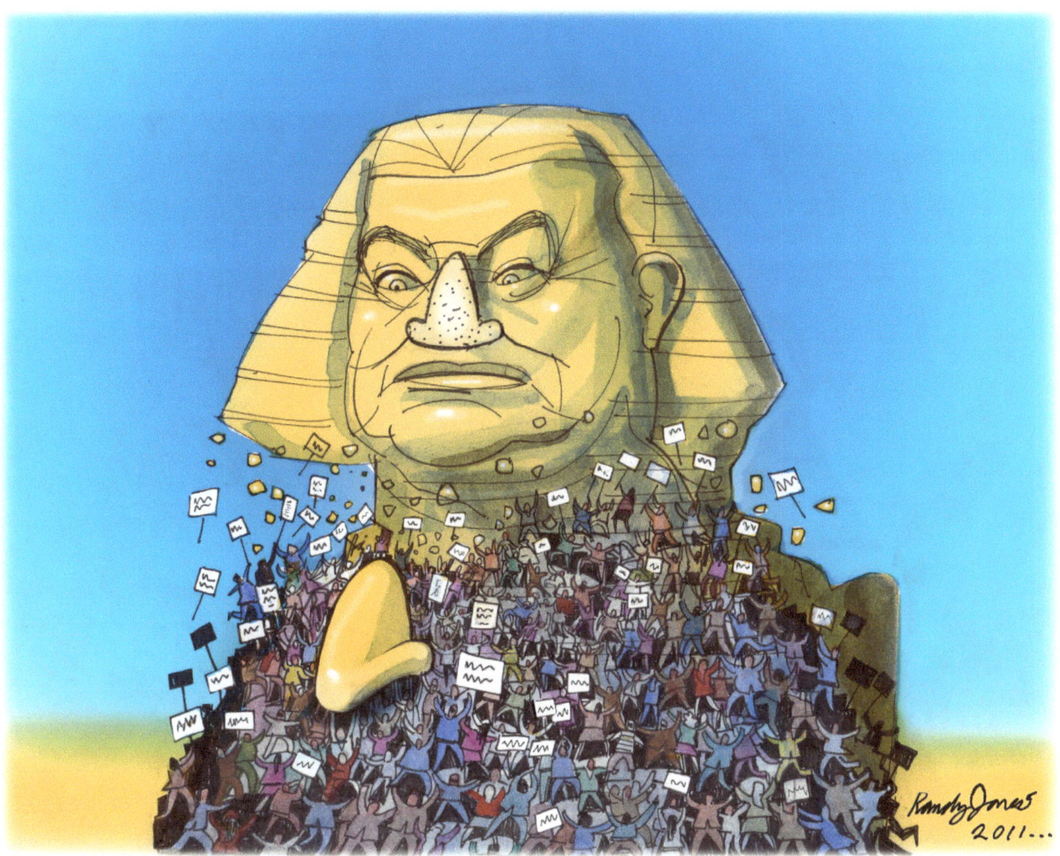

Randy Jones • Mubarak Under Siege • Pen, Ink & Watercolor

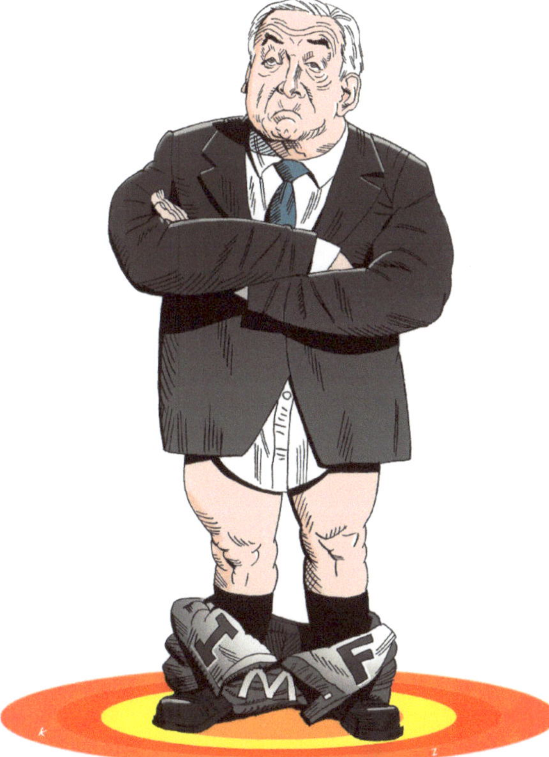

Martin Kozlowski • Strauss-Kahn Scandal
Pen, Ink & Digital Color

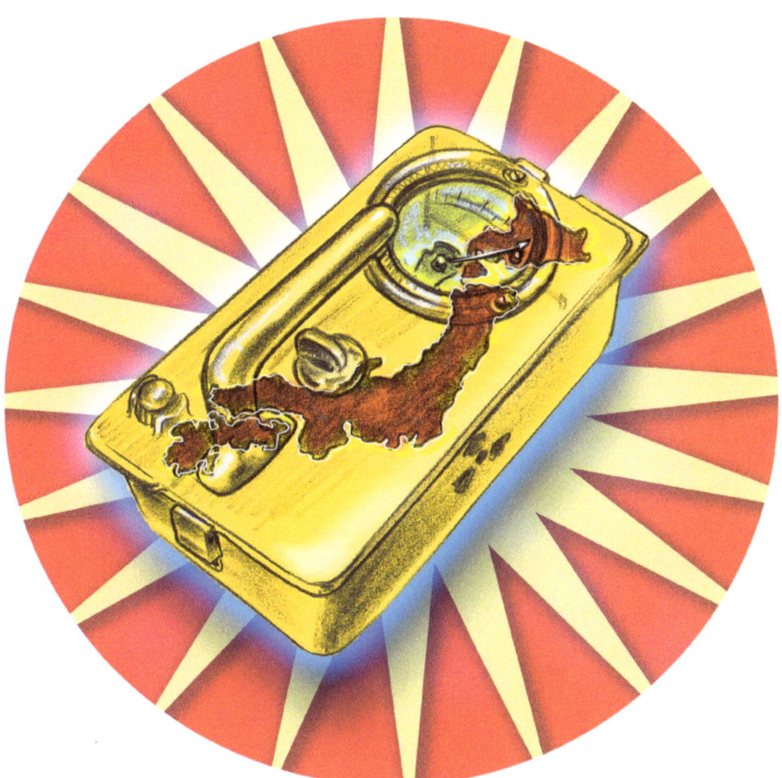

Thomas Kerr • Japan's Radiation Threat • Pencil & Digital Color

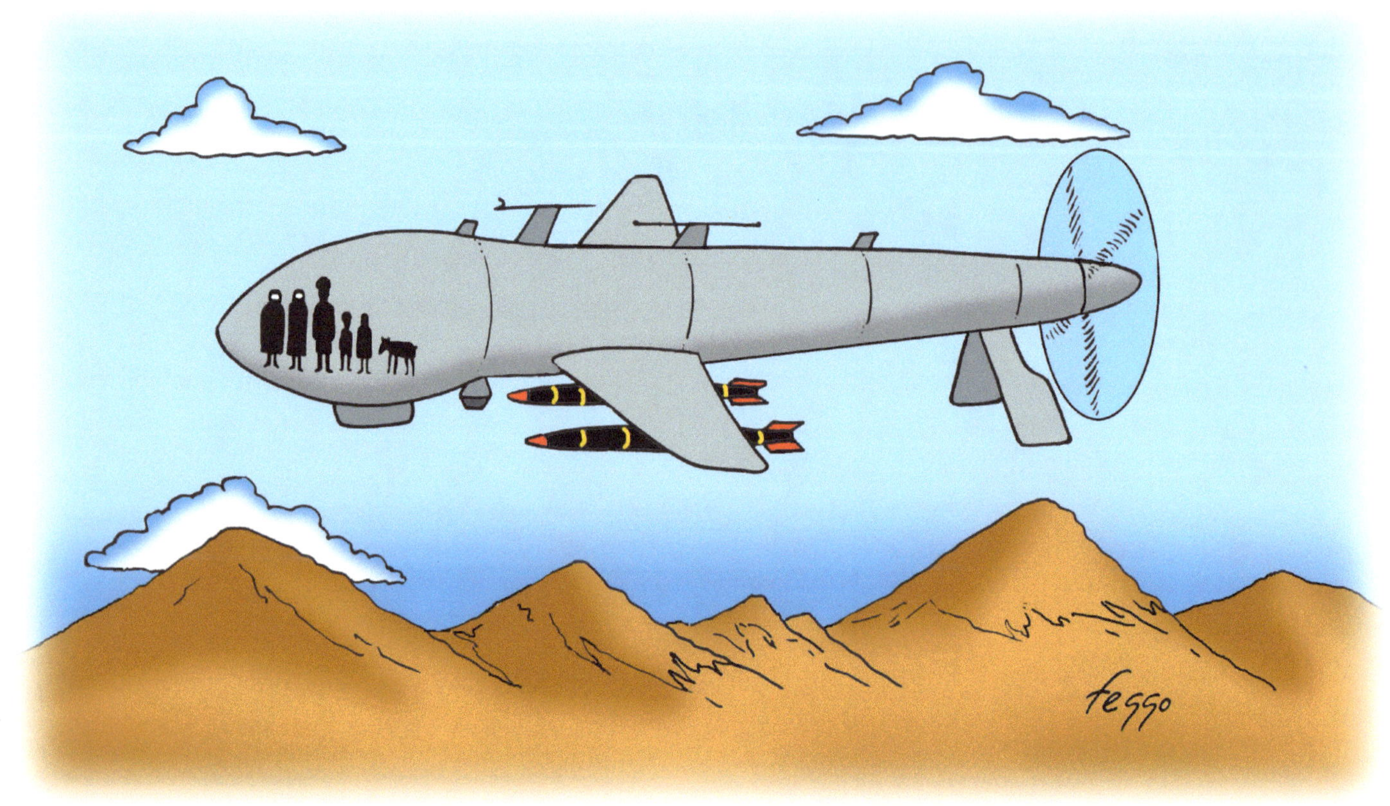

Felipe Galindo • Predator Drone Kills • Pen, Ink & Digital Color

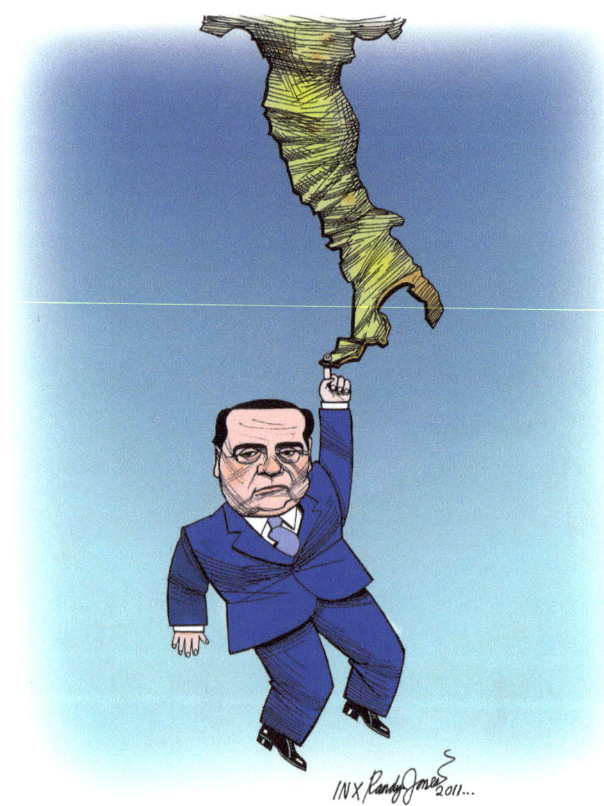

Randy Jones • Italy Boots Berlusconi
Pen, Ink & Digital Color

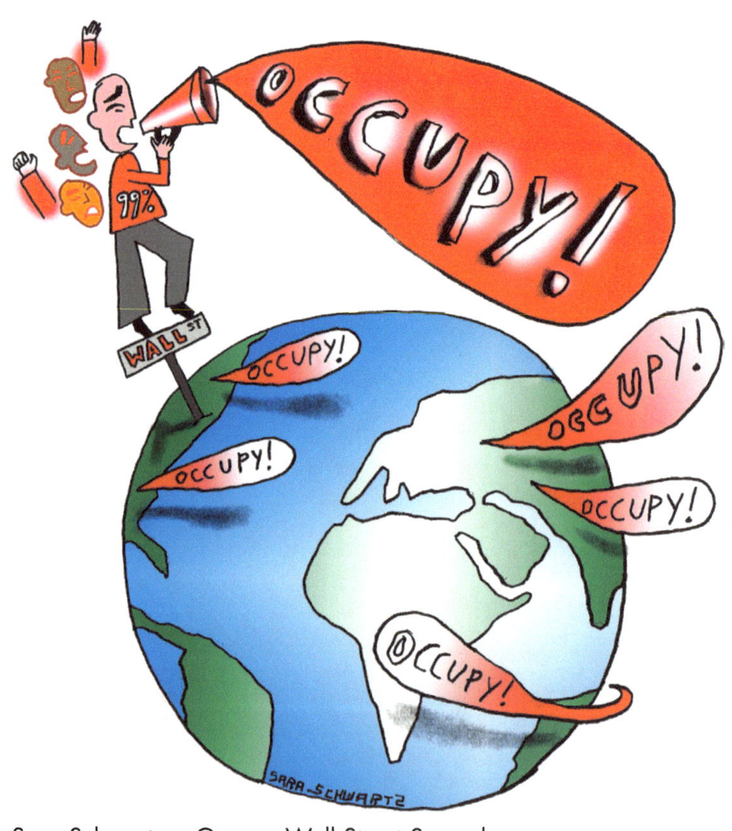

Sara Schwartz • Occupy Wall Street Spreads
Pen, Ink & Digital Color

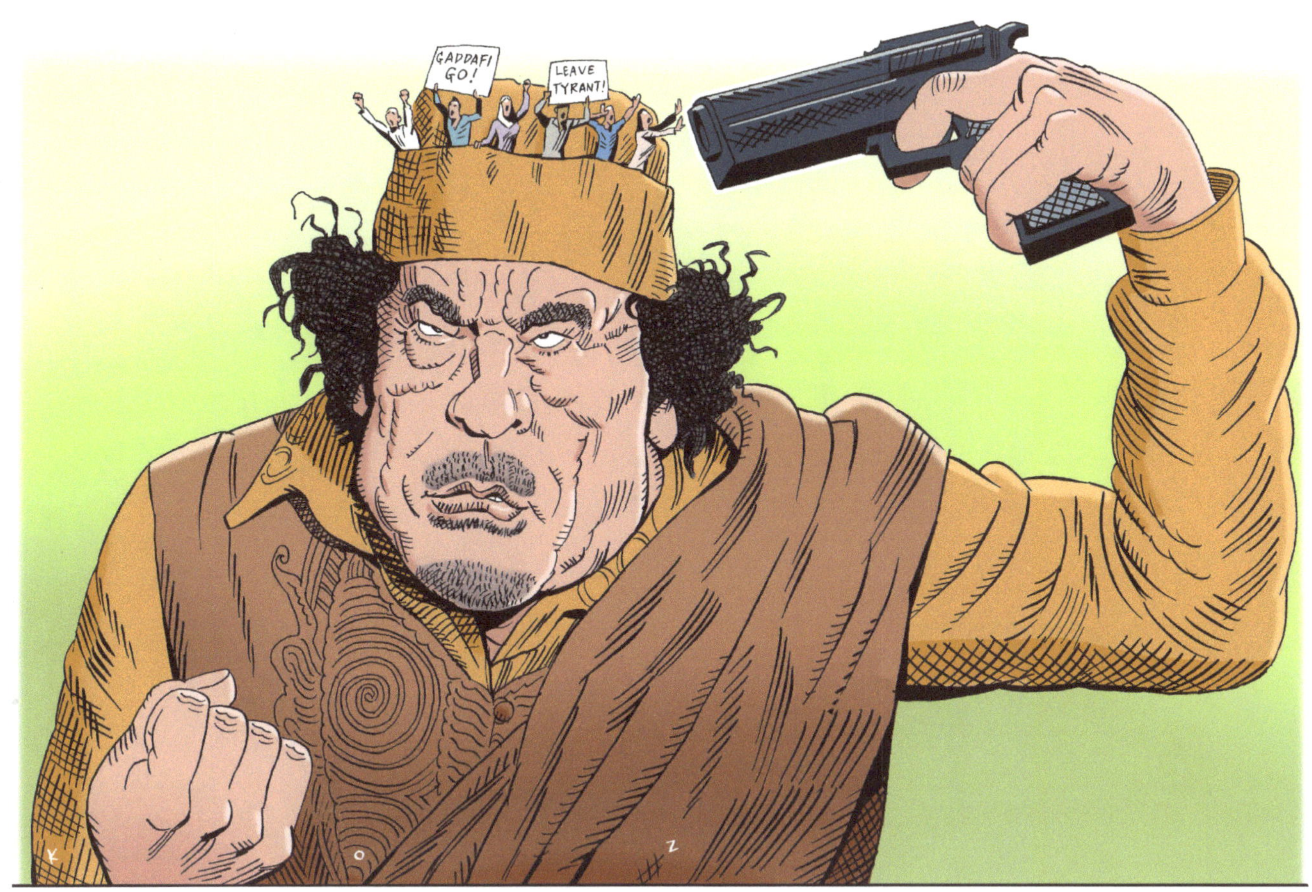

Martin Kozlowski • Gaddafi Attacks Libyans • Pen, Ink & Digital Color

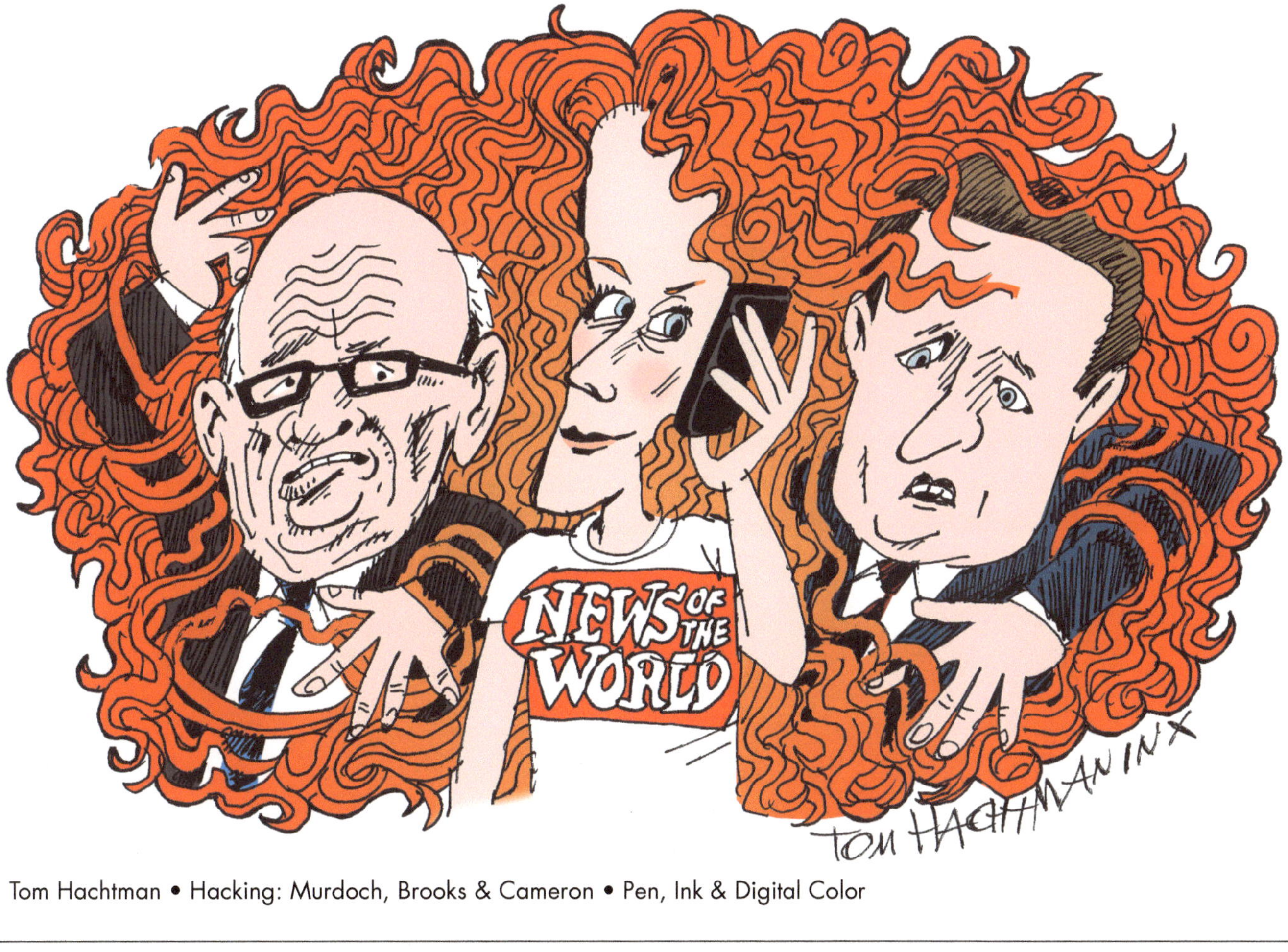

Tom Hachtman • Hacking: Murdoch, Brooks & Cameron • Pen, Ink & Digital Color

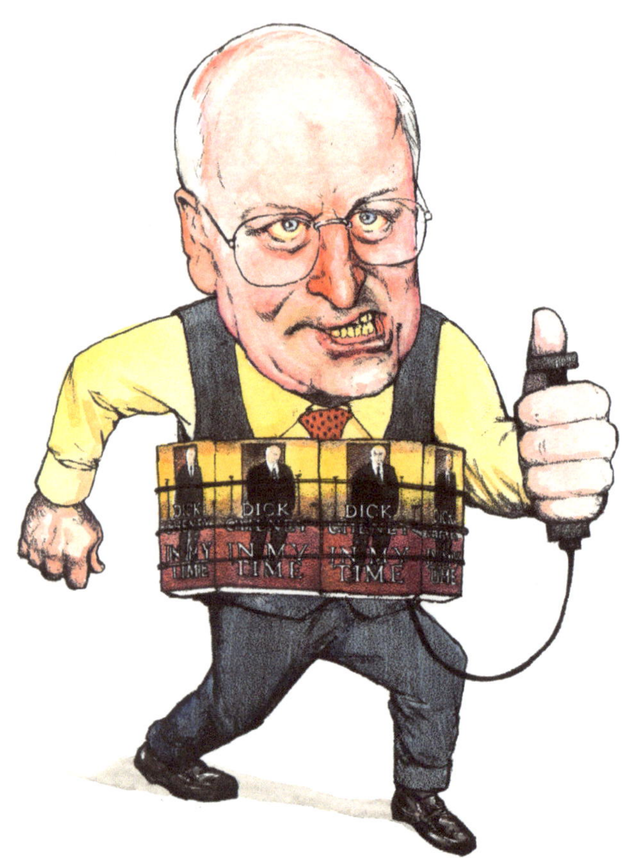

David Chelsea • Cheney's Explosive Memoir
Pen, Ink & Digital Color

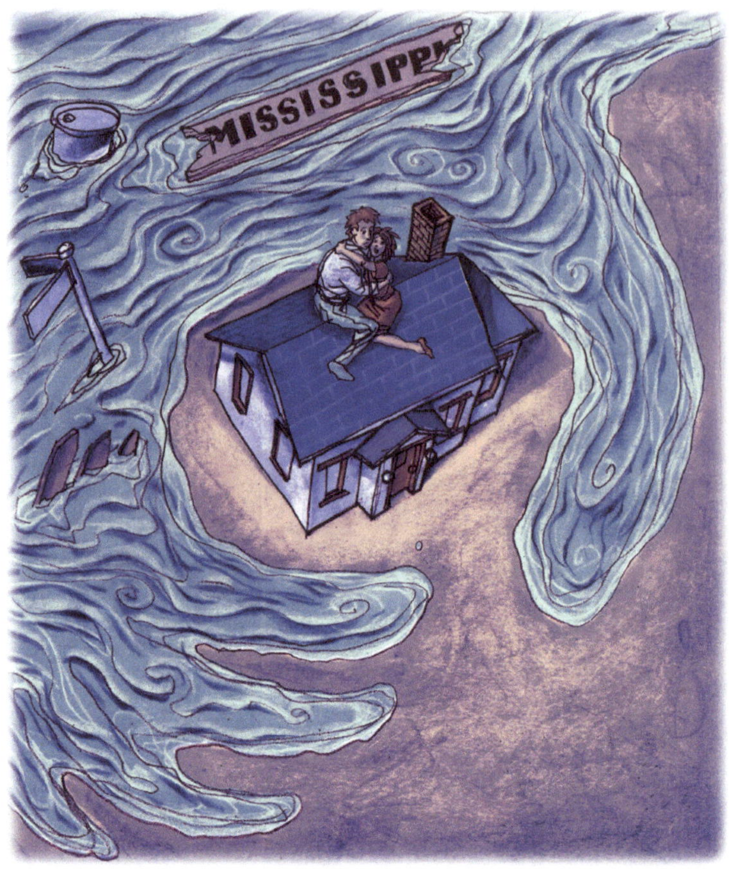

David Klein • Mississippi Floods • Pencil & Digital Color

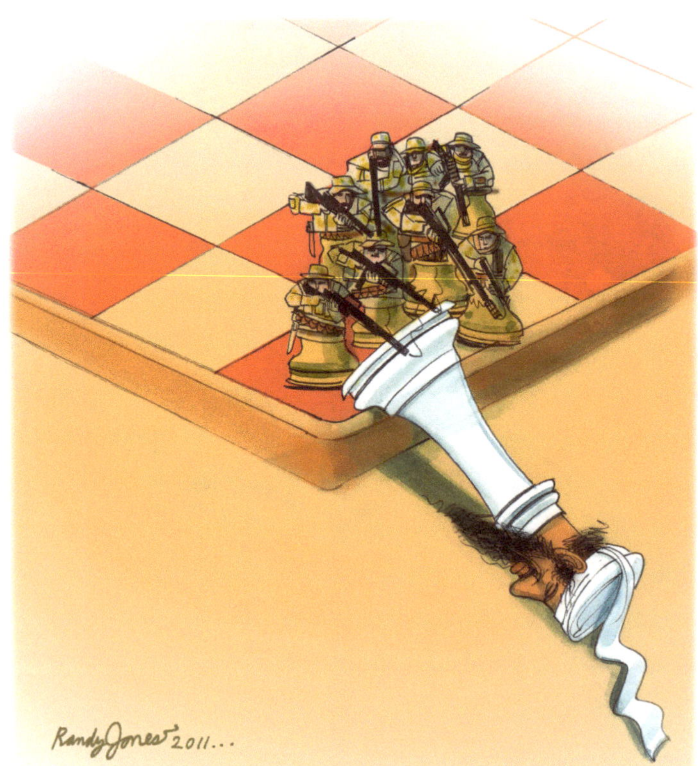

Randy Jones • Checkmate: Osama bin Laden Falls
Pen, Ink & Watercolor

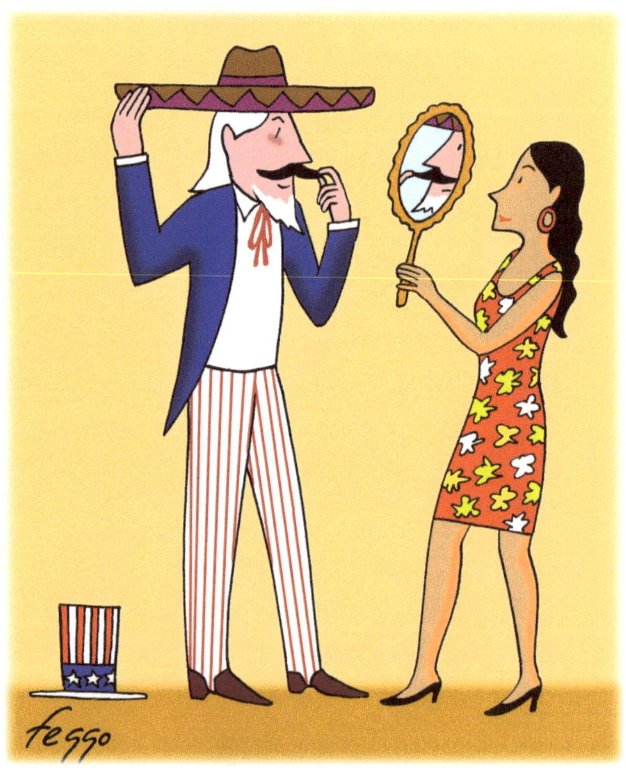

Felipe Galindo • Hispanic Population Boom
Pen, Ink & Digital Color

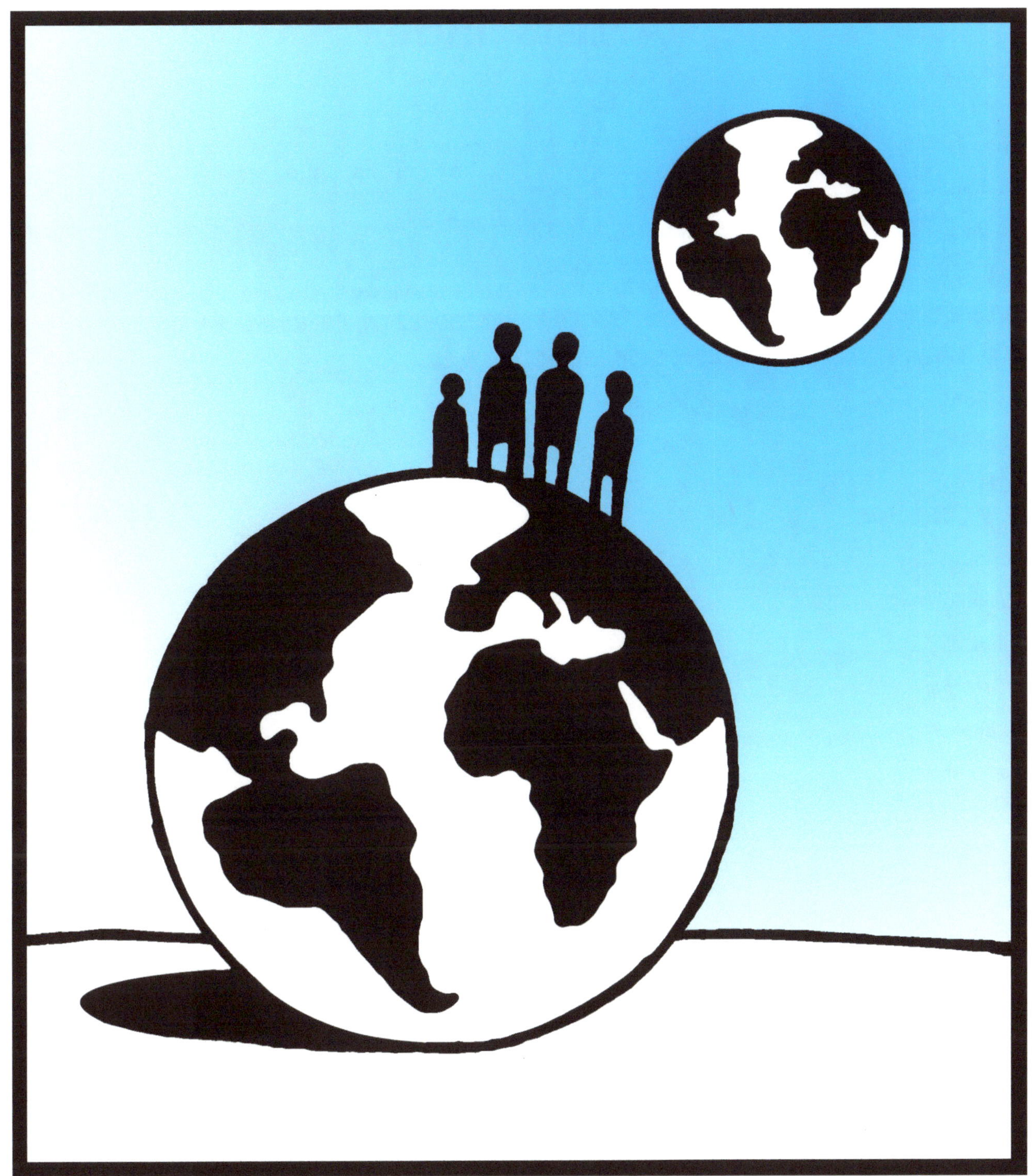

Igor Kopelnitsky • Gap Between Rich & Poor • Digital Media

The artists who have joined the band of INXsters — for the long or the short of it — represent many of the top talents in the field of illustration over the last 30 years. Outside of INX, their work has appeared in every major newspaper and magazine in the U.S. and abroad. They have won the most prestigious prizes in the industry. They have published best-selling children's books, contributed cartoons to *The New Yorker*, and drawn movie posters for Oscar-winning films. They've created comic strips, designed packaging, written and illustrated graphic novels, published monographs and memoirs, made fine art, and participated in countless exhibitions.

This is an exceptionally talented group of diverse individuals who have each excelled in their vocation. Two admirable characteristics that they all share, a passion for their craft and a deep engagement with the times in which they live, have probably never had purer expression than in their work for INX.

Artists' Index

INX: Three Decades and Counting

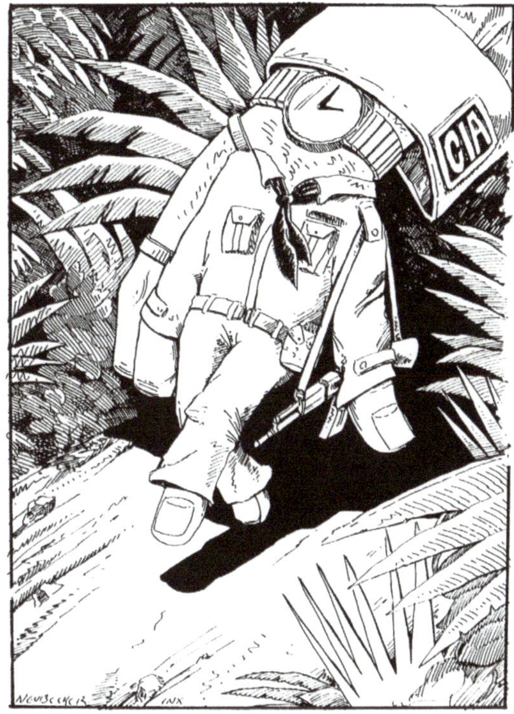

Robert Neubecker • CIA in Central America
Pen & Ink • 1981

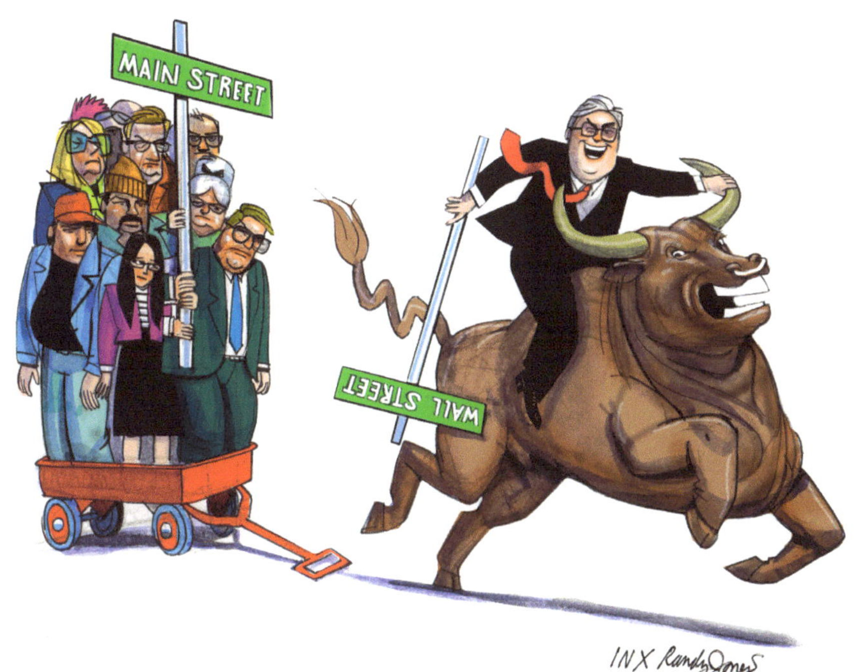

Randy Jones • Wall Street Surges, Main Street Lags
Pen, Ink & Watercolor • 2009

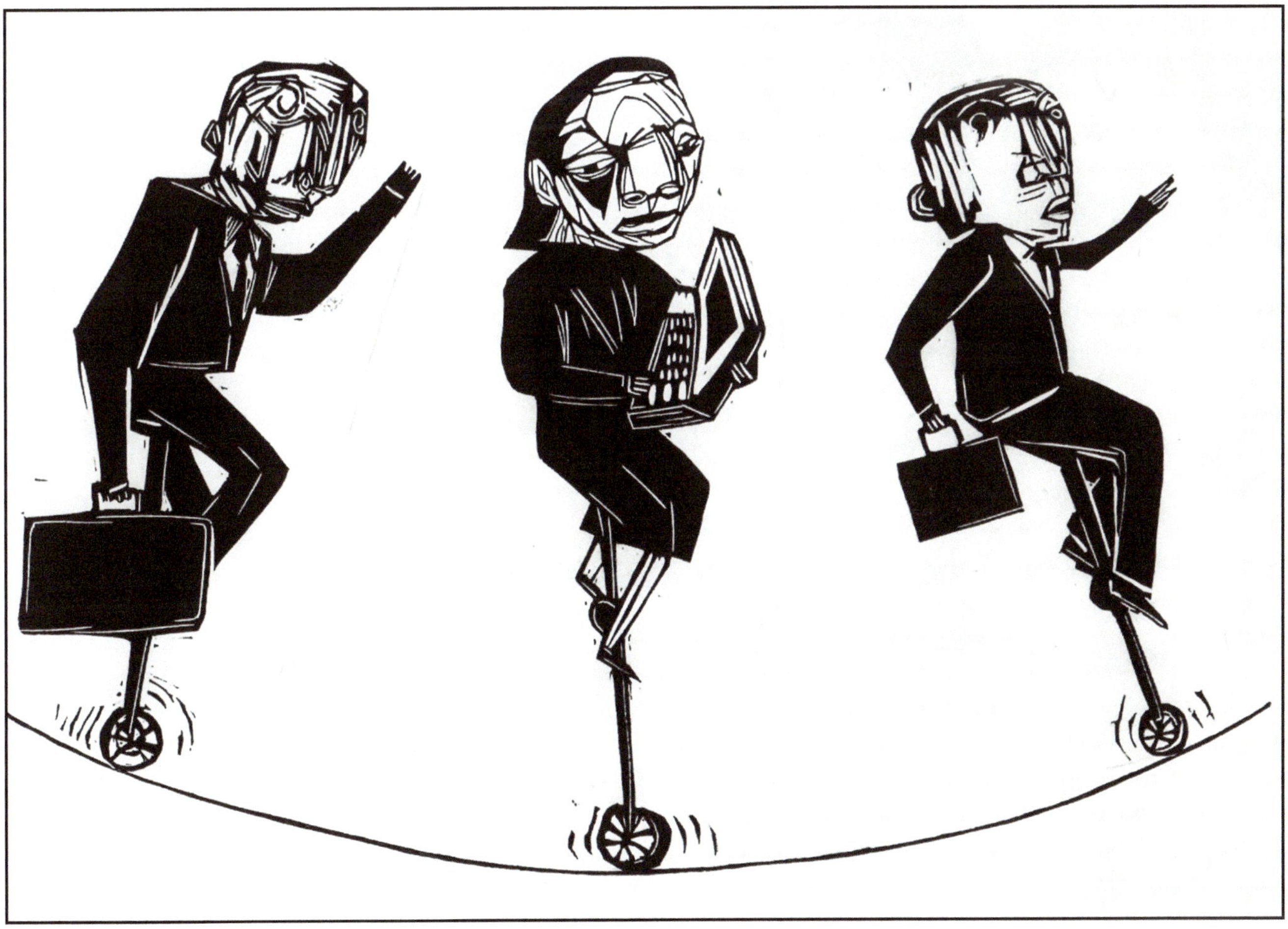

Jordin Isip • Corporate Balancing Act • Linocut • 1993

CPSIA information can be obtained
at www.ICGtesting.com
Printed in the USA
LVHW071707220120
644441LV00003B/45